Marketing Management for Nonprofit Organizations

Adrian Sargeant

Senior Lecturer in Nonprofit Marketing
Henley Management College

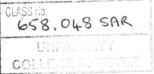

OXFORD
UNIVERSITY PRESS

OXFORD
UNIVERSITY PRESS

Great Clarendon Street, Oxford OX2 6DP

Oxford University Press is a department of the University of Oxford.
It furthers the University's objective of excellence in research, scholarship,
and education by publishing worldwide in

Oxford New York

Athens Auckland Bangkok Bogotá Buenos Aires Calcutta
Cape Town Chennai Dar es Salaam Delhi Florence Hong Kong Istanbul
Karachi Kuala Lumpur Madrid Melbourne Mexico City Mumbai
Nairobi Paris São Paulo Singapore Taipei Tokyo Toronto Warsaw

with associated companies in Berlin Ibadan

Oxford is a registered trade mark of Oxford University Press
in the UK and in certain other countries

Published in the United States
by Oxford University Press Inc., New York

© Adrian Sargeant 1999

British Library Cataloguing in Publication Data

Data available

Library of Congress Cataloging in Publication Data
Sargeant, Adrian.
Marketing management for non-profit organizations /
Adrian Sergeant.
p. cm.
Includes bibliographical references and index.
1. Nonprofit organizations—Marketing. I. Title.
HF5415.S275 1999 6589.048—dc21 98-36853

ISBN 0-19-877566-0 (pbk.)
ISBN 0-19-877567-9

10 9 8 7 6 5 4

Typeset by Hope Services (Abingdon) Ltd.
Printed in Great Britain
on acid-free paper by
Bookcraft Ltd.
Midsomer Norton, Somerset

bs

Marketing Management for Nonprofit Organizations

Preface

NONPROFIT MARKETING has finally come of age. Rising from its status as a relatively obscure variant in the early 1970s, it is now widely accepted that marketing has much to offer a variety of different categories of organization. This is a considerable feat of recognition, for it was only a few years ago that one would have been severely chastised in many nonprofit circles for even daring to mention the 'M' word in public.

Perhaps part of the reason for marketing's increasing acceptance in the sector is due to the broadening and softening of its definition. Marketing is no longer defined as the provision of required goods and services at a profit. The focus has switched to the satisfaction of consumer wants and, more generally, to sensitively serving the needs of a particular society. Thus marketing has begun to lose something of its association with the relentless pursuit of profit and has evolved into a philosophical approach to the management of an organization that has just as much relevance for 'profit' and 'nonprofit' alike.

In recognition of this somewhat wider definition of marketing there are now a variety of texts on the market which address its specific application to one or more nonprofit sub-sectors. Broadly speaking, this literature can be divided into two categories—highly theoretical texts written for an academic audience and 'how to do it' books written by practitioners for the benefit of their peers. Both categories of approach clearly have a valuable role to play, but the development of this dichotomy is perhaps unfortunate as both categories of author/audience could have much to offer one another. The approach taken in this text is therefore to combine the experience of practitioners working in each nonprofit sub-sector, with the available academic research. As the reader will later appreciate, the amount of research in some areas of nonprofit marketing is often sadly lacking, but, where it is available, it can prove a valuable aid to shaping the approach a particular organization might take to its market.

The text has been written primarily for use by undergraduate and postgraduate students, taking nonprofit marketing as an optional part of their studies. It has thus been structured to reflect the usual content of such course modules—namely, an introduction to marketing, the development of a marketing plan, and the complexities of marketing in a number of specific nonprofit contexts. It will however also be of interest to practitioners seeking to learn from the activities of marketers/researchers working in other parts of the nonprofit sector. A broad range of issues will be addressed and sufficient marketing concepts and frameworks introduced to allow the reader to approach the development of a marketing plan for their own organization with confidence.

The general approach adopted in this text has thus been to divide the subject into three sections. In the first of these sections, the scale and scope of the nonprofit sector will be explored. The ICNPO (International Classification Of Nonprofit Organisations) will be introduced as a means of conceptualizing the great diversity of organizations that can be considered as nonprofit in nature. Clearly the exact categories of organizations that will be nonprofit in a given society will vary, depending on the historical development of that society, its relative degree of economic sophistication, the relative degree of state involvement and the existence of appropriate infrastructure supports. Nevertheless the ICNPO constitutes an effective framework through which to analyse the work of nonprofits. In the first section of this text, therefore, marketing's relevance to a variety of these categories of nonprofit will be established and a number of the typically expressed reservations towards the concept explored.

In the second section of the text, the implementation of marketing will be discussed at both philosophical and functional levels. With regard to the former, Chapter 2 will examine how a nonprofit might attain a market orientation, the benefits that this might bring, and the specific organizational actions that might be required to bring this about. Chapters 3 and 4 will then move on to consider the subject of marketing planning and guide the reader through the necessary steps that will facilitate the development of a marketing plan for a given organization. Thus, the intention of this section of the text is to facilitate a discussion of how marketing should typically be managed in a nonprofit context. The reader will be introduced to a series of concepts and frameworks which have a general relevance to all nonprofit organizations.

In the third and final section of the text, marketing's specific application to fundraising, arts organizations, education institutions, healthcare organizations, and the social marketing of ideas will be explored. These chapters have been designed to build on the general framework for marketing planning given earlier. The reader will be appraised of the key influences on the marketing function in each case and a number of the specific nuances of marketing in each particular nonprofit sub-sector. Whilst this section has therefore been designed for the reader to 'dip in and out of', a number of the issues discussed in each chapter have a relevance for all nonprofit organizations. These 'application' chapters have been carefully structured so as to minimize any overlap of coverage and the reader will hence find that each chapter deals with a different mix of nonprofit marketing issues—such as direct/database marketing, the achievement of a marketing orientation, the management of service quality and the development of a marketing communications campaign.

Of course, this latter section of the text could be criticized on the grounds of scope. Whilst it is now almost universally accepted that fundraising, arts, and social marketing can now legitimately be regarded as nonprofit marketing activity, a number of readers may question the inclusion of the chapters relating to healthcare and education. These latter chapters have been included here because such activities *are* most definitely nonprofit in nature in a number of different countries. Even in the USA, where much healthcare marketing is for-profit in nature, for example, there remain a number of nonprofit healthcare institutions which could stand to benefit from marketing at both conceptual and practical levels. Moreover in the UK, where perhaps a more hybrid system of healthcare is beginning to develop, the marketing of healthcare will benefit much more from the concepts and frameworks introduced in this text than it would from a standard for-profit approach. This is simply because the healthcare environment exhibits many of the same characteristics as other categories of non-profit—that is, there is a distinction between the markets for resource attraction and resource allocation, there is a need to achieve a balance between the satisfaction of individual customer requirements and the longer-term 'satisfaction' of society as a whole—and there are also a greater number of different publics that each institution must address, even if no exchange (in the economic sense of the term) actually takes place between them and the institution concerned. Such complexities are characteristic of the majority of nonprofit marketing and the content of this text will hence be of particular relevance.

The argument for the inclusion of education institutions is very similar. Not only do they face the same environmental conditions outlined above, but the resources of any educational institution are almost always directed in their entirety towards the development of their educational mission. Very few such institutions have the need to generate a return for shareholders and indeed many educational institutions are now charitable in status. It would therefore seem somewhat churlish to suggest that anything other than a nonprofit approach to marketing would be most appropriate. In compiling this text it was thus felt that an 'inclusive' approach would be preferable, since readers always have the option of ignoring those sections that they perceive as lacking in relevance. It is the sincere hope of this author, however, that the text *will* be considered as a whole, since there are always lessons to be learnt from best practice in other sectors and one should never be afraid of borrowing good ideas—whatever their source.

I hope the text meets your needs.

Acknowledgements

I am very grateful to all those who helped me to complete this text. Specifically I would like to thank my PhD students, Saadia Asif and Mahadzirah Mohamad, whose work on service quality and internal marketing was a frequent source of inspiration.

I would also like to thank Karen Rothwell of the RSPB, the staff of the Camborne School of Mines and the Development Office of the University of Exeter, Frank O'Friel of the Richmond Community Healthcare Hamlet, Fifi Butler from Performing Arts Management, David Hamilton-Peters of the Royal National Theatre, and Nedra from Weinreich Communications, Greenbrae, Califorfnia. Without their support and assistance it would not have been possible to develop the case studies that appear in this volume.

Grateful acknowledgement is made to all the authors and publishers of extract material which appears in this book.

Contents

PART A

An Introduction to Marketing in the Nonprofit Sector

IT IS THE PURPOSE of this introductory section to introduce the reader to the scale and scope of the nonprofit sector. As the reader will later appreciate, there is considerable academic debate currently raging over the issue of what should, and should not, be considered nonprofit in nature. Since this text has been designed for use in a variety of settings and contexts, the author has deliberately adopted a fairly broad perspective of the sector, on the basis that readers may then select the content that they perceive as having the greatest relevance to their own specific organization or requirements.

This introductory section will also trace the development of the marketing concept, demonstrate its relevance to nonprofit organizations and illustrate the form that marketing activities might normally take. Specific issues, such as the attainment of a marketing orientation, or the development of a marketing plan are reserved for the second section of the text.

Introduction

Objectives

By the end of this chapter you should be able to:

(1) define and describe the extent of the nonprofit sector;

(2) understand the development of the nonprofit sector and its relationship with other elements of society;

(3) define the role of marketing as it applies to a nonprofit organization;

(4) respond to typically encountered objections to marketing in the nonprofit context;

(5) distinguish between product, sales and market orientations;

(6) describe the components of a typical marketing mix.

Why Nonprofit?

Given that it is our intention to examine the application of marketing to the nonprofit (NFP) sector, it is important to begin by defining the category of organization to which this text is addressed. Over the years many authors have developed widely differing terminology for what is ostensibly the same type of organization. Of course, all the terminology varies in scope but there is considerable overlap and confusion. Texts may therefore be found which refer to NFPs, NGOs, NFGOs, PVOs, the 'Voluntary Sector', and the more general 'Third Sector'. Dig a little deeper and you may even find texts referring to subgroups of organizations such as QUANGOs, BONGOs, GONGOs, FONGOs, and my personal favourite, PONGOs.

For the sake of simplicity, however, the term 'nonprofit' will be used throughout this text to embrace all the various types of organization listed above. The marketing principles contained herein are capable of being applied to all and it would therefore seem inappropriate to lapse into semantic hyperbole. For those that are interested however, Table 1.1 provides enlightenment.

Table 1.1
**Common
Mnemonics**

Mnemonic	Description
NFP	Not For Profit Organization
NFGO	Not For Gain Organization
PVO	Private Voluntary Organization
NGO	Non Governmental Organization
GONGO	Government Organized Non Governmental Organization
QUANGOs	Quasi Autonomous Non Governmental Organizations
BONGOs	Business Organized Non Governmental Organizations
FONGOs	Funder Organized Non Governmental Organizations
PONGOs	Political Non Governmental Organizations

For our purposes:

A nonprofit organization may be defined as one that exists to provide for the general betterment of society, through the marshalling of appropriate resources and/or the provision of physical goods and services. Such organizations do not exist to provide for personal profit or gain and do not, as a result, distribute profits or surpluses to shareholders or members. They may however, employ staff and engage in revenue-generating activities designed to assist them in fulfilling their mission.

This definition correlates strongly with the use of the term in the US and comfortably embraces all the specific contexts of NFP marketing which will be considered in this text.

A Classification of Nonprofits

Before developing an explanation of how marketing can apply to a diverse range of nonprofit organizations, however, it is useful to be able to categorize those organizations according to the nature of the work that they are engaged in. Fortunately a variety of typologies exist. In North America, for example, the National Taxonomy of Exempt Entities (NTEE) assigns a four-digit code to each distinct category of nonprofit, non-governmental organization in the US. The first digit defines the purpose of the organization. The second and third digits define the major focus of the organization's programmes, whilst the fourth defines the nature of the primary beneficiary group.

A similar system has now been developed for the purposes of international comparison. The ICNPO (International Classification of Non Profit Organizations) is illustrated in Fig. 1.1.

Whilst the ICNPO system has enormous advantages in that we may now compare the performance of the nonprofit sector across international boundaries, it is not without some difficulty in its application. The reader will appreciate that the work of many nonprofits will cut across the neatly defined categories listed in Fig. 1.1. A charity such as the International Red Cross, for example, is engaged in projects which could be classified under many of the headings provided.

It is also worth noting that not all the categories listed will have a relevance to each society around the globe. Salamon and Anheier (1992), for example, suggest that there

Group I: Culture and Recreation

Organizations and activities in general and specialized fields of culture and recreation

I 100 Culture
Media and Communications
Visual Arts, Architecture, Ceramic Art
Performing Arts
Historical, Literary and Humanistic Societies
Museums
Zoos and Aquaria

I 200 Recreation
Sports Clubs
Recreation and Social Clubs

I 300 Service Clubs

Group 2: Education and Research

Organizations and activities administering, providing, promoting, conducting, supporting and serving education and research

2 100 Primary and Secondary Education
Elementary, Primary and Secondary Education

2 200 Higher Education   Fundraising Organisations
Higher Education

2 300 Other Education
Vocational/Technical Schools
Adult/Continuing Education

2 400 Research
Medical Research
Science and Technology
Social Sciences, Policy Studies

Group 3: Health

Organizations that engage in health-related activities, providing health care, both general and specialized services, administration of health care services and health support services

3 100 Hospitals and Rehabilitation
Hospitals
Rehabilitation

3 200 Nursing Homes
Nursing Homes

3 300 Mental Health and Crisis Intervention
Psychiatric Hospitals
Mental Health Treatment
Crisis Intervention

3 400 Other Health Services
Public Health and Wellness Education
Health Treatment, Primarily Outpatient
Rehabilitative Medical Services
Emergency Medical Services

Group 4: Social Services

Organizations and institutions providing human and social services to a community or target population

4 100 Social Services
Child Welfare, Child Services, Day-care
Youth Services and Youth Welfare
Family Services
Services for the Handicapped
Services for the Elderly
Self Help and other Personal Social Services

4 200 Emergency and Relief
Disaster/Emergency Prevention and Control
Temporary Shelters
Refugee Assistance

4 300 Income Support and Maintenance
Income Support and Maintenance
Material Assistance

Group 5: Environment

Organizations promoting and providing services in environmental conservation, pollution control and prevention, environmental education and health, and animal protection

5 100 Environment
Pollution Abatement and Control
Natural Resources Conservation and Protection
Environmental Beautification and Open Spaces

5 200 Animals
Animal Protection and Welfare
Wildlife Preservation and Protection
Veterinary Services

Group 6: Development and Housing

Organizations promoting programmes and providing services to help improve communities and the economic and social well-being of society

6 100 Economic, Community and Social Development
Community and Neighbourhood Organizations
Economic Development
Social Development

6 200 Housing
Housing Associations
Housing Assistance

6 300 Employment and Training
Job Training Programmes
Vocational Counselling and Guidance
Vocational Rehabilitation and Sheltered Workshops

Group 7: Law Advocacy and Politics

Organizations and groups that work to protect and promote civil rights, or advocate the social and political interests of general or specific constituencies, offer legal services, and promote public safety

Fig. I. I: **Cont.**

7 100 Civic and Advocacy Organizations
Advocacy Organizations
Civil Rights Associations
Ethnic Associations
Civic Associations

7 200 Law and Legal Services
Legal Services
Crime Prevention and Public Safety
Rehabilitation of Offenders
Victim Support
Consumer Protection Associations

7 300 Political Organizations

Group 8: Philanthropic Intermediaries and Volunteerism Promotion

Philanthropic organizations and organizations promoting charity or charitable activities

8 100 Philanthropic Intermediaries and Volunteerism Promotion
Grantmaking Foundations
Volunteerism Promotion and Support
Fundraising Organizations

Group 9: International Activities

Organizations promoting greater inter-cultural understanding between peoples of different countries and historical backgrounds and also those providing relief during emergencies and promoting development and welfare abroad

9 100 International Activities
Exchange/Friendship/Cultural Programmes
Development Assistance Associations
International Disaster and Relief Organizations
International Human Rights and Peace Organizations

Group 10: Religion

Organizations promoting religious beliefs and administering religious services and rituals; includes churches, mosques, synagogues, temples, shrines, seminaries, monasteries, and other similar institutions, in addition to related associations and auxiliaries of such organizations.

10 100 Religious Congregations and Associations
Congregations
Associations of Congregations

Group II: Business, Professional Associations and Unions

Organizations promoting, regulating, and safeguarding business, professional, and labour interests

11 100 Business, Professional Associations and Unions
Business Associations
Professional
Labour Unions

Group I2: Not Elsewhere Classified
12 100 N.E.C.

are five sets of factors which are important in explaining the scope and scale of the non-profit sector in any one given country.

(1) *Heterogeneity*—The more diverse a given population, the larger the size of the non-profit sector is likely to be. This factor seems to derive from the needs of various ethnic communities to preserve and protect their own unique cultures and identities. In most cases this task can best be accomplished through the formation of a variety of nonprofit organizations, which are by definition less susceptible to influence from either government or the private sector.

(2) *Scope of the Welfare State*—The scope of a nonprofit sector will vary widely depending on the scope of government involvement in social welfare. The sector will usually expand to fill the most important gaps left by the state.

(3) *Level of Development*—Less developed countries are found to have more traditions of mutual aid and collaboration, but they lack the 'middle class' base which has proved important in the development of the nonprofit sector in the developed world. The middle classes have traditionally, by virtue of their position within a society, been quick to recognize the needs of the poorest, or most under-privileged segments of their population and been amongst the first to invest both their time and capital in the relief thereof. As economies make the transition from developing to developed, therefore, the number of nonprofit organizations is likely to increase substantially.

(4) *Legal Framework*—Interestingly, common law systems are found to be more conducive to the growth of the nonprofit sector than civil law systems.

(5) *Historical Traditions*—Historical and religious traditions can act either to encourage or discourage the voluntary sector. Each society thus evolves its own pattern of societal supports.

Having defined the extent of the NFP sector and examined some of the influences on its development, it is now worth saying a word or two about the significance of the sector in both developed and developing economies.

Significance of the Nonprofit Sector

The number of nonprofit organizations has grown enormously over the past twenty years. Not only have their numbers increased but the scope of their work has widened also, to the point where they are involved with almost every aspect of human endeavour—right across the globe. No longer can nonprofits be viewed as organizations involved in 'fringe' activities of dubious quality. Nonprofits play a major role in almost every society, helping to provide health, education, and social welfare to literally millions of disadvantaged people world-wide. Of course the relative size of the NFP sector varies from country to country as the following quotation from a recent Commonwealth Federation Report (1996) illustrates:

> In Britain there are estimated to be over 500,000 NGOs (Not for Gain Organizations). The turnover of the 175,000 of these that are registered charities is estimated at £17 billion per year. In Canada, the Canadian Environmental Network of NGOs has 2000 groups in membership. Zimbabwe has an estimated 800 NGOs, which have spent Z$300–400 million on projects since independence. One of these NGOs has an annual budget of over £600,000 and works with 80,000 rural families. In Sri Lanka one rural development NGO alone has 9000 paid fieldworkers and 41,000 local fieldworkers, working in 10,000 villages. . . . In Australia more than half of the country's welfare services are supplied by NFP charitable organisations. They are estimated to number more than 11,000 turning over a total of A$4.4 billion per year and mobilising an estimated 93 million volunteer hours.

In the first study of its kind, the John Hopkins Comparative Nonprofit Sector Project determined that in the seven countries for which they were able to assemble complete data (the US, the UK, France, Germany, Italy, Hungary, and Japan) the nonprofit sector employed the equivalent of 11.8 million full-time workers and contributed almost 5 per cent of the combined GDP of these countries. The traditional view of developed nations as two-sector societies can therefore now be challenged. The emergent nonprofit or third sector is taking on a new significance.

Figure 1.2 illustrates how nonprofits are now an integral part of the fabric of many societies. They are characterized by their concern with the disadvantaged, or with wider issues which impact on the general well-being of a particular society. They therefore have strong links with civil society in that they may be providing essential goods and services for the needy or under-privileged. They will also have contacts with government as they lobby for attention, apply for funding, compete for government contracts, etc. Nonprofit organizations may in addition have strong links with commercial

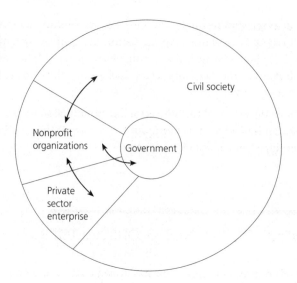

organizations either through the provision of goods and services, or to solicit funding on behalf of their beneficiary groups. Whilst the model in Fig. 1.2 is clearly a gross simplification of what, in reality, are often very complex and interconnected relationships, it does however highlight the significant role that the nonprofit sector has to play in many, both developed and developing, societies.

Current Developments in the NFP Sector

The nonprofit sector is currently undergoing a period of radical change. On a global scale there has been an explosion in the number of nonprofit organizations over the past thirty years, almost certainly in response to rapidly changing environmental, social, and economic conditions. These conditions have recently included the impact of climatic changes, increasing national debt, the emergence of new diseases, the breakdown of some traditional political structures, and an ongoing succession of armed conflicts.

Moreover, organizations such as the EEC (European Economic Community), the World Bank, and the International Monetary Fund have also influenced the development of nonprofits through their capacity to exert influence over the policies adopted by individual governments in a general trend towards globalization. Whilst such moves may be welcomed by some, it is undeniable that moves towards globalization are gradually leading to the erosion of national traditions and cultures. Such strategies are also serving to widen the gap between the 'haves' and the 'have nots' in the newly created global village. It is therefore no surprise that many new nonprofits have been created in response to these changes, and there are as yet no signs of a slowing of growth in this area.

Aside from the changing patterns of nonprofit provision world-wide, there are also considerable changes taking place in the way in which the sector operates within individual national boundaries. A detailed discussion of these issues is beyond the scope of this text, but it is worth noting that, in the UK, for example, many nonprofits are coming ever more to resemble business organizations in the manner in which they are operated or managed. Legislation such as the Community Care Act (1992), for example, has encouraged charities to bid for contracts for funding to provide services on behalf of local authorities. For many charities this has proved to be one of the most significant changes in their 400-year history. Hard-nosed contractual negotiations and business deals now sit alongside the more traditional collecting tins and flag days. Charities are no longer competing just with one another for funds, they are now competing with private companies (and other bodies) for the right to provide the services their mission suggests they should.

It is against this backdrop of change that this new text is set. It will explore the capacity of marketing to aid charities and nonprofits in general to survive in an increasingly hostile and demanding environment. Given this general objective it is time to consider what marketing actually is and how it can help serve the plethora of different categories of nonprofit organization alluded to above.

What is Marketing?

Many definitions of marketing exist, and with each new textbook that is published another definition is added to the list. Resisting the temptation to add my own, it is useful to begin by examining in detail some of the most well known and widely accepted. In the UK the most popular definition of marketing is that offered by the Chartered Institute of Marketing:

> Marketing is the management process responsible for identifying, anticipating and satisfying customer requirements profitably.

Ignoring for a moment the unfortunate emphasis on profit, there are two very striking components to this definition which are central to understanding marketing's role in any organization. In short, marketing is both a concept and a function. At a conceptual level, marketing represents a philosophy or approach to management that places the customer right at the centre of everything that an organization does. At a functional level it may be regarded as that part of the organization which gathers research, helps design new services, prices them, distributes them, and ultimately promotes them to the consumer. It is important though, that a wider perspective on marketing be retained. In too many organizations marketing is regarded only as this latter, somewhat narrow, functional field of endeavour and the conceptual level is ignored altogether. Marketing should not be seen as the preserve of a few personnel in the marketing department, but rather as a global approach to an organization's operations that should be adopted by all, irrespective of their position in the organization.

The concept of 'process' is also an important one since the 'process' of marketing in a genuinely marketing-led organization should start by determining customer needs and using these to form the basis of the products or services that the organization will supply. Indeed an understanding of customer requirements can offer an organization much more than the mere design of its market offering. Value can be created at every contact the customer has with an organization. If one understands what creates this value, it is possible to enhance the design of all an organization's systems with the simple goal of delivering the maximum possible value to the customer. The definition of marketing developed by Kotler and Fox (1987, 5) says far more about the mechanics of how this might be achieved:

> Marketing is the analysis, planning, implementation and control of carefully formulated programs designed to bring about voluntary exchanges of values with target markets for the purpose of achieving organisational objectives. It relies heavily on designing the organisation's offerings in terms of the target market's needs and desires and on using effective pricing, communication and distribution to inform, motivate and service the markets.

It is clear from both definitions that marketing is primarily concerned with identifying and satisfying the needs of an organization's customers and it is equally clear that the actual personnel responsible for fulfilling this role will not be exclusively those located in the marketing department. In the case of universities, for example, whilst the marketing department may well produce the prospectus and its associated advertising, the contact a student has with the admissions office, an academic in the selected department, the accommodation office, etc. will all be likely to have rather more impact on that student's ultimate decision about whether or not to study there. There is therefore a need for marketing to be embraced as a management philosophy which permeates all departments and all levels within an organization.

Regrettably, however, in some organizations the creation of a marketing department has been simply a knee-jerk response to falling sales. The purpose of the marketing department in such organizations is not to ensure the satisfaction of the organization's customers, but rather to hard sell failing products and services. It is no coincidence, for example, that many traditional universities have now created marketing roles and even whole marketing departments as they find themselves competing for students with the new universities from the ex-polytechnic sector. Rather than embrace the marketing concept and design new courses and services around the preferences of the market, many established organizations have simply looked to find better ways of selling their existing services. This is not what good marketing is all about. These two contrasting views of marketing are illustrated in Fig. 1.3.

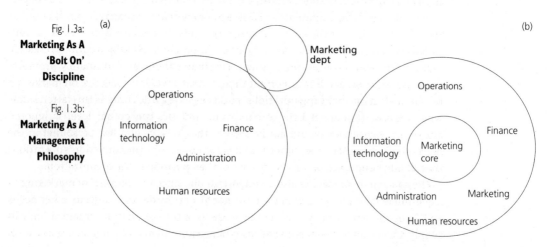

Fig. 1.3a:
Marketing As A 'Bolt On' Discipline

Fig. 1.3b:
Marketing As A Management Philosophy

In the first Figure (1.3a) marketing is regarded purely as a functional role which can be 'bolted on' to an organization, as and when circumstances require it. Nonprofits adopting this approach would tend to produce the products and services that the members of their board, often in isolation, decide are appropriate for the target group. Little or no effort would typically be made to ascertain the genuine needs of their customers, and failing demand would usually be met with ever more aggressive attempts to convince customers of the desirability of the existing products/services. The marketing function would therefore lack resources for activities other than promotion and would fail to have any real input to the strategic direction the organization might take. It is therefore with good reason that Malcolm MacDonald, one of the UK's leading authorities on marketing, refers to such departments as the 'Corporate Zit'.

By contrast an organization such as the one in Figure 1.3b, would regard marketing as the guiding philosophy which drives the whole approach to the management of the nonprofit. Such organizations plan their product/service provision in close consultation with customers and ensure that they are so structured/designed as to provide the maximum possible benefit and value to the ultimate users/beneficiaries. Moreover, each of the organization's systems are structured to enhance this value and every employee is specifically encouraged to regard marketing as his/her responsibility. The marketing function would be expected to engage in a wide range of activities, including market research, new product development, pricing, etc. and would have representation at the most senior level in the organization concerned. The details of how a change in emphasis from that depicted in Figure 1.3a to that in Figure 1.3b might be achieved is a subject to which we shall return in some detail in Chapter 2.

Certainly all organizations will want to consider and carefully manage the functional aspects of marketing in order to secure custom, but a focus solely on such activities will never actually involve the organization in genuine marketing. Indeed it is such narrow views of 'what marketing is' which have specifically contributed to earning the subject a bad name, particularly in some nonprofit quarters. Many arts organizations have until recently rejected the marketing concept because they saw it as being synonymous with selling, which by definition lowered the perceived quality of the service they were trying to provide. Indeed, when the author approached a senior member of staff in a neighbouring faculty recently to canvass views about arts marketing he was told quite categorically that the whole idea of marketing was quite 'reprehensible'. Whilst such one-word definitions of marketing have the merit of being easier to remember than those offered previously in this text, they represent a crass misunderstanding of what marketing is, and what it is trying to achieve. Genuine marketing both begins and ends with a thorough understanding of the needs of the customers that a particular organization exists to serve. The concept therefore has a clear relevance to *all* types of organization, whether they be motivated by profit or not.

The History of the Marketing Concept

Marketing ideas and concepts are certainly not new. Indeed the underlying concepts have been around for centuries. As long ago as 1776, Adam Smith, widely regarded as the father of modern economics, remarked that:

> Consumption is the sole end and purpose of all production; and the interest of the producer ought to be attended to, only so far as it may be necessary for promoting that of the consumer. The maxim is so perfectly self evident that it would be absurd to attempt to prove it. But in the mercantile system, the interest of the consumer is almost constantly sacrificed to that of the producer; and it seems to consider production, not consumption, as the ultimate end and object of all industry and commerce.

'Perfectly self evident' this concept may be, but in some quarters little appears to have changed over the past 220 years! Indeed it was not until comparatively recently that the idea of focusing on the needs and wants of consumers has come to the fore. Certainly until the beginning of the twentieth century much of British industry could be criticized for concentrating excessively on the economics of production. With an almost insatiable demand world-wide for the goods and services it could produce, there was little need to focus particularly on consumer needs, as someone, somewhere, would undoubtedly want the product. It is therefore no surprise to find that management theorists of the time were concerned with concepts such as 'efficiency' and regarded management as a pure science which could be explored and developed in an attempt to find 'the one best way of doing things'. Organizations from around this time could therefore be regarded as being production oriented. A typical structure for such an organization is given in Fig. 1.4.

Fig. 1.4: **Structure of a Typical Production Oriented Organization**

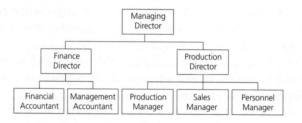

With the recession of the 1920s and 1930s, however, producers suddenly found themselves facing a considerable slump in demand. Being an efficient producer was no longer in itself enough to guarantee survival. Indeed the efficient production of inventory which could not be sold was a sure route to disaster. In recognition of this, a change in emphasis evolved. The sales function within the organization began to take on a new significance. A typical organization structure for what might be termed a sales oriented organization is shown in Fig. 1.5.

Once again organizations of the time were little concerned with the actual needs and wants of consumers. The focus was largely on how best to sell what the company could produce. It is worth noting in Fig. 1.5 how the sales function has risen to a more dominant position and appears to embrace all forms of contact with the customer, including the provision of customer service. The division between sales and the advertising and PR function is also worthy of note, particularly as the latter function was perceived

Fig. 1.5: **Structure of a Typical Sales Oriented Organization**

as being of far less significance. This is a division typical of the time and it reflects the dominant paradigm—the fervent desire to sell products to the customer.

It is interesting to note that whilst few genuinely production oriented organizations remain in business today, there are a large number of sales oriented organizations still in existence. Those organizations that have retained a sales orientation tend to be those that provide a product/service that will only ever have to be purchased once. It could therefore be argued that the concept of customer satisfaction is less an issue, since the organization will not be looking to solicit a repurchase. However, such a philosophy ignores the fact that consumers talk to one another and organizations can very quickly obtain a poor reputation for customer service. For proof of this, compile your own list of organizations that you consider to be sales oriented and ask a colleague to do likewise. My guess is that a comparison of both lists will reveal considerable similarity.

After the Second World War, the pattern of world trade was changed irrevocably. By the early 1950s, companies in the UK, for example, suddenly found themselves competing with organizations in America, Japan, and a revitalized Europe. Consumers were faced with a considerable choice of producer from whom to purchase. Moreover, the mushrooming of the mass media made consumers more generally aware of the range of purchase options that were open to them. Faced with this choice, consumers were finally able to exercise considerable power over producers and to elect to purchase only from those that they felt would adequately service their needs.

To be truly successful in these newly competitive markets, organizations needed to focus on customer needs and ensure that they met those needs better than could any of the competition. Organizations, therefore, finally began to recognize the importance of developing a customer or market focus and a new type of organization began to emerge. Figure 1.6 illustrates a structure typical of a market oriented organization.

Fig. 1.6: **Structure of a Typical Market Oriented Organization**

This new type of organization placed a high emphasis on the collection of marketing research and the use of it to identify customer needs. This information would then be used to inform new product development, to develop appropriate pricing strategies, to make the product accessible to the market, and, finally, to promote the advantages that it could offer the consumer and reassure them that it could meet their needs. As a result, the sales function is no longer of such importance. Indeed, if the marketing is handled correctly there may be no need to 'sell' the product at all—it should 'sell' itself. It is interesting to note, therefore, that the sales function in this example has now been subordinated to marketing in recognition that selling is simply one component of an overall marketing mix.

The Marketing Mix

The term 'marketing mix' warrants a little elaboration. Neil Borden first mooted the concept in 1953, likening the marketing task to the process of baking, where a number of ingredients have first to be assembled and blended (in appropriate proportions) together. A little more specifically, McCarthy (1960) was the first to suggest that there were four such ingredients to successful marketing which organizations needed to consider. He was responsible for introducing the now famous '4Ps' to marketing vocabulary and believed that adequate attention to each of these four key areas of marketing would ultimately result in corporate success. His mix consisted of the following four elements:

(1) *Product (or market entity)*—Marketers first need to be clear about the nature of their customers' requirements and use this knowledge to design products/services that will meet their needs. Marketers also need to have involvement in defining the range of goods or services that will be produced, for how long they will be produced and how they will be packaged.

(2) *Price*—As one would expect, this element refers to decisions taken in respect of the price that will be charged for the product or service, whether different types of customer will be charged differentially, what the discount and credit policies might be, etc.

(3) *Place*—Place refers to the channels or routes to market that it is intended to use. This would include a detailed analysis of the types of outlet to be used and a consideration of the physical distribution methods to be employed.

(4) *Promotion*—The final 'P' of McCarthy's mix refers to all the promotional tools that could be employed to stimulate an interest in the minds of consumers and ultimately an intention to purchase. 'Promotion' hence includes a consideration of advertising, sales promotion, direct marketing, public relations, personal selling, and exhibitions/trade fairs.

Of course this mix is a very simplistic framework and it has been much criticized over the years. One of the most lasting of these criticisms is that the mix is heavily oriented towards the marketing of physical products. Since most nonprofits are more concerned with services it is worth taking a brief look at an extension to the mix proposed by Booms and Bitner (1981). This time the authors refer to the '7Ps' of marketing where the additional three Ps are as follows:

(5) *Physical Evidence*—Service marketers also need to consider the nature of the environment in which the service will be delivered. Hence arts marketers need to consider the physical design and layout of their exhibitions to maximize visitor

interaction. Similarly hospitals need to ensure a bright, clean, and yet friendly environment for their patients.

(6) *Process*—The flow of the activities that will be encountered by service customers are also worthy of specific attention. Marketers need to consider the number of steps that will comprise the service and the extent to which customer involvement is necessary in the process.

(7) *People*—Arguably the most important ingredient of the service mix, since the people an organization employs are often part of the overall service experience encountered by the customer. This element hence involves a consideration of the employment, training, and motivation of individual members of service staff. A consideration of internal marketing communications is also usually included.

Of course marketing involves much more than simply looking at the four, or even seven Ps. Before a marketing mix can be developed, an organization must undertake a thorough analysis of its 'trading' environment and take careful account of its own internal capabilities. Only then will it be in a position to develop meaningful objectives for itself and develop key strategies and a marketing mix to secure them. The process by which all this is accomplished is outlined in detail in Chapter 4. For now it is important only to appreciate the role of marketing as a functional activity and the elements of the mix by which it is usually organized.

What can Marketing offer a Nonprofit Organization?

Having examined what marketing is, we are now in a position to explore the extent to which it can be of value to a nonprofit organization. There has been considerable debate over the years concerning whether the marketing concept can legitimately be applied to the management of such organizations.

In the late 1960s, Kotler and Levy (1969) were the first to open the debate on the relevance of the marketing concept to organizations working in the nonprofit sector. In their view marketing had the capacity to grow beyond its role as a narrow business activity and to take on a broader societal meaning. The authors defined marketing as: 'Sensitively serving and satisfying human need'.

Whilst this definition is somewhat broader than those introduced earlier it does draw attention to what good marketing can achieve in the NFP sector. It also has the merit of removing the emphasis on profit that was developed earlier in the CIM definition. After all, most nonprofits are by very definition less concerned with profit than they are with meeting some particular need in society. Marketing in this context is therefore concerned with facilitating an exchange process between an organization and its publics, so that some basic societal need can be fulfilled. The question therefore remains—whose need? Dare we refer to customers? The term has already been used in this text, and Kotler and Levy are in no doubt on this issue. The authors feel that all organizations have customers, whether they choose to refer to them as such or not. A list of typical customers for a variety of nonprofit organizations is given in Table 1.2.

Table 1.2
Nonprofits and Key Customer Groups

Category of Organization	Key Customer Groups
Charities	Volunteers
	Individual Donors
	Corporate Donors
	Charitable Trusts
	Recipients of Goods/Services
Arts Organizations	Visitors
	Audiences
	Corporate Sponsors
	Arts Funding Bodies
Healthcare Trusts	Patients
	Visitors/Relatives of Patients
	General Practitioners
	Insurance Companies
	Government Funders
Education	Students
	Alumni
	Industry
	Research Funders
	Local Communities
	Local/National Government

Viewing those groups in society that a nonprofit is designed to serve as customers is a very powerful notion because it forces those responsible for the marketing of such organizations to begin their planning processes by defining precisely the requirements of those customers. Think, for example, of those wonderfully boring museums we all encountered as children. Row after row of neat glass cases each displaying their sterile collection of antiquities. At least if you were physically fit you could drag yourself from one end of an exhibition to another, but what about those who were handicapped in some way? Until comparatively recently, few facilities were provided for the disabled, and museums were therefore largely perceived as unwelcoming by such categories of individual. Fortunately there has now been a sea-change of emphasis in the sector. The Albert Memorial Museum in Exeter, for example, has recently completely redesigned its displays. Market research revealed (not surprisingly) that visitors actually did not like to see everything behind glass. Sets were therefore created which now give an impression of walking through a particular age in history. There are also a few animated displays, and children can touch and feel some of the less fragile exhibits. Moreover, the whole collection has been designed so that those with a visual impairment can actually read the written commentaries and those who are confined to a wheelchair can still get a good view of the exhibits and not feel constricted.

What this example clearly illustrates is the difference between a product and a marketing orientation in the arts sector. At one extreme we have a picture of a museum which views its collection as the primary and indeed sole reason for its existence. At the other end of the spectrum we see a museum that is proud enough of its collection that it desires to encourage as many people as it can to come and enjoy it. Moreover, such museums want the visitor to be enthused by their collections and to go away believing that they have had an educational, yet entertaining, visit. In short, one form of museum is attempting to satisfy its customers whilst the other is not. Which of these should be regarded as performing the greatest service to society?

There are many clues in this simple example to what marketing can offer a nonprofit. Specifically the following benefits are worthy of note:

(1) Marketing can improve the levels of customer satisfaction attained—in the simple example outlined above the Albert Memorial Museum has been able to substantially improve levels of visitor satisfaction without compromising the integrity of the collection.

(2) Marketing can also assist in the attraction of resources to a nonprofit organization. Many nonprofits need to raise funds to support their work. Marketing tools and techniques can offer fundraisers substantial utility and afford them greater opportunities to fulfil an organization's mission.

(3) The adoption of a professional approach to marketing may help an organization to define its distinctive competencies. In other words, marketing can define what an organization can offer society that others cannot. This may be manifested in an ability to work with particular categories of people in society, or it may be manifested in the way in which such work is conducted. Whatever the case, if an organization can identify those areas where it can add value, over and above that which can be offered by 'competitors', it can refine those competencies and use them to enhance both fundraising and service delivery as a result.

(4) A professional approach to marketing also offers organizations a framework within which to work. A systematic approach to researching needs, setting objectives, planning to meet those objectives, and the instigation of formal control activities to ensure that they will actually be achieved, should minimize the wastage of valuable marketing resources.

Despite the obvious benefits that marketing can offer an NFP there are a number of important differences between the application of marketing in a for-profit and a not-for-profit context. Various authors have discussed these differences, and there is considerable debate about whether the differences are as real as they might at first appear. Nevertheless the following list developed by Lovelock and Weinberg (1990) may help to explain some of the complexities the marketing function in a typical nonprofit may encounter.

Multiple Constituencies

In a for-profit context the marketing function is concerned with developing goods and services which will then be sold to customers. This (hopefully!) will generate revenue which can then be used to purchase the raw materials necessary to produce the next generation of goods and services—and so on. In short there is only one constituency which needs to be addressed by the marketing function. In many charities however there are two constituencies, since the individuals who donate funds are rarely those that will actually be able to draw benefit from the services that the charity ultimately provides. In other words, there is a clear distinction between resource attraction and resource allocation.

From this simple description you can probably already see why the idea that multiple constituencies might be something unique to the nonprofit sector has been criticized by some writers. It has been argued, for example, that many business organizations draw income from a variety of sources, not necessarily just their primary customer group. Some may attract significant government funding or seek occasionally to raise funds from a new issue of shares. Thus marketers in business organizations can also find themselves dealing with multiple constituencies. It does seem safe to conclude however that the division between resource attraction and resource allocation is unlikely to be as clear-cut as it is in many nonprofit organizations.

Non-Financial Objectives

As Drucker (1990, 107) notes,

> performance is the ultimate test of any institution. Every non-profit institution exists for the sake of performance in changing people and society. Yet, performance is also one of the truly difficult areas for the executive in the non-profit institution.

Setting objectives which can then be used to monitor performance is a particular problem for nonprofit organizations because of the intangible nature of much of the service provided. It is also a problem because, as Drucker goes on to note, 'the results of a nonprofit institution are always outside the organisation, not inside'. Their results are therefore inherently more difficult to measure. This is not to suggest, however, that nonprofit organizations should not at least try to set targets—although the question then remains, to what should these relate?

It is probably fair to dispense with profit maximization theories in this sector. Most nonprofits are by definition little concerned with profit. They may however still be concerned with the concept of maximization, in the sense that they may have objectives which are concerned with input or output maximization. In the case of the latter, many nonprofits appear to perpetually find that demand always outstrips their capacity to supply. The charity for the homeless, Shelter, for example, would undoubtedly view its primary objective as being to help as many homeless people as possible. In the case of the former, some charities have as their goal resource attraction, on the basis that there will always be needs for them to meet. The charity Guide Dogs For The Blind is arguably one such organization, as it has been criticized for generating substantial reserves in recent years. The charity would argue however that it is very necessary for them to continue fundraising as, some day, all the guide dogs they have already supplied will need replacing.

It is also clear that the subject matter of any objectives set will differ from the for-profit sector. Nonprofits cover a very wide range of human interests and behaviours and this is reflected in the broad diversity of objectives they possess. The author has encountered objectives written in terms of the numbers of people aided, an individual's quality of life, changes in public attitudes, and even mortality rates!

Services and Social Behaviours rather than Physical Goods

The majority of nonprofits produce services rather than physical goods. Indeed many organizations do not even produce a service that one could clearly define. Some organizations exist simply to attempt to alter some form of social behaviour through either direct communication with the target group, or indirectly through the lobbying of government. Nevertheless, the distinction between services and products is an important one, since many charities do market services and doing so is an inherently more complex process than the marketing of physical goods. As Zeithaml *et al.* (1985) note, there are four key differences which should be taken account of, namely:

(1) *Intangibility*—When a customer purchases a physical good or service he/she can assess it by its appearance, taste, smell, etc. They can therefore 'confirm' their expectations about the properties of the product they are going to receive. With a service, however, the consumer has no way of verifying the claims of the producer until the service has actually been purchased.

(2) *Inseparability*—Physical goods are produced and then purchased by the customer. With services the process is the other way around. Services are sold first and then produced at the time of consumption by the customer. (In this sense production and consumption are said to be inseparable.) This means that producer and consumer have to interact to produce the service. Marketing a service therefore involves not only facilitating an exchange process, but also facilitating an often quite complex producer/consumer interaction.

(3) *Heterogeneity*—Allied to the previous point, since production and consumption are inseparable, there are few chances for a service supplier to carry out pre-inspection or quality control in the same way that one can with physical goods. Indeed monitoring and control processes are of necessity considerably more complex in the context of services.

(4) *Perishability*—Services cannot be stored in the same way that one can store food or electrical items in a retail outlet. If a theatrical performance begins with a half-empty house, or there are last-minute cancellations of a physician's appointments, those services have been lost for ever. Marketers, therefore, have a more complex balancing operation to perform to ensure that their services remain as optimally utilized as possible.

These differences are summarised in Table 1.3.

Table 1.3
Services are Different

Goods	Services	Resulting Implications
Tangible	Intangible	Services cannot be inventoried Services cannot be patented Services cannot be readily displayed or communicated.
Standardized	Heterogeneous	Service delivery and customer satisfaction depends on employee actions Service quality depends on many uncontrollable factors There is no sure knowledge that the service delivered matches what was planned and expected
Production separate from consumption	Simultaneous production and consumption	Customer participates in and affects the transaction Customers affect each other Decentralization may be essential Mass production is difficult
Non-perishable	Perishable	It is difficult to synchronize supply and demand with services Services cannot be returned or resold

Source: Zeithaml *et al.* (1996), *Services Marketing*, McGraw Hill, New York. Reproduced with the kind permission of McGraw Hill.

Where NFPs are concerned with physical behaviours rather than services, additional complications arise. Attempting to influence social behaviours will never be a non-controversial task, no matter how much benefit may ultimately accrue to society as a result of such endeavours. Organizations such as ASH for example—the anti-smoking campaign—continually face pressure from organizations with diametrically opposed views, such as nonprofits set up by smoker's rights activists. This is not competition in the way that one may define it in the for-profit context, but rather an attempt by one nonprofit to deride the work of another.

Public Scrutiny/Non-Market Pressures

Certain categories of organization within the NFP sector are open to intense levels of public scrutiny. The emergency services, local authorities, hospitals, and even universities are subject to regular public scrutiny. UK universities, for example, are subject to a comprehensive audit of the quality of their teaching and research every four years. In the healthcare sector the government white paper 'Working For Patients' has recently introduced the independent body, the Audit Commission, into the UK healthcare framework. The commission (which has been performing a similar function for Local Authorities for some years) now has responsibility for ensuring that the National Health Service continues to provide 'value for money'. Such public scrutiny simply does not occur on the same scale in a for-profit business context.

Indeed nonprofits have to contend with a variety of other non-market pressures. Whilst no one would claim for a moment that it is easy for a business organization to be able to forecast demand for its products, demand for the services of a nonprofit can fall away to nothing or literally double overnight. The nature of Oxfam's work overseas with Third World countries can change radically from year to year depending on political, economic, and climatic conditions. The very nature of a focus on the disadvantaged makes it almost impossible to know where future priorities might lie. As a further example, at the time of writing, the UK government has just decided to withdraw the provision of state benefits to those seeking political asylum in the country who do not declare this intention upon arrival. Their action has compelled the International Red Cross to supply food parcels to people who now have no means of supporting themselves. This is the first time Red Cross food parcels have been distributed in the UK in over thirty years—not therefore an easy action to predict.

The instability of the environment in which many nonprofits operate thus contributes to the fact that such organizations often have less control over their own destiny than their counterparts in the for-profit sector. Marketers in nonprofits therefore have a much more complex role to perform.

Tension between Mission and Customer Satisfaction

The final key difference that may be encountered in the nonprofit sector relates to the nature of some nonprofit missions. Many such organizations are compelled by their mission to take a long-term view of their relationships with their target markets. Health and welfare groups in the Third World, for example, may be promoting the use of contraception in direct conflict with the established patterns of local belief and culture. Similarly many theatres and arts centres have a mission to explore a wide range of art forms, not just to provide those forms of entertainment that they know will be well patronized by their local community. There is therefore a tension between the satisfaction of current customer needs and the fulfilment of a particular organization's mission. Short-term customer satisfaction may often have to be sacrificed by nonprofits as they take a longer-term view of the benefit they can offer to society.

The idea that organizations should take this longer-term view of the welfare of their 'customer' groups is a notion that one would rarely encounter in the for-profit sector. Business organizations make their money by satisfying the immediate needs of their customers today, and need therefore to devote the maximum effort to the achievement of this goal. One of the key advantages of a strong nonprofit sector is that the division between resource attraction and resource allocation affords a greater opportunity for a longer-term perspective to be adopted. Whilst the needs of the current customer group are important (and will be ignored completely at the organization's peril), nonprofits do have the luxury of being able to strike a balance between the short and long-term needs of their key customer groups. Hence the role of marketing in this context genuinely becomes one of 'sensitively serving the needs of society'.

Typical Objections to Marketing

Despite the benefits that marketing can provide, there have been a number of objections raised over the years when writers have mooted the possibility of its application to the nonprofit sector. The most common of such objections, usually raised by managers working in the sector, are dealt with below.

Marketing is not Necessary

This objection stems from a belief that the nonprofit is doing worthwhile work and is therefore worthy of support for its own sake. In the UK this idea has been particularly prevalent in the education sector where established universities have traditionally not felt the need to market their services, as they have expected students to research the quality of various institutions and to 'seek them out' to study a particular subject. The idea that academics are somehow 'intellectual monks', to whom people will turn for an education because of the perceived quality of an institution, is now hopelessly outdated. Students have a much wider choice of courses than they had even ten years ago and because of this can 'pick and choose' the institutions at which they want to study. Given that a much larger percentage of young people are being encouraged to enter higher education, the profile of the student body has also changed. As a result, all but the Oxbridge universities are now finding themselves having to compete hard to attract the brightest students.

Marketing Invades an Individual's Privacy

Marketing is viewed by some as intrusive, as it is seen as invading an individual's right to privacy. This criticism is perhaps a little more difficult to answer since at some point marketers will undoubtedly conduct research in an attempt to identify consumer needs. As Kotler and Clarke (1987, 22) point out:

> Market research in any consumer industry is invasive; market researchers may enter people's homes to ask about likes and dislikes, beliefs and attitudes, income and other personal characteristics. Moreover in

[the NFP sector], the research is more likely to cover sensitive areas individuals would prefer not to reveal to strangers.

Of course if organizations are to get close to their market and understand what requirements customers might have, a certain amount of marketing research will always be necessary. This is particularly so in the context of the NFP sector since, as we have already seen, the concern is often with services and social behaviours which are by definition more difficult for an organization to monitor. However if one considers that the ultimate aim of this research should be to benefit society as a whole, perhaps an occasional 'invasion of privacy' could be forgiven.

Of course market research is simply one way in which an individual's privacy can be compromised. Many forms of promotion are judged to be unwelcome and invasive. Advertising, direct mail, telemarketing, etc. have all attracted a bad reputation at one point or another for entering someone's home with unwelcome messages about an equally unwanted product or service. This is not however a criticism of marketing *per se*, but rather a criticism of the way that marketing tools have been employed by particular organizations. Poorly planned and executed campaigns may often target individuals who have no interest in the service being promoted and give the marketing profession a bad name. Neither does it make sense for nonprofits to engage in such activities as they waste valuable marketing resources. Instead organizations should look to refine their targeting and to develop a more focused campaign to promote their services only to those who would stand to benefit.

Marketing Lowers Perceived Quality

The author was recently approached by a university admissions officer who felt aggrieved that his university was going to begin actively marketing its undergraduate courses. He felt this would lower the perceived quality of those courses in the minds of potential students. In his words, his 'university will appear desperate' to attract students. On further enquiry what he was actually objecting to was the proposed advertising of his undergraduate courses. He may indeed have had a point since until recently the advertising of undergraduate courses was taboo in the UK. The existence of a gentlemen's agreement between universities to avoid unseemly competition precluded the use of advertising (except during the 'clearing' process). It would therefore be relatively unusual for a university to advertise and it may yet prove to have a detrimental effect on recruitment.

However, the reader will by now appreciate that marketing is much more than mere advertising alone and this criticism is therefore based on a false premise. The idea that the attainment of a customer focus would somehow result in a drop in the quality of service provision is frankly obtuse. There are regrettably, however, still a significant number of organizations who have failed to grasp the value of marketing as a concept and this objection is thus still one that is commonly encountered.

Marketing is Immoral

This objection also stems from a fundamental misunderstanding of the marketing concept. It is often raised because marketing is seen as manipulating consumers into purchasing goods and services that they don't really need. The origins of this objection are rooted in a failure to grasp the difference between marketing and sales. It is certainly true that a sales oriented organization continually strives to persuade customers to buy as much of their product or service as possible. Such organizations are little concerned with the genuine needs of customers. Market oriented organizations, on the other hand, have realized that such an emphasis is ultimately self defeating. Instead they focus on supplying customers with the services they actually need and make it clear who their target groups actually are, in an attempt to avoid unnecessary purchases by those who would be better served by another organization. If this sounds a little trite, it is worth remembering that this is simply good 'business' practice. Dissatisfied customers are estimated to discuss their experiences with an average of seven close friends, relatives, and colleagues. Making a sale at any cost can hence result in a significant amount of negative word-of-mouth 'advertising' and is ultimately self defeating.

Marketing will Stifle Innovation

This criticism is a little more subtle. It is raised by those who argue that a marketing oriented organization will attempt to studiously serve the needs of its target markets. It will concentrate ever harder on trying to exactly match its products/services with the profile of those demanded by its customers. In doing so, however, it will be unlikely to devote much time and effort to the development of radical new developments which could ultimately benefit society as a whole. Consumers do not generally enjoy change and are hence unlikely to recommend it to marketing researchers if asked.

Clearly there is a danger that marketing could force an organization unwittingly into a form of management myopia, but this pitfall is perhaps more relevant to a business organization where profit is the prime consideration. Since new-product development is an inherently risky strategy, a business organization will tend to demand considerable evidence that an investment in a new product/service is likely to pay off. In the nonprofit context, however, one could legitimately argue that managers have considerably more latitude in terms of how they choose to fulfil an organization's mission, particularly where there is a separation of resource attraction and resource allocation. Whilst one still has to be conscious that funders have their own agenda and would not wish to see a nonprofit engage in unnecessary risk it is certainly true that some funders may actually encourage the organization they are supporting to be innovative. This is the case with much arts funding and indeed evidence of the ability to innovate may well be one of the necessary criteria to be awarded such funding in the first place.

In essence these are the typical objections that are raised to marketing in a nonprofit context. Those readers who are interested in learning more about specific objections raised in the context of health care or education are advised to consult Kotler and Clarke (1987) or Kotler and Fox (1987).

Is Marketing gaining Acceptance?

Is marketing gaining acceptance in the nonprofit sector? The short answer to any such question must surely be yes; although certain parts of the sector have undoubtedly been more responsive than others. Charity fundraisers, for example, have long been making use of marketing tools and techniques. Indeed, fundraisers from the best-performing charities are now agency trained, and aware that to compete they must offer a very real service to their 'clients'. Thus in their dealings with the corporate sector, charities are increasingly seeking to work in partnership with their sponsors. This has in part been driven by an increasing acceptance of the need for marketing, but also by the expectations of the corporate customers themselves. The selection process employed by corporates to identify potential charity partners has moved away from a woolly pattern of corporate philanthropy to one where hard-nosed assessments are made of the direct benefits that could accrue from an association with a particular nonprofit organization. Indeed, in many cases charities are now required to pitch for the business. As Fendley and Hewitt (1994, 14) note, 'gone are the days of battleship ladies in intimidating hats . . . [trying to get] the chairman in a moral half-nelson.'

Staying with charities for the moment, there has certainly been an increase in the use of professionally qualified (or experienced) marketers from the for-profit sector. As Addison (1993) notes, heads of appeals are being increasingly drawn from the for-profit sector and, as trained professionals, they are bringing with them a variety of new skills. As a result many organizations have redefined their mission and/or their image. Donaldson (1994) for example, cites the case of the Save The Children Fund which redefined its mission in the late 1980s and now aims to 'make a reality of children's rights'. Adopting standard business practice, their Director General, Nicholas Hinton, has fought to ensure that everyone connected with the organization both understands the mission and strives to make it a reality. In a further example Braid (1994) identifies that the charity National Children's Home has recently rechristened itself NCH Action For Children at a cost of £50,000. Research by fundraisers indicated that, although the organization is the second largest children's charity in the UK, fewer than 8 per cent of the population had any awareness of it. The change of image was hence seen as essential so that the charity could strive for a clear positioning in the minds of potential donors.

It would be a mistake, however, to assume that an enhanced awareness of the benefits that marketing can offer is limited just to the realm of charity fundraising. Arts marketers too have come to recognize the utility that the concept can offer. Indeed in 1991 the consortium of Arts Council and Regional Arts Association Officers went on record as stating that marketing should be viewed as essential to increasing the perceived value of the arts in society (MANAR, 1991). In the healthcare sector marketing techniques have been found to raise both awareness of, and participation in, screening clinics, health promotion programmes, etc. Even in the social sphere, marketing has begun to touch all our lives, warning us of the dangers of smoking, alcoholism, and drug abuse, and ensuring that the most vulnerable groups within society receive the support and understanding they deserve.

In short the marketing concept has a great relevance for all nonprofit organizations. What is necessary now is to explain in more detail the range of marketing techniques that exist and how they can be organized in the development of a meaningful marketing plan. This is the focus of Part B of this text, whilst Part C is designed to relate the theory of marketing to the specifics of a number of nonprofit contexts. Marketing's application to fundraising, health care, the arts, education, and social marketing will therefore be examined in some depth.

Discussion Questions

1. Using examples from your own experience, distinguish between nonprofit organizations that have a product, sales, or a market orientation?
2. What are the key benefits that marketing can offer a nonprofit organization?
3. What typical objections may be encountered in attempting to introduce marketing to a nonprofit organization for the first time? How might these be countered?
4. What is meant by the term 'marketing mix'? How would you describe the marketing mix of your own organization?

References

Addison, J. (1993) 'The Selling of Giving', *Sales Promotion*, Oct, 30–3.

Booms, B. H. and Bitner, M. J. (1981) 'Marketing Strategies and Organisation Structures for Service Firms, Marketing of Services', in Donnelly, J. and George W. R., (eds) *Marketing Of Services*, Chicago, American Marketing Association.

Borden, N. H. (1964) 'The Concept of the Marketing Mix', *Journal of Advertising Research*, June, 2–7.

Braid, M. (1994) 'Children's Charity in Drive for Recognition', *Independent*, 1 Feb, 1.

Commonwealth Federation (1996) *NGOs What They Are and What They Do*, The Commonwealth Foundation, Webpage (http://carryon.oneworld.org/com).

Donaldson, L. (1994) 'Charities: A Man with a Mission', *Independent*, 29 Sept, 31.

Drucker, P. (1990) *Managing the Non-Profit Organisation*, Oxford, Butterworth Heinemann.

Fendley, A. and Hewitt, M. (1994) 'When Charity Begins with a Pitch', *Marketing*, 23 June, 14–15.

Kotler, P. and Clarke, R. N. (1987) *Marketing for Health Care Organisations*, Englewood Cliffs, Prentice Hall.

Kotler, P. and Fox, K. F. A. (1985) *Strategic Marketing for Educational Institutions*, Englewood Cliffs, Prentice Hall.

Kotler, P. and Levy, S. (1969) 'Broadening the Concept of Marketing', *Journal of Marketing*, Vol. 33, Jan, 10–15.

Lovelock, C. H. and Weinberg, C. B. (1990) *Public and Nonprofit Marketing*, 2nd edn, San Francisco, The Scientific Press.

McCarthy, E. J. (1960) *Basic Marketing: A Managerial Approach*, Illinois, Richard Irwin.

MANAR (1991) *National Arts and Media Strategy: Discussion Document on Marketing the Arts*, Marketing the Arts Nationally and Regionally (MANAR), London, Arts Council.

Salamon, L. M. and Anheier, H. K. (1992) *In Search of the Non-Profit Sector II: The Problem of Classification*, Johns Hopkins Comparative Non-Profit Sector Project, Baltimore, Johns Hopkins Institute for Policy Studies.

Smith, A. (1776) *The Wealth Of Nations*, Letchworth, Dent and Sons Ltd.

Zeithaml, V. A. (1985) 'How Consumer Evaluation Processes Differ Between Goods and Services', *Journal of Marketing*, Fall, 186–90.

Zeithaml, V. A. and Bitner, M. J. (1996) *Services Marketing*, New York, McGraw Hill.

The Implementation of Marketing

IT IS THE PURPOSE of this second major section of the text to introduce the reader to the tools and techniques that can be utilized to develop a nonprofit's approach to marketing at both conceptual and practical levels. In Chapter 2 we will examine how the marketing concept can be operationalized within a nonprofit context with a view to the attainment of a market orientation. Specifically the advantages of such a focus will be developed and a framework suggested within which a market orientation may be developed.

In Chapter 3 we will then move on to consider the practical application of marketing and specifically how a nonprofit organization might select and target those groups of customers it is considered most appropriate to serve. Deciding on an appropriate basis for the segmentation of a market, and isolating those individuals most likely to benefit from the nonprofit service, is an essential prerequisite to the development of a full marketing plan. It is this latter topic which forms the basis of Chapter 4, the final chapter in this section. Here the reader will be introduced to a marketing planning framework and a number of the essential tools and techniques that may be adopted to aid the development of an appropriately targeted plan.

On completion of this section, therefore, the reader should be in a position to develop an outline marketing plan for a nonprofit organization. The nuances of marketing's application to a variety of nonprofit sectors will then be developed in Part C of this text.

2

Developing a Marketing Orientation

Objectives

By the end of this Chapter you should be able to:

    (1) understand the key requirements for achieving a market orientation;

    (2) develop a customer focus in a given organization;

    (3) define and manage service quality in a given organization;

    (4) develop a competitor focus in a given organization;

    (5) design and implement a competitor monitoring system;

    (6) develop and enhance interfunctional co-ordination within a given organization;

    (7) design and implement an internal marketing strategy.

What is a Market Orientation?

In Chapter 1 we discussed the historic evolution of the marketing concept and traced its development through from early production and sales led organisations. The reader will recall that as organizations began to recognize the value of marketing not only as a functional activity, but also as a philosophy or approach to business, the first truly marketing oriented organizations were brought into existence. As we shall see, such organizations have a number of defining characteristics, which, it has been argued, allow them to achieve above average returns in their respective industries. Whilst in this text we are not concerned with the idea of returns in a strictly business sense it is instructive to see what can be learnt from these organizations. Before starting out on this path however, it is once again important to be clear about the terminology we intend to employ. What exactly do we understand by the term marketing orientation?

A variety of writers, such as Doyle (1987), Go and Pine (1995), and Palmer (1994), have previously used the term marketing orientation to describe an organization that has developed a strong focus on its customers. Such organizations begin serving the needs of a particular market only when they have a clear understanding of the requirements thereof. Similarly such organizations maintain close links with their customers and ensure that the delivered service consistently matches or exceeds market expectations. Kotler and Clarke (1987) therefore define marketing orientation as follows:

> A marketing orientation holds that the main task of the organisation is to determine the needs and wants of target markets and to satisfy them through the design, communication, pricing and delivery of appropriate and competitively viable products and services.

Regrettably however, as in other areas of marketing, the water has been muddied by the use of other, conflicting terminology. Expressing a similar idea, for example, Shapiro (1988) and Webster (1988) have preferred to use the term 'customer orientation' explicitly. Kohli and Jaworski (1990) on the other hand, utilize the label 'market orientation' for two key reasons. Firstly, as will be apparent from the comments in Chapter 1, marketing has suffered from something of an image problem in many organizations, particularly in the nonprofit sector. The use of the expression 'market' orientation is therefore likely to be less politically charged. Allied to this, the term tends to focus an attention on markets, not customers *per se*, and whilst many nonprofit managers have difficulty in recognizing the latter, most now concede to the existence of the former. The second key advantage is that marketing cannot then be accused of rampant imperialism, inflating its own importance within the organization. The construct is thus effectively removed from the province of the marketing department, instead involving all departments in the process of understanding and satisfying market requirements. The following definition of what we shall refer to here as 'market orientation' will therefore be employed throughout the remainder of this text.

> The generation of appropriate market intelligence pertaining to current and future customer needs, and the relative abilities of competitive entities to satisfy these needs; the integration and dissemination of such intelligence across departments; and the co-ordinated design and execution of the organisation's strategic response to market opportunities. (Kohli and Jaworski, 1990)

Having now settled on the terminology, it would doubtless be helpful to explore the concept in a little more depth. Narver and Slater (1990) have usefully distilled the definition given above into three behavioural strands—namely, customer orientation, competitor orientation, and interfunctional co-ordination—and argue that all three should be regarded as being of equal importance. These are illustrated in Fig. 2.1.

Customer orientation involves the organization in achieving a sufficient understanding of its target markets to be able to create superior value for them. Since in a service environment the creation of value is often highly dependent on the quality of customer interactions with staff, the achievement of a market orientation thus involves the development of an appropriate set of cultural attitudes which should ultimately permeate the whole organization (Deshpande and Webster, 1989).

The concept of a competitor orientation involves the organization in understanding the short-term strengths/weaknesses and long-term capabilities/strategies of both its current and future competitors. This is essential if the organization is to avoid being overtaken by competitive innovation (see, for example, Porter, 1985).

Fig. 2.1: **The Components of Market Orientation**

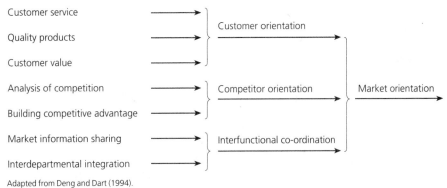

Adapted from Deng and Dart (1994).

Interfunctional co-ordination refers to how the organization utilizes its internal resources in the creation of superior value for target consumers. It is important, for example, for opportunities for synergy to be exploited across traditional departmental boundaries and for customer and competitive intelligence to be shared constructively between all those who stand to benefit. Indeed Kohli and Jaworski (1990) expand on the concept of interfunctional co-ordination in a detailed study of a number of market oriented organizations. The authors suggest that such organizations can be characterized as having:

(1) a close integration of the marketing function into the organisational structure and strategic planning process;
(2) a primary identification with the organization as a whole rather than individual departments;
(3) inter-departmental relations based on co-operation rather than rivalry.

We shall be utilizing the framework provided in Fig. 2.1 throughout the remainder of this chapter to examine in some detail how a marketing orientation might best be developed within a nonprofit organization.

Achieving a Customer Focus

An Overview

Before elaborating in any more detail on the organizational actions required to achieve a customer focus it is worth briefly returning to the question of the benefits that such a focus can bring. In the context of nonprofit organizations this analysis should be split between those customers who supply the funding and those who require it. In respect of the former, writers such as Kotler (1982) and Lamb (1983) draw a distinction in fundraising between what they view as campaign and development orientations, which may be regarded as equating with sales and market orientations respectively. As Fig. 2.2 shows, the emphasis in organizations with the latter form of emphasis is very much on researching donor needs and wants. Rather than simply attempting to communicate the needs of the organization to those who will hopefully feel disposed to give, the organization gives considerable thought to what the donor is likely to want from the exchange. Some individuals will doubtless want regular communications

Fig. 2.2: **Campaign and Development Orientations Contrasted**

	Focus	Target	Means	Ends
Campaign orientation	Inward upon the organizations' needs	Everybody	Intensive promotion	Money
Development orientation	Outward upon donors' wants and preferences	Specific individuals and groups	Co-ordinated development strategies	Mutually satisfying exchanges

Source: Lamb (1983). Reprinted with permission from *Fund Raising Management Magazine*, 224 Seventh St, Garden City, New York, 11530, USA (516/746-6700).

with the charity, others may give only once a year and expect to hear only at that time; some donors may want quite explicit recognition of their donation, and others may simply prefer to retain their anonymity. It should also be noted that certain categories of individual will feel predisposed to support different aspects of the organization's work, because they perceive a relevance to their own values, and even within these subsets of customers there will undoubtedly be those who will wish to give at somewhat higher levels than others. The targeting strategy of the charity should hence reflect these differences and not attempt to treat all donors identically. Donors do reward organizations that treat them as individuals and not as simply another name on the database, as the performance of organizations such as Botton Village will attest.

Aside from the benefits of enhanced customer satisfaction, benefits will also accrue because of the more effective use of fundraising resources. When one understands the needs of donors it is, for example, possible to get away from heavily promoting the cause. A greater understanding of donors can lead to the development of less aggressive strategies based on the development of relationships rather than the hard sell. Intensive promotion should therefore not be necessary in a truly customer focused organization.

Of course most nonprofits have customers in the sense not only of those individuals or organizations that supply funding, but also those individuals or organizations that consume it. The achievement of a customer focus amongst recipient groups has traditionally been harder for most nonprofits to accomplish because staff and even volunteers have historically failed to value these target groups. Bruce (1995) suggests that there are a number of reasons why this should be so, including:

(1) *Monopolistic position*—The position of many nonprofits in the market is one of a monopoly supplier. There can therefore be a danger that customers are so reliant on their services that such organizations may adopt a 'take it or leave it' attitude and fail to take the time to adapt their offerings to individual needs.

(2) *Demand far exceeds supply*—Often, even where competition does exist, the demand in many nonprofit markets for the services the organization can supply is so great that they can never hope to meet even a fraction of it. The temptation for nonprofits here is to tackle the most homogenous categories of need, since these are usually somewhat easier to serve in volume with an undifferentiated service. There may be occasions, however, when such categories of need are not the most pressing, and smaller groups of customers with more acute levels of need may find themselves ill-served by the standard services available.

(3) *Patronizing attitude of 'haves' to 'have nots'*—There is a particular danger of this phenomenon in markets where the demand is high for the service provided. Service

delivery staff may take the view that recipients are lucky to be amongst the 'chosen few' and should by implication feel only gratitude towards the supplying organization. The idea that recipients have the right to express any form of negative comment or criticism remains anathema to many.

(4) *Professional training encourages the view that 'I know what's best for you'*—Many nonprofit service providers are highly trained professionals, who possess expert knowledge in their field. They may therefore feel that they have a complete understanding of the needs of the recipient and thereby not be sensitive to signs of differing individual need.

(5) *Motivation of belief based organizations*—Nonprofits whose mission is to promote certain behaviours because of religious beliefs may fail to take a true account of the needs of their recipients. Indeed, service providers may strive to inculcate behaviour patterns that directly conflict with what the recipients perceive to be their needs. There is, of course, nothing inherently wrong with this approach, as it may cut to the heart of the reason for the nonprofit's existence, but even the most zealous of religiously oriented organizations may find their path somewhat easier if they begin by understanding current customer requirements. It is so much easier to plan a strategy if one understands where one is starting from.

(6) *Action oriented approach*—Historically one of the greatest strengths of the voluntary sector has been its ability to respond rapidly to changing patterns of need. Unconstrained by government bureaucracy or the profit needs of shareholders, voluntary organizations have been able to take immediate action, specifically tailored at a local level to alleviate the distress and/or suffering of those in need. Whilst the speed of response may legitimately be regarded as a very real strength, there are also key difficulties that can be encountered with this approach. Principal amongst these is the fact that fundamental *a priori* customer research is not widespread throughout the sector. This in turn can create a situation where the solutions proposed by voluntary organizations are sub-optimal from a customer's perspective because their real needs have not been fully understood.

Bruce is clearly not optimistic about the ability of nonprofits to achieve a genuine customer focus amongst their beneficiary groups. In many cases there remain very real difficulties to be overcome. Nevertheless the culture within the nonprofit sector is changing and it is fair to say that a great many organizations are beginning at least to wake up to the importance of satisfying their customers. We can now return to the question of how best this might be accomplished. As illustrated in Fig. 2.1, there are two dimensions to a customer orientation: the provision of quality services, and the creation of customer value. Each of these will now be considered in turn.

Service Quality

In its simplest form service quality is a product of the effort that every member of the organization invests in satisfying customers. More specifically, service quality has been defined as:

> The delivery of excellent or superior service relative to customer expectations. (Zeithamal and Bitner, 1996)

Quality . . . is behaviour—an attitude—that says you . . . will never settle for anything less than the best
in service for your stakeholders, whether they are customers, the community, your stockholders or the
colleagues with whom you work every day.   (Harvey, 1995)

[Quality is] providing a better service than the customer expects.   (Lewis, 1989)

At the heart of these and other definitions of quality lies the fact that perceived quality is what the consumer sees and is the result of a comparison between expectations of
service quality and the actual service received. Churchill and Suprenant (1982) were
amongst the first to moot the existence of what has come to be known as the 'disconfirmation paradigm'. Whilst this is a concept that has recently received criticism in
the literature, largely because there is no real evidence that the comparative process actually takes place, it does represent a useful starting point in our analysis.

Accepting for a moment that the disconfirmation paradigm is an appropriate way to
model customer perceptions of delivered service quality, a number of interesting
implications begin to emerge. Peters (1987), for example, argues that on this basis organizations should look to 'under-promise' and 'over-deliver'. In this way customer expectations will be low, their perceptions of delivered service quality high, and as a
consequence their satisfaction will also be high. The problem with this argument is
that expectations are learnt from experience, so this process will only work once. As
soon as consumers perceive a high standard of service, they will come to expect it on
subsequent occasions and could potentially be dissatisfied if their expectations are not
fulfilled. As a result, this author contends that by far the safest way of ensuring customer satisfaction is simply to consistently deliver to one's service promises.

The second interesting consequence of the disconfirmation paradigm is that it leaves
organizations looking to identify the criteria against which consumers build expectations. As Levitt (1981, 100) explains, this is not easy:

The most important thing to know about intangible products is that the customers usually don't know
what they're getting until they don't get it. Only then do they become aware of what they bargained for;
only on dissatisfaction do they dwell . . . .

Even where those factors important to overall satisfaction can be adequately
identified, organizations still have the task of setting objective measures of quality
and ensuring that they deliver against the targets that they set. Indeed, this is not an
easy task since, whilst the quality of physical goods can be measured quite satisfacto-
rily by monitoring variables such as durability, or the number of physical defects
(Crosby, 1979), in the case of services there is an almost total absence of objective
methods of assessment.

Some consolation can be drawn however, since it is not only the service providers
themselves who have difficulty in assessing the quality of their services. Consumers can
have equal difficulties in formulating their own individual assessments. Whilst the disconfirmation model looks quite neat in theory, in practice consumers can make quality assessments on the most superficial of cues. To explain why this might be it is worth
looking at the work of Nelson (1970) who drew a useful distinction between two categories of consumer goods, namely:

(1) *those high in search qualities*—which consumers *can* evaluate prior to making a purchase (e.g. size, colour, feel, smell);

(2) *those high in experience qualities*—where the attributes can only be discerned during
use, and hence (in most cases) after purchase. (e.g. taste, wearability, etc.).

For our purposes, however, Darnby and Karni (1973) helpfully add a third category:

(3) *Credence qualities*—these are characteristics which are difficult to evaluate, even after consumption. Many nonprofits offer services which are high on credence qualities (e.g. a heart operation or a charity donation).

The existence of these three qualities can best be conceptualized on a continuum. As can be seen from Fig. 2.3, different products/services have varying degrees of credence qualities. It will be inherently more difficult to assess the quality of a service that contains a high degree of credence qualities. Consumers may find it all but impossible to evaluate their experience. Nevertheless, marketers should not lose heart as the evidence suggests that in such cases consumers do use a variety of surrogate variables to evaluate such services. For example, in the case of a bypass operation consumers are unlikely to have the technical knowledge to appraise the skills of the surgeon—they might hence appraise service quality on the basis of the perceived professionalism of staff, the level of technology employed, the decor of their ward/building, etc. This is a simple but important concept to grasp as these criteria could quite easily be radically different from those that the hospital itself might use to evaluate the quality of the same operation (e.g. survival rates, number of medical complications, technical proficiency, use of resources, etc). Nonprofits must monitor service quality not only against their own internal criteria but also in terms of those that are likely to be used by the customer. In the case of services that are high on credence qualities, these dimensions can usually only be identified through research.

Fig. 2.3:
Continuum of Evaluation for Different Types of Products

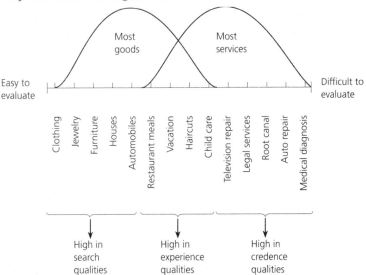

Source: Zeithaml *et al.*, *Services Marketing*, McGraw Hill, New York. Reproduced with the kind permission of McGraw Hill.

The Measurement of Service Quality

Given the difficulties alluded to above, the reader could be forgiven for believing that the measurement of service quality is an almost impossible task. A variety of methods of measurement have been advocated, but there is still considerable disagreement in the literature in respect of the best method to use. Ovretveit (1992, 23) argues in favour of a market focused approach. As he puts it:

The question is not the general 'What do customers think about our service?' but the more specific 'Which features of our service are the most important to potential, current and past customers in relation to the actions which the service wishes to influence, and how does the service compare to the alternatives on these features'.

It is therefore too simplistic merely to ask customers what they think about each dimension of the service. Every group of customers will have their own priorities in terms of those elements of the service that they perceive to be most important. Measuring every service component may therefore not be necessary and, where deficiencies are encountered, additional resources may only be required in those areas which will have the greatest impact on customer satisfaction.

It therefore seems clear that an organization looking to monitor service quality should:

(1) identify its key customer groups or segments;
(2) identify the key components of the service;
(3) assess the relative importance of each component for each customer segment;
(4) set performance targets for each key component;
(5) measure actual service performance against each target;
(6) prioritize necessary improvements;
(7) allocate investment accordingly.

Following such a procedure should ensure that where deviations are detected against the desired targets, scarce resources can be targeted at only those aspects of the service that are perceived to be of greatest importance. Of course, these factors will not be static over time and the process described above should be iterative.

Whilst many of the steps appear quite straightforward, step (5) is in reality somewhat problematic as in practice it is not an easy task to set about actually measuring service quality. Three broad approaches are possible.

(a) Counting Complaints

Clearly the most simplistic approach is simply to count the number of complaints that relate to each service provided, or each specific component thereof. This is clearly a very unsatisfactory method of monitoring service quality, as only a relatively low proportion of customers will actually take the trouble to complain. Most will simply rate the service as poor and look for alternative suppliers.

(b) Rating Service Attributes

A rather more sophisticated method of measuring service quality consists of deriving a list of service attributes and asking customers to rate their perceptions of each attribute, typically on a five or seven point scale.

In a study of student satisfaction with higher education (HE) institutions, for example, Stewart (1991) utilized a series of attitudinal statements with a likert scale for responses ranging from 'strongly agree' to 'strongly disagree'. The statements selected probed customer perceptions of each element of the traditional marketing mix, including:

(1) *Product*—the variety of curriculum, course scheduling, student evaluations of faculty, opportunities for personal growth via professional and leadership activi-

ties, academic advising, student interaction with faculty and administrators, library holdings and cultural, athletic, and social opportunities.

(2) *Price*—tuition expenses—finance packages available.

(3) *Place*—environmental issues—campus attractiveness and safety, availability of lounge facilities, study areas, and parking spaces. Health and library service offerings. Procedures for selecting dormitory and room-mate assignments. Adequacy of meals/other catering.

(4) *Promotion*—accuracy of promotional material—prospectus, departmental literature. Do students know where to go for advice, are they informed of extra-curricular activities on campus? Availability of information in respect of changes in curriculum procedures and requirements.

Importantly, the author also advocated the gathering of data relating to the perceived importance of each element. For each of the components of the HE service it is hence possible to plot the position of a given university's performance on a graph such as that in Fig. 2.4.

Fig. 2.4:
**Importance/
Agreement
Quadrants**

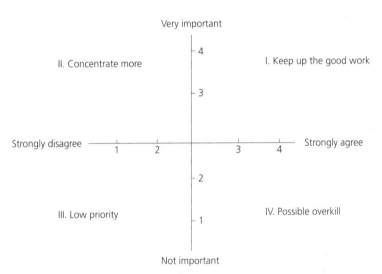

Service components falling within the top right hand segment are those that are both very important to customers and those areas where the university performs well. The level of service should clearly be maintained in these areas. Service components falling within the bottom right hand quadrant are those where the university performs well, but are considered to be areas of little importance by customers. Institutions should hence give consideration to whether resources directed to these areas could be better employed elsewhere.

In the case of service components falling within the top left hand quadrant, the advice would clearly be to concentrate any additional resources in these areas. They are perceived to be of considerable importance by customers, but the actual performance falls well short of the mark. Service components falling within the bottom left hand area can be seen to be under-performing, but such under-performance may not be of particular significance, since these dimensions are also perceived to be of little importance by those surveyed.

(c) The SERVQUAL Method

Perhaps the most famous of the techniques of service quality measurement is that proposed by Parasuraman *et al.* (1988). The authors posited the existence of four key service gaps (five if the aggregate gap is included). These gaps are together responsible for the difference between expected and perceived service quality.

Gap 1: Not knowing what customers expect—the difference between consumer needs and management's perceptions of those needs.
Gap 2: Not selecting the right service design—the difference between management perceptions of customer needs and the service standards set.
Gap 3: Not delivering to service standards—the difference between service specifications and actual service delivery.
Gap 4: Not matching performance to promises—the difference between the service promises made in external communications and the actual service delivered.

Parasuraman *et al.* (1988) evolved this concept of 'gaps' into a quantitative technique for measuring service quality known as SERVQUAL. This is based upon a generic 22-item questionnaire designed to cover the broad dimensions of service quality. The model has received widespread support in the literature, although it has been refined and adapted to make it suitable for application in a number of different sectors (see for example Babakus and Boller, 1992). The SERVQUAL instrument is illustrated in Fig. 2.5.

Fig. 2.5: **The SERVQUAL Instrument**

Directions: This survey deals with your opinions of —— services. Please show the extent to which you think firms offering —— services should possess the features described by each statement. Do this by picking one of the seven numbers next to each statement. If you strongly agree that these firms should possess a feature, circle the number 7. If you strongly disagree that these firms should possess a feature, circle 1. If your feelings are not strong, circle one of the numbers in the middle. There are no right or wrong answers—all we are interested in is a number that best shows your expectations about firms offering —— services.

		Strongly Disagree						Strongly Agree
E1	They should have up-to-date equipment	1	2	3	4	5	6	7
E2	Their physical facilities should be visually appealing	1	2	3	4	5	6	7
E3	Their employees should be well dressed and appear neat	1	2	3	4	5	6	7
E4	The appearance of the physical facilities of these firms should be in keeping with the type of services provided	1	2	3	4	5	6	7
E5	When these firms promise to do somthing by a certain time, they should do so	1	2	3	4	5	6	7
E6	When customers have problems, these firms should be sympathetic and reassuring	1	2	3	4	5	6	7
E7	These firms should be dependable	1	2	3	4	5	6	7
E8	They should provide their services at the time they promise to do so	1	2	3	4	5	6	7
E9	They should keep their records accurately	1	2	3	4	5	6	7
E10	They shouldn't be expected to tell customers exactly when services will be performed (-)	1	2	3	4	5	6	7
E11	It is not realistic for customers to expect prompt service from employees of these firms (-)	1	2	3	4	5	6	7
E12	Their employees don't always have to be willing to help customers (-)	1	2	3	4	5	6	7
E13	It is okay if they are too busy to respond to customer requests promptly (-)	1	2	3	4	5	6	7
E14	Customers should be able to trust employees of these firms	1	2	3	4	5	6	7
E15	Customers should be able to feel safe in their transactions with these firm's employees	1	2	3	4	5	6	7
E16	Their employees should be polite	1	2	3	4	5	6	7

E17	Their employees should get adequate support from these firms to do their jobs well	1	2	3	4	5	6	7
E18	These firms should not be expected to give customers personal attention (-)	1	2	3	4	5	6	7
E19	Employees of these firms cannot be expected to give customers personal attention (-)	1	2	3	4	5	6	7
E20	It is unrealistic to expect employees to know what the needs of their customers are (-)	1	2	3	4	5	6	7
E21	It is unrealistic to expect these firms to have their customers' best interests at heart (-)	1	2	3	4	5	6	7
E22	They shouldn't be expected to have operating hours convenient to all their customers (-)	1	2	3	4	5	6	7

Directions: The following set of statements relate to your feelings about XYZ. For each statement please show the extent to which you believe XYZ has the feature described by the statement. Once again, circling a 7 means that you strongly agree that XYZ has that feature, and circling a 1 means that you strongly disagree. You may circle any of the numbers in the middle that show how strong your feelings are. There are no right or wrong answers—all we are interested in is a number that best shows your perceptions about XYZ.

P1	XYZ has up-to-date equipment	1	2	3	4	5	6	7
P2	XYZ's physical facilities are visually appealing	1	2	3	4	5	6	7
P3	XYZ's employees are well dressed and appear neat	1	2	3	4	5	6	7
P4	The appearance of the physical facilities of XYZ is in keeping with the type of services provided	1	2	3	4	5	6	7
P5	When XYZ promises to do something by a certain time, it does so	1	2	3	4	5	6	7
P6	When you have problems, XYZ is sympathetic and reassuring	1	2	3	4	5	6	7
P7	XYZ is dependable	1	2	3	4	5	6	7
P8	XYZ provides its services at the time it promises to do so	1	2	3	4	5	6	7
P9	XYZ keeps its records accurately	1	2	3	4	5	6	7
P10	XYZ does not tell customers exactly when services will be performed (-)	1	2	3	4	5	6	7
P11	You do not receive prompt service from XYZ's employees (-)	1	2	3	4	5	6	7
P12	Employees of XYZ are not always willing to help customers (-)	1	2	3	4	5	6	7
P13	Employees of XYZ are too busy to respond to customer requests promptly (-)	1	2	3	4	5	6	7
P14	You can trust employees of XYZ	1	2	3	4	5	6	7
P15	You feel safe in your transactions with XYZ's employees	1	2	3	4	5	6	7
P16	Employees of XYZ are polite	1	2	3	4	5	6	7
P17	Employees get adequate support from XYZ to do their jobs well	1	2	3	4	5	6	7
P18	XYZ does not give you individual attention (-)	1	2	3	4	5	6	7
P19	Employees of XYZ do not give you personal attention (-)	1	2	3	4	5	6	7
P20	Employees of XYZ do not know what your needs are (-)	1	2	3	4	5	6	7
P21	XYZ does not have your best interests at heart (-)	1	2	3	4	5	6	7
P22	XYZ does not have operating hours convenient to all their customers (-)	1	2	3	4	5	6	7

NB. The statements should appear in a random order in a questionnaire and those phrased in the negative (-) should be reverse-scored prior to data analysis.

Source: Parasuraman, Zeithaml and Berry (1988). Reproduced with the kind permission of the JAI Press Inc, Greenwich, Connecticut.

The idea behind the questionnaire is essentially that:

$$Q = P - E$$

where

Q = the perceived quality of each item
P = the performance achieved in each item
E = the customer's expectations of performance in each item.

To measure the quality of each service dimension one therefore subtracts the expectations score from the performance score for each item. A high positive result would hence indicate a high perceived standard of service, whilst a high negative score would indicate a low perceived standard of service.

In testing the responses received to this instrument, the authors determined that service quality can best be viewed as having five underlying dimensions, namely:

Tangibles—physical facilities, equipment and appearance of personnel;
Reliability—ability to perform the promised service dependably and accurately;
Responsiveness—willingness to help customers and provide prompt service;
Assurance—knowledge and courtesy of employees and their ability to inspire trust and confidence;
Empathy—caring, individualised attention the firm provides its customers.

Hence a number of the statements in the questionnaire can be viewed as addressing the issue of reliability, whilst others together address the issue of responsiveness, etc. As a result the scale has a number of applications within a service environment. These include:

(1) Tracking service trends. SERVQUAL can be used over time to plot changes in customers' perceptions of key service components (i.e. responses to individual questions).

(2) Analysing each service dimension. Average 'difference' scores can be calculated for each of the five dimensions referred to above. The possibility also exists to average each of these to arrive at an overall measure of service quality which could then be tracked over time.

(3) Identifying the relative importance of each service dimension. A statistical technique known as regression can be used to isolate which of the five dimensions are felt by customers to be of the greatest importance. Resource allocation can then be planned accordingly.

(4) Determining whether specific groups of customers exist that prioritize differently the dimensions of service quality. If this should be the case each group can be profiled to determine its demographic and/or lifestyle characteristics (see Chapter 3).

(5) Tracking and comparing the service provided across different outlets and/or channels of distribution.

(6) Benchmarking against competitors. A separate series of 'perceptions' questions could be included in the instrument for each key competitor and the resultant information used for benchmarking purposes.

SERVQUAL has been found to be very effective in a variety of different contexts including health care, charity service provision, and even in evaluating the service provided by the arts. It could therefore be used to good effect by nonprofits in a variety of the ways alluded to above.

Customer Value

So far in this chapter we have talked about customer perceptions of service quality and identified three ways in which this might be measured. The reader will recall that the latter two methods allow the researcher to identify those attributes of the service from which the customer derives the most value and it is this latter concept that will be focused on here.

All service organizations, whether they be profit-making or not, are unlikely to provide a service which has only one ingredient. When an arts customer buys a ticket for a museum, for example, the opportunity to view the exhibits is not the only component of the service purchased. Qualities such as the ability to be able to interact with the display, to understand something of the history of the items, and to be able to have an occasional dialogue with staff might also be significant components of the experience. Identifying which of the dimensions are of most importance is of crucial importance, since it allows management to invest in those areas where customers derive the most value from their visit and cut costs in those areas which are not perceived to be of particular importance. This very simple idea has recently taken on a whole new significance because of the work of Jones and Sasser (1995). Consider the graph in Fig. 2.6.

The figure illustrates the satisfaction ratings recently obtained from a survey of customers to a one-off exhibition at an art gallery.

Fig. 2.6: **Customer Satisfaction with an Art Gallery Exhibition**

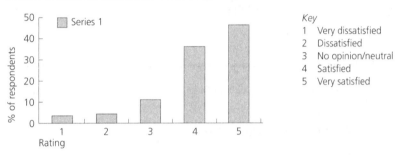

Putting yourself in the position of the manager of that gallery for a moment, would you be happy with these figures?

The conventional wisdom has always been that you should be. After all some 82 per cent of your customers are either satisfied or very satisfied. Consider an additional question.

Which category of customers should we be most concerned with?

Again the conventional wisdom has always been that we should work to improve the ratings that we are currently receiving from customers rating their satisfaction with the service as a 1, 2, or 3. Clearly they are not satisfied with the service and we need to improve what we offer these groups of customers.

If you were then told that the customers who rate their satisfaction as a 5 are six times more likely to purchase from you again than the customers who rate their satisfaction only as a 4, would your opinion change?

In a study which embraced a variety of different sectors Jones and Sasser concluded that this was a pattern of loyalty common to all the sectors studied. In the example quoted, even if *all* the customers who rated their satisfaction as a 5 repurchase, only 17 per cent of those who rated it as a 4 will do so. This revelation somewhat focuses the mind on the group of customers who should clearly be regarded as most important. If an organization can improve on the percentage of customers who rate their satisfaction as a 5, it can substantially improve on the levels of loyalty that will be exhibited as a result.

Before moving on, it is worth noting that the factor of six quoted above is not static across all industries and sectors: it will clearly depend on the availability of substitute services and the nature of the competition. For many nonprofit organizations providing comparatively unique services the factor is likely to be considerably lower, but even if it should prove to be as low as two or three, a significant difference will still exist between the loyalty patterns exhibited by the customers who consider themselves satisfied and those who consider themselves very satisfied.

The reason for elaborating on this research is a simple one. The key to moving customers from a 4 to a 5 is customer value. If you think back to some of your own experiences with service organizations, and in particular those that you might have been asked to evaluate, you can probably very quickly recall why you failed to award a '5' yourself to a particular organization. The organization almost certainly met your basic requirements, but did not excel in one area that was of particular importance to you. As a result organizations need to be particularly alert to those aspects of their service offering that customers perceive to be most important and ensure that they 'engineer in' value in these key areas. If loyalty is to be preserved and/or enhanced, customers must be made to feel that they have received an exceptional service.

Developing a Competitor Orientation

Analysis of Competition

The first step in developing a competitor orientation is once again research. Organizations with strong competitor orientations continually evaluate their positions in respect of each of their key competitors, in order to discover areas of strength and weakness and to find ways of strengthening their own competitive advantage (see for example Aaker, 1989, or Narver and Slater, 1990). The only way that this can be achieved is through the creation of an effective competitor monitoring system which generates benchmarking data in respect of each key aspect of competitor operations and alerts the organization to actual and potential competitive innovations. This benchmarking data allows a nonprofit organization to compare:

1. *Its own portfolio of provision against other actual or potential providers.* Whilst an often insatiable demand for nonprofit services ensures that most adequately managed organizations will continue to have the capability to provide some form of service to their client groups, some organizations may be guilty of providing services which might be more effectively provided by others in the market. Nonprofits, perhaps more than any other category of organization (by virtue of their use of third party funds), have a duty to ensure that they provide the most appropriate range of services to their recipient groups. They can only achieve this by monitoring competitive strengths and concentrating only on those areas where the organization in question has a comparative advantage. This may take the form of specialist expertise most closely suited to one form of need, or it may, for example, be the ease of access to one category of recipient group. A competitor orientation can hence optimize the use of resources across the sector as a whole and maximize the potential benefit to society as a result.

2. *The costs of providing goods and services to their recipient groups.* The level of need that a nonprofit is able to cater for relative to other service providers will not only be of concern to management but also to potential funders. Most will want to ensure that their funding is directed to the organization that is likely to have the most impact on the target beneficiary group. It is thus no surprise to learn that most Charitable Trusts require quite detailed information about the category and level of need that will be serviced, before their trustees will reach a decision in respect of whether an application for funding will be granted.

3. *The costs of fundraising.* All nonprofits who have to fundraise to conduct their primary activity should be concerned with the relative efficiency of each form of fundraising activity. They will want, for example, to ascertain from which sources major competitors derive their income and the fundraising techniques (such as direct mail, telemarketing, etc) that are used to solicit it. A comparison of both sources of funding utilized and the expenditures on each fundraising technique relative to income generated will aid management in targeting future scarce fundraising resources more effectively (see for example Sargeant and Kaehler, 1998).

The attainment of a competitor orientation has recently taken on a whole new significance for a great many nonprofits in the UK who now have to compete with private sector organizations for the right to provide services to their beneficiary groups. The UK government is now issuing contracts for a great many societal services, and both voluntary sector and private sector organizations are typically invited to tender. Competitive intelligence is therefore absolutely essential to track potential competitors and their past strategies and performance. Such data can be manipulated to ensure that an appropriate competitive strategy is developed which will maximize the likelihood of success in the competitive tendering process.

There are a number of stages involved in the development of a competitor intelligence system. These are listed below:

(1) *Specification of the benefits sought.* The process should begin with an identification of what the organization is wishing to gain from the system—e.g. the benchmarking of fundraising costs, delineation of competitor strengths and weaknesses, understanding of competitive portfolios, etc.

(2) *List the information requirements.* The exact nature of the competitor intelligence required should be specified. This should flesh out the list provided above and provide the specific information that will be required to achieve each of the benefits listed in (1).

(3) *Review published sources.* Referred to as secondary data, there are an increasing number of sources of information about nonprofit organizations. These include the government's Central Statistical Office, trade magazines/journals, reports published by the Charities Aid Foundation or NCVO (National Council of Voluntary Organizations), newsclippings, data gathered at trade exhibitions or fairs, and information published in an electronic format on the Internet.

(4) *Review internal sources.* One of the key assets in the gathering of competitor intelligence is your own 'workforce'. All individuals within the organization need to be made aware of the need to gather and pass on snippets of market intelligence. This may therefore require the design and implementation of a reporting mechanism whereby staff and/or volunteers can easily pass on any information they

learn. This process should be ongoing and not conducted on an annual or bi-annual basis.

(5) *Review and prioritize remaining information requirements.* At this stage it will be necessary to isolate the remaining information requirements. Given that there is still comparatively little secondary data available in respect of the nonprofit sector, there may be a large number of these, all of which will vary in terms of their importance to organizational decision making. The most pressing of these should be isolated, with a view to them forming the basis of a market research project, possibly involving the use of an external research agency.

(6) *Conduct primary research.* In marketing parlance the term given to data that is collected afresh with a specific purpose in mind is 'primary' data. There are a number of methods by which primary data can be accumulated including—postal and telephone questionnaires, personal interviews, and group discussions. A detailed discussion of the relative merits of each of these techniques is unfortunately beyond the scope of this text, but interested readers are advised to consult a good standard text such as Chisnall (1992) or Churchill (1995).

(7) *Organization and dissemination of information.* Once collected, data needs to be converted to a managerially useful format, when it can be legitimately regarded as 'information' for the first time. This will undoubtedly involve the merging of data from various information sources and the provision of a summary in report format to key decision makers and advisers. Such reports are typically generated monthly, but in a highly hostile or unstable competitive environment, organizations may find a weekly summary sheet a useful adjunct to their full monthly report.

Building Competitive Advantage

The design of a competitive information system and the gathering of competitive and benchmarking data is but the first stage of developing a competitor orientation. Having gathered information about other providers in the market, or key competitors for funding, the next stage is to use it to your advantage. Profiling competitor strengths and weaknesses can allow an organization to see where its performance lags behind the competition, but it can also highlight areas where it either outperforms the competition, *or has the capacity to do so.* These areas are key, because they could represent a major source of a competitive advantage that an organization has over its rivals. This can then form the basis of extremely powerful communications with all the categories of customer with whom the organization has contact. For example, if an organization by virtue of its extensive network of volunteers has the potential to be the lowest cost provider in a given market, this fact needs to be communicated strongly to all potential funders who will undoubtedly be looking for the organization that can make the most effective use of their resources. Similarly if an organization has the leading researchers working in a particular field on its payroll, this fact should be emphasized to both recipients and funders alike because it has the capacity to clearly identify the organization as a market leader and therefore position it as being the most worthy of support/patronage.

There are a number of bases which can be used to develop a competitive advantage. These include:

(1) *Low cost*. The key to the competitive advantage here is the fact that the organization can provide goods/services at lower cost than their major competitors.

(2) *Service quality/content*. Some organizations may elect to differentiate the standard of care that they provide to donors and/or their recipient groups. They may strive to make the service in some way unique in areas *that are important* to their customers. To be truly sustainable however, these distinctions in service quality/content should be difficult for competitors to emulate.

(3) *Access to resources*. As in the example quoted above, many nonprofits possess specialist expertise. This expertise in itself can serve to differentiate the organization from potential competitors in the minds of funders and recipients.

(4) *Access to recipients*. The channels used to deliver some services may be long and complex. Many Third World charities for example have developed complex infrastructures which enable them to reach the most needy societies at comparatively short notice when disaster strikes. This flexibility of response can in itself form the basis of a competitive advantage, as speed may be of primary importance to both funders and recipients alike.

Of course this list is not exhaustive but it does serve to illustrate one very key point. If an organization is not clear about why it is distinctive, neither will its potential funders or the recipients of the goods and services provided. In the case of the former, this will lead to cash shortages as funds are diverted to other organizations that are perceived as being more deserving. In the case of the latter, those most in need of the support of the organization may be reluctant to come forward to seek the help that could be available, because they fail to understand what is unique about the provision and hence why it might better match their pattern of need.

Enhancing Interfunctional Co-ordination

The reader will recall from our earlier discussion of Narver and Slater's (1990) work that the third and final component of a market orientation is 'Interfunctional Co-ordination' and that this in turn consists of two elements—namely, information sharing and inter-departmental integration. Such a distinction is unlikely however to be particularly helpful in practice since one would hope that one of the benefits to flow from increased integration would be improved information sharing. The distinction the authors draw could therefore be regarded as a little tenuous and for this reason the concept of interfunctional co-ordination will be dealt with here, as a whole.

Over the years much has been written about how enhancements could be made to the level of co-operation taking place between different departments within an organization. In recent years, however, a small body of literature has been building up which suggests that the key to achieving this enhancement might lie in applying the same marketing tools and concepts *within* an organization that have traditionally only been employed outside the organization, in its dealings with external customers. Not surprisingly this paradigm of thought has come to be known as 'internal marketing'.

Internal Marketing—The Philosophy

The whole concept of internal marketing is based on one simple premiss:

satisfied employees = satisfied customers

If one is able to recruit and maintain a motivated workforce and inculcate within them an understanding of the organization's mission and the needs and wants of its external customers, the argument runs that positive improvements in the quality of service provided by those employees to their customers should result. Moreover if employees can be encouraged to view *other employees* in the service chain as their customers and treat them with the standards of care normally reserved for external customers, overall levels of morale should begin to rise as everyone within the organization begins to notice an improvement in the quality of service provided to them by other members of staff. The resultant 'customer'-driven culture, it is argued, should have a knock-on effect into dealings with external customers, who should also notice a difference in the quality of service provided.

The reader will doubtless be relieved to discover that there is now a sizeable body of evidence to suggest that this is indeed the case (see for example Berry, 1987; Bowen and Schneider, 1985; Gronroos, 1981a and 1981b; and Tansuhaj *et al.*, 1988). The quality of employee interaction *is* strongly correlated with perceived (external) service quality. Given our earlier discussion of the Gap model, this should perhaps come as no surprise since the quality of employee interactions can clearly have the capacity to influence each of the gaps Parasuraman *et al.* (1988) identify. The quality of the delivered service will be strongly correlated with the extent to which:

(1) employees feed back information to management in respect of customer requirements;
(2) management and staff pool their expertise to match service specifications to the needs of the target customer groups;
(3) staff are encouraged to deliver to the service standards set and, moreover, receive the support of their colleagues, where necessary, to do so;
(4) staff are kept regularly informed of the content of external communications and have the opportunity to feed back their views on the same to management.

Internal marketing activity can help facilitate each of these processes. So what exactly is meant by the term internal marketing? Once again, there is little academic agreement about its use. Internal marketing has been variously described as:

viewing employees as internal customers, viewing jobs as internal products that satisfy the wants of these internal customers while addressing the objectives of the organisation.   (Berry, 1981)

a philosophy for managing the organisation's human resources based on a marketing perspective. (George and Gronroos, 1989)

the spreading of the responsibility for all marketing activity across all functions of the organisation and the proactive application of marketing principles to 'selling the staff' on their role in providing customer satisfaction within a supportive organisational environment.   (Gilmore and Carson, 1995)

(describing) the work done by the company to train and motivate its internal customers, namely its customer contact employees and supporting service personnel to work as a team to provide customer satisfaction.   Kotler (1997)

At the heart of these various definitions lie two basic principles. First, internal marketing is seen as a mechanism for spreading the responsibility for marketing across the whole organization, whilst the second key idea is that to achieve this effectively each employee should be encouraged to regard their successor in the service chain as an internal customer, not merely as a colleague.

Other authors, such as George (1990), have chosen to focus on the two roles that internal marketing can perform in an organization. In the first it may be viewed as a tool to help individuals to understand the significance of their roles and to create an awareness of how these roles relate to others within the organization. The aim of this approach is to improve cross-functional co-ordination and co-operation. The second role the author envisages is to promote, develop, and sustain the ethos of customer service for internal as well as external customers. Piercy and Morgan (1994, 5), meanwhile, propose a rather more elaborate set of internal marketing 'goals'.

(1) gaining the support of key decision makers for organizational plans;
(2) changing the attitudes and behaviours of employees and managers who are working at key interfaces with customers and distributors;
(3) gaining commitment to making the marketing plan work;
(4) managing incremental changes in the culture from 'the way we always do things' to the 'way we need to do things to be successful'.

Internal marketing thus has a variety of benefits that it can offer a nonprofit organization. Of course actually identifying goals and benefits is one thing—making them a reality quite another. In the next section we will therefore examine some of the internal marketing tools and techniques that are available.

Internal Marketing Techniques

There are a variety of techniques that could legitimately be regarded as components of internal marketing. Helpfully Gronroos (1981a) draws a distinction between what he sees as the strategic and tactical levels of internal marketing. Whilst these levels should not be viewed as being carved in stone—because what are strategic issues for some, will only be tactical concerns for others (and vice versa)—it does constitute a useful framework within which to group the essential ideas.

(a) Strategic Internal Marketing

Gronroos argues that each of the following dimensions of organizational management can be regarded as strategic internal marketing activity.

(i) Adoption of Supportive Management Styles

If an internal marketing programme is to be developed and implemented, it must have the complete support and backing of senior management. Encouraging staff to view colleagues and volunteers as customers requires a major change in organizational thinking, and without top-level support the change is unlikely to occur. Staff need to be given the time necessary to develop internal service standards and plan ways in which performance could be monitored against them. This will only occur if senior staff are seen to support the initiative.

(ii) Supportive Personnel Policies

One of the fundamental ideas underlying internal marketing is that individuals should be matched with the job(s) to which they are most suited. This requires careful recruitment and job and career planning for all individuals within an organization. Many nonprofits have long put effort into attracting personnel with the right skills and attitudes for customer-facing roles, but perhaps rather less effort is typically applied to matching the right 'type' of person to the right job role internally, even if skill sets can be seen to match.

(iii) Customer Service Training

Critical to the achievement of a market orientation is customer service training. Staff need to understand the importance of both internal and external customers and how they should be treated. It is helpful if staff are developed from the outset with this form of training as they can then be involved in the setting of appropriate service standards and the monitoring thereof. In short they should be allowed to 'own' the process and hence not fear the results that might accrue. One of the key mistakes made by many organizations initiating a customer focus for the first time is that the systems that should be used to monitor and enhance service standards are used only as a 'stick' to beat those staff who are seen to be 'underperforming'. This is one way of guaranteeing a considerable resistance to change.

(iv) Customer Focused Planning Procedures

The author was introduced some years ago to a model known as the 'Iceberg of Ignorance'. Based on research, it posits the very simple idea that the higher up an individual might be in their organizational hierarchy, the more 'ignorant' they are likely to be of the requirements of their customers. It's an interesting idea since, taken to its logical conclusion, it would suggest that to really get on in this life, one should aspire to ignorance! Perhaps more constructively, however, the iceberg provides a very graphic illustration of a concept, an understanding of which still manages to elude a great many organizations. The idea is presented visually in Fig. 2.7.

At the bottom of the iceberg are positioned the front line staff who, as a consequence of their job role, have a fairly complete understanding of the customer's requirements and problems. In the case of most service providers these individuals are interacting with customers on a daily basis and if problems are encountered they will be the first to

Fig. 2.7: **The Iceberg of Ignorance**

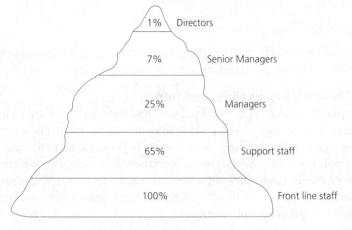

- 1%   Directors
- 7%   Senior Managers
- 25%   Managers
- 65%   Support staff
- 100%   Front line staff

be aware of them. The higher up the iceberg you climb, the less in touch personnel become. A typical charity director will only be acquainted with around 1 per cent of the problems experienced by recipients of his/her goods/services. Even the lowest levels of managerial staff may get to learn of only 25 per cent of the problems/difficulties experienced by their customers.

It is therefore quite perverse that many organizations continue to plan their future from the top down. In reality those who have the most responsibility for strategic planning often have the least understanding of the key issues at stake. For this reason, the adoption of an internal marketing perspective should facilitate the involvement of staff at all levels within an organization in the planning process. Whilst it may be physically impossible (and probably not very desirable!) for all staff to be present when strategy is decided upon, there is absolutely no excuse for not seeking input and/or suggestions from those staff most frequently interacting with customers, as one of the first steps in the planning process.

(b) Tactical Internal Marketing

Tactical internal marketing considerations include the following.

(i) Training

Whilst a commitment to customer service training should often be considered a strategic issue, as it will concern all individuals within an organization, there is also a case for investment in informal and ongoing training, the requirements of which will be specific to particular divisions or functions. Periodic training of volunteer fundraisers would, for example, fall under this general heading.

(ii) Encouragement of Informal and Interactive Communication

Staff from different functional areas within the organization should be encouraged to communicate with each other informally, as well as formally in the course of performing their job role. Literally any form of communication which gets away from the traditional 'memo' would be desirable. Inter-disciplinary meetings, social events and the informal monitoring of internal service levels should greatly facilitate this goal. One voluntary sector organization recently built the factor 'delivery against internal service standards' into its criteria for the award of performance-related pay. This encouraged staff from all departments to develop informal links and communicate more effectively with each other, thereby maximizing the likelihood of overall performance in this key area.

(iii) Formal Internal Communications

Formal internal communications include newsletters, updates, briefing documents, etc. These serve a useful purpose in that they can convey developments to staff quite economically and explain often complex changes to the nature of service provision. The better of these documents also serve to promote a feeling of organizational identity rather than a series of departmental identities which can often lead to internal conflict and competition.

(iv) Internal Market Research

A prerequisite to the attainment of internal customer satisfaction is understanding those elements of the service that are perceived as being most important, and concentrating efforts accordingly. Whilst this might sound a little obvious many non-profit organizations have been slow to recognize that volunteers in particular usually come to an organization with a series of expectations and requirements which, if not met (at least in part), will lead to the high attrition rates currently experienced by many within the sector. Internal market research should therefore be regarded as essential.

(v) Cross-disciplinary Teams

This is a further technique that can be used to promote greater co-operation between departments. Teams are brought together of staff working in often quite disparate sections of the organization. These teams work together to solve quality and/or other organizational problems and report back their suggestions to management. Staff thereby have the opportunity to work with others and to understand a variety of different organizational perspectives.

(vi) Staff Secondments

Some organizations approach the problem of inter-functional co-ordination in a rather different way. They allow staff to experience what it might be like to work in another department with whom they will ultimately have much contact, by seconding them there for a period of several weeks or months. This allows them to experience at first hand problems of internal service quality and to see these difficulties from the perspective of their internal customer.

(vii) Suggestion Schemes

The question of staff input to the strategic planning process has already been dealt with above. However, in most organizations the planning process, if it happens at all, will tend to happen only once, or at most twice, a year. In such circumstances a mechanism for communicating good ideas to senior managers quickly and efficiently may well be called for. Ideas are often collected centrally in a box, or a hotline is provided to staff so that they can speak directly to a senior executive. Staff suggestion schemes sometimes, but not always, reward the best of the ideas presented.

Once again, this list is in no way exhaustive, but it should serve to provide an appreciation of the many techniques that can be used to promote inter-functional co-ordination and thereby enhance the overall level of market orientation attained.

Summary

In this chapter we have examined the components of a market orientation. We stated that it may be thought of as having three behavioural dimensions—namely, customer orientation, competitor orientation, and inter-functional co-ordination. A customer orientation involved developing an understanding of the dimensions of the service that were perceived to be of greatest importance by customers and engineering value in these key areas. Three methods of measuring delivered service quality were discussed and in particular the characteristics of one of the most commonly used techniques, SERVQUAL, were explored.

The achievement of a competitor orientation was shown to deliver a number of strategic benefits to a nonprofit organization and involve the creation of an effective competitor monitoring system. This, it was argued, could provide valuable data against which to benchmark performance and suggest key areas to management that could be used as the basis for a sustainable competitive advantage. Finally, the issue of inter-functional co-ordination was explored and the concept of internal marketing introduced as one route to the attainment thereof. A variety of both strategic and tactical applications were described.

The achievement of a market orientation thus involves an equal focus on each of these three dimensions and can potentially offer a number of benefits to an organization in terms of both its use of resources and the pattern of market responses it develops. In many ways it can be regarded as the embodiment of the marketing philosophy within an organization. The reader will appreciate that if equal weight and emphasis is given to each of the three dimensions alluded to above, the organization will evolve a new 'way of doing business' which focuses far more on the markets that the organization serves (both internal and external) and the needs thereof. We can therefore now go on in Chapter 3 to examine in greater detail the first of the functional components of marketing and in particular to discuss how an organization might select appropriate groups of external customers to target with its goods and services.

Discussion Questions

1. What are the key components of the service provided by your organization, or one with which you are familiar? Which of these are perceived as being of most importance by your external customers? How might you measure your performance in these key areas?

2. What data should a nonprofit collect and monitor in respect of its key competitors for both funding and service provision? From which sources might this data be obtained?

3. With reference to your own organization, or one with which you are familiar, outline what you believe to be its key source of competitive advantage. How does this differ from the advantage possessed by the key competitors?

4. What is internal marketing? To what extent do you believe it is a valid concept?

5. With reference to your own organization, or one with which you are familiar, describe how you might set about enhancing levels of inter-functional co-ordination?

References

Aaker, D. (1989) 'Managing Assets and Skills: The Key to Sustainable Competitive Advantage', *California Management Review*, Vol. 31, No. 2, 91–106.

Babakus, E. and Boller, G. W. (1992) 'An Empirical Assessment of the SERVQUAL Scale', *Journal of Business Research*, Vol. 24, 253–68.

Berry. L. L. (1981) 'The Employee as Customer', *Journal of Retail Banking*, Vol. 3, March, 33–40.

Berry, L. L. (1987) 'Service Marketing is Different', *Business*, Vol. 30, No. 2, 24–9.

Bowen, D. E. and Schneider, B. (1985) 'Boundary Spanning-Role Employees and the Service Encounter: Some Guidelines for Management and Research' in Czepiel, J., Solomon, M. and Suprenant C. (eds.) *The Service Encounter*, Lexington, Lexington Books, 127–45.

Bruce, I. (1995) 'Do Not For Profits Value Their Customers and Their Needs?', *International Marketing Review*, Vol. 12, No. 4, 77–84.

Chisnall, P. (1992) *Marketing Research*, Maidenhead, McGraw Hill.

Churchill, G. A. (1995) *Marketing Research: Methodological Foundations*, Hinsdale Ill., The Dryden Press.

Churchill, G. A. and Suprenant, C. (1982) 'An Investigation into the Determinants of Customer Satisfaction', *Journal of Marketing Research*, Vol. 19, 491–504.

Crosby, J. (1979) *Quality is Free*, New York, McGraw Hill.

Darby, M. R. and Karni, E. (1973) 'Free Competition and the Optimal Amount of Fraud', *Journal of Law and Economics*, Vol. 16, April, 67–86.

Deng, S. and Dart, J. (1994) 'A Multi-factor, Multi-items Approach', *Journal of Marketing Management*, Vol. 10, 725–42.

Deshpande, R. and Webster, F. (1993) 'Corporate Culture, Customer Orientation and Innovativeness in Japanese Firms: A Quadrad Analysis', *Journal of Marketing*, Vol. 57, 23–37.

Doyle, P. (1987) 'Marketing and the British Chief Executive', *Journal of Marketing Management*, Vol. 3, No. 2, 121–32.

George, W. (1990) 'Internal Marketing and Organisational Behaviour. A Partnership in Developing Customer Conscious Employees at Every Level', *Journal of Business Research* , Vol. 20, No. 1, 63–70.

George, W. R. and Gronroos, C. (1989) 'Developing Customer Conscious Employees at Every Level—Internal Marketing', in Congram, C. A. and Friedman, M. L. (eds.) *Handbook of Services Marketing*, AMACOM.

Gilmore, J. and Carson, C. (1995) 'Managing and Marketing to Internal Customers', in Glynn, W. J. and Barnes, J. G. (eds.) *Understanding Service Management*, Chichester, Wiley.

Go, F. M. and Pine, R. (1995) *Globalization Strategy in the Hotel Industry*, London, Routledge.

Gronroos, C. (1981a) 'Internal Marketing—An Integral Part of Marketing Theory', Proceedings, AMA Services Marketing Conference, 236–8.

Gronroos, C. (1981b) 'Internal Marketing—Theory and Practice', Proceedings, AMA Services Marketing Conference, 41–7.

Harvey, T. (1995) 'Service Quality: The Culprit And The Cure, *Bank Marketing*, June, 24–8.

Jones, T. O. and Sasser, W. E. (1995) 'Why Satisfied Customers Defect', *Harvard Business Review*, Nov/Dec, 88–99.

Kohli and Jaworski (1990) 'Market Orientation: The Construct, Research Propositions and Managerial Implications', *Journal of Marketing*, Vol. 54, April, 1–18.

Kotler, P. (1982) *Marketing for Nonprofit Organisations*, 2nd edn, Englewood Cliffs, Prentice Hall.

Kotler, P. (1997) *Marketing Management: Analysis, Planning and Control*, 9th edn, Englewood Cliffs, Prentice Hall.

Kotler P. and Clarke R. N. (1987) *Marketing for Healthcare Organisations*, Englewood Cliffs, Prentice Hall.

Lamb, C. W. (1983) 'Non Profits Need Development Orientation To Survive', *Fund Raising Management*, Aug, 26–30.

Levitt, T. (1981) 'Marketing Intangible Products and Product Intangibles', *Harvard Business Review*, Vol. 59, May/June, 94–102.

Lewis, B. (1989) 'Quality in the Service Sector. A Review', *International Journal of Bank Marketing*, Vol. 7, No. 5, 4–12.

Narver, J. C. and Slater, S. F. (1990) 'The Effect of a Market Orientation on Business Profitability', *Journal of Marketing*, Oct, 20–35.

Nelson, P. (1974) 'Advertising as Information', *Journal of Political Economy*, Vol. 81, July/Aug, 729–54.

Ovretveit, J. A. (1992) 'Towards Market Focused Measures of Customer/Purchaser Perceptions of Service', *Quality Forum*, Vol. 18, No. 1, 21–4.

Palmer, A. (1994) *Principles of Services Marketing*, Maidenhead, McGraw Hill.

Parasuraman, A., Zeithaml, V. A. and Berry, L. L. (1988) 'SERVQUAL: A Multiple Item Scale for Measuring Consumer Perceptions of Service Quality', *Journal of Retailing*, Vol. 64, No. 1, 12–40.

Peters, T. J. (1987) *Thriving on Chaos: Handbook for a Management Revolution*, New York, HarperCollins.

Piercy, N and Morgan, N. A. (1994) 'The Marketing Planning Process: Behavioural Problems Compared to Analytical Techniques in Explaining Marketing Plan Credibility', *Journal of Business Research*, Vol. 29, No. 3, 167–78.

Porter, M. (1985) *Competitive Advantage*, New York, Free Press.

Sargeant, A. and Kaehler, J. (1998) *Benchmarking Charity Costs*, West Malling, Charities Aid Foundation.

Shapiro, B. P. (1988) 'What the Hell is "Market Oriented"', *Harvard Business Review*, Nov–Dec, 119–25.

Stewart, K. L. (1991) 'Applying a Marketing Orientation to a Higher Education Setting', *Journal of Professional Services Marketing*, Vol. 7, No. 2, 117–24.

Tansuhaj, P., Randall, D. and McCullough, J. (1988) 'A Service marketing Management Model: Integrating Internal and External Marketing Functions', *Journal of Services Marketing*, Vol. 2, Winter, 31–8.

Webster, F. E. (1988) 'The Rediscovery of the Marketing Concept', *Business Horizons*, May–June, 29–39.

Zeithaml, V. A. (1985) 'How Consumer Evaluation Processes Differ Between Goods and Services', *Journal of Marketing*, Fall, 186–90.

Zeithaml, V. A. and Bitner, M. J. (1996) *Services Marketing*, New York, McGraw Hill.

3

Market Segmentation

Objectives

By the end of this chapter you should be able to:

(1) define market segmentation;

(2) distinguish between market segmentation and product differentiation;

(3) explore the efficacy of a range of segmentation variables in a variety of different contexts;

(4) assess the viability of particular market segments.

Introduction

Before considering the development of a marketing plan for a nonprofit organization it is necessary to define in some detail the nature of the target group that will be addressed. Chapter 2 has already highlighted the importance of a customer focus and the detailed understanding of a market that such a focus can bring. What the chapter did not discuss, however, is how one might define the most appropriate groups of customers to address and the market variables that might best be used for this purpose. Central to this task is the concept of market segmentation.

What Is Market Segmentation?

As we have seen in Chapter 2 the customers of many organizations have a diverse set of needs and wants. This makes it difficult for an organization to maximize the benefit it can offer customers, since those aspects of a service that one individual will find appealing may well not appeal to another. Thus, while an organization could achieve economies of scale by treating all customers as if they were alike, it would run the risk of alienating particular groups of customers who could find that their specific needs were not being met. Indeed if a standardized (or mass marketing) approach is taken there is a very real risk that the organization will fail to meet the requirements of any of its customer groups.

On the other hand, if an organization attempts to satisfy the needs of all its customers individually it will inevitably find that the cost of so doing is prohibitive. Clearly there is a need to find some form of balance between these two extremes of strategy. The key to getting to grips with this complexity is undoubtedly the concept of market segmentation, which Kotler (1991, 66) defines as:

> the task of breaking the total market (which is typically too large to serve) into segments that share common properties.

In a similar vein Simpson (1994, 564) defines it as

> the process of dividing up a market into two or more parts, each having unique needs and then developing products and related marketing programs to meet the needs of one or more of these segments.

Many examples of successful market segmentation abound. In consumer markets, for example, it would hardly be viable to produce a brand of breakfast cereal and expect to be able to market the product to every possible consumer in the market-place. Rather, companies prefer to concentrate on targeting a particular sub-market or segment with a uniquely tailored product and marketing mix. Hence there are cereals which appeal to the children's market, cereals which appeal to individuals who might be dieting, cereals which appeal to those who prefer a hot breakfast, and so on. In the same way a not-for-profit organization will need to isolate specific groups of clients that it will want to target with an equally specific marketing mix. Charity fundraisers, for example, will want to segment their database to identify the heaviest donors to their organization and ensure that such individuals receive an especially differentiated standard of care, both to reflect their value to the organization and to ensure that they remain loyal to it over time. Market segmentation is hence an essential feature of the modern marketing mix and in short may be regarded as one of the most fundamental concepts in marketing.

Market Segmentation versus Product Differentiation

The development of the concept of segmentation is attributed to Wendell R. Smith in a paper first published in 1956. Smith (1956, 6) suggested that:

> segmentation is based upon developments on the demand side of the market and represents a rational and more precise adjustment of product and marketing effort to consumer or user requirements. In the language of the economist, segmentation is disaggregative in its effects and tends to bring about recognition of several demand schedules where only one was recognised before.

Smith drew a distinction between market segmentation and product differentiation which he saw as alternative strategies. In particular he saw product differentiation as being:

> concerned with the bending of demand to the will of supply . . . [in which] . . . the differentiator seeks to secure a layer of the market cake, whereas one who employs market segmentation strives to secure one or more wedge-shaped pieces.

Hence product differentiation may be most appropriate in those markets where distinct segments of customers do not exist and where, in effect, one may be found to be competing with all the other suppliers in that market. It has been argued that a lot of charity fundraising activity may fall into this category. Writers such as Schlegelmilch (1979) have determined that the donors to one type of charity (e.g. Welfare, International Aid, Animals, etc.) do not differ significantly from donors to other types of charity. If true (and there has been considerable debate on this issue), this would make it impossible for charities to segment the market for donor recruitment activity and hence target individuals who might be predisposed in some way to giving to their particular cause. In such circumstances organizations would have little alternative but to differentiate themselves from other charities by emphasizing and developing some aspects of their operations or service which have been found to be important to potential donors.

Product differentiation is therefore likely to be characterized by heavy promotional spending, the purpose of which is to define in a unique way what the organization stands for and what it can offer in relation to competitors in the market-place. In some cases the product/service may even command a premium price, since consumers may perceive a strong difference between it and the alternative offerings available. This perceived difference may be real (and created by adding value in some way for consumers/donors) or it may be imaginary and created purely through the effective use of promotional activity.

There are clearly many ways in which product/service differentiation could be accomplished and, using the catch-all term 'market entity', Staudt *et al.* (1976) conclude that the following approaches are possible:

(1) *Physical differentiation of the market entity*—where the design of the product/service is enhanced in some way to distinguish it from the competition.
(2) *Psychological differentiation of the market entity*—where the imagery associated with the product/service is formulated to be in some way unique.
(3) *Differences in purchasing environment*—the outlets through which the product/service is marketed or delivered may offer features which differentiate it from the competition.
(4) *Difference by virtue of physical distribution capability*—thus customers may find that the products/services are delivered more efficiently or on a more timely basis than would be available from another supplier.
(5) *Difference in after purchase assurance of satisfaction in use*—after sales service can also be used for the purposes of differentiation, perhaps through the provision of a higher quality service than that offered by competitors. This may be of particular relevance to fundraisers who could seek to reassure donors that their monies have been used to good effect.
(6) *Differences in prices and terms of sale*—it is also possible to differentiate on the basis of the charges that will be made to consumers, the forms of payment that are

accepted, the duration over which payment may be made, and the detailed terms of the sales contract itself.

It should be noted however that the preceding list focuses on the nature of the product/service and it is almost certainly this focus which has led to only moderate success for companies following a differentiation strategy (Ogwo, 1980). Even where an organization has elected to pursue a strategy of differentiation, customer needs and wants are still a primary consideration. Organizations must elect to differentiate themselves in those areas that are perceived by the customer as being important. This is an idea developed further in Chapter 4.

Is Segmentation a Viable Strategy?

In contrast to a strategy of differentiation, however, a strategy based on market segmentation begins with a thorough analysis of all the needs/wants of an organization's customer base. This information is then used to determine whether distinct patterns of needs exist and whether it would be possible/desirable to exploit those needs with a uniquely tailored marketing mix. Of course to do so would involve the organization in considerable additional expense, since one has then to develop not one, but two or more separate marketing mixes—one to address each of the market segments identified. Tynan and Drayton (1987, 303) argue that:

> at a superficial level the theory of market segmentation appears to conflict with basic economic theory. The tailoring of a product to meet the needs and wants of a market segment militates against long production runs and the resulting economies of scale.

The same would also be true in the case of an organization which was involved purely in the provision of a service. If management decide to tailor their services to a variety of subsets of customers they will need to arrange a separate pattern of delivery for each. Specialist staff, training, information technology, and infrastructure support may be required for each segment, thereby adding significantly to the costs of the service provision.

To understand why segmentation may be still be a viable strategy one needs to understand the origins of the concept. It arose out of rationing after the second world war, increasing technological progress, increasing social mobility, and the wider spectrum of consumer needs and wants that these changes created (Crimp, 1985). Companies were thus able to identify specific groups of needs and concentrate all their efforts on satisfying the needs of one or more such groups. Thus although economies of scale might have been lost, the companies concerned were able to instigate savings since they could target their marketing mixes much more specifically at their target groups and minimize wastage. It was no longer necessary, for example, to advertise in the mass media, as more specific channels of communication could be identified. Manufacturers also found that concentrating all their efforts on specific segments of customers tended to generate consumer loyalty and firms in the long run were able to avoid tough price competition with 'own brands'.

Not all writers agree, however, that segmentation is a viable strategy and although they are small in number it is worth briefly considering their views. Bliss (1980), for example, has suggested that while many marketing managers acknowledge the rationale of segmentation, many are dissatisfied with it as a concept, partly because it is inapplicable or difficult to apply in many markets, but also because emphasis is too often given to the technique of segmentation at the expense of the market itself and the competitive situation which exists. Writers such as Resnik *et al.* (1979, 100–6) have also addressed this issue and have suggested that changing values, new lifestyles, and rising product costs all argue the case for what they call 'counter segmentation'. This they define as an aggregation of various parts of the market rather than subdivision. However, the majority of writers do agree that market segmentation is for most a viable option of considerable strategic importance.

The General Approach to Segmenting a Market

A number of different methods may be used to segment the market. Green (1987) suggested that these methods could be categorized as being either *a priori* and cluster based or *post hoc*. An *a priori* approach is based on the notion that the marketer decides in advance of any research which basis for segmentation he/she intends to use. Typically this might involve categorizing customers according to their projected usage pattern (e.g. heavy, medium, or light user) and demographic and/or psychographic characteristics (see below). The marketer would then carry out research to identify the attractiveness of each segment and, on the basis of the results, make a decision as to which segment or segments to pursue. *Post hoc* segmentation, however, involves the marketer in carrying out an amount of initial research into the market place. This research might highlight attributes, attitudes, or benefits which relate to particular groups of customers—information which may then be used to decide how best to divide the market. In practice, whether *a priori* or *post hoc* segmentation is undertaken will depend on the relative degree of experience a marketer has within a given market. In cases where the marketer is close to the market and has considerable experience of it an *a priori* approach may best suit the company's needs. Alternatively, where the marketer has little knowledge, a *post hoc* method of segmentation may well be most appropriate.

Criteria for Segmenting Consumer Markets

Over the years a plethora of different variables have been used as the basis for market segmentation. Fortunately the majority of these can now be grouped as follows:

1. Demographic
2. Geographic and Geodemographic

3. Behavioural
4. Psychographic

Each of these classes of variables will now be considered in turn

I Demographic Variables

It may be possible to segment a market on the basis of variables such as age, gender, socio-economic group, family size, family life cycle, income, religion, race, nationality, occupation, or education. These are collectively known as demographic variables. This method of market segmentation is particularly popular in consumer markets since consumer wants, needs, and preferences are often highly correlated with these characteristics. The other reason for the popularity of demographic segmentation is a historical one. Such data has been collected over a great many years and hence much is known about the consumer behaviour of each target group. One may purchase, for instance, data relating to the media exposure of each individual demographic category.

It should be noted that it is now rare for an organization to use one demographic variable in isolation: rather, they now tend to use some combination of the same (Stanton, 1978). Despite their popularity they are seen by many as offering only a low utility primarily because they are based on descriptive rather than causal factors and hence cannot be relied upon as accurate predictors of future behaviour. Despite these reservations their use is still widespread. A selection of such variables will therefore now be considered in turn.

(a) Age

Age has frequently been used as the basis for segmentation since purchasing patterns are clearly related to an individual's age. One interesting reason for this observation may have been revealed by a study carried out by Philips and Sterthal (1977) who concluded that age differences result in changes to the sources of information a particular individual will use. Age was also shown to affect the ability to learn and the susceptibility to social influence. Clearly these are all factors which could influence purchasing behaviour and all three have a relevance to the not-for-profit sector.

(b) Gender

Kotler (1991) notes that an individual's gender has proven to be a good indicator of a propensity to buy a particular product or brand. In particular he cites cosmetics, clothing, magazines and toiletries. Gender has proven to be a useful criteria in the nonprofit sector too, as it seems that heavy charity donors are more likely to be female (CAF, 1996). Much social marketing may also have to be designed on the basis of a segmented approach by gender. For example, attitudes to safe sex, abortion, and healthcare screening have all been found to vary significantly by gender and communications messages must be tailored to reflect this.

(c) Family Life Cycle

Segmentation conducted on this basis is based on the premise that demand for goods/services will vary depending on the stage that customers have reached in terms of the development of their family. Segmentation can hence be based on whether individuals are single, married, married with children, etc. The idea is certainly not new. It was first postulated by Rowntree at the beginning of the century. However, the model now in most common usage is that first presented by Wells and Gubar (1966), and illustrated in Fig. 3.1.

Fig. 3.1: **The Family Life Cycle**

Stages in the Family Life Cycle	Buying Patterns
1. Bachelor Stage: Young single people living at home	Few financial commitments—recreation and fashion oriented
2. Newly Married Couples: Young, no children	High purchase rate of consumer durables—buy white goods, cars, furniture
3. Full Nest 1: Youngest child under six	House buying is at a peak. Liquid assets are low—buy medicines, toys, baby food, white goods
4. Full Nest 2: Youngest child six or over	Financial position is improving—buy a wider variety of foods, bicycles, pianos
5. Full Nest 3: Older married couples with dependent children	Financial position is improving still further. Some children now have jobs and wives are working. Increasing purchase of desirables—buy furniture and luxury goods
6. Empty Nest 1: Older married couples, no children at home, head of household still in workforce	Home ownership is at a peak—savings have increased and financial position improved. Interested in travel, recreation and self education. Not interested in new products—buy luxuries and home improvements
7 Empty Nest 2: Older married, no children living at home, head of household retired	Substantial reduction in income. Buy medical products and appliances that aid health, sleep and digestion
8. Solitary Survivor in the Workforce	Income still high but may sell home
9. Solitary Survivor, Retired	Same medical and product needs as group 7. Substantial cut in income. Need for attention and security

Source: Wilson et al. (1994). Reproduced with the kind permission of Butterworth-Heinemann, Oxford.

As a composite model (made up of age, number of years married, ages of children, and working status), the concept of the family life cycle has proven to be more useful than simple segmentation based on age alone (Lansing and Kish, 1957). It is however not without its critics, since it is based on the conventional nuclear family. When one views the current pattern of family life within the UK this model is clearly no longer completely valid. The model, for example, takes no account of the high divorce rate and subsequent increase in one person households and has a somewhat outdated view of women. Women are now able to work a larger proportion of their lives and are able to continue working even during the early years of their child's development. Despite the criticisms, however, the model is still in wide usage and has been proven to be a good indicator of a propensity to purchase certain categories of services (see for example Dominguez and Page (1984)).

In recent years a new version of the family life cycle has emerged which also takes account of an individual's aspirations and behaviour patterns as they progress through the phases of the lifecycle model. Four main stages of the life cycle are defined and these are then subdivided by income and occupation. The resultant model, known as SAGACITY, is shown in Fig. 3.2.

This model clearly improves on the earlier family life cycle since an individual's needs will clearly be related not only to his/her position in their life cycle but also to their occupation and relative income level. The definition of a typical segment would

Fig. 3.2: **The Sagacity Model**

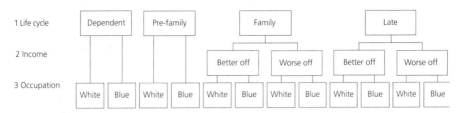

Source: Research Services Ltd., 1982, Reproduced with kind permission.

hence involve all three variables, and on the basis of these one would then be in a position to identify the purchasing patterns of the individuals concerned.

A further variation on this theme was supplied by Levy (1992) who suggests that the demographic variable career phase could be used as the basis for segmentation particularly in the market for continuing education. This has clear implications for both colleges and universities who could closely monitor the needs of a variety of career phase segments and determine, on the basis of such intelligence, which were likely to be the most appropriate to serve with their particular educational programmes.

(d) Income/Occupation

Income has also been proven to be a further useful base for segmentation and, despite difficulties in identifying a true picture of income for a particular group of consumers (i.e. taking account of the black economy and traditional reluctance to disclose such data), has been shown to be a good indicator of a propensity to purchase certain categories of products or services, or even to give to certain categories of cause (see for example Allt, 1975 or Slocum and Matthews, 1970).

A more common method of segmentation however is to be found by combining income and occupation into a single model. Since its conception in the UK, the National Readership Survey (NRS) has classified readers of press/magazines into one of six categories according to social grade. Buyers of magazine/press advertising space may then use this data to select media which provide a high concentration of readers belonging to one or more of their target groups. The NRS classification is shown in Table 3.1.

Table 3.1
Socio-Economic Groupings

Social Grade	Example Occupation
A	Senior Professional/Managerial
B	Middle Professional/Managerial
C1	Supervisory Management—Clerical
C2	Skilled Manual Labour—e.g. Electrician
D	Unskilled Manual—e.g. Labourer
E	Unemployed, Students etc.

It should be noted, however, that the system is now almost fifty years old and therefore based on a time when society was considerably more stable than it is at present. As Chisnall (1992, 210) notes, 'originally the grading system was intended to reflect the impact of life-style, income, and status; but society has been in a state of flux for (many) years'. Social strata no longer exist in the way that they once did. Educational opportunities are now spread through all societal levels and many wives are now providing a second income for their households, making it difficult to identify a 'head of household' on whose profession a categorization could be based. The system is further flawed because it takes no account of customer lifestyles, needs, or aspirations—in short, it says nothing about consumers as people. All of these characteristics clearly have the capacity to influence one's choice of product or service and, since the social grading system was based on the fundamental premiss that people's propensity to purchase certain categories of products would depend primarily on their level of income, its use must surely be called into question. Monk (1970) concluded that the social grading system was still in widespread use because:

(1) from a technical standpoint occupation is relatively stable and reliable at the data collection stage.

(2) It is a reasonable general purpose classification in that it is useful for most product fields without necessarily being the most ideal for any particular product fields.

2 Geographic and Geodemographic Segmentation

Geographic Segmentation

It has been argued that in terms of historic development, segmentation on the grounds of geography was the first to develop. Until quite recently transportation systems would have limited the access that some firms had to more distant geographical markets. They therefore had little choice but to set up their businesses in close proximity to a key concentration of potential buyers. Given that many nonprofits are set up with the objective of supplying services to a particular geographic community this may be a very effective (and necessary!) method of segmenting the potential market for a wide variety of such organizations. However, segmentation on the basis of geography represents a very broad-brush approach to segmentation and can supply little in the way of fine detail, particularly when one is investigating consumer markets. By contrast 'geodemographics' is an attempt to improve significantly on some of the limitations of the simple geographic model.

Geodemographics

The study of geodemographics arose from work carried out by Webber in 1973. He was originally interested in studying urban deprivation in Liverpool and classifying neighbourhoods using techniques of cluster analysis to produce a system containing 25 separate neighbourhood types. Each exhibited different mixes of problems and required a different type of social policy. Each neighbourhood was also defined in terms of its population, housing, and socio-economic characteristics. With the collaboration of the census office he was later able to extend this analysis and derive 38 separate neighbourhood types with which he was able to classify the UK as a whole.

The next significant development came when Baker (1982), of the British Market Research Bureau, identified that Webber's system had considerable potential for controlling the activities of the Target Group Index (TGI). He was able to identify that certain neighbourhood groups displayed a particular type of purchasing pattern. In short, similar neighbourhoods tended to buy similar types of products. The techniques of geodemographics have recently been refined and a variety of commercial systems are now in existence. In the UK the most well known of these is undoubtedly a system produced by CACI, called ACORN (A Classification Of Residential Neighbourhoods). The full classification system is shown in Table 3.2.

Table 3.2
**The ACORN
Classification
System**

Acorn Groups 1991	% of population
Wealthy Achievers, Suburban Areas	14.0
Affluent Grays—Rural Communities	2.2
Prosperous Pensioners, Retirement Areas	2.8
Affluent Executives, Family Areas	3.4
Well Off Workers, Family Areas	7.0
Affluent Urbanities, Town and City Areas	2.5
Prosperous Professionals, Metropolitan Areas	2.5
Better Off Executives, Inner City Areas	4.0
Comfortable Middle Ages, Mature Home Owning Areas	13.7
Skills Workers, Home Owning Areas	10.8
New Home Owners, Mature Communities	9.9
White Collar Workers, Better Off Multi Ethnic Areas	4.0
Older People Less Prosperous Areas	4.4
Council Estate Residents, Better Off Homes	10.9
Council Estate Residents, High Unemployment	3.6
Council Estate Residents, Great Hardship	2.4
People In Multi-Ethnic Areas, Low Income	2.8

Source: © CACI Limited, 1998. All Rights Reserved. ACORN and CACI are registered trademarks of CACI Ltd.

Users of the ACORN system can take an individual's postcode and identify the type of housing that that individual lives in, approximately what income they have, whether they are house owners or tenants, and approximately what stage they are in their family life cycle. They can also identify details of those product categories most likely to be of interest to the individual in question. This is a powerful marketing tool since an organization can request that its database be profiled and, if certain ACORN categories are found to predominate, the information can then be employed to good effect by targeting other households which have a similar profile. This would ensure that only individuals who are more likely to have an interest in (or need for) an organization's services will be selected for contact. The ACORN system can therefore help save valuable marketing resources, particularly when one considers that the subsequent purchase of lists of prospects is relatively inexpensive.

It should be noted that a number of other companies are now offering geodemographic systems on a commercial basis. These systems include MOSAIC, PINPOINT, and FINPIN.

Behavioural Segmentation

Kotler (1991, 272) defines behavioural segmentation as dividing buyers 'on the basis of their knowledge, attitude, use, or response to a product'. He goes on to say that 'many marketers believe that behavioural variables are the best starting point for construct-ing market segments'. There are many bases for segmentation under this general cate-gory, among them: benefit segmentation, brand loyalty, user rate, user status, and usage situation.

(a) Benefit Segmentation

Almost certainly the best known writer concerning benefit segmentation was Haley (1968). His research related to the toothpaste market and he identified four benefit seg-ments: seeking economy, protection, cosmetic, and taste benefits. In Haley's view the benefits identified in each case are the primary reason for the existence of true market segments. Interestingly his analysis showed that each benefit group was associated with distinct sets of demographic, behavioural, and psychographic characteristics. For example, the category seeking decay prevention were found to have large families, use as a consequence large amounts of toothpaste, and were conservative in nature. All this information is clearly valuable to toothpaste manufacturers, who can use it to buy space in media channels which reach the target group cost effectively and, more im-portantly, design promotional straplines (unique selling propositions) that will appeal to the target market. A single product or brand may indeed be dedicated specifically to the needs of that target audience.

The concept of benefit segmentation has also been explored in the nonprofit sector. Cermak, File, and Prince (1994), for example, have attempted to derive a benefit seg-mentation of potential donors. However, their study was based not on the behaviour of members of the 'donor market' but rather on an analysis of the reasons why decision makers in charitable trusts choose to make donations to a particular cause. The au-thors identified four distinct benefit segments, namely:

Affiliators—donors who benefit through social affiliation and the opportunity to exer-cise humanitarian impulses.
Pragmatists—donors who are primarily motivated by the tax advantages that might accrue from a donation.
Dynasts—donors who give because there is a family tradition of giving.
Repayers—donors who seem to give because of a need to reciprocate—perhaps because someone close to them has benefited from the cause.

An understanding of the key benefits sought by such donors could hence be of im-mense value to fundraisers in facilitating the design of appropriate marketing com-munications.

Benefit segmentation may be particularly useful where a particular product/service category already exists. It will then be somewhat easier to encourage individuals to list the benefits sought and subsequently use this as the basis for segmentation. As an ex-ample of this Brown (1992) carried out a benefit analysis of the fitness market. He identified that while considerable attention had been paid to the fitness and wellness needs of people by healthcare and related marketing organizations, little research had been carried out directed at identifying the market segments for fitness based upon consumer's perceived benefits of fitness. His study resulted in the definition of three distinct segments of fitness customers, namely:

(1) *Winners*—those who tend to do whatever it takes to get ahead in life and have re-alised the importance of becoming and remaining physically fit.

(2) *Dieters*—those who are mainly interested in weight control and physical appearance, using exercise to obtain these goals.

(3) *Self Improvers*—those who see exercise as a way to feel better.

From the perspective of a GP looking to encourage his/her patients to adopt better standards of fitness, it would hence appear that there are three distinct sets of benefits that patients could view as directly resulting from an exercise regime. By implication promotional material could be produced which would be likely to strike a chord with each segment.

(b) Brand Loyalty Status

The second technique encompassed by behavioural segmentation is that of brand loyalty status. This is an attempt to segment consumers on the basis of their purchase/usage patterns. Wilson *et al.* (1994) identify the following four segments.

(1) *Hard-core Loyals*—consumers who buy one brand all the time. Hence a buying pattern of AAAAA may be used to represent the consistent purchasing pattern of brand A.

(2) *Soft-core Loyals*—consumers who buy from a limited set of brands on a regular basis. Their purchasing pattern may be represented by AABABB.

(3) *Shifting Loyals*—consumers who switch loyalty on a regular basis. Their purchasing pattern may be represented by AABBCC.

(4) *Switchers*—consumers who show no loyalty to any one brand. This group may be considered especially susceptible to special offers or be attracted by regular variety. Their purchasing pattern may be represented by ABBCACB.

If, however, one is considering the use of loyalty as the criterion for segmentation, one should also consider the difficulties that might be encountered in the measurement thereof. What appear to be brand-loyal purchase patterns might in reality reflect habit, indifference, a low price, or the non-availability of other brands. There is therefore a need to probe what lies behind the purchase patterns observed. Even when various degrees of loyalty in the market-place have been identified it is not always a straightforward exercise to take advantage of this information. Whilst one can clearly identify one's own 'hard-core loyals', etc., it may not be easy to identify those of other organizations. The utility of the concept will hence depend on the extent to which each segment also exhibits a unique set of demographic or lifestyle characteristics. Knowledge of these details may lead to the development of a strategy designed to influence traditional patterns of loyalty, specifically targeted at those groups of consumers most likely to respond. Soft-core loyals purchasing competing services may, for example, be a particularly worthwhile segment to address.

(c) User Status

A further popular method for segmenting the market is to utilize data relating to product/service usage rate. Customers may be classified according to whether they are heavy, medium, or light users of the product and treated accordingly. This method may be particularly useful, since it is often a relatively small percentage of the market that accounts for a large percentage of consumption. Twedt (1964) argued that in many markets 20 per cent of the customers account for 80 per cent of the consumption. Thus there would be considerable utility in profiling those consumers who exhibit high usage rates. Not only can existing heavy users then be treated with an appropriate level of care, but other individuals in society who have a similar profile can be targeted in an attempt to get them to sample the organization's services. This method does however have the drawback that not all heavy consumers are usually available to the same provider because they are seeking a different set of benefits. For example, regular theatre attenders may be subdivided by a preference for different categories of performance.

Psychological Segmentation

The term psychological segmentation covers a multitude of different marketing sins. Many of the criteria that have been developed under this general heading have been discredited over the years, whilst others remain hotly contested. In general, it is probably fair to say that, the further one moves away from purely psychological variables towards those that include some physically observable (and hence measurable) element, the greater the degree of utility that will be offered. The use of two of the more contentious psychological variables, namely 'personality' and 'attitude' is discussed below.

(a) Personality

In attempting to go beyond the simple demographic approaches to segmentation, market researchers have unashamedly hijacked two sets of techniques from clinical psychology. The first approach involved utilizing what are known as standardized personality inventories and was proposed by Koponen (1960). The author administered a standard test of personality to almost 9,000 Americans. Essentially this involved the respondents choosing a series of statements that they could most closely identify with. The statements were so constructed as to measure the strength of a number of specific human needs. These are illustrated in Fig. 3.3.

When the author compared this data with known purchasing habits he was able to identify purchase patterns that appeared to be linked to personality variables. He found, for example, that heavy male smokers expressed higher needs for sex, aggression, achievement, and dominance than their non-smoking counterparts. Heavy smokers were also found to have significantly lower needs for compliance, self-depreciation and association. From a nonprofit perspective this could be highly significant since it paints a very clear picture of one segment of customers that one might wish to target with an anti-smoking campaign.

The second approach to using personality techniques involved applying the theories and models used in clinical psychology to design motivational research. The aim of such research was to understand why individuals choose to behave in the way that they do. Dichter (1964) was among the first to experiment with the use of these techniques in marketing research, and many other researchers quickly followed suit. At the time their work was very popular but this was due, at least in part, to the highly entertaining explanations it offered for routine purchasing behaviour. Cigarettes apparently were bought for their sexual symbolism and garden hoses could be sold to women as a 'symbol of the futility of genital competition' (see Schiffman and Kanuk, 1994).

Achievement	To rival and surpass others, to do one's best, to desire prestige, accomplishment, ambition success
Compliance	To accept leadership, to follow willingly, to let others make decisions, submission, deference, conformity
Order	To have things arranged, to be organized, to be clean, tidiness, neatness, organization
Exhibition	To be the centre of attention, to have others notice you, to make an impression on others, vanity and self dramatization
Autonomy	To seek freedom, to resist influence, to defy authority and coercion, independence and freedom
Association	To form friendships and associations, to participate in groups, to do things with others, affiliation and companionship
Analysis	To understand others, to examine motives, to analyse your own behaviour, understanding and introspection
Dependence	To seek aid, to be helped by others, to be guided and advised, helplessness
Dominance	To control others, to be a leader in groups, to influence others, control and supervision
Self-depreciation	To feel inferior to others, to accept blame, to accept punishment, masochism and shame
Assistance	To help others, to be sympathetic, to protect others, helpfulness and support
Change	To do new things, to do different things, to change daily routine, variety and novelty
Endurance	To stick to a task, to work hard at a job, to complete anything undertaken, persistence and toil
Heterosexuality	Willingness to talk about sex, to be attracted to the opposite sex, to go out with the opposite sex, love and desire
Aggression	To attack, assault or injure, to belittle, harm, blame, to punish, sadism and violence

Source: Koponen (1960).

Wells and Tigert (1971, 250) note that early studies into motivation were met with a substantial amount of criticism from the establishment, who felt that motivational research was 'unreliable, invalid, unobjective, too expensive, liable to be misleading and altogether an instrument of the devil'. It is worth noting therefore that the use of personality as a basis for segmentation has met with considerable debate over the years. The numbers of studies that have confirmed its usefulness and those who dismiss it are roughly similar. Whatever the truth of the matter the relevance of personality variables for segmentation strategy must be called into question. With the conflicting information that has been accumulated it would seem wise to look for other alternatives on which to base marketing strategy.

(b) Attitudes

These have been used as the basis for segmentation by a number of organizations but they have particular relevance to the nonprofit sector where many marketing campaigns are aimed at changing societal attitudes to certain types of behaviour (for example smoking, drinking). Many such campaigns assume, however, that there is a definite link between attitudes and actual purchase behaviour. Such a link has yet to be proved conclusively. Opinion is sharply divided between those authors who believe there is a causal link (for example McGuinness *et al.*, 1977, Crespi, 1977, and Howitt and McCabe, 1978) and those that believe there is not (for example, Fishbein, 1967, Ajzen and Fishbein, 1973, and Pinson and Roberto, 1973).

Nevertheless, despite the disagreement a variety of studies do appear to have employed attitudinal data to good effect. As an example, Allen and Maddox (1990) made use of attitudinal variables to segment the market for blood donations. An analysis of postal survey data revealed that there were four distinct clusters or segments of opinion about the process of giving blood. Three of the four clusters identified exhibited moderate to strong degrees of scepticism regarding blood donation, but for a variety of different reasons. This indicated a need to dispel distinct sets of disinformation and uncertainties. The authors concluded that simple generic appeals would therefore prove ineffective at appealing to all the target segments and they therefore suggested focusing specific promotional messages at specific target segments.

4 Psychographic Segmentation

Psychographic or lifestyle segmentation is an attempt to move away from earlier views of people expressed mainly in behavioural, demographic, and socio-economic terms. In this case individuals are grouped in terms of their hobbies/interests, feelings, aspirations, etc. In modern times this represents one of the most powerful criteria which can be used for market segmentation, since a mass of lifestyle data now exists relating to the readership of a whole variety of different publications, making it possible to target individuals on this basis very cost effectively.

Kotler (1991, 171) defines lifestyle as a

person's pattern of living in the world as expressed in the person's activities, interests and opinions. Lifestyle (therefore) portrays the whole individual interacting with his/her environment.

It may therefore be considered as distinct from personality. Personality variables describe the pattern of psychological characteristics that an individual might possess, but say nothing of that individual's hobbies, interests, opinions, or activities. Lifestyle data, however, can supply these missing variables.

Boyd and Levy (1967, 38) assessed the implications of the lifestyle concept and drew the following conclusions:

Marketing is a process of providing customers with parts of a potential mosaic from which they, as artists of their own lifestyles, can pick and choose to develop the composition that for the time seems the best. The marketer who thinks about his products in this way will seek to understand their potential settings and relationships to other parts of consumer lifestyles and thereby to increase the number of ways they fit meaningfully into the pattern.

A number of early lifestyle classification systems are to be found in the literature; among them Wells (1975, 201) who questioned some 4,000 male respondents and using the technique of factor analysis was able to derive the simple classification system shown in Table 3.3. Wells was also able to define the media and product usage of each group described in the table. The utility of this very simple classification lies in its ability to suggest effective promotional strategies that can be used with each segment. Group 4, for example, may well be deemed an appropriate target for arts marketers promoting a series of live classical music concerts. If so, price may be less of an issue for this group and, rather than trying to compete with other arts events on this basis, marketers may instead try to emphasize the quality of their events and price them to reflect this.

However, as the reader will no doubt appreciate, classifications such as this are very vague and it should hence be no surprise to learn that writers such as Young (1971) warn us that this form of general societal segmentation system can never have the

Table 3.3
**Wells's
Psychographic
Classification
System**

Group I. The Quiet Family Man—8% of total males

He is a self sufficient man who wants to be left alone and is basically shy. Tends to be as little involved with community life as possible. His life revolves around the family, simple work and television viewing, has a marked fantasy life. As a shopper he is practical, less drawn to consumer goods and pleasures than other men. Low education and economic status, he tends to be older then average.

Group 2. The Traditionalist—16% of all males

The man who feels secure, has self esteem, follows conventional rules. He is proper and respectable, regards himself as altruistic and interested in the welfare of others. As a shopper he is conservative, likes popular brands and well known manufacturers. Low education and low or middle socio-economic status. The oldest age group.

Group 3. The Discontented Man—13% of all males

He is a man who is likely to be dissatisfied with his work. He feels passed by life, dreams of better jobs, more money and more security. He tends to be distrusting and socially aloof. As a buyer he is risk conscious. Lowest education and lowest socio-economic group, mostly older than average.

Group 4. The Ethical Highbrow—14% of all males

This is a very concerned man, sensitive to people needs. Basically a puritan, content with family life, friends and work, interest in culture, religion, and social reform. As a consumer he is interested in quality, which may at times justify greater expenditure.

Group 5. The Pleasure Oriented Man—9% of all males

He tends to emphasise his masculinity and rejects whatever appears to be soft or feminine. He views himself as a leader among men. Self centred, dislikes his work. Seeks immediate gratification for his needs. He is an impulsive buyer, likely to buy products with a masculine image. Low education, lower socio-economic class, middle aged or younger.

Group 6. The Achiever—11% of all males

This is likely to be a hardworking man, dedicated to success and all that it implies, social prestige, power, and money. Is in favour of diversity, is adventurous about leisure time pursuits. Is stylish, likes good food, music, etc. As a consumer he is status conscious, a thoughtful and discriminating buyer. Good education, high socio-economic group, young.

Group 7. The He Man—19% of all males

He is gregarious, likes action, seeks an exciting and dramatic life. Thinks of himself as capable and dominant. Tends to be more of a bachelor than a family man, even after marriage. Products he buys and brands preferred are likely to have self-expressive value, especially a man-of-action dimension. Well educated, mainly middle socio-economic status, the youngest of the male groups.

Group 8. The Sophisticated Man—10% of all males

He is likely to be intellectual, concerned about social issues, admires men with artistic and intellectual achievements. Socially cosmopolitan, broad interests. Wants to be dominant and a leader. As a consumer he is attracted to the unique and fashionable. Best educated and highest status of all groups, younger than average.

Source: Reprinted with permission from *Journal of Marketing Research*, published by the American Marketing Association, Wells W. D. (1975) 12(2), 196–213.

same degree of accuracy as that produced by a product-specific approach. As a result Young argues that the only way to utilize psychographic variables to their best effect is to analyse them in the context of a particular product/service—a view shared by Wells (1975). This is an important argument because it suggests that organizations would be well advised to look to those lifestyle variables that are most closely associated with their organization and explore first the potential for segmentation on these grounds.

Indeed, many examples are to be found in the literature of researchers who have adopted this product-specific approach. In a general study of health care Rubinger (1987) has identified nine psychographic segments which define how consumers view the provision thereof:

(1) *Quality Minded Users*—the largest group nation-wide, look for the best health care at any cost.
(2) *Ready Users*—the second largest group—they represent a very receptive market for health care and will readily accept whatever is available.
(3) *Independently Healthy*—participate in sports, are concerned about nutrition, and pay more for health care.
(4) *Avoiders*—stay away from health care.
(5) *Naturalists*—seek alternatives to traditional health care.
(6) *Family Oriented Users*—believe their children's health to be paramount, interested in nutrition, wellness, and family.
(7) *Clinic Cynics*—sceptical about all forms of organized health care.
(8) *Generics*—see no difference between healthcare provision from one institution to another.
(9) *Loyalists*—find one institution and stay with it.

There are many implications for marketing strategy that come out of this research, since certain segments can clearly be targeted with campaigns either to address their specific needs or to facilitate a change in attitude. A great number of studies may be found in the literature which make exactly this point and demonstrate how an understanding of customer lifestyles makes it possible to select media which reach those customers cost effectively and to select promotional messages which a particular group will find intuitively more appealing.

Given the enthusiasm in the literature for the use of psychographic variables it is not surprising to learn that most national/international advertising agencies now have their own classification system to assist in campaign planning. There are also a number of commercially available systems. Among these is a system known as VALS (Values and Lifestyles Segmentation) which attempts to measure and segment people based on their goals, motivations, and values. People in twelve different countries have now been categorized. Developed in the USA by Arnold Mitchell of the Stanford Research Institute, the system categorizes people into one of nine lifestyle groups, namely:

(1) *Survivors*—who are generally disadvantaged and who tend to be depressed, withdrawn, and despairing;
(2) *Sustainers*—who are disadvantaged but who are fighting hard to escape poverty;
(3) *Belongers*—who tend to be conventional, nostalgic, conservative, and generally reluctant to experiment with new products or ideas;
(4) *Emulators*—who are status conscious, ambitious, and upwardly mobile;
(5) *Achievers*—who make things happen and enjoy life;
(6) *I Am Me*—who are self engrossed, respond to whims, and are generally young;
(7) *Experientials*—who want to experience a wide variety of what life can offer;
(8) *Socially conscious*—people with a marked sense of social responsibility and who want to improve the conditions of society;
(9) *Integrateds*—who are psychologically fully mature and who combine the best elements of inner and outer directedness.

The designers of VALS believe that individuals can be seen to pass through a number of development phases with the integrated stage being seen as the ultimate. In terms of marketing each segment can be seen to have very different needs, and hence products and services could be designed to focus specifically on a particular group of people. Helpfully, it is possible to purchase lists of individuals who can be categorized as belonging to one or either of these segments, so targeting can now be greatly enhanced.

There are many other systems available commercially, most of which work on a similar principle, although the variables tested in each case are slightly different. It would therefore be advantageous prior to utilizing one of these systems to have carried out some initial market research to identify specifically which lifestyle variables are significant in a given market. Other commercially available systems include Young and Rubicam's 4Cs and Taylor Nelson's Monitor.

A Cautionary Note

Having extolled the virtues of lifestyle segmentation it is important to be clear about their use in a not-for-profit setting. Many of the systems now available were designed primarily with the commercial sector in mind. They may therefore not offer the same degree of utility to the nonprofit sector, particularly given the observation of Young (1971) who suggested that, to use lifestyle data effectively, only those variables of direct relevance to the work of a particular organization should be selected. Having sounded this word of caution however, many of the largest lifestyle houses in the UK *do* now gather data in respect of nonprofit products and services. As a result it is now possible to buy lists of individuals who have a propensity to give to particular charitable causes and, moreover, to profile these individuals to ascertain whether they exhibit any other lifestyle characteristics which might suggest appropriate promotional messages and acceptable modes of contact. It is also possible to buy lists of individuals with an interest in specific categories of the arts, further/higher education, and aspects of health care. At the time of writing, this service is relatively inexpensive, costing typically only around £80–150 per 1,000 names and addresses, depending on the degree of refinement (i.e. number of criteria) required. It should be noted however that, for smaller nonprofits, even this low cost may be prohibitive as most lifestyle houses have a minimum order quantity of 5–10,000 names.

Criteria for Segmentation of Industrial Markets

Many nonprofits will be concerned not only with individuals in society but also with corporate organizations, particularly those which have the potential to act as sponsors of certain nonprofit activity. Indeed, as will be shown in Chapter 5, the support of corporate donors remains an important source of income for the voluntary sector. As a result it is worth briefly examining the criteria that can be used as the basis for segmentation in industrial markets.

Fortunately, the consensus to emerge from the literature is that it is possible to use many of the same criteria in industrial markets as one would typically use in consumer markets (see, for example, Nicosia and Wind, 1977). Wind and Cordozo (1974), however, suggest that industrial segmentation should be considered in two stages. The first stage involves defining the segments in terms of industry demographics, size, industrial sector, Standard Industrial Classification (SIC) code, and product usage. The second stage they advocate is to define the segments in terms of the behavioural characteristics of their decision making units or buying centres. The result is a hybrid segmentation system which reflects not only the type of business, but the manner in which it operates. To help illustrate the variety of criteria that are available it is worth briefly reviewing the work of Bonoma and Shapiro (1983) who developed one of the most comprehensive reviews of industrial segmentation currently available. The criteria that the authors identify are given in Table 3.4. The authors originally suggested that these criteria are arranged in descending levels of importance. In the specific context of the nonprofit sector, however, many of the criteria towards the bottom of the list can actually offer considerably more utility than those towards the top. As an example, charities will look particularly to solicit support from corporate organizations that have a track record of loyalty to their suppliers. It takes time to establish relationships and a charity can invest considerable amounts of time and money securing appropriate corporate partnerships. They clearly have a vested interest in ensuring that once established these relationships prove to be as enduring as possible and to a certain extent this can be researched upfront.

Similarly the purchasing approaches adopted might also form the basis for appropriate market segmentation. Those organizations that are looking for a genuine degree

Table 3.4

Criteria for Segmentation of Industrial Markets

Demographic Industry Type—which industries that buy the product should be focused on? Company Size—What size companies should be focused on? Location—What geographical areas should we focus on? **Operating Variables** Technology—What customer technologies should we focus on? User Status (i.e. heavy, medium, light)—Which type of user should be concentrated on? Customer Capabilities—Should customers having many or few needs be concentrated on? **Purchasing Approaches** Buying Criteria—Should customers be targeted that are looking for price, quality or service, etc? Buying Policies—Should customers requiring leasing facilities, for example, be targeted ? Current Relationships—Should the company focus only on those customers with whom a relationship already exists? **Situational Factors** Urgency—Should customers requiring immediate delivery be targeted? Size of Order—Should customers requiring large or small orders be targeted? Applications—Should customers requiring only a certain application of the product be targeted? **Personal Characteristics** Loyalty—Should only companies exhibiting high degrees of loyalty to their suppliers be targeted? Attitudes To Risk—Should risk taking or risk avoiding customers be targeted? Buyer-Seller Similarity—Should companies with similar characteristics to the seller be targeted?

Source: Bonoma and Shapiro (1983).

of commercial gain to accrue from their involvement with a nonprofit organization should be approached rather differently from those that are likely to view their association purely as a philanthropic activity.

Since criteria such as company size and location will clearly determine the likelihood and amounts of funding to be supplied it would seem that charities should give the greatest consideration to a mix of demographic, purchasing approach, and personal characteristic variables, when designing an appropriate commercial segmentation system.

Criteria for Evaluating the Viability of Market Segments

The reader will by now appreciate the diversity of variables that could potentially be used as the basis for market segmentation. Whilst there are many potential segments that an organization could look to pursue, it is almost certain that only a few of them will actually be worth exploiting. The difficulty facing marketers is exactly how to evaluate the possibilities.

In practice there are seven criteria that can be used to evaluate the potential offered by each segment proposed. Only if the analysis is favourable in each case should the segment be pursued. The segment must be:

1. *Measurable*—The market should be easily measurable and information about the segment and its characteristics should therefore either exist or be obtainable cost effectively.
2. *Accessible*—It should be possible to design a distinct marketing mix to target the segment cost effectively. One would therefore need to look for example at appropriate channels of distribution and media opportunities which could be used to target customers cost effectively with the minimum of wastage.
3. *Substantial*—It should be cost effective to market to the segment. Clearly the segment should be large enough in terms of sales volume (or small with sufficiently high margins) to warrant separate exploitation.
4. *Stable*—The segment's behaviour should be relatively stable over time to ensure that its future development may be predicted with a degree of accuracy for planning purposes.
5. *Appropriate*—It should be appropriate to exploit a particular segment given the organization's mission resources, objectives, etc.
6. *Unique*—The segment should be unique in terms of its response (to marketing activity) so that it can be distinguished from other segments.
7. *Sustainable*—Sustainability is an issue that is rapidly gaining in importance. It refers to the extent to which particular categories of customer can be sustained by the organization. The National Trust, for example, would hope to attract only conscientious walkers to their coastal paths: those that will treat the countryside with respect, stick to the signposted paths, take home their litter, etc. Not every

segment of society will thus be sustainable and marketing activity must hence be carefully targeted.

Criterion six warrants further elaboration. A segment may meet all of the other criteria but may behave identically to other segments in terms of its response to different types and timing of strategy. If this is the case, Kotler and Andreasen (1991, 170) identify that 'although it may be conceptually useful to develop separate segments in this way, managerially it is not useful'. As an example, if two segments of attenders at arts events both enjoy the same category of performance, both expect the same level of service at the venue, and both exhibit the same sensitivity to price, it is not managerially useful to continue to regard them as unique, even if they differ in demographic or lifestyle terms, since the organization will treat both these segments of customers alike. Differential treatment is only appropriate where there is some form of differential response.

Fig. 3.4:
Hypothetical Responses of Two Markets to Fundraising Activities

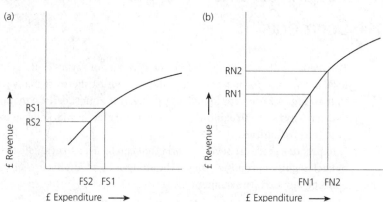

Source: Kotler and Andreasen (1991) *Strategic Marketing for Nonprofit Organisations*, 5th edn., © 1996. Adapted by permission of Prentice Hall Inc, Upper Saddle River, NJ.

As a further example Fig. 3.4 shows the allocation of a fundraising budget between two geographically separate markets, North and South. It can be seen from the slope of the two graphs that the North is more fundraising elastic (i.e. more sensitive to fundraising expenditure) than the South. The points FS1 and FN1 represent equal fundraising expenditures in the two markets. This allocation strategy yields total response results of (RS1 + RN1). However if the expenditure is shifted around between the two regions and £2,000 is moved from the South to the North, then the total amount raised will rise (RS2 + RN2) even though total expenditures are unchanged. Clearly fundraisers should continue shifting their fundraising budget to the North until such time as the incremental gain in one market just equals the incremental loss in the other. One would normally take advantage of any differential responsiveness until there is no variation in total responsiveness given any small changes that might be instigated. It should also be remembered that in this simple example the only variable under consideration was fundraising expenditure. In reality segments may exhibit differential responsiveness to a wide range of differing criteria and these data can be utilized to great effect in marketing planning. Clearly if no differential responsiveness is exhibited one might question the value of segmenting the market on that basis since no managerial advantages accrue.

Summary

Market segmentation may be regarded as one of the most fundamental concepts in modern marketing. It affords nonprofit organizations the opportunity to break down the overall market for their goods and services and to group together customers with similar needs and wants. A separate and distinct marketing mix can then be designed and implemented for each segment.

A variety of variables can be used as the basis for market segmentation including demographic, geodemographic, behavioural, and lifestyle variables. In practice it is now common for most organizations to use a variety of these and to develop composite forms of segmentation that relate most closely to the needs of the markets being exploited. Of course, not every segment identified by management will be found to be worth exploiting and a variety of criteria have been discussed that could be used to determine their suitability or otherwise.

Perhaps the greatest contribution that a careful consideration of segmentation issues can make to an nonprofit organization lies in the necessity for management to develop a thorough understanding of their markets and the individual categories of customers that they serve. Segmentation cannot happen without it! The knowledge gained, however, is invaluable in that it will greatly inform decision making in respect of every other aspect of the marketing planning process. A knowledge of the segments that will be served helps focus the information search that normally precedes the development of a marketing plan. It can also help in the development of meaningful objectives and dictate to a nonprofit organization the form that its marketing mix should most usefully take. Indeed, as previously noted, if the circumstances demand it, separate marketing mixes may need to be developed for each individual segment it is decided to address.

It is for this reason that a discussion of segmentation issues has been provided here in preparation for a more detailed look at the whole marketing planning process in Chapter 4. Whilst segmentation is an integral part of that process, it is also a necessary prerequisite thereof.

Discussion Questions

1. Distinguish between market segmentation and product differentiation. To what extent would you agree that they should be regarded as alternative strategies?
2. How might a charity such as the RNLI proceed to segment the market for potential donors to its organization? What issues would it need to consider?
3. With reference to your own organization, or one with which you are familiar, identify the basis that is currently used for market segmentation amongst potential funders and/or users of the nonprofit products/services. How might this be improved/refined?
4. As the marketing manager of one of the UK's leading healthcare trusts, prepare a presentation to the Board of Trustees explaining how a strategy of segmentation could help the Trust to market its services more effectively.

References

Ajzen, I. and Fishbein, M. (1973) 'Attitudinal and Normative Variables as Predictors of Specific Behaviour', *Journal of Personality and Social Psychology*, Vol. 27, No. 1, 41–57.

Allen, J. and Maddox, N. (1990) 'Segmenting Blood Donors by their Perceptions and Awareness about Blood Donations', *Health Marketing Quarterly*, Vol. 7, No. 1, 177–93.

Allt, B. (1975) 'Money or Class: New Light on Household Spending', *Advertising Quarterly*, Vol. 44, Summer, 6–9.

Baker, K. (1982) quoted in Clark, E. (1982) 'Acorn Finds New Friends', *Marketing*, 16 Dec, 13.

Bliss, M. (1980) *Market Segmentation and Environmental Analysis*, unpublished MSc. Thesis, University of Strathclyde.

Bonoma, T. V. and Shapiro, B. P. (1983) *Segmenting the Industrial Market*, Lexington, Lexington Books.

Boyd, H. W. and Levy, S. J. (1967) *Promotion: A Behavioural View*, Englewood Cliffs, NJ, Prentice Hall.

Brown, J. D. (1992) 'Benefit Segmentation of the Fitness Market', *Health Marketing Quarterly*, Vol. 9, No. 3, 19–28.

CAF (Charities Aid Foundation), (1996) *Dimensions of the Voluntary Sector*, West Malling, CAF.

Cermak, D. S. P., File, K. M. and Prince, R. A. (1994) 'A Benefit Segmentation of the Major Donor Market', *Journal of Business Research*, Vol. 29, No. 2, 121–30.

Chisnall, P. (1992) *Marketing Research*, Maidenhead, McGraw Hill.

Crespi, I. (1977) 'Attitude Measurement, Theory and Prediction', *Public Opinion Quarterly*, Vol. 41, No. 3, 285–94.

Crimp, M. (1985) *The Marketing Research Process*, 2nd edn, London, Prentice Hall.

Dichter, E. (1964) *Handbook of Consumer Motivations*, New York, McGraw Hill.

Dominguez, L. V. and Page A. (1984) 'Formulating a Strategic Portfolio of Profitable Retail Segments for Commercial Banks', *Journal of Economics and Business*, Vol. 36, No. 3, 43–57.

Fishbein, M. (1967) *Attitude Theory and Measurement*, New York, John Wiley and Sons.

Frank, R. E. (1967) 'Correlates of Buying Behaviour for Grocery Products', *Journal of Marketing*, Vol. 31, No. 4, 48–53.

Green, P. E. (1977) 'A New Approach to Market Segmentation', *Business Horizons*, Vol. 20, No. 1, 61–73.

Haley, A. T. (1968) 'Benefit Segmentation: A Decision Oriented Research Tool', *Journal of Marketing*, Vol. 32, No. 3, 30–5.

Howitt, D. and McCabe, J. (1978) 'Attitudes do Predict Behaviour—In Mails at Least', *British Journal of Social and Clinical Psychology*, Vol. 17, No. 3, 285–6.

Koponen, A. (1960) 'Personality Characteristics of Purchasers', *Journal of Advertising Research*, Vol. 1, No. 1, 6–12.

Kotler, P. (1991) *Marketing Management: Analysis, Planning, Implementation and Control*, 8th edn, Englewood Cliffs, Prentice Hall.

Kotler, P. and Andreasen, A. (1991) *Strategic Marketing for Non-Profit Organisations*, New Jersey, Prentice Hall.

Lansing, J. B. and Kish L. (1957) 'Family Life Cycle as an Independent Variable', *American Sociological Review*, Vol. 22, No. 5, 512–19.

Levy, D. R. (1992) 'Segment Your Markets', *Association Management*, Vol. 44, No. 8, 111–15.

McGuiness, J., Jones, A. P. and Cole, S. G. (1977) 'Attitudinal Correlates of Recycling Behaviour', *Journal of Applied Psychology*, Vol. 62, No. 4, 376–84.

Market Research Society (1984) *Market Research Society Yearbook*.

Monk, D. (1970) *Social Grading on the National Readership Survey*, London, Research Services Ltd, (JICNARS).

Nicosia, F. and Wind, Y. (1977) 'Behavioural Models of Organisational Buying Processes', in Nicosia, F. and Wind, Y. (eds) *Behavioural Models of Market Analysis: Foundations for Marketing Action*, Hinsdale, Ill., Dryden Press, 96–120.

Ogwo, O. E. (1980) *An Analysis of the Psychographic and Demographic Correlates of Consumer Credit Behaviour*, Unpublished Doctoral Dissertation, University of Strathclyde.

Philips, L. W. and Sternthal, B. (1977) 'Age Differences in Information Processing: A Perspective on The Aged Consumer', *Journal of Marketing Research*, Vol. 14, No. 4, 444–57.

Pinson, C. and Roberto, E. L. (1973) 'Do Attitude Changes Precede Behaviour Changes?', *Journal of Advertising Research*, Vol. 13, No. 4, 33–8.

Resnik, A. J., Turney, P. B. B. and Mason, J. B. (1979) 'Marketers Turn Towards Countersegmentation', *Harvard Business Review*, Vol. 57, No. 5, 100–6.

Rubinger, M. (1987) 'Psychographics Help Health Care Marketers Find and Serve New Market Segments', *Marketing News*, Vol. 21, No. 9, 24 April, 4–5.

Schiffman, L. G. and Kanuk L. L. (1994) *Consumer Behaviour*, 5th edn, Englewood Cliffs, Prentice Hall.

Schlegelmilch, B. B. (1979), 'Targeting Of Fund Raising Appeals', *European Journal Of Marketing*, Vol 22, 31–40.

Simpson, J. A. (1994) 'Market Segmentation for Appraisal Firms', *Appraisal Journal*, Vol. 60, No. 4, 564–7.

Slocum, J. W. and Matthews, H. L. (1970) 'Social Class and Income as Indicators of Consumer Credit Behaviour', *Journal of Marketing*, Vol. 34, No. 2, 69–74.

Smith, W. R. (1956) 'Product Differentiation and Market Segmentation as Alternative Marketing Strategies', *Journal of Marketing*, Vol. 21, No. 3, 3–8.

Stanton, W. J. (1978) *Fundamentals of Marketing*, 5th edn, New York, McGraw Hill.

Staudt, T. A., Taylor, D. A. and Bowersox, D. J. (1976) *A Managerial Introduction to Marketing*, Englewood Cliffs, Prentice Hall.

Twedt, D. W. (1964) 'How Important to Marketing Strategy is the Heavy User?', *Journal of Marketing*, Vol. 28, No. 1, 301–35.

Tynan, A. C. and Drayton, J. (1987) 'Market Segmentation', *Journal of Marketing Management*, Vol. 2, No. 3, 301–35.

Wells, W. D. (1975) 'Psychographics: A Critical Review', *Journal of Marketing Research*, Vol. 12, No. 2, 196–213.

Wells, W. D. and Gubar, G. (1966) 'Lifecycle Concept in Marketing Research', *Journal of Marketing Research*, Vol. 3, No. 4, 355–63.

Wells, W. D. and Tigert, D. J. (1971) 'Activities Interests and Opinions', in Engel, J. F. (ed), (1972) *Market Segmentation, Concept and Applications*, Holt and Rinelot Winston.

Wilson, R. M. S., Gilligan, C. and Pearson, D. J. (1994) *Strategic Marketing Management*, Butterworth Heinemann.

Wind, Y. and Cordozo, R. (1974) 'Industrial Market Segmentation', *Industrial Marketing Management*, Vol. 3, No. 1, 153–65.

Young, S. (1971) 'Psychographics Research and Marketing Relevancy', in King, C. W. and Tigert, D. J. (eds) *Attitude Research Reaches New Heights*, Chicago, American Marketing Association, 220–2.

4

The Marketing Planning Process

Objectives

By the end of this chapter you should be able to:

(1) conduct a thorough marketing audit of a nonprofit organization;

(2) derive specific, measurable, achievable, relevant, and time-scaled marketing objectives;

(3) analyse, select, and discuss key marketing strategies;

(4) derive a tactical marketing mix for a not-for-profit organization;

(5) specify appropriate marketing resources to achieve stated objectives;

(6) define appropriate control criteria.

Introduction

It is the purpose of this chapter to provide a framework for use by those interested in developing a marketing plan for a nonprofit organization. It will specify the key headings that would normally be utilized and explain many of the models and/or frameworks which can be helpful in defining both marketing strategy and tactics. It should be noted however that this chapter should in no sense be regarded as comprehensive. There are many excellent texts on the market whose sole purpose is to address the marketing planning process. What follows should therefore only be regarded as an overview of the subject as it relates to the nonprofit sector.

A simple marketing planning process is illustrated in Fig. 4.1. It should be noted that there is no one right way in which to write a marketing plan, and the style and format will hence vary considerably from one organization to another. Indeed there are almost as many different formats as there are authors of marketing texts! Nevertheless

Fig. 4.1: **The Marketing Planning Process**

Mission Statement

Organizational Objectives

Marketing Audit

a) *PEEST Analysis*
■ Political
■ Economic
■ Environmental
■ Socio-cultural
■ Technological

b) *Market Analysis*
c) *Competitor Analysis*
d) *Analysis of Publics*
e) *Analysis of Own Organisation*

SWOT Analysis

Marketing Objectives

Key Marketing Strategies

Tactical Marketing Mix
■ Product/Service
■ Price
■ Place
■ Promotion
■ People
■ Process
■ Physical Evidence

Budget

Scheduling

Monitoring and Control

the process outlined in Fig. 4.1 has the merit of including what are considered to be the key ingredients of a typical marketing plan—namely, an analysis of where the organization is at present, where it would wish to be in the future, and the detail of how it proposes to get there.

Mission and Organizational Objectives

Many organizations find it helpful to begin the development of their marketing plan by restating their mission and organizational objectives. This helps to focus the minds of those responsible for marketing on the issues which are considered to be of paramount importance for the organization as a whole. It also assists them in delineating those aspects of the organization's role which warrant further investigation in the detailed marketing audit which follows. If an arts centre, for example, has the mission of supporting new forms of art and encouraging local talent, it will not only have to spend time and resources in identifying these in the first place, it will also have to examine the nature of potential audiences for these new art forms as they begin to emerge. A good mission therefore has the capacity to guide the direction that the organization will take and ensure that the use of valuable marketing resource is optimal.

A number of nonprofit organizations have to date resisted the temptation to develop a mission statement, feeling perhaps that to do so would be to adopt yet another business practice which many such organizations still actively resent. They believe that mission statements serve as little more than promotional hype and serve no useful managerial purpose. Such views are short-sighted, however, as good mission statements can act as a reference point from which it is possible to derive appropriate and clear organizational objectives. To facilitate this, the more useful mission statements address in general terms the reasons for the organization's existence and, as noted by Abell (1980), contain reference to most, if not all, of the following ingredients:

(1) the customer groups that will be served;
(2) the customer needs that will be met;
(3) the technology that will be employed in satisfying these needs.

A glance through a selection of nonprofit publicity material reveals that many nonprofits have been intuitively writing mission statements for years, even if they prefer to use alternative terminology such as 'aims', 'purpose', or 'philosophy'. In truth the terminology is unimportant. What matters is that the organization can summarize in a few words its *raison d'être*. Not only does this aid planners in the manner described above, but it can become a remarkably useful reference point for potential donors, or those who might stand to benefit from the goods/services being provided. Supporters and potential beneficiaries can see at a glance what the organization is trying to achieve and confidently initiate some form of relationship if they feel it will be appropriate.

A selection of 'missions' are given below.

In 1978, the World Wildlife Fund decided that its 'purpose' was:

> to raise the maximum funds possible from UK sources and to ensure that the funds are used wisely for the benefit of conservation of the natural environment and renewable natural resources with emphasis on endangered species and habitats.

The Elizabeth Svendsen Trust for Children and Donkeys has as its stated 'aim':

> to bring enjoyment and pleasure into the lives of children with special needs and disabilities and the satisfaction that comes with the achievement of learning riding skills.

The Horder Centre for Arthritis describes its 'philosophy' as follows:

> The Horder Centre exists to improve the quality of life primarily to people stricken with arthritis. The mainsprings of our philosophy are:
>
> ■ to provide professional help by all available methods for people suffering the pain and disabling effects of all forms of arthritis.
> ■ to restore maximum independence and alleviate pain wherever possible.
> ■ to remain at the forefront of the battle against arthritis as a Centre of Excellence.

The reader will appreciate that in all these examples there is a noticeable absence of figures. Mission statements should address what the organization wishes to achieve, but in such a way that the mission can be adopted consistently for a reasonable period of time. It should not be necessary to readdress the mission on an annual basis, since it should serve only to provide the most general of signposts.

Indeed the specific detail of what an organization seeks to accomplish within each planning period would normally form part of the content of the organizational objectives. Drucker (1955) isolated what he believed to be eight aspects of operations where organizational objectives could be developed and maintained. These have been modified slightly below to relate them more specifically to the context of nonprofit organizations.

(1) Market standing
(2) Innovation
(3) Productivity
(4) Financial and physical resources
(5) Manager performance and development
(6) Worker/Volunteer performance and attitude
(7) Societal needs to be served
(8) Public responsibility

Clearly each of these areas has some relevance for marketers even if many of them do not specifically relate to the marketing function. It is important however to realize that these objectives are stated for the organization as a whole to work towards. Their achievement will require a co-ordination of effort across all divisions/departments within the organization. Managers with responsibility for finance, human resources, service delivery, etc. will all have their part to play in ensuring that the organization delivers what it says it is going to deliver. It is for this reason that it is common practice to restate such objectives at the beginning of a typical marketing plan. Marketers should then be able to isolate what they as individuals need to be able to achieve over the planning period to facilitate the achievement of these wider objectives. There would be little point, for example, in the marketing department raising vast sums of money for causes that are not perceived as congruent with the organization's goals, whilst failing to raise sufficient sums for those that are. A restatement of the corporate objectives can therefore serve as an important focus for the marketing plan which follows.

The Marketing Audit

The marketing planning process can be conceptualized as having three main components:

(1) Where are we now?
(2) Where do we want to be?
(3) How will we get there?

The marketing audit specifically addresses the first of these issues. As such it is arguably the most crucial stage of the whole planning process since without a thorough understanding of the organization's current position it will be impossible for planners to develop any kind of vision of what they would wish to accomplish in the future. The marketing audit is essentially a detailed review of any factors which are likely to impinge on the organization taking into account both those generated internally and those emanating from the external environment. The marketing audit is thus a systematic attempt to gather as much information as possible about the organization and its environment and, importantly, how these might both be expected to change and develop in the medium and long term futures. A typical framework for a marketing audit is given below.

I PEEST Factors

It is usual to begin the audit process by examining the wider environmental influences which might impact on the organization. Often these may be factors over which the organization itself has little control, but which will nevertheless crucially impact on the organization at some stage in the future. The framework utilized for this analysis is typically referred to as a PEEST analysis and comprises the following elements.

- Political
- Economic
- Environmental
- Socio-cultural
- Technological

In each case the aim is to accumulate a list of all the pertinent factors and how these are expected to change over the planning period. It is best at this point in the process not to spend too much time deliberating about the impact that these factors might have on the nonprofit organization, but rather to note them, detail how they might change, and move on. The danger of precipitating a discussion at this stage—as the author has found to his cost—is that other clues as to the impact these PEEST factors might have will tend to emerge as the audit process progresses. It is therefore better to consider potential impacts '*en masse*' when the audit itself is complete. A sample PEEST analysis for a nonprofit concerned with raising public awareness of the impact of modern industrial practices on the quality of the environment is presented in Fig. 4.2.

2 Market Analysis

The second stage of the audit involves conducting a thorough analysis of the markets in which the nonprofit perceives itself—and, importantly, is perceived by its customers—as operating. Chapter 2 has already detailed the dangers of developing too myopic a view of the market that will be analysed and it is important therefore that this is developed from the customer's perspective.

The other complexity associated with this stage of the analysis derives from the fact that nonprofits often have two or more markets in which they may be considered as operating. At a very minimum the marketer is likely to have to deal with the distinction between the market for the goods and services of the organization (resource allocation) and the market for the acquisition of those resources (resource attraction). This section of the audit should therefore be structured to consider in detail the factors relevant to each. The precise content of this section of the audit will clearly vary from one organization to another, but Fig. 4.3 contains a number of suggestions in respect of each of the categories of data that might be found useful at this stage.

Political Factors

Attitudes of Government
Legal Framework
Fiscal Framework
Government Contracts
Activities of Pressure Groups

Economic Factors

Employment
GNP Trends
Interest Rates
Inflation
Business Cycles

Environmental Factors

Environment Protection Legislation
Levels of Deterioration
Sustainable Practices
Activities of Major Polluters
Location/Development of Major Polluters

Technological Factors

Government Investment in Research
Development of New Materials
Sources of Technology Transfer
Manufacturing Practices

Socio-cultural

Attitudes to Recycling
Awareness of Environmental Decay
Consumer Lifestyles
Demographic Patterns
Content of School Education
Major Influences on Consumer Behaviour
Patterns of Consumption

Fig. 4.3:
Analysis of
Nonprofit
Markets

Resource Allocation	Resource Acquisition
Size, growth and trends, (by both value and volume)	Size growth and trends, (by both value, volume and category of support)
Principal needs to be met—characteristics	Needs of prospective supporters
Patterns of need	Patterns of giving/Donor behaviour
Geographic concentration of need	Ability to segment donor market
Physical resources available in market to meet need	Current/Anticipated fundraising practices
Relevant trade bodies—Associations—public/private/ voluntary	Principal channels of communication
Trade practices/Behaviour of other bodies	
Ability to pay within overall market	
Common methods of distribution	
Principal methods of communication	

3 Competitor Analysis

There are essentially three categories of competitors who are worthy of investigation at this stage in the audit.

(1) *Competitors for Resources*—i.e. other nonprofit organizations who seek to attract resources from the same sources as the nonprofit in question.

(2) *Competitors for Provision of Nonprofit Services*—nonprofits may also encounter competition from other organizations who seek to provide the same services as themselves. Increasingly this competition may come from for-profit organizations who may decide to compete, for example, for government service contracts.

(3) *Organizations with Competing Missions*—many nonprofits now exist whose primary goal is to persuade society to adopt new forms of purchasing, smoking, or sexual

behaviours. Such nonprofits typically encounter opposition from other organizations which exist to further exactly the opposite forms of behaviour. In such circumstances these organizations should clearly be regarded as competitors and subject to an equally detailed level of analysis.

To be able to compete successfully in their chosen markets nonprofits need to have a sound understanding of the behaviours of organizations who might be regarded as competitors, and to attempt to determine what their future strategies might be. It is also helpful to understand something of the capabilities of each major player and to define clearly their individual strengths and weaknesses. The following checklist could therefore be used as the starting point for analysis, although it should be noted that the specific factors an organization will need to examine is likely to vary considerably from case to case:

- contact details of each competitor
- size and geographic location(s)
- financial performance
- resource capabilities
- past strategies
- tactical marketing mixes employed
- key alliances formed
- major strengths and weaknesses.

4 Analysis of Publics

Kotler and Andreasen (1991, 89) use the term 'publics' to refer to:

> a distinct group of people, organisations, or both, whose actual or potential needs must in some sense be served.

The term 'public' is therefore more general in its meaning than the concept of 'customer' and embraces every group whose needs must be taken into account by the focal organization. For a registered charity this might typically include individual donors, funding bodies, the local community, the general public, media, recipients of goods and services, the organization's own staff, volunteers, etc. It is therefore important that the focal organization understands the needs and behaviours of these target groups, so that they might be taken account of in the subsequent development of strategy. In particular the following information could prove useful:

- identification of each key public
- requirements/needs/wants of each group
- basis (if any) for market segmentation
- buying/giving behaviours
- attitudes
- media exposure
- patterns of change in any of the above.

5 Analysis of Own Organization

Having now analysed every important component of the external environment it is important to conclude with an examination of the capabilities of the focal organization. A detailed audit should be undertaken of the organization's current marketing activity and its overall performance in respect of previous marketing goals. The following checklist is indicative of the categories of information that might typically be regarded as relevant, but in no sense should it be regarded as exhaustive.

Resource Attraction Activities:

- fundraising income (subdivided by source, e.g. individual, corporate, and trust donations)
- fundraising income (subdivided by method of fundraising employed, e.g. direct mail, telemarketing, etc.)
- income from contracts
- sales (subdivided by channel) and margins achieved
- attractiveness of service provision to potential funders
- marketing procedures
- marketing organization
- marketing intelligence systems
- marketing mix.

Resource Allocation Activities:

- sales/service take-up rates (subdivided by location, market segment, and service category)
- market share analysis
- cost effectiveness of services being provided
- marketing procedures
- marketing organization
- marketing intelligence systems
- marketing mix.

Clearly, conducting a marketing audit can be a very time-consuming process and, given that it is good practice to conduct an audit each year, it can place considerable demands on organizational resources. Nevertheless, the benefits that the audit can offer in terms of enhanced management decision making far outweigh the costs that might be incurred. Indeed if the auditing process is instituted on an annual basis, most of the necessary mechanisms for the gathering of data will have been put in place in the first year, and hence the costs in both time and effort should subsequently fall substantially.

Regrettably, however, many organizations continue only to take the trouble to complete this exercise when they are facing a crisis. Faced with decreased demand for their services, or a dramatic reduction in funding, organizations begin to panic and only then seek the reasons for these occurrences. Had a systematic approach to environmental scanning been adopted, not only would they have been less likely to have been taken by surprise, but the development of suitable strategies to counter the problems might already be well under way.

SWOT Analysis

Clearly at this stage the output from the marketing audit may be regarded as little more than a collection of data, and in this format it is as yet of little value for planning purposes. What is required is a form of analysis which allows the marketer to examine the opportunities and threats presented by the environment in a relatively structured way. Indeed it should at this point be recognized that opportunities and threats are seldom absolute. An opportunity may only be regarded as an opportunity, for example, if the organization has the necessary resource strengths to support its development. For this reason it is usual to conduct a SWOT analysis (Strengths, Weaknesses, Opportunities, and Threats) on the data gathered during the marketing audit. This is simply a matter of selecting key information from the audit and presenting it under one of the four headings. The important word here is 'key'. It is important that some filtering of the data gathered at this stage is undertaken so that the analysis is ultimately limited to the factors of most relevance for the subsequent development of strategy.

The principal aim of the SWOT analysis is to allow the organization to find a fit between its internal capabilities and the opportunities and threats presented by the external environment. This idea is represented diagramatically in Fig. 4.4. It can also assist managers by focusing their attention on areas where there are either gaps in their knowledge or high levels of uncertainty. In the case of the latter it may prove necessary to make a series of assumptions about the manner in which the environment will change to facilitate the SWOT analysis. If so, these should be kept to a reasonable minimum and made as specific as possible. This will aid planners in subsequently estimating outcomes from the strategies ultimately prescribed.

Fig. 4.4: **SWOT Analysis**

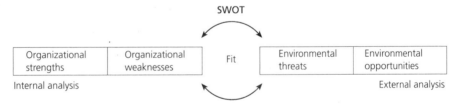

Source: Lancaster, G. and Massingham, L. (1988) *Essentials of Marketing: Text and Cases*. Reproduced with the kind permission of McGraw Hill.

On completion of the SWOT analysis the organization should be in a position to develop strategies which maximize the potential offered by the market opportunities (drawing on organizational strengths), whilst at the same time looking to minimize the likely effects of any weaknesses or perceived threats in the environment. The output from the SWOT analysis should also help inform the development of appropriate marketing objectives, since it should at this stage be clear what the most appropriate means of achieving the organizational objectives (stated earlier) will be.

Setting Marketing Objectives

The importance of setting objectives in a not-for-profit context has long been under-rated. As Drucker (1990, 107) notes:

> In a non-profit organisation there is no such (thing as a) bottom line. But there is also a temptation to downplay results. There is the temptation to say: We are serving a good cause. We are doing the Lord's work. Or we are doing something to make life a little better for people and that's a result in itself. That is not enough. If a business wastes its resources on non results, by and large it loses its own money. In a non-profit institution though, it's somebody else's money—the donor's money. Service organisations are accountable to donors, accountable for putting the money where the results are, and for performance. So, this is an area that needs special emphasis for non-profit executives. Good intentions only pave the way to Hell!

Objectives are an important part of the plan as they are the only mechanism by which its success can be measured. If a plan achieves its stated objectives we might reasonably conclude that it has been a success. Without them, one can only speculate as to the planner's original intent and the effectiveness of the activities undertaken have no benchmark against which to be assessed. Valuable resources could be being wasted, but the organization would have no mechanism for identifying that this was in fact the case.

As a minimum therefore, marketing objectives for nonprofits should address the following two issues:

(1) The match between the services produced and the markets that those services are intended to serve. Thus objectives should specify the services that will be provided and for whom.

(2) The level of resource that it is intended to attract to support the services identified at (1) above.

It is also important to realise that the style in which the objectives are written is also a significant issue. Objectives are only of value if it is possible to use them as an aid to managing the organization's resources and hence vague terms and needless ambiguity should be studiously avoided.

> Vague objectives, however emotionally appealing are counter-productive to sensible planning and are usually the result of the human propensity for wishful thinking which often smacks more of cheerleading than serious marketing leadership. What this means is that while it is arguable whether directional terms such as decrease, optimise, minimise should be used as objectives, it seems logical that unless there is some measure, or yardstick, against which to measure a sense of locomotion towards achieving them, they do not serve any useful purpose.   (MacDonald, 1984, 88)

Hence, to be managerially useful, good objectives should exhibit the following characteristics; they should be:

(1) *Specific*—related to one particular aspect of marketing activity. Objectives which relate simultaneously to diverse aspects of marketing activity are difficult to assess since they may require the organization to use different techniques of measurement and to look across different planning horizons. Attempting to combine activities might therefore lead to confusion, or at best a lack of focus.

(2) *Measurable*—Words such as maximize or increase are not particularly helpful when it later becomes necessary to assess the effectiveness of marketing activity. To be useful, objectives should avoid these terms and be capable of measurement. They should therefore specify quantifiable values whenever possible—for example, to achieve a 20 per cent market share, or to produce a 5 per cent reduction in smoking, nation-wide.

(3) *Achievable*—Marketing objectives should be derived from a thorough analysis of the content of the marketing audit, not from creative thinking on the part of managers. Objectives which have no possibility of accomplishment will only serve to demoralize those responsible for their achievement and serve to deplete resources that could have had a greater potential impact elsewhere.

(4) *Relevant*—Marketing objectives should be consistent with the objectives of the organization as a whole. They should merely supply a greater level of detail, identifying specifically what the marketing function will have to achieve to move the nonprofit in the desired direction.

(5) *Time-scaled*—Good objectives should clearly specify the duration over which they are to be achieved. Not only does this help to plan the strategies and tactics by which they will be accomplished but it also assists in permitting the organization to set in place control procedures to ensure that the stated targets will indeed be met. Thus monthly 'sub-targets' for each form of fundraising could be set and corrective action initiated early in the duration of a plan , as soon as a variance is detected

Thus good marketing objectives should be SMART! (Specific, Measurable, Achievable, Relevant, Time-scaled.)

Having now outlined the 'rules', it might be helpful to actually demonstrate what a typical nonprofit marketing objective might look like. In the context of arts marketing, a marketing objective for a theatre might take the form:

> To achieve a 20 per cent increase in student attendance at all performances between 15 October and 10 December 1997.

In a fundraising context the objectives might read:

> To attract £200,000 in voluntary income from individual donors by the end of the calendar year.

> To attract £50,000 of (cash) corporate support by the end of November 1997.

Key Strategies

Having specified the objectives it is intended that the plan will achieve, it is now possible to address the means by which these will be accomplished. These 'means' are termed 'marketing strategy' and it is useful to consider this in relation to the following three categories

(1) Overall Direction
(2) Segmentation Strategy
(3) Positioning Strategy

Each will now be considered in turn.

I Overall Direction

There are essentially four key strategic directions that an organization could follow if it is looking to achieve growth. These are illustrated diagramatically in Fig. 4.5. All the options involve making decisions about the range of services that will be provided and the markets into which they will be delivered. Each strategic option will now be considered in turn.

Fig. 4.5: **The Ansoff Matrix**

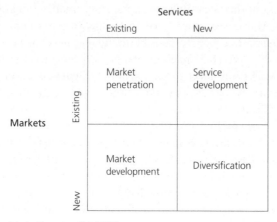

Adapted from Ansoff, I. (1968).

(a) Market Penetration

This option involves the organization in attempting to gain a greater number of sales in its existing markets. The existing range of services continues to be marketed to the existing market segments and no changes are planned to either. There are many ways in which a nonprofit could look to penetrate the market, including finding some way to reduce the price charged for the service, enhancing promotional activity, improving distribution facilities, or, more likely, maximizing output. Many charities, for example, face almost unlimited demand for the services they currently supply and could hence gain greater penetration simply by looking for ways to maximize the output from their own organization.

In cases where demand is less buoyant however, or where the charity has a comparatively low level of awareness amongst its target audience, the organization may have to resort to intensifying its marketing activity to stimulate the additional demand that it requires. If there are competitors in the market this may prove to be no easy task as additional 'sales' may have to be gained at their expense. This is perhaps less of a problem in an expanding market as there may be sufficient increases in demand per annum to allow all competing organizations to realize their growth objectives without having to compete directly with others in the sector. In static or declining markets, however, the reverse is true and additional sales will only be generated by stealing them from others competing within the same market.

(b) Service Development

Service development will normally be an attractive option where the organization does not perceive sufficient opportunities for growth by continuing merely to deliver its existing services. The demand for service development may also be driven by demands from customers as, for example, many local authorities have discovered in recent years. Faced with such a situation an organization may decide that it is appropriate to develop other services which the members of its existing markets may utilize. Indeed for some organizations a continuing strategy of service development may be the sole reason for their existence. Those, for example, which provide care to patients suffering from terminal illness will continually seek to develop their services as levels of medical and technical knowledge are expanded.

It should be noted however that service development is inherently more risky than market penetration, since substantial investment is often required to develop new services and there is no absolute guarantee that once developed they will be favoured by the organization's current customer groups.

(c) Market Development

Market development involves the organization in continuing to provide its current range of services, but extending the range of markets into which they will be delivered. The nonprofit can hence elect to target additional market segments, to exploit new uses for the service, or both. A strategy of market development may be most appropriate where a given organization has distinctive expertise which it can offer. In such cases it may make more sense to target other segments rather than dilute the available expertise by attempting to broaden the range of service on offer.

Indeed a number of nonprofit organizations may be forced into a strategy of market development even in circumstances where they have yet to completely satisfy demand in their existing markets. The housing charity Shelter, for example, has found it necessary to support the homeless in an increasingly larger percentage of Britain's towns and cities, whereas only a few years ago it could have concentrated solely on a small number of these, secure in the knowledge that it was addressing the needs of the majority of individuals at risk.

(d) Diversification

This is perhaps the most risky of all the four potential growth strategies. It involves the nonprofit in beginning to deliver services of which it has no experience, and supplying these to completely new groups of customers. The degree of risk the organization is subjecting itself to will depend on whether the diversification is either *related* or *unrelated*.

In the case of *related diversification* the organization is continuing to operate within broadly the same sector but is attempting to do something new for the first time. The rush to create retail outlets for charities in the 1980s would have constituted related diversification for the organizations involved, since they had long had experience of fundraising, but perhaps little, if any, of running a successful retail enterprise.

Unrelated diversification is perhaps less common since this would involve an organization in a radical departure from its existing services/markets. This may be necessary for some nonprofits who find that their *raison d'être* has ceased to exist, as when, for example, a cure is found for the disease, the relief of whose sufferers they exist to serve. Government legislation can also force organizations into unrelated diversification. For example, many of the oldest charity trusts in the UK were originally formed with the express purpose of maintaining bridges, highways, etc. Now that local authorities have statutory obligations to look after the transport networks within their boundaries the objects of these trusts have been changed over time to allow them to support other worthwhile causes, many of which, on the face of it, bear no resemblance whatsoever to the original reasons for the trust's creation.

(e) Are there other Strategic Directions?

For the sake of completeness it is worth noting that not every organization may wish to achieve growth. Ansoff's matrix, as depicted in Fig. 4.5, assumes that this is the case and ignores the other strategic options available which include:

Do Nothing—where the organization takes a conscious decision not to alter current strategy.

Withdraw—where the organization decides to sever its links with a particular service/market.

Consolidation—which involves the nonprofit in seeking strategies that will allow it to maintain its current market position. This should not be confused with the 'do nothing' option since the strategies necessary to support a current strategic position are unlikely to be identical to those that allowed an organization to create it in the first place.

2 Segmentation Strategy

The second key strategy that must be decided upon is how the markets in which the nonprofit is operating will be segmented. This ensures that the organization has a clear view of those customer groups it exists to serve. The previous chapter has already examined in some detail the criteria that may be employed to segment both consumer and industrial markets. At this stage in the marketing plan the nonprofit will want to specify exactly how each market in which it is operating will be segmented and, within that, specifically those segments that it is proposed to address. Aside from specifying those segments that the organization is already addressing, if a strategy of market development or diversification has been decided upon it will also be necessary to identify the new segments that will now be targeted. Marketing planners can then ensure that a coherent marketing plan is developed which will capitalize on any potential synergies that might be gained from the strategy/tactics used to develop each segment.

3 Positioning Strategy

Once the organization has decided appropriate targets for the marketing plan to address, it will be necessary to develop a strategy that will shape the image that the nonprofit wishes to project in the minds of those targets. This is in essence what marketers refer to as 'positioning' and it may be defined as:

> the act of defining in the minds of the target market what a particular organization's services can offer in relation to the others on the market.

It is therefore essential that the organization understands how its various customer groups perceive it in relation to the other 'suppliers' in the market. For example, imag-

Fig. 4.6: **Initial Positioning of Bloomsville University**

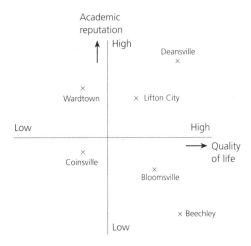

ine that a university (let's call it Bloomsville) wanted to identify how it was perceived by prospective undergraduate students. It understands that students are attracted to it for a number of reasons, but decides to investigate how it is positioned to other institutions in respect of just two of these—its academic reputation and the quality of life it offers to its students. The process would begin by some exploratory research to determine how the university and each of its competitors was rated on these two dimensions. A perceptual map could then be developed like the one depicted in Fig. 4.6. Bloomsville administrators could then see at a glance how their university was perceived in relation to others. It seems quite clear from the figure, for example, that although the quality of life offered by the university is perceived as being quite reasonable, the university has a relatively poor academic reputation. This may be a reputation that is entirely deserved and felt by the management to be a reasonable perception, in which case no further action might be necessary. If, however Bloomsville academic research is actually quite respected in the academic community and/or the university has recently figured well in the latest Research Assessment Exercise (RAE), management might take the view that this perception is unacceptable and initiate action to improve it. A communications plan could thus be implemented which would highlight recent Bloomsville research success in an attempt to shift its relative positioning in the manner indicated in Fig. 4.7. Clearly further research would then be necessary to track the implementation of the communications plan, to ensure that it was having the desired effect in the market.

Summary

The 'Key Strategies' section of the marketing plan should make it clear to the reader what direction the nonprofit intends to take to achieve its organizational objectives. In particular the services to be provided and the markets that will be served should be clearly identified, together with a detailed specification of each selected market segment and the needs thereof. This section of the plan should also specify how the organization intends to position itself within each of its key markets. The fine detail of how this will be achieved is provided in the section below.

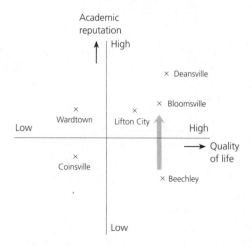

Fig. 4.7: **Final Positioning of Bloomsville University**

Before moving on, however, it is important to draw a distinction in our discussion between the terms 'strategy' and 'tactics'. There is often considerable room for confusion between these two terms and it is important that their meaning be fully understood. Essentially there is a difference of scope between them, with the term 'strategy' being used to refer to the general approach that an organization might take towards the fulfilment of its objectives. The term 'tactics', on the other hand, is used to denote the fine detail of exactly how the strategy will be implemented. Thus the marketing strategy that a museum might adopt with the stated objective of increasing the number of visitors to its premises in 1998 by 10 per cent, might read as follows:

> To attract a greater percentage of local residents to the permanent exhibition (market penetration).
>
> To target tourists and other visitors to the city to the permanent exhibition (market development).
>
> To develop a lecture service for schools where lectures would be provided on selected topics relating to the National Curriculum (service development).

Whilst the strategies give a clear indication of the directions that the museum will take to increase its visitor numbers, they do not specify the detail of how each strategy is to be developed and implemented. This level of detail is left to the tactical section of the plan where the details of exactly how, for example, more local residents will be attracted to the museum will be explored. This might include modifying the exhibition itself, re-examining admission fees, enhancing advertising in the local press, etc. Indeed the tactical component of the plan will also outline the budget for each activity and specify a schedule illustrating the timing of each marketing activity.

The Tactical Marketing Mix

I Product/Service

(a) The Components of Products and Services

The starting point for examining this component of the marketing mix lies in determining the requirements of the target market. What needs do the target segments have and how can they best be satisfied? Armed with this knowledge marketers can then ensure that the products and services their organization provides are appropriately tailored to the needs of each of their customer groups.

The marketing literature presents a variety of frameworks for the analysis of the components of a product/service and these provide a useful guide for examining and defining the market entity that the organization is looking to provide. Kotler, for example, distinguishes between the core, tangible, and augmented aspects of a service whilst Levitt focuses on a service's generic, expected, and augmented components. In each case the analysis is based on the idea that any service can be seen as offering a basic set of features from the point of view of the consumer. Beyond this, services are augmented by a variety of additional features which associate it with a particular supplier, differentiate it from competing services, and make it in some way distinctive.

Kotler's perspective is presented in Fig. 4.8. Adopting this model in the nonprofit sector aids the marketer in clarifying the components of the service that they are offering to both recipients of goods and services and also to those that elect to fund such activities. The 'core' service from the perspective of the donor, for example, is arguably the knowledge that one has contributed to a worthwhile cause. In the case of health care the core product is undoubtedly the diagnosis and programme of treatment prescribed. At this point however the service is only being defined in terms of the generic available in the market. One would hope for example that two or more competent physicians would reach the same conclusion in respect of a patient's ailment. Similarly most charities are capable of providing a 'feelgood' factor to one degree or another. In short, it is unlikely that the core service will vary much from one organization to another. It may be thought of as being simply the minimum necessary to satisfy the needs of the customer.

The tangible component of the service is of particular importance since recent research indicates that consumers are more likely to purchase and re-purchase a service

Fig. 4.8:
**Components
of a Product**

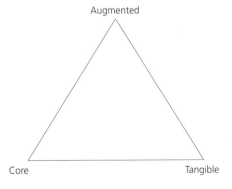

Augmented

Core   Tangible

if they can take away something tangible from the experience. Enhancing the tangible nature of the service can also serve to reduce risk from the perspective of the purchaser (see for example George and Berry, 1981, or Palmer, 1994) and act as a useful reminder of their experience which can assist in word-of-mouth advertising amongst friends and colleagues. In the fundraising context the tangible part of the service would therefore include the 'thank you' tokens which are typically received for making a donation in the street. Whilst rewarding a donor for his/her generosity such tokens also serve the ancillary purpose of providing a protection against further requests for donations.

In the healthcare context the concept of tangibility would more usefully relate to the quality of the environment provided for patients. Many hospitals and private clinics now give considerable thought to the physical design and layout of those areas where patients and their loved ones are likely to spend time. As obvious as this may sound there is now a considerable body of research to suggest that in the absence of other evaluative criteria, patients will tend to rely on these tangible cues to judge the quality of the service they receive.

The reader will therefore appreciate that giving consideration to the tangible components of their service may be one way in which a nonprofit could look to differentiate their service from that supplied by potential competitors. Given that the core product is widely available, however, it is unlikely that simply adjusting the tangible components of the service will in itself be enough to create and sustain an advantage over the competition. The augmented part of the service is the real key to this issue. Whilst the consumer is paying for a certain core experience and will doubtless be happy if he/she receives it, the augmented component goes in some way beyond what the consumer was expecting. It may be thought of as value added, which can be used to draw a distinction in the minds of consumers between the service provided by one organization and that provided by another. Returning to our earlier examples for a moment, there may be many ways in which both organizations could augment their service. Donors could receive personalized mailings, individual attention from staff, invitations to visit a particular project to see how their money has been used, a commemorative plaque, etc. In the healthcare context the service could be augmented by the quality of information provided to relatives, allowing greater time for a patient–physician dialogue, access to support groups, personal follow-ups by hospital staff when the patient has returned home, etc. Clearly, augmenting the service in any of the ways described would be costly, but the rewards in terms of enhanced customer satisfaction and hence loyalty to the organization could well be worth the initial investment.

Together these three components form the basis of the market offering. Each component should be considered both in isolation and as a part of the complete service offering. This latter point is of particular significance since all three aspects of the service have the capability to communicate a message to the customer and it is hence essential that each of the three dimensions reinforces the message communicated by the other two. Whilst a useful starting point in the analysis, however, a consideration of the mere components of a market entity will in itself not be enough. In the case of many nonprofits, the organization is offering much more than merely one or more service offerings to the market. Nonprofits can also offer considerable value to the customer through an association with their 'brand'.

The American Marketing Association defines a brand as:

a name, term, sign, symbol, or design, or a combination of them, intended to identify the goods or services of one seller, or group of sellers and to differentiate them from those of competitors.

A brand therefore has the capacity to convey considerable meaning to a target group and an association with this in a nonprofit context may well be more important to a target group than the actual product/service being offered. The NSPCC's Happy Kids brand, for example, is a considerable asset to the organization, as it is an instantly recognizable entity in its own right. It successfully conveys something of the values, attributes, culture, and personality of the charity. As a consequence, the NSPCC has been able to utilize the brand for additional revenue generation and has successfully 'shared' the brand recently with a number of corporate sponsors who, in return for cash support, have benefited themselves from the favourable imagery the brand has offered their products/services. Thus the creation and/or management of a nonprofit's brand image can be a critical issue for marketers to address.

(b) Service Life cycle

Returning to the issue of the product/service offering, however, one of the most fundamental concepts in marketing is the idea that a market entity will pass through several discrete stages from the moment it is first introduced until it is ultimately withdrawn from the market. An understanding of these stages can greatly aid a marketer as the appropriate tactics for the successful management of the service will often vary greatly between each stage of its life. Wilson *et al.* (1994, 274) summarize the implications of the life cycle concept thus:

(1) services have a finite life;
(2) during this life they pass through a series of different stages, each of which poses different challenges to the seller;
(3) virtually all elements of the organization's strategy/tactics need to change as the service moves from one stage to another;
(4) the profit potential of services varies considerably from one stage to another;
(5) the demands upon management and the appropriateness of managerial styles also vary from stage to stage.

This idea is illustrated in Fig. 4.9. During the introductory stage of the life cycle the service will take time to gain acceptance in the market and sales will hence be relatively low. At this stage the organization will be unlikely to have recouped its initial set-up and development costs and profitability remains negative. Over time, as the service begins to gain acceptability in the market, sales will experience a period of sustained growth and provision of the service should at this stage become profitable. With the passage of time, the level of sales will eventually begin to level off as the market becomes saturated, until ultimately the service becomes obsolete and sales begin to decline. At this stage the organization may wish to consider discontinuing the service, as with the lower volume of sales, the costs of provision may prove prohibitive.

The life cycle concept has been much criticized over the years but it can still offer marketers considerable utility in that it can help to define the form that the marketing mix might take at each stage. As an illustration of this point, consider the role of advertising in the marketing mix. At point (A) in Fig. 4.9 the role of advertising would

Fig. 4.9: **The Service Life cycle**

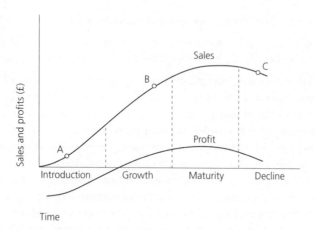

almost certainly be to inform the potential market that the service exists and the potential benefits that it might offer. Raising awareness would hence be a key objective at this stage. As the service moves to point (B) in the life cycle, however, the nature of the market has changed. If the new service has been particularly innovative it will be unlikely that competitors have stood idly around watching developments. Instead they will probably have entered the market with their own version of the service at this stage and the objectives of the advertising will thus need to change. A continual emphasis on raising awareness would be inappropriate since it would only serve to increase the overall level of demand in the market and thus benefit the advertiser and all the competition alike. Instead, a rather more useful objective might be to differentiate the service offered from those provided by the competition. The emphasis would change to identifying a clear positioning in the minds of target consumers. By the time that the service moves to point (C) in its life cycle, advertising support may be withdrawn altogether to reduce costs, or additional monies may be spent to 'prop up' ailing demand in the market.

Whilst I have focused here solely on how the model can assist the planning of advertising, it is clear that equal utility could be offered to any other ingredient of the marketing mix. In most cases, pricing, distribution, and even the characteristics of the service itself will be modified as the life cycle progresses. Indeed the model can also be used to help charities think about the nature of their provision. In such cases it is often helpful to move away from the concept of a service and to attempt to visualise the life cycle of a need. Bryce, for example, makes the point that many nonprofits are addressing fairly specific needs within society. These may remain very stable from one generation to the next or they may change fairly rapidly. The need to deal with the design of a vaccine for Polio has now been dispensed with, but the arrival of the Aids virus poses a new threat. Disasters and emergencies create a somewhat more transient need, hence the likely life cycle of a need can have important planning implications, particularly when you consider that some needs are perceived by donors as being more immediate and worthwhile than others.

As with their counterparts in the for-profit sector however, nonprofits normally have more than one service available at any one time and the life cycle concept has the significant drawback that it tends to focus management attention on each service individually without viewing the organization's portfolio as a coherent whole. Indeed a nonprofit organization may be viewed as a set of activities or projects to which new ones are intermittently added and from which older ones may be withdrawn. These activities and projects will make differential demands on, and contributions to, the organization as a whole. Hence some form of portfolio analysis might prove a useful tool in deciding how the service mix might be improved, given the resource constraints that are valid at any one time.

(c) Portfolio Analysis

MacDivitt and Asch (1987) suggest that nonprofits should conduct a regular analysis of the portfolio of services that they look to provide. The model the authors propose is depicted in Fig. 4.10. To utilize the model it is necessary to begin by examining in detail the components of the two axes, namely external attractiveness and internal appropriateness. If we consider first the question of external attractiveness, this relates to a particular organization's ability to attract resources. Not all an organization's services will be equally attractive to potential funders and, whilst most charities would not exclude the provision of a service simply because it was perceived by donors as unsavoury, few would argue that the ability to raise funds was not an issue. Whilst the specific factors will undoubtedly vary from one organization to another, the degree of support donors are willing to give a particular activity is likely to depend on:

(1) the level of general public concern;
(2) likely trends in public concern;
(3) numbers of people aided;
(4) immediacy of impact on beneficiary group.

Fig. 4.10: **A Nonprofit Portfolio Model**

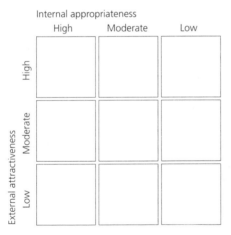

It is important to recognize that this list is not exhaustive and the beauty of this model is that organizations can utilize whatever factors they perceive as being relevant to their own environment and circumstances.

Turning now to the question of internal appropriateness, this relates to the extent to which the service 'fits' the profile of the organization providing it. In other words, is provision appropriate, given the skills, expertise, and resources available within the organization. Relevant factors here might include:

(1) the level of previous experience with the activity;

(2) the perceived importance of the activity;

(3) the extent to which the activity is compatible with the organization's mission;

(4) the extent to which the organization has unique expertise to offer.

Once again this list can be expected to vary from context to context, and an organization should look to identify those factors which are most pertinent to its particular circumstances.

Having now defined the components of both internal appropriateness and external attractiveness, the reader will appreciate that not all the factors identified could be seen as having equal importance to a given organization. For this reason it is important to weight the factors according to their relative importance. This is illustrated in Table 4.1. The reader will note that the weights for the components of each axis should all add up to 1. In the example given, the numbers of people the organization can aid is seen as being a more important determinant of external attractiveness than the question of how immediately the assistance can be provided. Donors to this organization do not appear to have any difficulty in taking a long-term view of the impact of their support.

Table 4.1
Calculation of
External
Attractiveness

Vertical Axis	**Weight**	**Rating**	**Value**
External Attractiveness			
Level of Public Concern	0.2	5	1.0
Likely Trends in Public Concern	0.3	3	0.9
Numbers of People Aided	0.4	8	3.2
Immediacy of Impact on Beneficiary Group	0.1	7	0.7
Total	1.0		5.8

The next step is to take each activity in which the organization is engaged and give it a score from 1 (very poor) to 10 (excellent) in terms of how it measures up against each of the components listed. To make this process clear a fictional example (let us call it Activity A) has been worked through in Tables 4.1 and 4.2. Considering first the question of how externally attractive this activity might be, it is clear that public support for it looks set to decline in the future and it is for this reason that a relatively low rating of 3 has been awarded against this factor. The activity does have the merit however of having an immediate and beneficial impact on a large number of people and somewhat higher ratings are therefore awarded for these factors. Multiplying the weights by the ratings assigned produces a value for each factor. Summing these values gives an overall score for (in this case) the external attractiveness axis of 5.8.

Table 4.2
Calculation of
Internal
Appropriateness

Horizontal Axis	**Weight**	**Rating**	**Value**
Internal Appropriateness			
Level of Previous Experience	0.1	5	0.5
Perceived Importance of the Activity	0.2	2	0.4
Compatibility with Mission	0.5	6	3.0
Possession of Unique Expertise	0.2	7	1.4
Total	1.0		5.3

Similarly, in the case of the internal attractiveness axis, each factor is assigned a weight. Each activity in which the organization is engaged is given a rating according to its performance in respect of each factor. Once again 1 = Very Poor 10 = Excellent. Returning to our analysis of activity (A), Table 4.2 makes it clear that the charity has only moderate experience to offer and does not view its provision as being particularly important (even though it would appear to come within the organization's mission). However, the charity does have fairly unique expertise which it could offer to recipients. The result is an aggregate score of 5.3 on the internal appropriateness axis.

Fig. 4.11: **Utilizing the Portfolio Model**

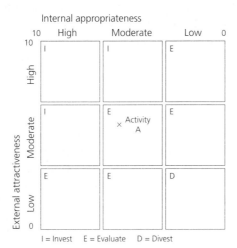

I = Invest   E = Evaluate   D = Divest

These figures can now be plotted on the matrix in Fig. 4.11, where the position of activity (A) has been clearly indicated. If it is conceptually useful, some organizations choose to take the analysis one stage further and draw a circle around the plotted position, the diameter of which is directly proportional to the percentage of overall expenditure that is allocated to each activity. In this way managers can see at a glance how funds are allocated between each of the services in the portfolio. Of course, for this to happen, all the services that a particular organization provides would be plotted in this way and then an analysis undertaken of the health (and balance) of the portfolio as a whole. Depending on the location of each activity within the matrix, the organization can then either look to invest further in its development, divest the activity and use the resources elsewhere, or subject the activity to further evaluation if the position still remains unclear.

Activities falling in the top left hand corner of the matrix are clearly those which are perceived as fulfilling an important need in society and the attraction of funding is unproblematic. The organization also appears well placed to provide these services as it has the necessary expertise and/or experience in house. The activities are also more likely to be seen as being compatible with the organization's mission and are hence excellent candidates for continuing investment.

Activities falling in the bottom right hand corner, however, are clearly activities which could be causing an unnecessary drain on resources. They are not seen as being important by society and are not compatible with the organization's mission. Indeed there may be other potential providers who could provide a much higher quality of service. Activities in this area of the matrix should then be scrutinized with a view to divestment. After all, if the activity is difficult to raise funds for, and the organization is not good at providing the service anyway, what could be the possible rationale for continuing? Of course, this is only a model and the activity would have to be scrutinized very carefully before a divestment decision was taken, but the analysis has at least yielded considerable insight into the potential for valuable resources to be conserved and perhaps put to other, more appropriate uses.

This leaves the question of activities falling within the central diagonal, such as the one in our fictional example. These should be carefully evaluated as they are only moderately appropriate for the organization to provide and they have only limited external attractiveness. It may be that there are very good strategic reasons for continuing to offer these services, or it may equally be that they could comfortably be left to another better qualified, organization to supply. Further analysis would clearly be warranted.

2 Price

The second of the ingredients of the marketing mix concerns issues connected with price. In a not-for-profit context, price can take on many guises and could take the form of entrance fees, tuition fees, service charges, donations, contributions, etc. In many organizations, particularly those with a good or service to sell, the pricing decisions may be almost identical to those taken in the for-profit sector. For other organizations, however, the 'price' charged to the beneficiaries may well be kept to an absolute minimum, and indeed may even be set at zero. Such practices definitely do not have parallels in the for-profit sector, unless they are an integral part of a co-ordinated attempt to gain market share at any cost—witness, for example, the recent newspaper price wars in the UK.

(a) Price versus Cost

To begin a discussion of price in the nonprofit context it is useful to start with an understanding of costs. All transactions with an organization—be it in relation to the sale of physical goods, or the handing over of a £20 donation—have costs associated with them. These costs essentially break down into one of three distinct types (Rados, 1981). In other words:

> Total Costs = OOP costs + Opportunity Costs + AO costs
> where
> OOP costs = Out Of Pocket Costs
> and
> AO = All Other Costs.

To aid us in a discussion of these three different types of cost, we will consider the example of a charity donor who intends to attend a gala event in support of her local hospice. She understands that at the end of this event she will be asked to give around £50 to support the cause, and this would tend to be what most organizations would consider to be the cost to her of her continuing support. They would be wrong! To get to the gala, our donor would incur some form of travelling expense, either on public transport or in her own domestic car. She may also have to pay a baby-sitter and use the telephone to put off any other appointments which she might have had planned. All these together may be viewed as OOP expenses.

Our donor will also incur opportunity costs by attending the gala. Put simply, opportunity costs are the value of an opportunity passed up or foregone. She may have had the opportunity of attending the theatre, going to a friend's birthday party, enjoying a candlelit dinner for two, or earning an extra few hours of overtime at the office. Whilst only in the latter example is she actually out of pocket, a value could equally well be placed on the enjoyment she would gain from any of the other three alternatives. Since she has decided to forgo these in favour of attending the charity gala, the value of the next most attractive alternative can be viewed as the opportunity cost of attending.

Of course, there may be other costs associated with the evening. She may arrive a little late to find that no car parking places remain and she may have to spend time walking from one nearby. If it's a wet evening, this may be more than just a slight inconvenience. When she actually gets to the gala, the seating may be uncomfortable, she may find the staff not very welcoming, and the best of the food could already have been eaten. What a night! This final category of costs we may call AO costs and, when added to the opportunity costs and out of pocket costs, we can derive the total cost of the evening to our valiant donor.

It is important to recognize that total costs can often amount to significantly more than the actual price paid, because it is the perception of total price that is the important factor. Whilst easily able to afford the £50 donation, the donor in this instance may well fail to attend similar events in the future as the sum of all the other costs could have persuaded her that the evening was too expensive. Charities, and indeed all nonprofits, need to be sensitive to these issues. There would be little point, for example, in setting the price for theatre tickets without considering variables such as the attractiveness of the performance (affecting the value of the opportunity cost), or the costs to the audience of physically getting to the venue. In the case of the latter, if there are theatres more conveniently located, audiences will not have to incur the same level of transportation cost and may take this into consideration when they decide which of their local theatres to attend. This is an important concept to grasp, since in manipulating price a nonprofit can often be more creative than merely tinkering with whatever charge it happens to make for the goods and services it provides. Staying with our theatre example, negotiation with third parties might result in free car parking, special late night transport (to get people home after the performance), or a discount at a local restaurant to enable the theatre to market the evening as a package and thereby impact on opportunity costs.

(b) Setting the Price

There are a variety of ways in which an organization can go about setting price, namely:

(1) *Cost Plus.* Identifying what it costs to provide the service and adding on a profit margin if appropriate.
(2) *What they can afford.* Setting the price to match the organization's expectations of what the recipient group can afford to pay.
(3) *Competitor matching.* Identifying what competitors are demanding for their products/services and setting your own price accordingly.
(4) *Pricing to achieve organizational objectives.* Price can also be used as a tool to affect the overall levels of demand for the service in the market. The higher the total cost (see above) to the market, the less demand for the service there is likely to be. Nonprofits can therefore use price to achieve the organization's objectives in terms of the penetration a given service provision will have.

(c) Price Discrimination

The methods of price setting outlined above all make the assumption that all the organization's customers will pay a set price. This is not necessarily the case. Often nonprofits will have quite different categories of customers with widely ranging abilities to pay. Arts organizations, for example, will undoubtedly want to cultivate their student audience as they will ultimately form 'the audience of tomorrow' but they recognize too that this segment of the market are more susceptible to price than say a professional couple in their fifties. The answer is to price discriminate between these two segments and to charge a different price to each segment of the market. Price discrimination is a widespread practice amongst nonprofits and there are a variety of bases on which such discrimination can be based:

(1) *Market Segment*. As in the example above, the organization charges different segments of customers different prices for the service provided. Hence museums might offer discount packages to students, OAPs, family groups, schools, etc.
(2) *Place*. Theatre tickets are usually sold according to the desirability of their location. Customers will therefore pay very different prices for the same performance depending on where they elect to sit.
(3) *Time*. Discrimination by time could take may forms. For example, performance prices could vary at different times of the day, entrance fees could vary by season to encourage off-peak demand, last minute discounts could be offered on unsold theatre tickets to fill the auditorium, etc.
(4) *Service Category*. Often an organization will elect to offer several grades of service, many of which could be perceived as exclusive—the first night of a show for example, or a celebrity opening. Although the additional costs associated with the creation of such an exclusive event will clearly need to be taken into consideration when pricing, organizations often charge well in excess of what it actually costs them to provide these 'add-ons'. Certain categories of customers are often prepared to pay for the prestige of being able to take advantage of this exclusivity.

3 Place

The 'place' element of the marketing mix is concerned with issues such as the degree of accessibility to a service required, how the service will be distributed to clients, the level of control required over any intermediaries that might be used, and the geographical coverage for the service that is desired. Therefore, whilst the place element of the marketing mix has a clear relevance for organizations of all kinds, be they profit-making or not, there are perhaps additional complexities to be encountered in the nonprofit sector. Each of these will now be considered in turn.

(a) Service Accessibility

Service accessibility refers to the degree to which the customers of a particular organization should have easy access to the service being provided. Because of the inseparable nature of services, there are often few choices for nonprofit organizations other than to site themselves as close as possible to the target market. The difficulty for some nonprofits, however, is that they have two (or more) such targets. They must site themselves appropriately for both resource providers and resource consumers and there are often trade-offs that must be made between the two.

In the case of resource providers, location is important for the following reasons:

(1) Many nonprofits rely on the services of volunteers and must clearly have regard for where such individuals might typically live. It is much easier to attract volunteers if they do not have far to travel from their home.

(2) Location can greatly facilitate fundraising. If a charity can be seen to have a local presence, it will be somewhat easier to raise funds from both individual and corporate donors (see, for example, Sargeant and Stephenson, 1997).

(3) Location also needs to be considered in respect of the accessibility that will be offered to donors to make a donation. Many charities thus adopt a fairly intensive pattern of distribution attempting to make their collection boxes available in as many different locations as possible.

In terms of resource consumers, location is important for the following reasons:

(1) Nonprofits need to consider how accessible their services will be to members of their target market. Where the service is aimed at persons with some form of disability, any service will clearly need to be provided as close to their home as possible. For many visually impaired persons, for example, the requirement to use public transport to access a day centre provision would deter many from attending.

(2) There is an intrinsic link between the physical locations selected and the coverage that might be gained of the target market. Organizations must thus consider the geographical spread of their recipient base and select those areas with the highest concentrations of need.

(b) Channel/Route to Market.

For many nonprofit organizations, obtaining an appropriate route to market can be problematic at best. For-profit organizations have the 'luxury' of a plethora of channels of distribution that could be appropriate. These might include wholesalers, retailers, agents, distributors, franchises, etc. Clearly a typical manufacturer will have to determine which particular channels are likely to suit its needs best and then seek to develop relationships with these to encourage intermediaries to stock and perhaps promote the product. The key difference in the for-profit sector, however, is that manufacturers generally have a series of 'carrots' which they can use to motivate intermediaries to stock—such as variable commission rates, bulk discounts, merchandising assistance, dealer competitions, and so on. For most nonprofit organizations these options do simply not exist. Many services for the elderly, for example, are distributed primarily through the good auspices of social service or housing departments. Social workers receive no commission for passing on contacts to nonprofit organizations and do so simply because of the regard that they have for their clients.

The additional complexity of managing nonprofit channels of distribution is well illustrated by the following case.

Case Study 4.1: **Non-Maintained Special Schools**

Within the current legislative framework there are a number of schools within England and Wales which provide a specialist education for children with a variety of disabilities. Local Education Authorities currently have a duty to provide the best possible education for children irrespective of their level of disability. This encourages local authorities to create provision within their area for children with more common disabilities, such as learning disabilities, for example. In the case of children with a disability that is less common it is possible that an LEA will be unable to find appropriate provision within one of its own schools. Under such circumstances the LEA may decide to send a child to receive their education in a non-maintained special school, perhaps located outside their area. These organizations are charitable in status and rely for their funding on the fees paid by LEAs.

Under the terms of the 1981 Education Act, LEAs are under an obligation to integrate as many children as possible into mainstream schools, a move which while clearly in most children's interest, is certainly one which saves the LEA the expense of financing a number of special education places. Moreover, under the Act LEAs have a duty to take into account the wishes of parents in respect of a child's education. Thus if a decision in respect of a particular child is borderline, the wishes of the parent should influence the LEA to make the choice that the parents desire. In cases where the LEA and parents fail to reach agreement an appeals procedure may be instigated.

These extremely complex arrangements leave many non-maintained special schools with something of a marketing dilemma. Such organizations often have no alternative but to rely on the goodwill of intermediaries to pass on details of the services that they can provide. Advisory teachers employed by LEAs are the key source of information for parents, as are social workers and medical specialists, none of whom receive any remuneration from the non-maintained sector. Indeed one could argue that the one key intermediary, the LEA, has a vested interest in persuading parents to send their child to a mainstream school as it could then avoid the substantially higher fees payable to the specialist sector. Whilst there is no evidence that this actually occurs in practice, the potential for a conflict of interest is clear. Fig. 4.12 illustrates the percentage of the school population that has been receiving a special education, year on year, since 1979.

To compound this dramatic drop in numbers it is almost impossible for special schools to gain access to parents of potential students directly. Mailing lists of individ-

Fig. 4.12:

Percentage of Pupil Population placed in Special Schools

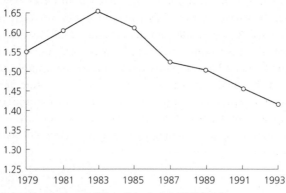

Source: Compiled from Audit Commission Analysis of DFE Statistics.

uals with a particular disability simply do not exist, and neither would it be desirable to create them. This makes it difficult for such organizations to communicate to parents the very real benefits that their schools can sometimes offer over a mainstream education.

Faced with these difficulties non-maintained special schools must therefore learn to deal with an extremely complex pattern of distribution, over the majority of which they can exert no control.

(c) Customer Perceptions of the Channel

In its simplest form this might involve decisions about the decor of the premises (relatively simple surroundings may suggest to potential donors for example, that donations are not being wasted on spurious decorations). More usually it may involve a consideration of the image that the channel might hold in the minds of potential customers. A decision may be taken for example, not to use the technique of outbound telemarketing in the mix at all, since in the minds of many donors it is still associated with the 'hard sell' techniques of the mid 1980s and is therefore seen as an unacceptable intrusion.

Those nonprofits that are involved in fundraising activities may instead make use of a range of distribution channels, including direct marketing, agents, volunteers, and, if collecting boxes are used, possibly a range of different retail outlets. Interestingly, Horne and Moss (1995) determined that collection box yields vary significantly between different categories of retail outlets and they should therefore be selected with care. The retail types associated with the highest yields are (in descending order) takeaways, cafés, bars, newsagents, supermarkets, and ironmongers. Soft furnishings, sports, and clothes shops were found to be the outlets with the smallest yields.

(d) The Emergence of Electronic Channels

The comparatively recent emergence of a range of new technologies has opened up a whole new range of opportunities for nonprofits not only to communicate with their market, but also to deliver their services to their clients. Many nonprofits now boast Internet sites where enquirers can link up 'live' and download information about the organization, its services, staff, facilities, etc. Whilst the majority of these electronic sources are as yet reactive, in the sense that they deal positively with enquiries, the opportunity exists in the future for nonprofits to take a more proactive stance and to actively market themselves through the medium of the Internet. Indeed a number of organizations are already making a very creative use of the medium.

A number of universities in the USA are now embracing the Internet as a means of delivering their programmes. Live conferences with staff and indeed whole educational programmes can now be delivered on-line. Such developments not only increase the number of fee-paying students that might be attracted to an institution, but because of the inherently convenient mode of delivery, many mature learners who would not have the time to return to a traditional classroom environment are being encouraged to return to their studies (see Exhibit 4.1).

The World Wildlife Fund (WWF) has also been benefiting from the creative use of new technology by the commercial organization 'e-cards'. The organization's website

Exhibit 4.1

THE FOLLOWING article appeared in the LA Times on Sunday, February 6, 1994

Advanced Degrees Earned

■ **Home study:** Lectures, class discussions, papers and exams are done via computer. Busy students set their own schedules.

By JANNY SCOTT
TIMES EDUCATION WRITER

D r. Iver Juster's idea of a good time is getting a master's in business administration. Business fascinates him, and the degree couldn't hurt in his career as a physician-executive.

But there was never time. Juster has a family and works 60 hours a week as a medical director for a Cerritos health maintenance organization. In spare moments, he is an insatiable consumer of workshops and home study courses.

Then last year, Juster heard about an MBA program offered entirely by computer. All the lectures, class discussions, papers and exams took place on-line. Students came and went on their own schedules, signing on before work or after midnight. If they kept up, participated in class, did their papers, and passed the tests, they could have an MBA within 2½ years. It was perfect for Juster.

Now the HMO director signs on the University of Phoenix's on-line MBA program—usually before dawn, armed with a cup of coffee, at his home computer in Long Beach. But he has also logged on from a dance camp in Sequoia National Park over the Labor Day weekend. And from time to time he lugs his laptop to a Thai restaurant near his

office and squeezes in some on-line time over lunch.

He spends 15 to 20 hours a week on schoolwork. By late next year, if all goes well, Iver Juster MD will become Iver Juster MD, MBA.

Juster is one of a growing number of busy adults—higher education's "new majority," whom schools have begun courting with a high-tech bag of tricks capable of offering courses, degree programs, even an entire college education, to people who need never set foot on a campus.

The New Jersey Institute of Technology in Newark, for example, offers a bachelor of arts in information systems via videotapes and a system of computer conferences it calls the virtual classroom. In the near future, Cal Poly San Luis Obisbo plans to offer videotaped lectures and demonstrations combined with self-paced tutorials, electronic mail and conferencing.

Several other California state universities plan to offer college courses to students in rural high schools, relying entirely on videotapes, printed materials sent by mail, and computer and telephone conferencing. Northern Virginia Community College offers foreign language teaching by voice mail, enabling teachers miles away to correct a student's accent.

"We have multiple senses, right?" said Sally M. Johnstone, director of the Western Cooperative for Educational Telecommunications in Boulder, Colo. "So we might have some video, some computing, some audio conferencing, some faxing back and forth of quick written material. There's now a whole basket of

technological tools that can be used."

About 1,000 students are enrolled in the University of Phoenix on-line degree programs. About 1,500 students have taken on-line courses through Connected Education Inc. in White Plains, N.Y., since 1985. And thousands of others have taken classes and earned degrees through other forms of long-distance learning.

Prices vary. A single three credit course through Connected Education costs $1,344. Juster's MBA will end up costing $16,000 to £17,000, he figures. In most cases, the telephone calls necessary to link up with an on-line service are local or toll-free.

Part of the appeal of distance learning is obvious: In most cases, no one has to be any place at a (particular) time. An engineer, say, who hopes to keep abreast in a rapidly evolving field and be positioned for a lucrative promotion can take long business trips and even be transferred cross-country without ever missing a class or exam.

Barry Galloway, 40, of Springfield, Va., designs training programs for companies. He works for a consulting group but wants to eventually go out on his own. So he recently got a master of science degree in instructional and performance technology from Boise State University via computer rather than attend the University of Maryland, 90 minutes away.

Margie Whiteleather, 28, of Ashland, Ohio, found other advantages. She has an undergraduate degree from Yale College. Now she is working her way, on-line, toward a

Off Campus and On-Line

master's degree in media studies from the New School for Social Research in New York City through Connected Education. Naturally shy and reticent in 'in-person' classes, Whiteleather says she participates more on-line.

Students with impaired hearing or for whom English is a second language also thrive on-line. In addition, prejudices are undermined. "I don't know if these people are white, black, yellow, fat, thin, tall, overweight or have a speech impediment," says Mark Eisley, who runs the Boise State program. "Things that might cause a bias or a hesitation to participate aren't there."

For college administrators, too, distance courses are suddenly hot. Faced with dwindling resources, rising demand and shifting student demographics, schools in states such as California are finding it makes sense to try educating people at home or at work rather than squandering scarce money on new buildings that future students will be too busy to reach.

"Many universities are starting to see that this could be a path out of the problems they are facing, in terms of more students than they could possibly educate in their current buildings or with their current faculty," said Lin Foa, deputy director of the Annenberg CPB Projects in Washington, which supports the development of courses and course materials to improve the quality of and access to education.

But how good is this form of education? Students seem pleased, although they say some teachers use the technology more effectively than others. Some students feared that

their courses would be too easy, but have been pleasantly surprised. It's easy to fall behind, they say; motivation and self-discipline help.

Unfortunately, few programs have been systematically evaluated. "Not enough effort has been put into assessment, frankly," said Jay Donahue, a senior program officer at the Fund for the Improvement of Post Secondary Education at the U.S. Department of Education.

The evaluations that have been performed are encouraging, researchers say. In New Jersey, researchers offered identical undergraduate and graduate courses on-line and in person over three years.

When they compared each group's exams and grades, the only significant differences had occurred in the computer science courses. The on-line students had done better.

Starr Rozanne Hiltz, a pioneer in the use of computer conferencing in education who conducted the experiment at New Jersey Institute of Technology in Newark and Uppsala College in East Orange, believes the main advantage of on-line classes is that they encourage collaborative, or group learning. Students work more closely with one another, and the role of the professor shifts.

"There is a change in the role of the lecturer, from someone who stood up there expounding truth with a capital T, to a kind of learning facilitator and coordinator who pulls together a set of resources, issues and questions," she said. It is much more possible to give up group assignments and require teamwork because the technology

negates the usual barriers of getting together.

Remarkably, some evaluations have found that students and faculty prefer distance education because there is more student-faculty interaction, particularly when computer conferencing is used. "My on-line students are more personal with me than my traditional students," Hiltz said.

Some professors, however, have other concerns. Sondra Farganis teaches social theory at the New School for Social Research and is about to teach her first on-line class. The prospect thrills and fascinates her. But she wonders if she will be able to convey her passion for her subject.

"I would worry about it turning into a kind of chatty talk show," said Robert Plitio, a writer and poet who is also embarking upon teaching his first on-line course at the New School. "In a classroom discussion, a teacher provides a lot of focusing and redirection."

There are legal, ethical and logistic questions as well. Should faculty be evaluated differently than in the past if they are teaching on-line? What about copyrights? And if the professor agrees to videotape a course for later use, can the university continue to use the videotape long after the teacher has left for another job?

But while those issues are sorted out, Juster moves methodically toward graduation. "A day doesn't go by that I don't apply something that I've learned," he said.

Exhibit 4.2

WWF E-Card

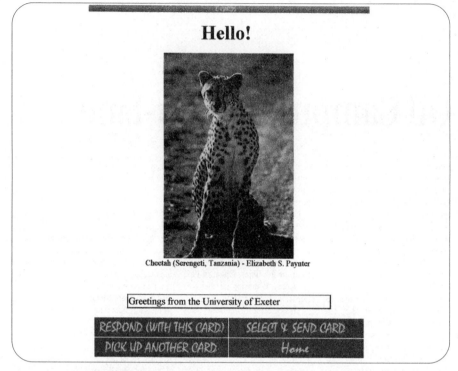

offers Internet 'surfers' the opportunity to send an e-card to their friends and loved ones. An e-card is essentially an electronic postcard and users can select the photograph that they would eventually like to appear on their recipient's screen. An example is given in Exhibit 4.2. It costs the user nothing to send the card, but by participating in the scheme they earn a donation for the WWF by being exposed to advertising on the e-card order page. The service provides an excellent example of the considerable benefits that can accrue from 'partnerships' between commercial and nonprofit organizations.

4 Promotion

The promotional element of the mix is responsible for the communication of the marketing offer to the target group. Promotion is:

> the process of presenting an integrated set of stimuli to a market with the intent of evoking a set of responses within that market set . . . and . . . setting up channels to receive, interpret and act upon messages from the market for the purposes of modifying present company messages and identifying new communication opportunities.   (Delozier, 1976)

It can be used for a variety of purposes within the marketing mix, typically:

(1) to inform potential customers of the existence and benefits of the service;
(2) to persuade potential customers that the benefits offered are genuine and will adequately meet their requirements;
(3) to remind members of the target group that the service exists and of the key benefits that it can offer;
(4) to differentiate the service in the minds of potential customers from the others currently on the market, i.e. to clearly define the positioning of the service.

However, before moving on to examine the elements of the communication mix and how they can be used to achieve the purposes outlined above, it will be instructive to begin by a short analysis of the communication process. Fig. 4.13 illustrates a simple model of communication. The source of the communication message is simply the organization that intends to communicate with its market. To enable it to do so, it must decide on the message that it wishes to convey—what does it want to convey about itself and what action (if any) would it like members of the target group to take on receipt of the message. In a social marketing content, this might involve the organization in trying to get across the dangers of unprotected sex in exposing people to the risk of Aids. The message might be a simple one—that 'unprotected sex puts you at risk of Aids'. However, the reader will appreciate that simply transmitting this message to the target market would be unlikely to be successful. To begin with, people react in different ways to fear appeals such as this and many might screen out the message as a result. Others might not perceive the message as being relevant to them because they do not perceive their lifestyle as putting them at risk. It is normal therefore for communications messages to be encoded.

Fig. 4.13: **A Simple Model of Communication**

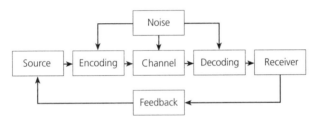

Encoding involves the source in deciding what the communications will actually contain to get across their message to consumers. In essence this is the creative treatment that is applied to the message to ensure that when it arrives at the receiver he/she decodes it as being of relevance to them and acts on it. This may be done, for example, by using perfectly ordinary-looking people in the commercials/advertising, conveying the selfishness of putting those you love at risk, explaining that aids can affect all sections of society, etc. Of course, there is no guarantee that when the message is received it will be decoded in the manner in which the source had originally intended. There are a variety of factors which can interfere with a communications message and these are typically referred to as noise.

Noise acts to distort the message or to prevent its reception by the receiver. It can thus take many forms including:

(1) a lack of attention on the part of the receiver;
(2) heavy promotional spending by other competing organizations;
(3) selection of inappropriate media;
(4) poor creative treatment, resulting in ambiguous messages;
(5) poor perception of source—if it is not regarded as credible the message may be ignored;
(6) environmental distractions—the message may be received under conditions that make it impossible for the recipient to concentrate.

It is thus important for an organization to try to minimize the effects of noise by selecting the most appropriate communication channels available to reach their target market. They can also help reduce noise by giving adequate thought to the encoding process and making sure that the promotional budget allows the organization to gain an appropriate 'share of the voice'. Clearly this is not an easy process to manage and it is hence essential to ensure that there are mechanisms in place to gather adequate feedback from the target market. If messages are either not being received, or are being decoded and 'wrongly' interpreted, it will be essential for the source organization to take corrective action immediately. Indeed it would be usual to test all forms of marketing communications prior to exposing them to the market, although even this is no guarantee of success. There is hence a need for the monitoring of marketing communications to be ongoing.

It is clear from the model in Fig. 4.13 that the promotional element of the marketing mix involves the establishment of a dialogue with customers, the quality of which can vary considerably depending on the nature of the communication channel selected and the degree to which noise has the capacity to interfere with message reception. Of course this model is very general and does not address issues which relate to the use of specific promotional tools. These are essentially advertising, sales promotion, public relations, and direct marketing—collectively referred to as the communications mix. We will now give a brief consideration to each of these elements in turn.

(a) Advertising

Kotler (1994, 627) defines advertising as 'any paid form of non-personal presentation and promotion of ideas, goods or services by an identified sponsor'. Advertising can be placed in a variety of media, including television, radio, cinema, newspapers, magazines/trade press, and outdoor (poster and transport advertising). With an ever increasing number of promotional media becoming available it is becoming ever more difficult to identify those media which offer the most appropriate use of promotional resources. Essentially one is looking to find the media which can reach the largest number of members of the target market at the lowest price. Thus the measure of 'CPT' (Cost Per Thousand) is used by many organizations to make comparisons between the use of various media. CPT is calculated very much as you would expect. If the cost of a full-page advertisement in a national newspaper circulated to 3 million readers is £9,000, the cost per thousand is £3. This figure can then be used to compare between the various media options available. It is however a very simple measure and it is necessary to be very clear about the profile of the media audience. If the profile does not match your requirements exactly (and it rarely does), you may be underestimating the CPT figure since you could be communicating with a large number of people who are not in your target market.

Media can also be selected on the basis of how many competitors use the medium, since if a large number of competitors are present the returns accruing to each advertiser are likely to be less than they would be in a publication where it is possible to enjoy a wider 'share of the voice'. It may also be important for many nonprofits to consider the environment of the medium. Does the medium offer an environment that is appropriate for the message being conveyed? There would be little point for example in placing an advert for a modern art exhibition in a publication whose editorial was generally critical of such art forms. Similarly the term 'environment' can be applied to the environment in which the message is received. Some media, such as specialist trade journals, demand a lot of concentration from readers, making it possible to provide much more detailed information about the product/service in advertisements. Television advertising, on the other hand, offers little opportunity in this regard since it commands little attention. Indeed many people leave the room, perhaps to make a coffee, when the commercial break begins.

(b) Sales Promotion

The term sales promotion in the nonprofit sector refers to:

> any immediate stimulation to buy (or to give a donation) that might be provided at or near the point of sale.

Hence the purpose of sales promotion is to prompt the customer to engage in a transaction with the nonprofit. It is thus more immediate in its effects and therefore favoured in times of budgetary constraint since an immediate return on the investment can be demonstrated. The same, regrettably, cannot be said of advertising, whose effects are considerably less tangible and certainly longer term. Sales promotion activity includes the provision of free gifts, discounts, premiums, leaflets, contests, display material, or demonstrations. The key to the selection of successful sales promotion activities undoubtedly lies in selecting something which reflects the needs and wants of the customer group and offers them something which they will find intrinsically to be of value. This may be as simple as an introductory discount on a service to tempt customers into sampling, or it may be something altogether more elaborate. In the fundraising context, for example, the simple poppy which indicates a donation to the British Legion has a very powerful and emotive appeal. It offers a potential donor the opportunity to associate with a nation's grief and thanksgiving, and indeed this promotion is so powerful that most people of prominence ensure that they wear one at least a week before Remembrance Sunday. The donor in this case is receiving a very real, if intangible, benefit. Other organizations allow donors to 'sample' their product and as a result guide dogs and even air ambulances can each have their part to play in a promotion. (The Cornish Air Ambulance Service recently charged donors for an opportunity to look inside the ambulance.) If the donor is able to share in a unique experience and is made to feel involved in the charity, fundraising will be greatly enhanced. It should also be noted that sales promotions can have a more mundane role to fulfil in that they allow volunteers to have something to sell and ensure (in the case of flags, pins, and stickers) that the donor is protected from further requests to give.

(c) Public Relations

Public relations (PR) is often confused with publicity, crisis management, lobbying, etc. In fact PR can embrace all these elements, but it should in itself be regarded as having a somewhat wider function within an organization. One of the most frequently used definitions of PR is as follows:

> Public relations is the management function that evaluates the attitudes of important publics, identifies the policies and procedures of an individual or an organisation with the public interest, and executes a program of action to earn understanding and acceptance by these publics.   (Public Relations News, 27 Oct 1947)

Hence it is concerned with the development of each of the organization's publics and might typically involve an organization in proceeding through the stages outlined in

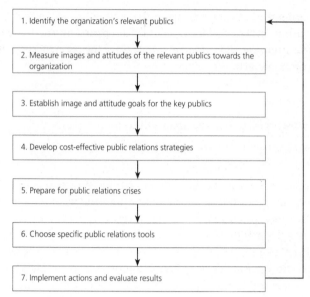

1. Identify the organization's relevant publics

2. Measure images and attitudes of the relevant publics towards the organization

3. Establish image and attitude goals for the key publics

4. Develop cost-effective public relations strategies

5. Prepare for public relations crises

6. Choose specific public relations tools

7. Implement actions and evaluate results

Source: Kotler and Fox, *Strategic Marketing for Educational Institutions* © 1985. Adapted by permission of Prentice Hall, Inc, Upper Saddle River, NJ.

Fig. 4.14. The process therefore begins with an analysis of the current perceptions of each of an organization's publics. Those perceptions are then assessed to see how desirable they might be from the organization's perspective and, where weaknesses/ambiguities are identified, a programme of PR can be developed to address them. The process Kotler and Fox advocate also makes it clear that it is important for an organization to plan for potential crises, however unlikely it may be that these might occur. If an organization has plans to deal with all potential contingencies, then should the unthinkable happen it will be well placed to implement a cogent response.

There are a variety of public relations tools that an organization could utilize to develop the desired perceptions amongst its target publics. These include:

(1) *Production of written material.* This might include leaflets, flyers, magazines, annual reports, and volunteer newsletters.

(2) *Organizational identity media.* Most nonprofits today have some form of corporate identity which features prominently in the organization's stationery, brochures, signs, and business cards. These are what might be referred to as organizational identity media and it is essential that through the careful use of design, logos, etc. all these media conform to a standard format and convey a consistent message to the publics targeted.

(3) *Publicity.* The PR department can often identify newsworthy activities within the organization and seek to promote these amongst the various media. The problem with such 'free advertising' is that there is no guarantee the media will elect to cover it; unlike advertising which must be sent to the media and paid for, publicity must be sent to the media and prayed for!

(4) *Provision of expert speakers.* Many nonprofits have unique expertise or act as the mouthpiece for a particular section of society. In such circumstances it is important that all the key media understand that this expertise exists, so that should an occasion arise where an expert comment is called for, they know exactly who to approach. For this reason many universities now produce a publication called

'Who Can Speak on What', or something similar, which can be distributed to regional and national media, in the hope they will use it to source subject specialists for expert comment.

(5) *Telephone helplines.* Many nonprofits who provide a service to members of the public are already providing very successful telephone helplines which provide help and guidance to those in need. Many of the medical charities, for example, provide a 24-hour helpline which sufferers and/or their relatives can ring for reassurance and guidance. Given that it now costs very little to provide a toll-free or Freephone number many nonprofits are now prepared to cover the costs of this activity themselves as part of a co-ordinated PR strategy.

Nonprofits generally have very complex audiences to whom they must communicate their message. This audience may be made up of current and potential sponsors, the media, the business and local community, their own volunteers and the recipients on whose behalf they are working. Given this complexity it is not surprising that public relations takes such a prominent place in the marketing mixes of many nonprofit organizations. Unfortunately, public relations has a much less obvious price tag than media advertising, and its results are perhaps even more difficult to assess. It remains, however, an important tool for many organizations, primarily because of the impact it can have on the market. Messages carried through third parties are perceived by the public as having greater credibility than messages conveyed in advertising, where the organization perhaps has a tendency to portray itself in an overly positive light.

(d) Direct Marketing

Currently a major growth area in marketing, direct marketing is increasing in importance for a great many organizations. Traditionally charities have been perceived as being particularly strong in this field, with their creative use of the marketing database putting them very much at the forefront of developments. Direct marketing can of course take many forms, the most common of which are briefly described below:

1. *Direct Mail.* With the increasing sophistication of database technology it is now possible to refine the contact strategies that nonprofits have with a wide range of customers. A theatre, for example, can look back over the purchase histories of its clients and write to those who it knows from past experience will be interested in certain categories of performance. Similarly charities can use their knowledge of the database to treat high value donors somewhat differently from low value donors and target direct mail shots at the time of year that specific segments of donors find most acceptable. Indeed nonprofits that make wise use of their database are moving away from a broadbrush approach to market segmentation and are beginning to develop almost one to one dialogues with their customers.

Most modern databases also allow a nonprofit to profile its customer base. Whilst the data so gained can be used to help develop existing customers, it can also be used to good effect to target other potential service users in society who match the profile of existing customers. With a proliferation of consumer and industrial lists now available, nonprofits can target prospective customers in a way that could only be dreamed of a mere twenty years ago. This is a subject that will be returned to in considerably more depth in Chapter 5.

2. *Telemarketing*. Whilst it would as yet be comparatively rare for a nonprofit to attempt telemarketing activity in house, unless it was on a particularly small scale, there are now a number of specialist agencies who offer telemarketing expertise to the nonprofit sector. It can be used for either inbound of outbound activity. Inbound activity remains the most common, whereby a Freephone or toll-free number is provided for clients and/or donors to contact the organization free of charge. The number is frequently quoted in all other forms of marketing communication and the telemarketing service provided free of charge to make the exchange process more accessible to clients. Outbound telemarketing is still rather less common, although growing in popularity. At a recent general election, for example, the Conservative Party made every effort to contact all the voters of a marginal seat in Cornwall by telephone to ensure that they were able to get their message across to potential waverers. Similarly many charities now call prospective donors on spec to solicit donations.

3. *Door-to-door*. Door-to-door canvassing and/or selling remains a popular way of fundraising for many, particularly 'local' charities. It can also be a very effective means of raising awareness of the activities of an organization, or canvassing to reach prospective volunteers.

4. *Personal selling*. Whilst this is perhaps less common in the nonprofit sector, there may be a number of organizations who find it desirable to maintain a direct salesforce which can negotiate on a one-to-one basis with prospective clients and/or funders. This is likely to be more appropriate where an organization has a small number of high value clients or where the clients are narrowly concentrated in a small geographical area. In such circumstances the increased overhead of employing a sales team may be justified in terms of the quality of the contact/service that will be provided.

5 People

To an organization providing a service to clients, the people element of the marketing mix is arguably the most important. After all, it may reasonably be argued that the people *are* the organization, whether they be paid employees or unpaid volunteers. Interestingly the latter category of staff are more prevalent than many people believe. Lynn and Smith (1992), for example, identified that almost half of the adults in the UK will engage in some form of voluntary activity over the course of a typical year. Indeed Bruce and Raymer (1992) identify that on average, for every paid employee retained, the larger charities utilize the services of 8.5 volunteers

Ensuring that all staff, whatever their status, deliver a service of the highest quality is a key issue for all nonprofits. The inseparability of services makes it impossible to distinguish between service production and service delivery and it is the people of the organization who are therefore responsible for both. In this section of the marketing plan the nonprofit must therefore give consideration to the people skills that it will need to provide its service and, indeed, to deliver every component of the marketing plan. This can then be matched against the profile of the existing human resources and appropriate gaps identified. The organization can then ensure that those 'gaps' are represented in the recruitment programme and that the appropriate person specifications are in place. On some occasions it may be possible to plug these gaps by the recruitment of full-time or part-time staff. On others it may be more appropriate to look to the recruitment of suitably qualified volunteers. Hind (1995) suggests that before recruiting paid staff, a process which results in a considerable drain on organizational resources, the organization should ensure that their recruitment is absolutely necessary. To determine this he suggests that paid staff are only necessary under the following circumstances:

(1) specialist expertise is required on an ongoing basis;
(2) continuous attention is needed to tasks which must be performed in accordance with the organization's timetable and in compliance with its formal procedures and standards;
(3) roles (exist) requiring the management of other staff or large groups of volunteers.

Of course, if the attraction of volunteers is the preferred option it is useful to understand something of an individual's typical motivations for volunteering. If the tasks for which volunteers are sought are not capable of satisfying volunteer requirements an organisation may be left with little choice but to opt for the paid alternative. Fenton *et al.* (1993) identified that the following three categories of volunteer motivation predominate.

(1) *Demonstrative Motivation.* Individuals who volunteer for this reason are essentially seeking some form of ego reward. They donate their time because they believe that some form of social recognition will follow.
(2) *Social Motivation.* The researchers found that this was the most common form of motivation and involves individuals volunteering because they see it as an active form of giving to support charity. It is seen as an opportunity to socialize with other volunteers and to feel collectively that they are doing good.
(3) *Instrumental Motivation.* Less commonly expressed than the other two, individuals who volunteer for this reason are doing so simply because they feel the need to help others. They feel they have a duty to help others less fortunate than themselves.

It is, of course, usually much easier to develop and retain existing staff/volunteers than it is to attract new ones. The second focus of this section of the plan is hence to identify what steps need to be taken to retain existing personnel. By far the easiest way of achieving this is probably to survey those who decide to leave and, having discovered the reasons for dissatisfaction, implement any changes that may be necessary to ensure that problems are corrected. One can also ensure that an ongoing dialogue is maintained with existing staff so that they do not feel compelled to leave in the first place! In the case of volunteers, it would also be advisable to ensure that the organization responds to the various categories of motivation identified above and understands in some detail what it is that the volunteers actually want to get out of their relationship with the organization. Retention strategies can then be developed taking account of these needs.

6 Process

When marketers talk of process, they are talking about the process that a particular client group must go through to purchase and enjoy the service being provided. Clearly for a service organization every aspect of the encounter that a customer has with staff will be important. Each stage of the service will be evaluated by customers and many will have the capability of having a substantial impact on the overall level of satisfaction experienced. The question is, however, which elements of the process are deemed by the customer to be most important. To answer this it is often useful to draw a flow chart of the various components of the service that the customer experiences. An example is shown in Fig. 4.15. Although this is a gross simplification of the process that one might go through in purchasing and enjoying an evening at the theatre, it does at least serve to illustrate that the process consists of a number of specific encounters with the organization. Each of these may of course be broken down into a number of sub-encounters. Take for example the telephone reservation process; there are a number of components to this, including the length of time you would have to wait to have your call answered, the efficiency and friendliness of the operator, and the accuracy with which he/she performs his/her role. For the moment however we will stick with the general process depicted in Fig. 4.15. The reader will appreciate that not every aspect of the service will be equally important. The provision of a cloakroom, clean toilets, and the existence of a bar may be relatively unimportant for the segment of customers addressed. If research is conducted which identifies those aspects of the service on which the customer places most importance, the organization can invest in those areas, ensure that they are of the highest quality, and hence enhance overall customer satisfaction. Conversely, in those areas that are considered unimportant, the organization can look to minimize cost and perhaps even remove that aspect of the service altogether, utilizing the resources saved in other areas that are perceived as being important. The idea of engineering customer value in this way was first suggested by Porter (1985) who referred to the concept discussed above as the Value Chain. In his view it represents an essential tool for organizations to use in appraising their service process with a view to enhancement.

Fig. 4.15:
Flow chart of a
Visit to the
Theatre

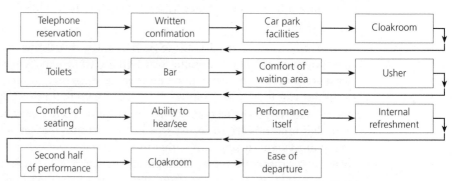

7 Physical Evidence

The final ingredient of the service marketing mix is physical evidence. Since the service product is largely intangible it is important for the organization to focus on those tangible cues that do exist and to ensure that they convey appropriate messages to the consumer about the quality of the service he/she is purchasing. As has already been identified (section 1 above), in the absence of a physical product consumers will use tangible cues to make their judgements in respect of service quality. In a typical organization these cues may include:

(1) *Premises*. Thought will obviously be given in the healthcare context, [...] to the physical design of waiting areas. They should generally be cle[...] able and informative, in the sense that reading materials may be left [...] informing them of various aspects of the services that are available.

(2) *Facilities*. The appearance of the facilities on offer is also important. In selecting a school, for example, parents are unlikely to rely totally on the reputation that a school has in a given area. They are also likely to inspect for themselves the facilities that it has to offer and may ask to see the sports, library, and IT provisions.

(3) *Dress*. The presentation of the staff can help reinforce the corporate image that the organization is looking to project. Smart, attractively presented staff can imply quality, in the absence of other cues, and may reassure potential customers of the professionalism offered by a particular organization.

(4) *Reports*. The written communications of the organization may also be regarded as tangible cues. The annual report and the 'sales' brochure will both be used to evaluate the service. In selecting a course of study at a University, for example, unless a visit to the site is planned, prospective students may have little more to build their perception of quality on than the presentation of the prospectus and its contents.

Summary of the Tactical Marketing Mix

We have now examined each of the ingredients of a typical service marketing mix. In developing a marketing plan an organization will need to give careful consideration to each of these seven elements, whilst at the same being careful not to fall into the trap of viewing each ingredient in isolation. The mix should be viewed as a collective whole and opportunities for synergy will only be exploited if it is regarded as such. Each ingredient of the mix should consistently reinforce the 'message' being conveyed by the others. To ensure that the plan does represent a coherent whole, the author should ensure that the organization's approach to each of the seven Ps is presented in the plan in a clear and easy-to-read format. It should then become obvious whether flaws or ambiguities are present, and corrective action can be taken.

Budget

Having detailed the steps that will be necessary to achieve the marketing objectives, the writer of the plan should then be in a position to cost the various proposals and to derive an overall marketing budget for the planning period. Of course, in reality life is just not that neat. Cost will undoubtedly have been in the minds of marketing planners even before they commenced the marketing audit. At the very least the development of a suitable budget is likely in practice to have been an iterative process, with proposals being re-evaluated in the light of budgetary constraints.

There are a variety of ways of determining the marketing budget. The ideal would clearly be to specify the strategy and tactics that are felt necessary to achieve the marketing objectives, and then to cost these to arrive at an overall budget. This is usually referred to as the 'task method' of setting a marketing budget. Of course, in reality this method is seldom employed since financial pressures from senior management, the budgeting/accounting practices of the organization, and uncertainty about resource attraction all hamper the derivation of an appropriate budget. In practice, therefore, budgets tend to be set by the following methods:

(1) *Percentage of last year's sales/donations.* There is a danger with this method, however, in that if the organization has been suffering from poor performance of late, reducing the marketing budget in line with sales/donations could actually serve to worsen the situation. Clearly, when sales or donations fall there is a strong case for enhancing not reducing the marketing budget.

(2) *Percentage of budgeted year's sales/donations.*

(3) *Competitor matching.* Estimating the amounts spent on marketing by the competition and matching their resource allocation.

(4) *What can be afforded.* Perhaps the least rational of all the methods of budget calculation, this method involves the senior management of the organization deciding what they believe they can afford to allocate to the marketing function in a particular year. Little or no reference is made to the marketing objectives, nor to the activities of competitors.

Irrespective of the method actually used, in practice it would be usual to specify how the eventual budget has been allocated and to include such a specification in the marketing plan itself. It would also be normal for an allowance to be made for contingencies in the event that monitoring by the organization suggests that the objectives will not be met. Sufficient resources should then exist for some form of corrective action to be taken.

Scheduling

The reader will appreciate that a large number of tactics will have been specified in the main body of the plan. To ensure that these tactics are executed in a co-ordinated fashion over the duration of the plan, it is usual to present a schedule which clearly specifies when each activity will take place. This would often take the form of a Gantt chart (an example, for a fundraising campaign, is given in Fig. 4.16). If the responsibilities for various marketing activities are split between different departments/sections of the organization, the schedule will act as an important co-ordination mechanism. Indeed if responsibilities are split in this way it would be usual to add an additional section to the plan specifying the individual postholder who will have responsibility for the implementation of each component of the plan.

Fig. 4.16: **Schedule of a Fundraising Campaign**

Activity	Jan	Feb	March	April	May	June	July	Aug	Sept	Oct	Nov	Dec
Direct Mail		x	x							x	x	
Press Advertising	x			x			x			x		x
Display Advertising (Posters)											x	x
Telemarketing		x				x			x		x	x

Monitoring and Control

As soon as the plan has been implemented, marketing management will then take responsibility for monitoring the progress of the organization towards the goal specified. Managers will also need to concern themselves with the costs that have been incurred at each stage of implementation and monitor these against the budget. Thus control mechanisms need to be put into place to monitor:

(1) the actual sales/donations achieved, against the budget;
(2) the actual costs incurred against those budgeted;
(3) the performance of individual services against budget;
(4) the overall strategic direction that the organisation is taking—i.e. will the overall corporate objectives be achieved in a manner commensurate with the organization's mission.

If variances are detected in any of these areas, corrective action can then be initiated, if necessary by utilizing the resources allocated for contingency specified above.

Discussion Questions

1. Explain the relationship between corporate objectives and marketing objectives.
2. Distinguish, with examples, between marketing strategies and tactics.
3. What would you describe as the key components of the fundraising product?
4. What benefits would a portfolio analysis typically offer a nonprofit organisation? What disadvantages/drawbacks can you see in using the approach advocated?
5. With reference to your own organization, or one with which you are familiar, identify the key costs that will be experienced by both your donors and the recipients of your goods or services. What are the implications of these costs for your pricing decisions?
6. What channels of distribution might typically be used by:
   (1) A modern art museum
   (2) A Third World charity looking to solicit funds
   (3) A library service for elderly persons with a visual impairment?
7. In what ways might the communications mix utilized by a University Development Office (i.e. the fundraising office within the university) differ from that adopted by a charity concerned with raising funds for cancer research?
8. 'Promotion is not the only element of the marketing mix that can communicate with customers. All seven elements of the service mix have the capacity to communicate with the customer.' Discuss.

References

Abell, D. F. (1980) *Defining The Business: The Starting Point of Strategic Planning*, Englewood Cliffs, Prentice Hall.

Ansoff, I. (1968) *Corporate Strategy*, London, Penguin Books.

Bruce, I. and Raymer, A. (1992) *Managing and Staffing Britain's Largest Charities*, VOLPROF, Centre for Voluntary Sector and Not-for-Profit Management, City University Business School, London.

Bryce, H. (1992) *Financial and Strategic Management for Non-Profit Organisations*, Englewood Cliffs, Prentice Hall.

Delozier, M. (1976) *The Marketing Communication Process*, McGraw Hill.

Drucker, P. F. (1955) *The Practice of Management*, London, Heinemann.

Drucker, P. F. (1990) *Managing the Non-Profit Organisation*, Oxford, Butterworth Heinemann.

Fenton, N., Golding, P. and Radley, A. (1993) 'Thinking about Charity: Report of a Pilot Study into Public Attitudes to Charities and Volunteering', in *Researching the Voluntary Sector*, West Malling, Charities Aid Foundation.

George, W. R. and Berry, L. L. (1981) 'Guidelines for the Advertising of Services', *Business Horizons*, Vol. 24, July–August.

Hind, A. (1995) *The Governance and Management of Charities*, Barnet, Voluntary Sector Press.

Horne, S. and Moss, M. (1995) 'The Management of Collecting Boxes: Analysis of Performance and Site Location', *Journal of Nonprofit and Public Sector Marketing*, Vol. 3, No. 2, 47–62.

Kotler, P. (1994) *Marketing Management: Analysis, Planning, Implementation and Control*, 8th edn, Englewood Cliffs, Prentice Hall.

Kotler, P. and Andreasen, A. (1991) *Strategic Marketing for Nonprofit Organisations*, Englewood Cliffs, Prentice Hall.

Kotler, P. and Fox, K. (1985) *Strategic Marketing for Educational Institutions*, Englewood Cliffs, Prentice Hall.

Lynn, P. and Smith, D. (1992) *The 1991 National Survey of Voluntary Activity in the UK*, Berkhamsted, Volunteer Centre UK.

MacDivitt, H. and Asch, D. (1989) *Block 1: Formulating Policy*, B881 Strategic Management, Milton Keynes, Open University Press.

McDonald, M. H. B. (1984) *Marketing Plans: How to Prepare Them, How to Use Them*, London, Heinemann.

Palmer, A. (1994) *Principles of Service Marketing*, Maidenhead, McGraw Hill.

Porter, M. E. (1985) *Competitive Advantage: Creating and Sustaining Superior Performance*, New York, Free Press.

Rados, D. L. (1981) *Marketing for Non-Profit Organisations*, Dover, Massachusetts, Auburn House.

Sargeant, A. and Stephenson, H. (1997) 'Corporate Giving—Targeting the Likely Donor', *Journal of Nonprofit and Voluntary Sector Marketing*, Vol. 2, No. 1, 64–79.

Wilson, R. M. S, Gilligan, C. and Pearson D. J. (1992) *Strategic Marketing Management*, Oxford, Butterworth Heinemann.

Specific Applications

HAVING NOW EXAMINED the operationalization of marketing at both philosophical (market orientation) and functional levels (marketing planning) it is now appropriate to move on to consider its specific application to a variety of nonprofit sub-sectors and contexts. The reader will appreciate from Chapter 1 that the term 'nonprofit' can legitimately be applied to an incredibly diverse population of organizations. For this reason it is intended to concentrate here only on what might be regarded as the most significant classifications of nonprofit activity either in terms of the sheer numbers of organizations that are embraced in a particular subset, or in terms of the impact that they might have on society. Marketing's application to fundraising, arts organizations, education institutions, healthcare organizations, and the development of social ideas, will therefore be discussed in turn.

The reader will appreciate that in the course of one brief chapter it will not be possible to do justice to every aspect of marketing within a particular sub-sector, but a number of the key issues will be addressed. Moreover the text has been structured to ensure that each chapter deals with different elements of marketing, or the marketing planning process. Thus whilst each chapter can be read in isolation, the reader is encouraged to treat this part of the text as a coherent whole, since a number of the issues raised in the context of one category of nonprofit activity are of just as much relevance for the sector as a whole.

Specific Applications

5

Fundraising

Objectives

By the end of this chapter you should be able to:

(1) describe the changes currently taking place in the fundraising environment and appreciate the implications thereof for fundraising strategy;

(2) distinguish between donor development and donor recruitment and plan fundraising activity for both;

(3) develop, plan, and implement corporate fundraising activity;

(4) develop, plan, and implement trust fundraising activity.

Introduction

Charities and their associated fundraising activity have a long history in the United Kingdom. Their origins can be traced to the seventeenth century and to the Charitable Uses Act of 1601 which introduced the term charity into the legal and fiscal framework of the UK for the first time. Since then charities have been responsible for providing a range of societal supports. Interestingly the preamble to the 1601 Act is still the starting point in determining charitable status and therefore what causes may be considered charitable in nature.

> The relief of aged, impotent and poor people; the maintenance of sick and maimed soldiers and mariners, schools of learning, free schools and scholars in universities; the repair of bridges, havens, causeways, churches, seabanks and highways; the education and preferment of orphans; the relief, stock or maintenance of houses of correction; marriages of poor maids; the supportation, aid and help of young tradesmen, handicraftsmen and persons decayed; the relief or redemption of prisoners, or captives and the aid or ease of any poor inhabitants concerning payment of fifteens, setting out of soldiers and other taxes. (Preamble to the Charitable Uses Act 1601)

Of course over the years the law has been amended and clarified, but the original Act still remains a valid starting point in determining whether an activity can be deemed charitable or not.

If the definition of 'charity' has remained static over the past 400 years, the fundraising environment most definitely has not! Early fundraising activity was largely limited to working with individuals, and hence was characterized by the building of networks of contacts and the cultivation of specific and carefully guarded relationships. Of course much major gift fundraising is still conducted in this way, but even in this sphere the pattern of giving has become phenomenally more complex. To begin with, even a mere century ago, the number of individuals who would have been worth cultivating in this way would have been relatively small. Wealth was historically concentrated in the hands of a few wealthy industrialists or landowners. Indeed much early charitable activity was undertaken at the whims of such individuals who were free to indulge their own favourite causes as time and money permitted.

In the modern era, many new sources of charitable income have emerged. These are listed in Fig. 5.1. Of course not all of these sources of income come within the scope of a typical fundraisers remit. The majority of fundraising departments have three key target groups only and, in the case of larger charities, may be structured to reflect the somewhat unique needs of each. For this reason it is intended that this chapter will examine fundraising techniques that may be used with individual donors, corporate donors, and trusts/foundations (including the national lottery). By way of an introduction, however, it is useful to begin by examining the changing fundraising environment. As we saw in Chapter 4, a thorough understanding of the 'trading' environment is an essential prerequisite to the development of any form of marketing strategy.

Fig. 5.1:
Sources of
Sector Income

- Individual Donations
- Legacies
- Sale Of Goods and Services
- Rent/Investment Income
- Tax Benefits
- Grants From:
  - Central Government
  - Local Government
  - Europe
  - Trusts/Foundations
  - National Lottery

Source: Pharoah (1997). Reproduced by kind permission of The Charities Aid Foundation.

The Fundraising Environment

Despite the range of funding sources outlined above many charities are now facing a genuine struggle for survival and many more are facing a situation where they are having to make cutbacks both in the variety and quality of the care that they provide. Why should this be so? There are a number of relevant factors which should be considered, primarily:

(1) the slow growth in voluntary income attracting to the sector;
(2) the growth in the number of registered charities;
(3) the nature of the new causes entering the sector;

(4) the performance of the major players;

(5) the advent of the national lottery.

In respect of the first point, there appears to have been a slow but steady increase in the amount of voluntary income attracting to the charity sector. The difficulty fundraisers have lies in determining the exact extent of this increase. Definitional problems and the fact that various 'tracking' studies all employ different methodologies makes the identification of reliable data on this issue problematic. One of the more indicative studies (because of its sole focus on fundraising charities), that produced by the Charities Aid Foundation, indicates that the growth experienced by the top 500 charities has been only 2.6 per cent in real terms from 1992 to 1997.

Compounding the problem of this relatively small growth rate has been the continued emergence of ever greater numbers of registered charities, many of whom will, by definition, be seeking to carve out their own slice of the fundraising cake. At the time of writing there are well over 182,000 registered charities in the UK and the total continues to grow at around 3,000 per annum. Fundraisers will therefore find themselves competing with ever increasing numbers of new charities each year.

In itself this would be less of a problem, if the nature of these new causes reflected the profile of the causes already in existence in the sector. Sadly this is not the case. Many of the new charities that have recently registered have causes that are altogether more appealing to the philanthropic public. Many schools and hospitals are now actively seeking funds from individual and corporate donors, where they might have relied completely on the state no more than ten years ago. It is a sad fact that it is easier to raise funds to educate a child than to house the homeless or feed a starving farmer in the Third World, yet who is to say which cause is actually more worthwhile. Indeed the overall pattern of giving in the UK is somewhat distorted, at least from the perspective of some foreign eyes. The Donkey Sanctuary, for example, is able to attract higher levels of voluntary income than the mental health charity MENCAP, whilst the Battersea Dogs Home is able to attract significantly more support per annum than the Terrence Higgins Trust. It seems clear therefore that the nature of the cause can have a dramatic effect on the fundraising capacity of an individual charity. Given the emotive appeals of many of the new organizations entering the sector, existing charities with less 'sexy' appeals will be worst hit by the changes.

A further factor which has contributed to the enhanced competitiveness of the sector is the performance of the major players. Data from Helms and Passey (1996) indicates that those charities with a total income exceeding £10 million continue to experience growth rates of around 14 per cent per annum. Whilst most analysts do not expect this trend to continue into the longer term, such enhanced performance must be a source of major concern to smaller charities, particularly given the earlier observation that the overall increase in income to the sector has been only a fraction of this amount.

The final major change to take place in the UK in recent years has been the introduction of the National Lottery. The lottery has been much maligned since its introduction in 1994 and perhaps unfairly. At the time many charities complained bitterly of the substantial drop they were experiencing in income. Whilst its impact on different forms of fundraising activity has yet to be established (and hence its inclusion here as a potential threat), there is no evidence to suggest that the introduction of the lottery has had any impact on overall levels of individual giving since its introduction. Indeed, as will be shown below, individual giving has actually increased in real terms since 1994. The key issue for many fundraisers has therefore been, not how to stem a decline in individual giving, but instead how to convince one of the lottery boards that their charity might be deserving of its support. In the three years since its introduction over £1.5 billion of funding has been awarded to UK charities and the lottery has hence become a major new source of income for the sector. Whether this funding is as accessible as it might be by all categories of charitable cause is quite another matter, and is beyond the scope of this book.

There are of course many other factors which have recently impacted on fundraising activity, including the introduction of new database technologies, a new legislative framework and increasing levels of management sophistication. Considered together, these factors have all contributed to the creation of a very dynamic fundraising environment and one which fundraisers will fail to take account of at their peril. It is for this reason that a detailed marketing audit (see Chapter 4) is as necessary a prerequisite to a fundraising plan as it is to the overall marketing plan of a nonprofit organization. The derivation of realistic (and appropriate) fundraising objectives and strategies will only be possible when an organization understands how the forces acting in the environment will impact on the actions that it decides to take. Fundraisers, in common with other marketers, cannot afford to operate in a vacuum.

The Fundraising Plan

The fundamental components of the marketing plan introduced in Chapter 4—namely the marketing audit, marketing objectives, strategies, and tactics—are all of equal relevance to the task of planning the activities that will be undertaken to raise funds for a particular organization. There is still a need for a comprehensive audit and the thoughtful derivation of fundraising objectives in the light of the information obtained.

Fundraisers will also wish to consider the overall strategies that they wish to pursue to raise the level of funds indicated in the objectives. This will undoubtedly involve apportioning effort amongst the various potential types of funder and within these groups the specific segments that will be addressed. The positioning of the organization within each segment will also warrant consideration at the strategic stage of the plan since it will be important to define quite clearly the values and imagery that the organization wishes to portray. It should also be made clear how these might differ from those of potential competitors for funds. At a tactical level, the fine detail of exactly how the objectives will be achieved is provided. In some organizations the tactical section of the plan is organized using the four or seven P framework proposed earlier, whilst, more usually for a fundraising plan, it will be structured using headings which reflect each key fundraising target (i.e. individual donors, corporate donors, and trusts). A separate tactical marketing mix will then be delineated for each of these targets. To complicate matters a little further, however, it would also be normal for a charity to draw a distinction, under the heading of individual donors, between donor recruitment and donor development activity. In the case of the former, the aim of the marketing is to attract new donors into the organization for the first time, whilst in the case of the latter the aim is to retain and develop these donors over an extended period of time. The structure therefore proposed for a fundraising plan is summarized in Fig. 5.2. Since many of these issues have already been explored in the preceding chapter it is intended here to concentrate solely on the tactical aspects of fundraising from individuals, corporate organizations and trusts.

Fig. 5.2:
**Structure of a
Fundraising
Plan**

Marketing Audit

SWOT Analysis

Fundraising Objectives

Fundraising Strategies

Fundraising Tactics

a) *Individual Giving*
   i) Donor Recruitment Activity
       Tactical Marketing Mix
   ii) Donor Development Activity
       Tactical Marketing Mix

b) *Corporate Giving*
   Tactical Marketing Mix

c) *Trust/Foundation Giving*
   Tactical Marketing Mix

Budget

Schedule

Monitoring and Control

Fundraising from Individual Donors

Donor Recruitment Versus Donor Development

Recruiting donors into the organization for the first time is probably the most difficult task that fundraisers ever have to accomplish. Most donor recruitment activity is perceived as a business of some risk, since it is unlikely that the resources expended on it will be immediately recouped. Expenditure on donor recruitment activity should thus be viewed as a long-term investment. Charities rarely do more than break even in conducting recruitment activity *per se*, but once 'warm' donors have been brought into the organization, the charity can begin to draw considerable benefit from the relationship it has with these individuals as these begin to develop over time.

Not all 'warm' donors will be treated alike however. A minority of those recruited will be worth substantially more to the organization than their peers, and where it has been identified that an individual is prepared to commit large sums of money, it is likely that he/she will be isolated from the general donor base and developed by specialist major gift fundraisers. Even in the case of smaller charities who may not have this degree of specialization in their fundraising departments, it is still almost certain that such individuals will receive a highly personal service from the most senior members of fundraising staff.

As to the majority of newly recruited donors, however, they are likely only to have given quite small sums of money. Despite this, such individuals are clearly enthusiastic about the nature of the cause and are therefore likely to respond again if asked to give in the future. Such individuals can therefore be targeted at regular intervals with requests to give further sums. Indeed as time passes they may also be targeted with requests to convert to covenanted giving, requests to encourage other supporters to join, or perhaps even a request to consider leaving the charity a legacy in their will. It is at this development stage that the relationship with these donors becomes truly profitable and begins to justify the initial investment.

Of course, given that donor development activity is inherently more profitable than donor recruitment, there is a danger that charities may focus too much on their existing donors at the expense of generating a sufficient supply of new donors who will provide the strongest revenue streams in times to come. Whilst there are no clear rules about what proportion of fundraising expenditure should be allocated to each form of activity, it is likely that in an established charity the ratio will be 80:20 in favour of development. Both forms of fundraising are discussed below.

Donor Recruitment Activity

There are really two approaches to the targeting of donor recruitment activity, the choice of which will depend on both the length of time the charity has been established and the degree of sophistication achieved in terms of record keeping. The two possible approaches are either:

(a) *A priori*—where the organization decides in advance of fundraising activity those categories of individual who are likely to be worth targeting. This 'gut feel' approach may be the only one possible if the charity is new and has no record of dealing with donors, or where record keeping has in the past been poor and where, hence, very little is known about existing donors to the organization.

(b) *Post hoc*—where the organization analyses the profile of its existing donors and utilizes this information to help it select future prospects. This latter approach clearly requires the organization to have either kept accurate and detailed records in respect of its donors, or to be willing to conduct additional market research to capture such information.

(a) The *A Priori* Approach

Considering first the *a priori* approach, the key question that fundraisers must ask is: 'What type of person will be likely to give to my cause?' We saw in Chapter 3 that there are a variety of demographic, lifestyle, and behavioural variables that could be used to select potential donors, but of all these criteria, which are likely to be the most successful?

At the first level of refinement, fundraisers will be likely to want to isolate charity donors (and preferably high value donors) from non-donors. They will then (of course) wish to isolate those that are likely to want to support their category of cause from the general mass of charity supporters. Fortunately a number of studies have recently been conducted that might guide them in the attainment of this goal.

Considering first the utility of geographic and demographic variables, Miller (1974) used a statistical tool known as 'regression' to identify demographic and socio-economic variables associated firstly with a propensity to donate to the US Lung Foundation and secondly to predict the size of their individual donations. Areas containing large populations and numerous families with high incomes and interest from dividends were found to be the most lucrative donors. Similarly Mindak and Bybee (1971) identified that a family's relative position in its life cycle was a good indicator of giving to the March of Dimes and Birth Defects Campaign in Travis County, USA. Beik and Smith (1979) were also able to utilize socio-economic data and relate this to the postcodes of potential donors who were more likely to give.

In a later study Smith and Beik (1982, 212) replicated these findings, quoting a national survey of philanthropic activity which identified that the 'heavy half' concept was equally applicable to the charity sector. 'About half the households, 48%, had incomes below $10,000, but accounted for only 18% of the dollar contributions. A similar proportion of households with incomes between $10,000 and $30,000 contributed a little over half the donations. The 4% of households with income over $30,000 provided 29% of the total giving'. Contributions were also found to be related to age and education although these lagged significantly behind income in terms of predictive power.

In the UK, the Charities Aid Foundation (1994) has carried out an extensive survey of charity donors. They found that charity donors are slightly more likely to be female (81 per cent of women give compared with 77 per cent of men) and that the propensity to donate is highest among the 25–34 age group. The 35–44 age group gives the highest average amount. The study also found that the propensity to give was highest amongst the sick and disabled (93 per cent made a donation) with retired people less likely to donate. In terms of socio-economic grouping the researchers found that the propensity to donate is highest among upper managerial and professional groups (AB). Not surprisingly the propensity to donate has also been seen to increase with the level of household income.

Recently attention has also focused on the use of psychographic or lifestyle variables. For example, Yavas *et al.* (1980, 43) in their study of donors to the United Way in America, conclude that 'donors appear to be more sympathetic, loving and helpful than non-donors'. In addition Schlegelmilch (1979) shows that attitudinal and lifestyle variables improve the prediction of whether an individual will give versus chance by 32 per cent. Similarly, in the US, the Yankelovich (1985) survey of American giving reported that the most important characteristics of the generous buyer are all related to the donor's perceptions and values. Perceptions of financial security, the availability of discretionary funds, attendance at religious services, and whether an individual volunteers time for charity were all shown to be good indicators of a propensity to give.

The literature further suggests that geodemographic variables can offer charities considerable utility and a number of major charities have been using the commercially available systems to good effect. Hansler and Riggin (1989) cite the example of the Arthritis Foundation in America which has recently used VISION to improve the response rate to its volunteer recruitment campaign. A selection of VISION segments and their propensity to volunteer time to charity is shown in Fig. 5.3. The graph warrants a little explanation. The vertical axis has been arranged as an index, with the point (0)

Fig. 5.3:
**VISION Profile
Bar Chart**

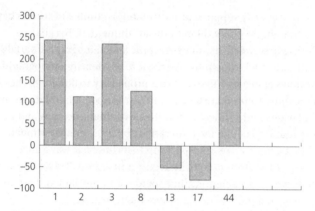

Segments above the line 0 (like No. 44—Prairie People) volunteer more often than 17 (Carports and Kids) and 13 (Little League and Barbecues).
Source: Hansler and Riggin (1989). Reprinted with permission from *Fund Raising Management Magazine*, 224 Seventh St, Garden City, New York, 11530, USA (516/746-6700).

representing the average propensity to volunteer across the whole American population. Thus segments such as No. 44, which the suppliers of this system call 'Prairie People,' are considerably more likely to volunteer time to charity than members of segment No. 17 ('Carports and Kids') or segment No. 13 ('Little League and Barbecues').

There are thus a variety of different variables which can be used to select segments of individuals who would be statistically more likely to give time or money to charity than others. All these variables could potentially be used to define a set of parameters that could be used to purchase a commercially available list of individuals. The charity could then conceivably target these individuals with a direct mailshot or telemarketing campaign, secure in the knowledge that they are statistically more likely to respond.

In all these studies however the only distinction that has been drawn is that between donors and non donors. No attempt has been made to differentiate between those who might choose to support one category of cause and those who might choose to support another. There is a good reason for this; a healthy debate at the present time surrounds this issue. Writers such as Schlegelmilch and Tynan (1989) who carried out a survey of 800 Scottish households containing known donors, demonstrated that 'specific types of charities are not associated with specific segments'. They therefore concluded that charities were providing a commodity product, since donors' needs appeared to be largely similar. It should be noted, however, that the authors tested only a limited number of psychographic variables and that these were not closely related to the charitable product. It is this latter point that may explain why the academic research is so sharply at odds with the reported experience of practitioners within the sector. Pagan (1994), for example, reports that the RNID (Royal National Institute for the Deaf) has recently increased the response from its direct mail campaigns quite significantly by recognizing that their donors tend to have a religious interest and enjoy both gardening and reading the *Daily Telegraph*. Building these lifestyle variables into the criteria for donor selection from lists has increased the response rate to 'cold' direct mail from 0.6 per cent to 3.3 per cent. Lonsdale (1994) quotes the further example of the Terrence Higgins Trust whose potential donors appear to be predominantly young to middle aged, male, with a high disposable income, and a propensity to enjoy gourmet food. This is hardly a profile which would match that of many charitable organizations.

More recent work by Sargeant and Bater (1996) resolves this apparent contradiction by demonstrating empirically that charities may indeed segment the market very successfully on the basis of lifestyle variables. The authors also argue that in reality the scope for demographic segmentation of the charity market will depend on the nature of the cause. Charities which exist to serve the needs of a very narrow set of recipients are likely to find it easier to segment the market on demographic grounds. The Police Dependants Trust, for example, has a very narrow recipient base, and to suggest that potential donors could not be selected using the demographic variable 'occupation', would be intellectually puerile. Serving and ex-police officers would clearly be a key target market for this highly specialist organization. If however the charity appeals to a wider recipient group as, for example, do Save The Children or Barnados, then demographic segmentation of potential donors becomes somewhat more problematic. In the latter case one would appear to be competing for funds from a demographically homogeneous body of donors.

(b) The *Post Hoc* Approach

The *post hoc* approach to targeting potential new donors involves the organization in conducting a detailed analysis of its own database/records, or in conducting an element of primary research. Here the aim is to profile those individuals who currently give to the charity and target others in society who exhibit broadly similar characteristics. Thus, if the existing database is comprised primarily of married A/B women, other individuals who match that profile can be targeted by using those criteria to select appropriate media for marketing communications. In the case of direct marketing activity this may involve building these variables into the criteria for list selection, whilst for more general advertising activity, magazines and even poster sites can now be selected which can offer greater penetration amongst the specific target groups.

Larger organizations may however be in a position to take this analysis one stage further. Consider Fig. 5.4. Charities with larger databases will undoubtedly find that patterns of giving are not uniform. Individuals give wildly differing amounts to the causes that they elect to support, depending on their levels of disposable income and the enthusiasm with which they view their participation. A useful form of analysis might therefore be to categorize donors according to the sums of money that they typically

Fig. 5.4: **The Donor Pyramid**

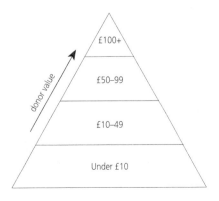

donate per annum. Thus a great number of donors may elect to give no more than £10 per annum. Substantially fewer will elect to give between £11 and £50 per annum and at the top of the pyramid, only a very small percentage of donors will be found to be giving over £100 each per year. These categories are of course purely arbitrary and any charity conducting this analysis will need to set appropriate 'cut-off' points of its own. Wherever the lines are drawn, however, it is important to realize that it is the profile of the people at the top end of the pyramid that fundraisers should be most interested in. These are, after all, the individuals who are giving the most to the charitable organization. If they have unique demographic, lifestyle, or behavioural characteristics it is important to use these as the criteria for list selection, etc., and not the criteria that define the profile of the database as a whole. By so doing the organization has a much better chance, not only of recruiting new donors, but of recruiting those who have a greater propensity to give larger sums.

Experienced fundraisers will appreciate that even this is a very simplistic form of analysis, but it does form a useful starting point. In charities where data has been studiously gathered for a number of years, it may be possible to take this analysis one step further and instead of using the value of the 'average' annual gift to map out the pyramid given in Fig. 5.4, it may instead be possible to use the variable 'lifetime value'. The simple variable 'average annual gift' is flawed since it neglects to take into consideration the longevity of the charity/donor relationship and the cash value of a donor's overall pattern of giving. The concept of lifetime value overcomes these shortcomings by deriving a monetary value for how much an individual donor will be worth to an organization over the duration of their relationship with it. As previously, the profile of those with a high lifetime value will be of inherently more interest to a charity than the profile of those with a low lifetime value.

The Opportunity

There are clearly a variety of criteria that can be used to target potential new donors to an organization and the good news is that in practice comparatively few charities are

Table 5.1
Criteria by which Potential New Donors are Selected for Contact

Criteria	Percentage of Respondents
Donor in Some Way Connected to the Cause	56.1
Geographic Location	40.7
Known Donor to Other Organisations	36.7
Income	31.6
Lifestyle	29.6
Age	28.6
Magazine Readership	23.5
Gender	21.4
Match to Database Profile	21.2
Geodemographic Variable	15.3
Other	10.2

Source: Sargeant (1996) 'Market Segmentation—Are UK Charities Making the Most of the Potential?', *Journal of Non Profit and Voluntary Sector Marketing* 1(2), 132–43. Reproduced with the kind permission of Henry Stewart Publications, London.

as yet making use of them. Recent data collected by Sargeant (1996) indicates that the variables that are currently utilized by the UK's top 500 fundraising charities are as illustrated in Table 5.1. The comparatively low percentages of charities using each method of identifying individual donors suggests that the targeting of new donors is still somewhat haphazard in the case of many organizations. This view is supported by the fact that only 21 per cent of fundraisers were involved in profiling their database to assist them in the pinpointing of other potential donors in the market. Given that almost 70 per cent of fundraising charities are currently engaged in the use of cold direct mail and a further 10 per cent in outbound telemarketing, there would appear to be a substantial opportunity for many organizations to hone the precision of this form of their direct fund-raising activities.

A particularly interesting aspect of these data is the relatively small but significant use of geodemographic and lifestyle variables. These figures almost certainly reflect the increasing sector-wide usage of commercially available targeting systems and bear testimony to the increasing sophistication of a number of charities' fundraising. This figure will doubtless increase over the next 5 to 10 years.

Fundraising from Existing Donors

Donor recruitment is but one aspect of charity fundraising. Once donors have been recruited the charity must then manage its relationship with those donors over time. The key to this management process is undoubtedly market segmentation (see, for example, May,1988).

Most charities now have a database (at least in the broadest sense of the word) but surprisingly few organizations appear to be using it to its full potential (Sargeant 1995). By segmenting the database and putting the data to work a charity can substantially increase its revenues. At the heart of segmentation in this context is what May (1988, 68) calls 'the ability to ask different donor groups for different amounts of money at different times'. This section will examine in some detail the mechanics of how this is to be achieved.

Assuming that a given charity has compiled a database, a number of criteria could be applied to that database to select donors for targeting with a particular campaign. Many of the variables we have already encountered, such as age, gender, income, geographic location, geodemographic coding, occupation, lifestyle, etc., could be used for this purpose. Clearly mailings with specific themes could be sent to target groups which experience suggests would be most receptive. In the context of database segmentation there are however a number of other variables that should be utilized, namely:

- original source of gift
- amount of highest/most recent donation
- date of most recent gift
- frequency of donation
- preferred timing of donation
- nature of the relationship required.

Considering each of these points in turn, data in respect of the original source of gift is useful since all individuals who give are unlikely to behave in a similar way. Direct mail donors, special event attendees, inquirers, sufferers, etc. will react differently to certain types of contact. If, for example, a donor has a history of attending fundraising events, but will not participate in other forms of fundraising activity, this fact needs to be recognized and taken account of in any future contact strategy.

Similarly the amount of the highest gift can enable a charity to develop a donor from a low value category (say £5 per annum) to a higher value category (say £20 per annum). It is now common practice for charities to ask for specific amounts when they write to donors. Often there are three or four alternative levels of giving included in a mailing and the donor is asked to tick a box to indicate the amount enclosed. Each level of giving is usually accompanied by an explanation of the impact that it will have on the recipient base. Most charities would also ensure that a final tick box allowed the donor to give any other amount they deemed appropriate. Asking for a specific sum has however been found to enhance the overall level of giving as donors are 'guided' to appropriate levels of support (Nichols, 1995). This is one of the reasons why so many television campaigns carry details on the screen of what a £5 donation, £10 donation, or £20 donation will accomplish. Of course when donors have been recruited to the organization, the level of donation requested by the tick boxes can be slowly increased over time. This may in turn require that several different versions of a mailing are produced in order that each value category of donor can be persuaded to give at a level at which they will find appropriate. It is to be hoped that this level will vary upwards with the passage of time. As a general rule of thumb it would be normal for a donor to be encouraged to give two or three times at the same level before any attempt was made to develop them in this way.

The date of the most recent gift is also an important database variable since to a certain extent it will control the date of the next contact that a charity will have with a particular donor. At the most simplistic level, this will help ensure that a donor who wrote a cheque for £100 yesterday is not burdened with another request for cash help tomorrow. Donors expect that the charities they support will maintain a dialogue with them and data needs to be managed intelligently to ensure that this is indeed the case.

Allied to this latter variable is the frequency at which donations are given by particular individuals. Often this may be once, twice, or three times a year and the patterns preferred by donors need to be respected. If one individual has a consistent record of giving twice a year it would seem a little foolish to write to them three or four times a year. Donors should be approached at a frequency that they find most comfortable to support. This makes the donor feel better about their relationship with the charity and avoids the wastage of valuable fundraising resources. A further point worthy of note in this section is the timing of individual donations. Many charitable donations are made in recognition of an anniversary or a special event such as Christmas. Once again, if a pattern begins to emerge, it would be sensible to respect the donor's wishes only to give at set times of the year and approach them only at those times. It is worth noting, however, that there is one key exception to this rule. Some charities do consciously make an effort to increase the frequency of donation as this is a further means of donor development and can often be more effective than asking directly for higher amounts of cash.

It can also be advantageous to combine a number of the preceding variables. If, for example, a charity focuses only on the amount of the last donation it might treat someone who gave £50 in January as a £10 donor if they happen to have given £10 in March. In fundraising terms this represents a big mistake since different categories of donors should receive different forms of communication, the 'value' of which reflects the level of support offered. Thus individuals who give more than £50 per year may receive different forms of communication than those who only give £10 a year.

There are of course a number of ways in which variables can be combined to ensure that the problem highlighted above is overcome. The easiest way of achieving this with most databases is simply to combine two variables and develop a coding system which acts to define each resulting segment of donors (see for example May, 1988). Such methods of segmentation are widely used (Sargeant, 1995) but, as will be explained, they are fundamentally flawed. Supposing for a moment that a charity has employed such a simple system of segmentation; they would be in a position to produce a graph such as the one reproduced in Fig. 5.5. In this example the charity has determined that low value donors will receive only a second class mailing, higher value donors a first class mailing, and the highest value donors, some form of personalized mailing which may include a small premium gift. Each shaded box thus represents a particular segment. In this example any individual who has given more than £25 within the last three years would receive a personalized mailing from the charity. Donors who gave a smaller sum, or who gave over £25 over three years ago would simply receive a mailing dispatched first class. Low value donors, or those who have given a considerable time ago, will receive a second class mailing. Finally, those donors who have not given for a considerable time would be dropped from the database altogether. As Rivlin (1990) points out such a system has the merit of being very simple to manage and the two most important factors in fundraising are taken account of.

Fig. 5.5: **Simple Two Variable Segmentation System**

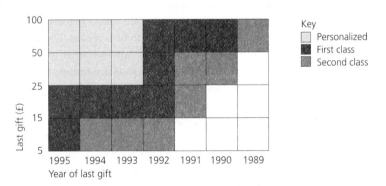

Before highlighting the difficulties associated with this form of approach, however, it is worth elaborating a little on the last point. Many charities are very adept at managing the data on their database and are really quite loath to part company with donors who either give at consistently low levels, or who last gave some considerable time ago. These donors are probably costing the organization more to support than they have ever contributed in return! Such individuals should be deleted from the database and offered as potential for reciprocal mailings. A great many charities will hence swop details of donors who have exhibited a disappointing level of commitment and some considerable benefit will usually result as many good new donors will be acquired in this way. This is because donors will usually only give at a low level for one of two reasons; the first is simply that this is all they can afford (and there is no real remedy for this!), but the second and more significant reason is that the charity they are supporting might not be perceived in their minds as being particularly deserving. Thus if this latter category of donors can be matched with an organization better suited to their 'needs' it would follow that higher levels of support will be forthcoming. This is indeed the case and reciprocal mailings can therefore be very effective.

Table 5.2 A History of Two Individual Donors	Donor A		Donor B	
	Date	*Amount*	*Date*	*Amount*
	Jan 1993	£20	Feb 1995	£20
	May 1993	£24		
	Nov 1993	£20		
	Feb 1995	£18		
	May 1995	£22		

To return however to the problems associated with the approach taken in Fig. 5.5, consider for a moment the case of the two donors in Table 5.2. Using the classification system postulated above, both these two donors would be classified in the same segment since the value of their last donation was between £15 and £25 and it was made in both cases during 1995. Using this simple form of segmentation, they would therefore be treated alike by the charity concerned. The profiles of these donors are hardly alike, however, and Donor A is of considerably more value to the organization than Donor B. Although building in the additional variable of 'frequency of donation' would solve this problem, it would be administratively burdensome for a charity since it would lead to a doubling of the number of segments that must be tracked. Rivlen (1990) therefore proposes that charities should undertake a regression analysis which could incorporate as many variables as were felt to be relevant. The aim in this respect is to build up a picture of the net worth of each donor and hence to estimate how much that person will give both over the next twelve months and even (if records permit) how much they might be expected to give over the lifetime of their association with the charity. Typically a charity may develop five such value segments and have a separate strategy for approaching each. Clearly the two donors in the example would then be classified into different segments, each of which could be addressed with an appropriate contact strategy. Fortunately many of the latest software tools available will perform this form of analysis, eliminating the need for fundraisers to have a detailed understanding of the statistics involved to use them effectively. For those readers interested in learning more about the technique, however, there is an excellent text on the subject produced by Hair *et al.* (1991).

The final of the variables that can be used to assist in donor development is the catch-all 'nature of the relationship that is required'. The very highest value donors may be looking for only personal forms of contact with the charity, whilst others will be content to receive regular newsletters, telephone calls, or mailshots. Surprisingly few organisations however, actually ask donors what form they would like their relationship with the charity to take. Would donors prefer to be contacted at set times of the year? Do they prefer to be prompted to give by regular requests for donations? Are they interested in visiting the charity? Would they like to receive newsletters/updates? Are they concerned always to receive an acknowledgement of their gift? Would they like to

Exhibit 5.1:

**Botton Village
Donor Response
Form**

Let Botton help you

Your support means a great deal to us and we want to help you in return. Please decide exactly how you want us to stay in touch by ticking the relevant boxes below.

Choose when you want to hear from us

1. At the moment we send you four issues of *Botton Village Life* **a year:**
- ☐ *I would prefer to hear from you just once a year, at Christmas.*
- ☐ *I would like you to keep me up to date with Botton's news through* Botton Village Life, *but I do not wish to receive appeals.*

2. At the moment we contact you just once a year:
- ☐ *I would like to receive all four issues of Botton Village Life.*

3. If you would rather NOT receive information:
- ☐ *I would prefer you not to write to me again.*

4. Choose whether you'll help us find new friends:
From time to time we agree with other carefully selected charities to write to some of each other's supporters. This can be a very valuable way to find new friends.
- ☐ *I would prefer not to hear from any other organisations.*

Choose what you'd like to receive

5. Our video of life in Botton
Our first video, *Botton Village: A Very Special Place*, is to be replaced with a new version. This is currently in production and we hope that our new video will be completed towards the end of 1997. We will let you know in our newsletter as soon as stocks are available. Meanwhile, you are welcome to borrow a loan copy of the existing video for one month.
- ☐ *Please send me your video on a month's free loan.*

6. Our *Sounds of Botton* audio tape
Our tape follows villager Jane Hill as she tours the village and meets her friends. It will give you a unique insight into life at Botton.
- ☐ *Please send me the Sounds of Botton tape. I enclose a cheque for £3.*

7. Our information for visitors
Visitors are always welcome at Botton. If you can, please give us a ring in advance on (01287) 660871. We can supply details of the opening times of our workshops and a map of how to get to Botton.
- ☐ *Please send me your information for visitors.*

How else can we help?

8. Explaining the various methods of giving you can use
Please send me:
- ☐ *'Ways of giving to Botton' information leaflet.*
- ☐ *Deed of Covenant form only.*
- ☐ *Gift Aid form only, for gifts of £250 upwards.*

9. Providing a helpful guide to making a Will
We produce *The Simple Guide to Making a Will* which is full of useful, impartial information. Of course, if you do decide to remember Botton in your Will, we would be very grateful.
Please send me my free copy of The Simple Guide to Making a Will, currently applicable only in England and Wales.
I would like the ☐ *standard print* ☐ *large-print version.*

10. Sending you past issues of our newsletter
Interesting stories from the village's history feature in past issues of our newsletter, *Botton Village Life*. You may ask for any of the past issues you would like, or another copy of ones you may have mislaid.
- ☐ *Please send me a set of back issues (1-20).*
- ☐ *Please send me issue no _____ (nos 21 upwards).*

11. Giving you details about Camphill in the UK
Botton Village is just one of the many communities which are part of the Camphill movement. If you want to know about other Camphill centres, we will be happy to help.
- ☐ *Please send me details of Camphill centres around the UK.*

Above: left to right are shown our Sounds of Botton tape, guide to making a Will, the Botton video, and a back issues set of Botton Village Life newsletter.

Do you want a word with someone?
Our office team of Fran, Alison, Rebecca, Jackie and Marion is here to help you. Just ring our helpline (01287 661294) or our switchboard (01287 660871), 9am to 4pm weekdays, and one of us will be pleased to talk to you. Do let us know if you have moved to a new address, if we are sending you more than one copy of our newsletter by mistake or if there is anything else you would like to tell us.

transfer to covenanted giving? Exhibit 5.1 contains a copy of a mailing distributed to donors to the charity Botton Village soon after they have made a donation for the first time. It shows quite clearly how donors can be offered quite differentiated forms of contact strategy, which not only enthuses the donor about the service he/she has received, but also conserves valuable fundraising resources as materials will not be dispatched to donors who have no interest in receiving them. The information Botton Village gathers can then be combined with data pertaining to the value of each individual donor and he/she can then be allocated to one of a variety of different segments, each of which will be developed with an appropriate contact strategy in the months that follow.

Work by Sargeant (1996) suggests that as with donor recruitment activity, comparatively few fundraising charities are taking full advantage of the opportunities to segment their database and to develop appropriate standards of care for differing categories of donors. Table 5.3 indicates the variables that charities would typically hold on their database, together with those that would typically be utilized to aid in the selection of donors to receive a particular campaign.

As one would expect charities are collecting a variety of data in respect of the amounts that individuals have given to their organization. Variables such as the amount and frequency of donation, together with a detailed giving history are clearly those which predominate. What is surprising however is the extent to which this information is under-utilized in the development of fundraising appeals when there is considerable evidence in the literature that effective fundraising appeals are based on a sound contact strategy which can be tailored to the needs of individual groups (or seg-

Table 5.3 **Charity Use of Database Variables**		
Variable	% of Respondents Holding Data on Charity Database	% of Respondents Utilising Data in the Selection of Donors to Receive a Particular Campaign
Date of Last Donation	96	60
Amount of Most Recent Donation	94	55
Frequency of Donation	74	49
Gender	58	13
Nature of Connection with the Organization (if any)	54	32
Preferred Mode of Donation	41	12
Record of Correspondence	38	12
Marital Status	29	4
Age	28	16
Preferred Date of Donation	20	16
Income/Profession	14	14
Hobbies/Interests	8	7
Net worth of Donor / Lifetime Value	5	5
Presence of Children in the Household	4	1
Attitudinal Data	4	3
Religion	4	4
Media Consumption	3	1
Membership of Voluntary Organizations	3	0
Level Of Education	1	1
Other	5	5

Source: Sargeant (1996) 'Market Segmentation—Are UK Charities Making the Most of the Potential?', *Journal of Non Profit and Voluntary Sector Marketing* 1(2), 132–43. Reproduced with the kind permission of Henry Stewart Publications, London.

ments) of donors (see, for example, Nichols, 1991). Indeed perhaps the most disappointing aspect of Table 5.3 is the fact that whilst almost all charities record the amount of the most recent donation, only half of this number will actually use this information to guide their choice of future contact strategy. In fundraising, as in the commercial world, some customers are worth far more to an organization than others. This should at the very least be reflected in the choice of the standard of care that high value donors receive. The defection of a high value donor to a competing organization will after all cost an organization far more (and in more than simply cash terms) than the defection of a low value donor. Correspondingly more effort should therefore be applied to the encouragement of loyalty amongst higher value customers.

Donor Recognition

With this latter point in mind it is worth briefly giving consideration to the question of how loyalty might be developed. At its most basic level the key to loyalty lies in maintaining a meaningful dialogue with donors over time. Donors (particularly high value donors) need to feel that they are appreciated and that their 'efforts' on the charity's behalf have actually made an impact. Moreover they expect that the charity will recall their past deeds and understand a little about them as individuals. Thus more successful fundraisers use every opportunity they can to develop and extend a dialogue with their donors. A colleague from a major wildlife charity ensures that he speaks personally to each of his major donors at least twice a year. In the early stages of his relationship with a high value donor he keeps a careful record of the donor's family circumstances (name of spouse, age of children, etc.) and any hobbies/interests that they might have. As any good salesperson will know, such intelligence is an invaluable tool as it allows the fundraiser to quite literally continue a conversation with a donor the next time they speak to them without the need to perform a devastating feat of memory. This particular colleague uses the information on hobbies and interests for a second purpose—if he comes across a newspaper or magazine article that he thinks would be of interest he will forward it to the donor concerned. A very low cost mechanism for enhancing value!

Of course there are a variety of other more formalized ways in which donors can be 'rewarded' either for their loyalty or for the amounts that they give. Some of the more common forms of what are termed 'donor recognition programmes' are listed below:

(1) *Newsletters*. Currently the most common form of 'reward', these serve to inform donors of the use to which their funds have been put and can act as a useful reminder of the donor's association with a charity, particularly if newsletters are sent at intervals complementary to other forms of contact.

(2) *Invitations to events*. Where charities have a site which donors may visit, donors may be extended an open invitation to visit, or alternatively open days can be held when donors can be specifically encouraged to visit. This category of reward may also take the form of invitations to special functions such as general meetings, dinners, galas, etc.

(3) *Citations in charity literature*. Often the annual reports of charities will feature the names of the highest value donors. Donors can also be thanked through acknowledgements in charity magazines or other promotional material.

(4) *Personalized communications.* As indicated above, higher value donors may receive uniquely personalized communications and may only be contacted by the most senior fundraising staff within the charity.

(5) *Premium materials/gifts, etc.* These are clearly going to be most effective where the premium directly relates to the nature of the cause and, whilst they should always be used with caution, are capable of adding considerable value to the charity/donor relationship. Perhaps the most unusual example the author has encountered would be the environmental charity which, instead of sending all its high value donors the usual thankyou letter, sent them all a pair of inflatable reindeer antlers!

(6) *Plaques/certificates of acknowledgement.* This is still a practice in its infancy in the UK, but is relatively commonplace in the USA. High value donors will be sent either a bronze, silver or gold plaque to acknowledge their donation, depending on the overall value thereof.

Despite the opportunities, donor recognition is still a practice which is under-developed in the UK. Whilst a few large charities have become very adept at building long-term relationships, particularly with high value donors, many still perceive that all their donors should be treated the same, irrespective of their overall value to the organization.

Case Study 5.1: **Celebrating the Million—The RSPB**

Background

The RSPB has recently celebrated the recruitment of its millionth member. Given that in 1988 the organization had a mere 500,000 individuals on its database, something of a sea change has taken place in the manner in which the organization promotes itself to its target markets.

Central to the RSPB strategy was the development of a formal five-year plan, the groundwork for which was undertaken in 1992. The organization began by undertaking a comprehensive review of its operations and carefully defining all the key conservation issues that it was necessary to address during the next five-year period. From this, the organization was then able to calculate the income stream that would be required and planners quickly realized that for all the objectives to be met they would have to double their net income by the year 2000.

Historically over 90 per cent of the organization's income has been derived directly from individuals in the form of membership subscriptions, donations, and legacies. Faced with what seemed like the impossibility of achieving a quantum leap in the levels of income attracted from these sources the organization decided to undertake a complete review of *all* its fundraising activity.

The audit identified three key areas in which improvements could be made, namely:

(1) *Face-to-face fundraising*—with visitors to RSPB reserves, local groups and high value donors;

(2) *Corporate fundraising*—where a potential existed to develop ongoing relationships with companies rather than one-off sponsorship;

(3) *Database marketing*—fundraisers were very much aware of the powerful correla-
tion between the number of members in the organization and the net income attracted. Whilst membership subscriptions were in themselves an important
source of revenue, committed members were often also willing to give additional
sums to support various appeals that the organization might run.

Aggressive targets were then set for each of these three areas and in particular the decision was taken to attempt to double the number of members to over one million during the next five-year period. Improvements were also to be made to the Return On
Investment (ROI) that would be achieved in the medium to long terms. The key to
achieving these goals can best be considered separately as recruitment and development activity.

Database Strategy—Recruitment

The RSPB, in common with most charities, takes full advantage of every opportunity to
encourage new members to join and uses a variety of promotional techniques to assist
in this goal, including face to face recruitment at its reserves and press, radio, and television advertising. By far the majority (typically 60–70 per cent) of new members, however, are recruited through direct-mail activity.

To help it target this latter activity the charity makes prolific use of marketing research data. For the RSPB the starting point is clearly the data already held on the database, such as gender, age, and geographical location. In itself however this information
is still very general in nature and insufficient to effectively target direct-mail activity.
Additional research is hence periodically undertaken with representative samples of
members/donors to establish both their lifestyle and attitudinal profiles. The former is
useful since it can greatly help in developing list selection criteria—the latter because
the data may be input to a variety of multi-variate statistical techniques including cluster analysis. Indeed by using this technique the RSPB has recently been able to determine that it is serving four distinct attitudinal segments of donors, namely:

(1) *Enthusiasts*. Individuals who are committed RSPB members and make every effort
to attend the programme of events which the organization arranges. For this
group the social interaction with other members is perhaps almost as important
as a passionate interest in the conservation of wild birds.

(2) *Birdwatchers*. These individuals support the RSPB because they are active birdwatchers and see membership as a natural complement to their hobby. They tend
not to attend meetings or events, but are no less active conservationists.

(3) *Garden Bird Enthusiasts (A)*. Individuals, probably in their 50s or 60s who enjoy nature and who join the RSPB to support its conservation work. They are enthusiasts as opposed to experts on wild birds, but this in no sense detracts from their
enjoyment thereof.

(4) *Garden Bird Enthusiasts (B)*. This group are very similar to the above, but they differ
in two important respects. They are generally younger than members of segment
(A) and support the RSPB for its work in protecting the environment rather than
preserving bird life *per se*.

Importantly, it has now proved possible to utilize this information to tailor the promotional messages used to contact specific target audiences. However, even when the

organization has decided on the content of an individual mailing for each segment, considerable effort is expended to ensure that it will have the desired effect. Focus group discussions may well be used to ensure that the promotional themes are appropriate, and two or more versions of a mailing will normally be tested with a representative sample of the chosen segment of members. Exhibit 5.2 illustrates three envelope designs that were piloted for a recent membership recruitment campaign. In this case it was only the envelope design that varied although the RSPB also tests the effectiveness of any promotional incentives it might include, such as a pen, sticker, video offer, etc. to ensure that any additional expenditure would be justified by the higher response rate it generated. Through research the charity has thus been able to greatly refine the precision of its recruitment activity.

Database Strategy—Membership/Donor Development

The first year of a new membership is critical. When members are recruited the primary objective in their first year is to get them to renew. Since over 80 per cent of members now join by direct debit, this task is much easier than it would have been, even a few years ago—the natural attrition has now been all but eliminated. During this critical period efforts are made to welcome members into the organization and get them used to the level of involvement that they will have in the years that follow. Later in the first year of membership, members may also be approached with a view to soliciting an additional donation from them for the first time. The timing of this 'ask', however, has been found to be critical.

A recent piece of marketing research has shown fundraisers that new members are significantly more likely to donate when they feel that the RSPB has fulfilled its part of the membership 'bargain' first. People who receive their first appeal mailing before the receipt of their first quarterly magazine were found to be 50 per cent less likely to respond. RSPB marketers therefore now ensure that all new members receive at least one quarterly magazine before soliciting any form of additional donation.

The organization also strives to recognize that the four attitudinal segments identified earlier will each have different levels of knowledge about birds and wildlife habitats. Sending an early campaign letter to members of the garden bird enthusiast segments asking them to support the Corncrake is unlikely to generate a good response because it is a bird they are likely never to have heard of. A more general 'softer' appeal is therefore deemed more appropriate for these particular segments. As levels of knowledge and awareness are cultivated over time, the nature of the appeal mailing is adjusted accordingly.

Using the techniques of Chi Square Automatic Interaction Detection (CHAID) and cluster analysis the organization can also identify the distinguishing characteristics of donors/members and use this knowledge to understand how best to present their services to them. In particular behavioural, attitudinal, and demographic variables have all been found useful in distinguishing between legacy donors, high value givers, members who will take out an affinity card, etc. In effect, the charity can hence look at the profile of a particular new member and know (with a fair degree of certainty) how that individual is likely to behave over time. RSPB fundraisers can thus determine whether a new member is a good legacy prospect, affinity card prospect, etc., and tailor the communications strategy to bring them to this point.

Exhibit 5.2:
**Pre-Tested RSPB
Envelopes**

Donor recognition is also a significant issue for RSPB fundraisers. Donors are individually thanked for each donation and feedback is regularly provided, either on an individual basis or through the *Birds* magazine, to keep donors informed as to the progress of a particular project and how their funds have been used.

All these key strategies allow the RSPB to maintain an almost individual dialogue with particular segments of members/donors and perhaps more importantly to build a closer relationship with each. Indeed, these relationships can be enhanced in a variety of other ways. Fundraising mailings can be structured to prompt gifts at specific levels. Such prompts are usually at odd-number levels (for example, £18.33) designed to reflect very specific and tangible benefits to bird populations. Although the RSPB team has found it difficult to develop donors past their own comfort level of giving, they have found it possible to increase the prompt levels *slowly* upwards and to increase the number of times people give. It is also possible to segment the database and to draw a distinction between different value levels of giving. Higher value donors will thus receive a different version of an appeal mailing featuring higher level prompts.

Indeed particularly high value donors are often targeted with a uniquely individualized mailing. Whilst the nature of the appeal will be identical, the organization feels that by recognizing the importance of this category of donor and making them feel, in a sense, special, it can greatly enhance its relationship with this group over time. As an example, the RSPB recently launched a land purchase appeal, which was targeted at a significant proportion of the database. Lower value donors received a standard mailing pack, whilst donors who had given over £1,000 during the previous year were sent a pack of correspondence relating to the land purchase, including the relevant council papers. Research had shown that donors in this category were more responsive to reasoned/rational argument and the mailing was hence designed specifically to appeal to them. It also served to indicate to this segment that the organization valued their commitment to the point at which it was willing to treat them a little differently from the other more general categories of supporter.

Nor is it just the high value donors to whom the charity is devoting attention. The RSPB had long recognized that it had a core of members who were either unable or unwilling to become donors. In many cases, it was felt that this might reflect the financial circumstances of the individual rather than any less commitment to the cause. In recognition of this, the RSPB now promotes ways in which individuals can help without spending money—for example, covenanting, selling raffle tickets, or taking out an RSPB Visa card. Many individuals who could not afford to give additional sums have been found to be more than happy to donate the time it takes to sell a book of raffle tickets on the charity's behalf. Indeed whilst the funds that this activity raises are worthwhile in themselves, this activity serves a greater purpose in that it brings a further segment of members into a much closer relationship with their charity. By so doing, there is a very real possibility that other forms of giving, such as legacies, may in the long term be enhanced.

At the core of all this activity is the RSPB's desire to make the most of its relationships with its supporters—and this is very much regarded as a two-way process. Aside from refining the precision of its direct marketing activity the charity has also continually invested in the development of its customer care. Ongoing research with members/donors ensures that the service provided by the organization closely matches that demanded by its customers. Only by ensuring that the relationship becomes mutually beneficial can fundraisers be sure that newly recruited donors will ultimately renew their membership and recommend the organization to others. A 'sales' oriented approach based on exploitation would clearly be in no one's interest and would ultimately be self defeating.

The Future

For all the progress that has been made over the past five-year period, the charity is still looking ahead. Plans are afoot to introduce an annual membership questionnaire which will capture attitudinal and media exposure data on an ongoing basis. This will then be recorded and stored on the database to make the targeting of particular forms of campaign even more effective than it is at present.

The focus of the next five-year plan will also change to reflect the need to develop the recently expanded database. Whilst it is still intended to achieve a growth in membership during each year of the subsequent plan, the focus will switch to improving the profitability of the relationship with those members already acquired. Having attracted a million members, the challenge is now to retain and develop them over time!

Individual Fundraising Approaches

So far in this chapter we have talked about how to target individual donors predominantly with some form of direct marketing activity. Before concluding this section therefore it is worth noting that a plethora of other fundraising techniques exist, many of which do not require anything like the degree of fundraising sophistication alluded to above. It is worth noting however that despite widespread participation in many of the forms of giving listed in Table 5.4, the revenues and costs generated by each activity will vary considerably from charity to charity. The work by Halfpenny and Lowe is, however, a useful starting point for fundraisers in determining which techniques might be worth investigation and further development. The authors surveyed a large number of charity donors to determine the percentage of all donors who give by a particular mode (illustrated in column 2 of the Table) and compared this data with what is known about the proportions of overall charitable income generated by each activity (see column 3). Three points are particularly worth noting from this Table. Firstly, whilst the various forms of charity collection remain important modes of giving, the revenues generated by such activities are considerably lower than many people believe. Whilst the costs are usually minimal, since many collections are undertaken by unpaid volunteers, they are perhaps a more useful device for raising a general awareness of the charity than for raising much needed funds. Secondly, the importance of trading income, particularly for the larger charities, is often underplayed. A significant percentage of overall charity income is generated by this means and although trading operations often differ widely in terms of profitability from one charity to another, it is clear that they can prove a very lucrative source of funds. Finally, the reader will appreciate that direct marketing techniques such as direct mail (appeal letters) and telemarketing currently have a relatively small role to play in generating funds for UK charities. Given the changing dynamics of the sector, however, and the ever lowering costs of computer databases, it is likely that this particular set of figures will change dramatically over the next five to ten years.

Table 5.4
**Modes of
Individual
Giving (1991)**

Method of giving	Percentage of all respondents giving by the method	Percentage of total donations
Door-to-Door Collections	37	6
Street Collections	32	4
Buying Raffle Tickets	31	7
Sponsoring Someone in an Event	23	6
Church Collection	14	8
Buy in Charity Shop	14	11
Pub Collection	11	2
Shop Counter Collection	11	1
Attend Charity Event	11	5
Buy in Jumble Sale	7	5
Subscription/Membership Fees	6	6
Buy through Catalogue	5	10
Collection at Work	5	2
Television Appeal	4	3
Buy Goods for Charitable Organizations	3	4
Appeal Letters	2	2
Appeal Advertising	1	4
Affinity Card	1	0.5
Telephone Appeal	0.5	0.5

Source: Halfpenny and Lowe (1993). Reproduced with the kind permission of the Charities Aid Foundation.

Fundraising from Corporate Donors

Patterns of Corporate Support

Recent survey work conducted by the Charities Aid Foundation (Pharoah, 1997) suggests that the overall level of corporate support for the voluntary sector has remained relatively stable in recent years, even if it continues to total less than 0.25 per cent of a typical company's pre-tax profit. Approximately £300 million is given in cash and non-cash assistance to the sector each year although there is some considerable debate surrounding the dispersion of these funds throughout the sector. Data from the National Council of Voluntary Organizations (NCVO) (Hems and Passey, 1996) suggests that the majority of charities have experienced a decline in corporate support because of the enhanced performance of the major players, whilst data from the Charities Aid Foundation suggests that the pattern of dispersion has actually been more uniform (Pharoah, 1997). It is possible that the great diversity of forms that corporate support can take are proving difficult to quantify and that differing methodologies are therefore generating quite different results. The most common forms that corporate support can take are listed below:

(1) *Cash support*—still by far the most common form of donation.

(2) *Sponsorship*—a form of giving which enables a charity function or event to take place that might not otherwise happen. Usually arrangements are made that will benefit both parties, perhaps through the provision of an adequate level of publicity and accompanying acknowledgements for the sponsor.

(3) *Secondment*—37 per cent of companies (surveyed) seconded staff to work with voluntary organizations in 1993/4.

(4) *Training*—this category includes payments for start-up costs and training of charity personnel.

(5) *Administrative support*—corporate staff may be involved in administering support programmes.

(6) *In-kind assistance*—where companies may elect to donate stocks and/or equipment for use in the pursuit of charitable causes.

(7) *Joint promotions*—this includes forms of joint sales promotions and the development of affinity card links.

After quantifying the value of donations by all the means listed above, Passey (1995) determined that total corporate support was allocated in the proportions illustrated in Table 5.5. The data show quite clearly that certain categories of cause will find it far easier to raise funds from corporate donors than others. To examine why this might be so it is useful to examine the underlying reasons why corporate donors elect to give to charity and how these patterns of thought have changed over the years. The literature suggests that there may be two distinct motivations for corporate giving. Ostergard (1994) reports that two paradigms of thought exist, namely the responsibility oriented paradigm and the opportunity based paradigm.

Table 5.5
Breakdown of Company Donations by Recipient Group

Category of Voluntary Activity	% Share of Total Support
Culture and recreation	11.7
Education and research	31.2
Health	26.8
Social Services	12.9
Environment	4.9
Development and housing	4.4
Law. Advocacy and politics	1.1
Philanthropic intermediaries	1.1
International	4.9
Religion	0.2

Source: Passey (1995). Reproduced with the kind permission of the Charities Aid Foundation.

(a) The Responsibility Oriented Paradigm

Historically this paradigm has predominated (Stroup and Neubert, 1987). Under this paradigm, corporate giving is viewed as a genuinely philanthropic activity where the primary objective is for the business to give something back to its community. Donations are made only because a particular cause is felt to be worthwhile and not because any form of gain will accrue to the donor. Indeed the causes supported may often bear no relationship to the business interests of the giver. The Exxon Education Foundation, for example, was widely admired until the late 1980s for being far removed from the world of big business. The programmes supported by the foundation bore absolutely no relation to the nature of Exxon's business interests. With the advent of 1989 and the Exxon Valdez oil spill, however, it became painfully clear to Exxon executives just how short-sighted this view had been. The company had missed an opportunity to forge links with charities which might conceivably have offered it a number of future benefits. With no long-term relationships having been established, for example with environmental groups, Exxon had nowhere to turn for advice and soon became the brunt of a torrent of criticism. By contrast Arco, a key competitor of Exxon, had been developing strategic links with environmental groups for a number of years and as a result has established a 'hotline' for advice should the unthinkable happen. They were also able to adapt their operational strategy to incorporate the advice offered by the environmentalists and hence minimize the future risk to their corporate identity. In short Arco had recognized the 'need' for a shift towards an opportunity based paradigm (Sterne, 1994).

(b) The Opportunity Based Paradigm

The opportunity based paradigm first began to emerge in the late 1960s and early 1970s with a number of organizations beginning to look for benefits of one form or another to accrue from their charitable giving. More recently authors such as Jones (1996) have noted what they call the emergence of 'strategic giving' which reflects what they perceive as a move towards fiscal efficiency and measurable effectiveness in charitable giving. Other writers, such as Pifer (1987), Mescon and Tilson (1987), and Wokutch and Spencer (1987) have identified a general shift towards what has become known as 'Dual Agenda' giving whereby organizations will be predisposed to giving to charities which have a good strategic fit with their own strategic objectives. As an example, Hunt (1986) points out that Hallmark chooses to support fine arts and design programmes in the hope that a supply of both employees and customers will be generated as a result.

It was probably in 1981 however that, in an attempt to raise funds for the restoration of the Statue of Liberty, a new dimension of corporate philanthropy really began to emerge. American Express referred to their programme of support as Cause Related Marketing (CRM), a phrase that switched the emphasis from purely what the business could do for the charity, to an equal focus on what the charity could do for the business. In defining cause related marketing in an address to his fellow business leaders, the senior vice president of American Express warned that:

> if your primary goal is to make money for a worthy cause, stay away from it. It's not meant to be philanthropy. Its objective is to make money for your business. (Kelley, 1991)

Varadarajan and Menon (1988, 60) define cause related marketing as a

> process of formulating and implementing marketing activities that are characterized by an offer from the firm to contribute a specified amount to a designated cause when customers engage in revenue providing exchanges that satisfy organizational and individual objectives.

CRM is thus concerned with the development of a win/win partnership where both parties derive broadly equal benefit. Those organizations that subscribe to the opportunity based paradigm will therefore be entering their relationship with a charity with a very clear idea of the set of benefits that they would expect to see accrue as a result.

In general there are four key categories of benefit that can accrue to a business as a result of its association with a charity.

(1) *Long-term strategic benefits*. Giving to some research charities may, for example, facilitate the development of a new technology which may be used by the donor organization in times to come. There may also be occasions when the recruitment of particular individuals is facilitated since an organization has been shown to 'care', or where highly skilled and qualified members of staff may be retained in the organization by virtue of a substantial investment in the socio-cultural infrastructure within the local community. As an example, Sterne (1994) reports that in the case of the Synoptics Corporation in the USA a rapid expansion programme made the recruitment of senior executives problematic. Potential applicants came not only with job expectations, but also other expectations of the company. The expectations of such employees therefore became a key driving force behind the creation of a community relations strategy which encompassed corporate giving, volunteering, matching gifts, and employee recognition programmes.

(2) *Community expectations*. There have been a number of well publicized examples where community expectations have led to a corporate donation either because the company has felt obligated to give or, perhaps more commonly, where it was felt that to give would enhance community relations to the point where the company could increasingly become a master of its own destiny. Richards (1995) cites the example of Procter and Gamble. With the advent of a new social responsibility programme headlines such as 'P and G know-how in fight against crime' and 'Procter to spend £15,000 on drugs booklet' have been commonplace in the press. This has had the fortunate effect that Procter and Gamble now finds it easier to have a say in the future of Newcastle where the firm is based.

(3) *Employee responsibility*. In many cases the organization may be motivated to give by the desires/concerns of its own employees. In this sense corporate giving can be seen to 'articulate' the social responsibilities of employees. An often cited example of this phenomenon is the Reebok Human Rights Now Tour with Sting and Bruce Springsteen in late 1980s. The tour probably didn't sell many shoes, but it gave the organization's young stakeholders a reason to be proud of their work. In a further example, Hallmark cards has developed a long-term relationship with the Children's Society. The charity are regular participants in the organization's sales conferences, which the company feels act as an excellent motivator for its sales force since the more they sell, the more the good cause benefits. The British Red Cross has even put in appearances at the AGM of City solicitors Freshmans. The aim here is for the company to provide a feel-good factor for delegates at the same time as explaining the benefits to shareholders of their continuing support.

(4) *Enhancing the bottom line*. If the company can be seen to 'care' by its key customer groups, there is a general expectation that sales may be enhanced as a result. Fendley and Hewitt (1994) cite the example of the NSPCC who have recently assisted the Yorkshire Building Society to introduce a new savings product for young savers. By using the NSPCC's Happy Kids brand which already extends to a range of children's clothing and greeting cards, the savings product gained something of an advantage in an already crowded market. In this case the NSPCC received £1 for each account that was

opened and 10 per cent of the gross interest paid twice a year. This one deal alone is estimated to have been worth at least £80,000 in its first year. Other successful examples in the UK of such practices include deals between the children's charity NCH and corporate sponsors Bisto and Securicor, estimated to be worth £125,000 and £110,000 respectively, and a new deal between White Horse and the RSPCA, worth in excess of £50,000.

There are clearly a variety of different reasons why businesses might elect to support charity, but it would be a mistake to believe, certainly in the UK, that the opportunity based paradigm is as widespread as the popular press might have one believe. In fact the majority of corporate giving (55 per cent) in the UK is still undertaken for purely philanthropic reasons. The key motivation for many corporate supporters is therefore no more hard headed or objective than would be the case in respect of most individual giving decisions (see Sargeant, 1997). What is interesting, however, is that whilst it is the responsibility based paradigm which remains the most dominant, those organizations who give for this reason tend to give far smaller amounts on average than those who subscribe to the opportunity based paradigm. Charities therefore need to give adequate consideration to which category of corporate donor they are likely to want to attract and tailor the approach accordingly. In the case of the former, literature which plays on many of the emotional appeals utilized with individual donors might be the most appropriate, whilst with the latter a more rational approach highlighting the benefits that can be offered in terms of press coverage, exposure in charity publications, networking with influential figures, etc. would clearly be preferable.

The key problem of course is deciding *a priori* which would be the best approach to use. The rationale for giving does not appear to be related to the size of the organization or the category of industry in which particular firms are operating. The only answer at present would appear to be a painstaking research process which carefully categorizes prospects according to their likely interests.

Targeting Corporate Donors

Stage 1

As the reader will by now appreciate there are a number of stages involved in soliciting corporate support. The first stage involves the charity in defining what it is looking to gain from potential corporate supporters. Whilst typically this might only be a target for cash donations, as was noted earlier corporate giving can take one of a number of different forms and it is hence important to be clear about exactly what the charity is hoping to get out of relationships from the outset.

The corollary of this of course is a consideration of exactly what the charity has to offer potential supporters—or at least what it is prepared to offer. Some charities may wish to maintain a degree of distance between the organization and its corporate supporters to avoid the risk of being put in a compromising situation in the future. Environmental charities in particular need to be very careful of those corporate organizations they initiate links with, and the degree of 'cosiness' that can be seen to develop between them. Then, should the need arise, they can still campaign for a change in industrial policies and even be overtly critical of the donor.

Stage 2

The second stage is perhaps the most difficult, for it is at this point that the charity needs to begin generating a list of potential contacts from whom it could look to solicit donations. Tables 5.6 and 5.7 contain a useful starting point in this analysis. Table 5.6 indicates those categories of business organization which typically offer the most support to charities, whilst Table 5.7 indicates those criteria that are normally used by such organizations to screen appeals that are targeted in their direction.

Table 5.6
Corporate Support by Industrial Category (SIC)

Industrial Category	Number of Companies Responding	Total Corporate Support (£000)	% of Total Support	Median Corporate Support (£000)
Manufacturing	56	49,013.0	32.9	213.5
Finance, Insurance and Real Estate	40	46,344.8	31.1	295.0
Mining	11	18,534.0	12.4	331.0
Retail Trade	14	18,431.0	12.4	421.0
Business Services	11	7,931.7	5.3	75.0
Transport and Communication	18	7,283.0	4.9	183.5
Construction	5	1,375.9	0.9	39.0
Wholesale Trade	8	922.9	0.5	118.3
Agriculture	0	0	0	n/a
Public Administration	0	0	0	n/a

Source: Passey (1995). Reproduced with the kind permission of the Charities Aid Foundation.

Table 5.7
Criteria used to Select Charities for Support

Criteria	% of Cases
Local Cause	62.5
Relevant to Business	43.8
Relevant to Staff	31.3
Size of Organisation	18.8

Source: Sargeant and Stephenson (1997) 'Corporate Giving—Targeting the Likely Donor', *Journal of Nonprofit and Voluntary Sector Marketing*, Vol. 2, No. 1, 64–79. Reproduced with the kind permission of Henry Stewart Publications, London.

Many corporate organizations will only give to causes that they perceive as local, perhaps because the charity is based in the locality of one of their manufacturing plants. Similarly the cause must often be perceived as being of relevance to the business and/or one which attracts the interest of staff. A significant number of corporate donors will also assess the relative size of the charity partner essentially for one of two reasons. Smaller firms will want to feel that their donation will have an impact and consequently they may elect only to support charities that are relatively small in size compared with their own annual turnovers. Larger organizations on the other hand may be looking for charity partners that can enhance their overall profile and they will hence be favourably disposed to approaches from the largest players in each charity 'market'.

At this stage of the process, the aim is for the charity to compile a list of loosely qualified 'suspects' who might be disposed to giving. This list will later be subjected to a higher degree of scrutiny (see below).

Stage 3

The third stage of the corporate fundraising process involves the charity in refining its list of contacts. Helpfully, Kotler and Andreasen propose a matrix which can assist fundraisers in this process (see Fig. 5.6).

Fig. 5.6: **Classifying Corporate Donors by Level of Interest and Giving Potential**

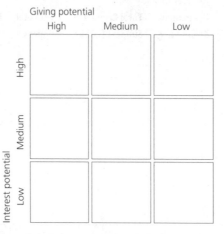

Source: Kotler/Andreasen, *Strategic Marketing for Nonprofit Organisations*, 5th edn © 1996. Adapted by permission of Prentice Hall, Inc, Upper Saddle River, NJ.

Clearly not every corporate organisation identified in the initial search stage will be felt equally likely to offer potential support. Neither will all organizations have an equal capacity for giving. Some organizations will quite rightly be regarded as hotter prospects than others and will therefore need to be isolated to receive perhaps a more personalized form of contact strategy. Plotting the position of each prospect in Fig. 5.6 can therefore assist a charity in prioritizing its prospects. The matrix is constructed in a very similar way to the portfolio matrix introduced in Chapter 4 (see p. 99 above for details). Essentially the charity must first identify those factors which will comprise each of the axes and then derive a score for each prospect which can then be used to plot their overall position in the matrix. In the case of 'Giving Potential' axis, there are a variety of factors which will impact on a firm's ability to give, including: financial performance, attitude of directors, giving policy, past record of giving, etc. Each of these factors can then be weighted for importance and each firm awarded a score in terms of how well they meet each of the criteria. An aggregate score for the horizontal axis can then be derived. Similarly there will be a variety of factors that will impact on the interest that the donor is likely to have in a particular charity. These might include: similarity of mission, similarity of target audiences, the need for favourable publicity, etc. Again a score can be derived for each factor and an overall score for the axis determined. At this point the prospect's position in the matrix can be plotted.

Organizations falling in the top left hand corner of the matrix are obviously candidates for personal attention from a charity's most senior fundraisers and a close and long-term relationship should be developed with these companies. Companies falling within the central diagonal are clearly worth contacting, but perhaps they may merit less attention in terms of a fundraiser's time. Indeed many of these organizations may be communicated with through the medium of direct mail, with subsequent personal follow-up if the response warrants it. Companies falling within the lower right hand corner of the matrix may either be contacted purely by direct mail (as this is comparatively inexpensive) or they may be dropped altogether from the charity's list of prospects.

Stage 4

As indicated above the fourth stage of the process involves the design and implementation of appropriate contact strategies for each category of prospects. This may involve the use of a variety of media including personal sales visits, direct mail, and telemarketing. It will also involve a careful tailoring of the 'offer' to ensure that only those aspects are emphasized that will have the most relevance for the potential prospect.

Stage 5

Stage 5 involves a careful monitoring of the overall process. This should be ongoing, so that if the desired response/success rates are not being achieved, questions can be asked and appropriate corrective action taken. The organization will also find it instructive to monitor the profile of those respondents who respond both favourably and unfavourably. This data will be invaluable in helping the charity to refine its selection of suitable corporate prospects in the future.

Of course the recruitment of new corporate donors represents the beginning of a series of relationships and charities must also give consideration to how these relationships will be developed over time. In particular the following questions are worth asking from the outset. Will particular members of staff be given responsibility for managing the relationships with specific corporate clients? Are appropriate mechanisms for providing the desired feedback to donors in place? What control procedures will be necessary to monitor the success of the relationship?

Fundraising from Trusts/Foundations

Charitable Trusts are organizations that exist to manage funds donated by an organization or individual (the donor or settlor), to the benefit of some beneficiary group. The beneficiaries are usually specified by the donor and it is the responsibility of the management of the trust (the trustees) to ensure that its funds are indeed used for this purpose. A great many trusts in the UK exist not to directly service the needs of the beneficiary group themselves, but rather to give grants to individuals or other charities in the furtherance of their objectives.

In the UK alone there are estimated to be well over 10,000 grant-making trusts which collectively give away over £1 billion for charitable purposes each year. However, they represent a very diverse population and whilst a few organizations give in excess of £10 million each, per annum, the majority of trusts are quite small in size and highly specialized in terms of the categories of cause that they will support.

In approaching trusts a seven-stage process is recommended, as follows.

1 Audit of Potential Projects

The first stage in trust fundraising will involve a careful analysis of all the activities that the organization is planning to carry out with beneficiary groups over the short to medium term (most trusts will not support projects which are likely to extend beyond a three-year time period). Those activities which can clearly be identified as specific projects should be isolated and evaluated for how attractive they are likely to be to an external funder. It is worth noting that many trusts will prefer not to fund projects which in their opinion are high profile enough to warrant the attraction of commercial support, and many will also shy away from the support of projects consisting largely of overhead costs or those which they believe should be government aided. Trusts are however interested in projects that are likely to have a high impact with the beneficiary group, are particularly innovative, and which can demonstrate an impact in a relatively short period of time.

Where potentially suitable projects have been identified, fundraisers will need to work closely with other charity staff to justify the need for each project and to derive a series of strong arguments in respect of why each is worthy of support.

2 Initial Trust Search

Having identified potentially suitable projects the next stage is to compile a short list of trusts that are, on the face of it, worthy of an initial approach. There are a variety of sources of information on trusts which can be used for this purpose and these tend to vary substantially in quality from country to country. In the UK the most commonly used source of trust information is the Directory of Grant Making Trusts, which lists the contact details for key trusts, information in respect of their giving behaviour, appropriate dates for application, and, importantly, the categories of cause supported. Other UK sources of information about trusts include the Charity Commission, Local Authorities, and the Directory of Trustees. Most other industrialized countries also have publications which can be scanned to locate trusts (for example, The Foundation Directory in the USA) and there is now even an International Foundation Directory in existence, for the benefit of those seeking to launch a more global appeal.

3 Network Search

The third stage in the process involves a charity in searching for any formal or informal links it might have with the trusts identified in stage 2 above. This is particularly important as the use of informal contacts can often have a very positive impact on the outcome of a grant decision.

Indeed, in his review of the status of trustees in the whole charity sector, Vincent (1988) was critical of the decisions made by trustees of grant making trusts:

> Is this [the decision] a matter of the personal whims of the trustee, or is there some objectivity in their decision making? At the present time it is very much a question of who you know.

Whilst few would doubt that all trusts would give serious consideration to a well-crafted proposal which was clearly covered by the objects of their organization, it is certainly the case that the exploitation of any personal contacts that might exist would certainly help to 'oil the wheels' of decision making. It must be remembered that charitable trusts receive many thousands of requests for support each year, and wherever possible it is important to stand out a little from this crowd. Many medium or large-sized trusts have comparatively large numbers of trustees to help share the administrative burden. The greater the number of trustees, the greater the likelihood that one or more of them might be known to someone associated with your own charity. It is therefore well worth while circulating the details of the larger trusts to which an application will be made to all key personnel, volunteers, or trustees who might conceivably have a contact. This contact could then be used to ensure that the application is made to the trust at the highest possible level. Literally every avenue should at this stage be explored to exploit any such contacts.

4 Prioritization and Matching of Prospects

Experience suggests that many trusts will have certain cut-off dates by which an application must be made. Others will be prepared to offer only small amounts of funding. Still others may offer funding for only a limited period of time. This variation will require fundraisers to prioritize those trusts to whom contact should be made so that the best possible use can be made of fundraising resources. Trusts should also be matched against those projects (identified in stage 1) which they are most likely to want to support.

5 Selection of Contact Strategy

The importance of networking has already been highlighted. It is clear that wherever possible the approach to a grant-making trust should be a personal one and ideally one which exploits an existing personal relationship between a trustee and someone associated with the applicant charity. Approaches where a personal contact is involved are clearly those that warrant the greatest effort since they are also likely to be the approaches that generate the most positive forms of response.

Where more personal forms of contact are not possible, it may still be possible to engage the trust administrator in a dialogue before the application is made. Often this can generate valuable information as the administrator will undoubtedly know the categories of project that are most likely to appeal to his/her trustees. In their role as gatekeeper they will also have a good understanding of what the trustees consider to be the key components of a successful application. This is all valuable intelligence which can help in stage 6—the application.

6 The Application

The written application should be carefully formulated and take account of any intelligence about the trust gathered at all of the preceding stages of the process. Applications to the larger trusts should always be made first since it is always more difficult to acquire early funding, and a few large donations to a project in the early stages can have the fortunate effect of encouraging other, smaller trusts, to contribute as time goes on. Applications to smaller trusts, which will typically only be made by letter, are thus normally left until last.

Applying to these smaller organizations, however, is a little more problematic since fundraisers are unlikely to be familiar with the individual needs and preferences of this category of organization. There is a need therefore to ensure that these written applications are crafted with a particularly high standard of care. Research with the administrators of 350 grant-making trusts conducted by Sargeant and Bater (1997) provides a useful insight into some of the more common pitfalls to avoid.

(1) *Not reading the requirements*. The temptation to adopt a shotgun approach to trust fundraising should be avoided. The production of vague letters of application which are then distributed *en masse* are unlikely to bear fruit and will almost certainly antagonize trust administrators who receive numerous such letters in their daily mailbags. Letters should be carefully crafted, taking account of the individual interests of each trust. Indeed, only those trusts should be targeted for whom the project is appropriate.

(2) *Providing too much/too little information*. Good applications should be short, concise and to the point. They should provide the trustees with all the information they require but avoid the temptation to oversell the project and bombard the trustees with needless amounts of background information. This will simply not be read and will only serve to detract from the overall quality of the application.

(3) *Poor Presentation*. A significant number of trust administrators complain that they receive scruffy hand-written applications that are difficult to decipher. Applications should be neat, well presented, and legible. They should not however be too 'plush' as this might, quite genuinely, create the impression that the applicant organization is awash with resources and does not require the funding anyway!

(4) *Not making the ask!* A surprising number of fundraisers avoid all the other pitfalls, but neglect anywhere in the application to state the total amount of funding that is requested. Many others fail to supply sufficient detail in respect of how the funds will be used. This is the one aspect of the application that is usually expected to be provided in some detail, as trustees need to evaluate each proposal they receive in terms of the impact it is likely to have with the beneficiary group. The 'ask' therefore needs to be clear and quantified.

7 Follow Up

The final stage of the process involves the charity in carefully recording details of both its successful and its unsuccessful applications. Even data pertaining to the latter can be immensely valuable as it may prove possible to contact the trusts concerned again at some later date. The experience gained at this stage can hence help inform the approach that is used on subsequent occasions. It may even be possible to obtain feedback from trusts to ascertain why a particular project was rejected. Any such approach would however need to be handled with care, as many trusts prefer not to divulge such information.

Perhaps more importantly, however, when a successful application for funding has been made, fundraisers will need to ensure that appropriate mechanisms for feedback are put in place so that the trust can be informed as to the progress of the project they are supporting. Only some 50 per cent of trusts will actually require such feedback as a condition of their support, but it is good practice to ensure that it is provided to all.

Even if trustees are unable to accept invitations to visit a project, or to read in great detail the impact it has had, the fact that the charity has taken the trouble to maintain a dialogue will undoubtedly pay dividends when subsequent applications are submitted in the future.

Summary

In this chapter we have examined three key areas of fundraising activity, namely fundraising from individuals, corporate organizations, and grant-making trusts. In the case of the former a distinction was drawn between donor recruitment and donor development activity. It has been argued that whilst it would be rare for donor recruitment campaigns to do more than simply break even, a careful profiling of existing donors to an organization can greatly enhance the response rates likely to be obtained. Moreover, if charity records permit, even greater utility can be gained by profiling only those individuals with a propensity to donate higher sums, and using this as the template from which to design the donor recruitment activity.

In the case of donor development, it has been argued here that charities should differentiate the standard of care, and hence the approach, that is used to develop donors based on the worth of each individual to the organization. In particular fundraising strategy should recognize the importance of keeping high value donors loyal to the organization, and to achieve this the design of an appropriate donor recognition programme could well be warranted.

A structure for planning the approach to corporate donors was also introduced, highlighting the importance of market segmentation as an aid to the targeting of organizations most likely to respond. Two key paradigms of corporate giving were described, with the responsibility oriented paradigm being shown to be predominant. It was noted, however, that organizations that give because they view their involvement with a charity as an 'opportunity' tend to give more on average than those with a more philanthropic perspective.

The chapter concluded with an analysis of trust fundraising. A structure for planning trust fundraising was introduced and the practicalities of fundraising from this target group were discussed.

There are thus many different categories of donor that a charity can elect to target. The appropriate balance for fundraisers to achieve amongst these three groups will undoubtedly depend on the size of the charity and the nature of its recipient group. Some categories of cause are inherently more appealing to individual donors, whilst others have an appeal that is perhaps more suited to the cultivation of corporate donors or charitable trusts. Whatever the balance that is most appropriate in a particular instance, there can be no substitute for a formal planned approach to the fundraising activity that will be conducted.

Discussion Questions

1. With reference to an organization of your choice, identify the key environmental influences currently acting on the fundraising function.
2. Why is it important for fundraisers to segment the donor market? What criteria might be employed for this purpose?
3. What do you understand by the term 'donor recognition programme'? Develop and outline such a programme for an organization with which you are familiar.
4. Many charities are now treating 'heavy' donors rather differently from those that give only small amounts to their organization. Are there any circumstances under which such a strategy would not be appropriate?
5. In your role as the fundraising director of a major charity, what advice would you offer to a junior colleague who is about to commence fundraising from grant-making trusts for the first time?

References

Beik, L. L. and Smith, S. M. (1979) 'Geographic Segmentation: A Fundraising Example', *Proceedings*, American Marketing Association, 485–8.

Charities Aid Foundation (1994) *Individual Giving and Volunteering in Britain*, West Malling, CAF.

Fendley, A. and Hewitt, M. (1994) 'When Charity Begins with a Pitch', *Marketing*, 23 June, 14–15.

Hair, J. F, Anderson, R. E., Tatham, T. and Black, W. C. (1995) *Multivariate Data Analysis with Readings*, New Jersey, Prentice Hall.

Halfpenny, P. and Lowe, D. (1993) *Individual Giving and Volunteering in Britain 1993*, West Malling, Charities Aid Foundation.

Hansler, D. F. and Riggin, D. L. (1989) 'Geodemographics: Targeting the Market', *Fund Raising Management*, Vol. 20, No. 10, 35–43.

Hems, L. and Passey, A. (1996) *UK Statistical Almanac*, London, NCVO.

Hunt, A. (1986) 'Strategic Philanthropy', *Across the Board*, July/Aug, Vol. 23, 23–30.

Kelley, B. (1991) 'Cause Related Marketing', *Sales and Sales Management*, March, 60.

Jones, J. (1996) 'Doing Good while Doing Well', *Black Enterprise*, Vol. 26, No. 7, 178–84.

Kotler, P. and Andreasen, A. (1991) *Strategic Marketing for Non-Profit Organisations*, New Jersey, Prentice Hall.

May, L. (1988) 'How to Build a Simple Segmentation System', *Fundraising Management*, May, 67–71, 111.

Mescon, T. S. and Tilson, D. J. (1987) 'Corporate Philanthropy: A Strategic Approach to the Bottom Line', *California Management Review*, Winter, Vol. 29, 49–61.

Miller, S. J. (1974) 'Market Segmentation and Forecasting for a Charitable Health Organisation', *Proceedings of the Annual Conference*, Southern Marketing Association, Atlanta, Georgia.

Mindak, W. A. and Bybee, H. M. (1971) 'Marketing's Application to Fundraising', *Journal of Marketing*, Vol. 35, No. 2, July, 13–18.

Nichols, J. E. (1991), *Targeted Fundraising*, Illinois, Precept Press.

Nichols, J. E. (1995) 'Developing Relationships with Donors', *Fundraising Management*, August, 18, 19, 47.

Ostergard, P. M. (1994) 'Fasten Your Seat Belts', *Fundraising Management*, March, 36–8.

Pagan, L. (1994) 'Testing out Support', *Marketing*, 12 May, 43.

Passey, A. (1995) 'Corporate Support of the UK Voluntary Sector' in CAF, (1995), *Dimensions of The Voluntary Sector*, West Malling, Charities Aid Foundation, 57–61.

Pharoah, C. (ed) (1997) *Dimensions of the Voluntary Sector*, West Malling, Charities Aid Foundation.

Pifer, A. (1987) 'Philanthropy, Voluntarism and Changing Times', *Journal of the American Academy of Arts and Sciences*', Winter, 119–31.

Richards, A. (1995) 'Does Charity Pay?', *Marketing*, 21 Sept, 24–5.

Rivlin, A. (1990) 'New Way to Manage a Database', *Fundraising Management*, July 1990, 33–8.

Sargeant, A. (1995) 'Market Segmentation in the Charity Sector—An Examination of Common Practice', *Proceedings of the MEG Annual Conference*, Bradford, July, 693–702.

Sargeant, A. (1996) 'Market Segmentation—Are UK Charities Making the Most of the Potential?', *Journal of Non Profit and Voluntary Sector Marketing*, Vol. 1, No. 2, 132–43.

Sargeant, A. (1997) 'Banishing The Battleship Ladies!—The Emergence of a New Paradigm of Corporate Giving', *Proceedings Academy of Marketing Conference*, Manchester, July, 903–16.

Sargeant, A. and Bater, K. (1996) 'Market Segmentation in the Charity Sector—Just What is the Potential?' *Working Paper 96/05*, University of Exeter

Sargeant, A. and Bater, K. (1997) 'Trust Fundraising—Learning to Say Thank You', *Journal of Nonprofit and Voluntary Sector Marketing*, forthcoming.

Schlegelmilch, B. B. (1979) 'Targeting of Fund Raising Appeals', *European Journal of Marketing*, Vol. 22, 31–40.

Schlegelmilch, B. B. and Tynan, A. C. (1989) 'The Scope for Market Segmentation Within the Charity Sector—An Empirical Analysis', *Managerial and Decision Economics*, Vol. 10, 127–34.

Smith, S. M. and Beik, L. L. (1982) 'Market Segmentation for Fundraisers', *Journal of The Academy of Marketing Science*, Vol. 10, No. 3, 208–16.

Sterne, L. (1994) 'Giving As They Grow', *Foundation News and Commentary*, 35(5), 42–3.

Stroup, M. A and Neubert, R. L. (1987) 'The Evolution of Social Responsibility', *Business Horizons*, Vol. 30, March, 22–4.

Varadarajan, P. R. and Menon, A. (1988) 'Cause Related Marketing: A Co-alignment of Marketing Strategy and Corporate Philanthropy', *Journal of Marketing*, Vol. 52, No. 3, 58–74.

Vincent, R. (1988) 'Charity Administration: Is it Time for an Institute of Charity Trustees?', *New Law Journal*, 29 April, 2–4.

Wokutch, R. E. and Spencer, B. A. (1987) 'Corporate Saints and Sinners', *California Management Review*, Vol. 29, Winter, 72.

Yankelovich, Skelly and White Inc (1985) *The Charitable Behaviour of Americans, Management Survey*, Washington DC, Independent Sector.

Yavas, U., Riecken, G. and Paremeswaren, R. (1980) 'Using Psychographics to Profile Potential Donors', *Business Atlanta*, Vol. 30, No. 5, 41–5.

6

Arts Marketing

Objectives

By the end of this chapter you should be able to:

(1) understand the contribution that marketing can make to the development of the arts;

(2) categorize and profile arts audiences to a variety of different events;

(3) use a box office database to facilitate the achievement of arts marketing objectives;

(4) describe the arts funding framework and appreciate the role of marketing in securing funding from both the Arts Council and corporate sponsors.

Introduction

It is the purpose of this chapter to explore many of the key issues currently of relevance to marketing in the arts sector. To achieve this, the chapter is divided into two major components. In the first, the relevance of marketing to the issue of audience development will be explored. The text will examine the available audience research and use this as the basis for a discussion of the formulation of appropriate marketing strategy, before moving on to consider the usefulness of the box office database in the completion of this task. The second and final component of the chapter considers marketing's application to the attraction of funding. In particular its relevance to securing both Arts Council funding and corporate sponsorship will be examined. The chapter will begin however, by exploring something of the nature of arts marketing and how its application may differ from that observed in other parts of the nonprofit sector.

Defining the Arts

It is important to begin this section by defining what we understand by the term 'arts'. For the purposes of this text, the definition first provided by the 89th US Congress (and later adopted by the Arts Council in the UK) will be employed, namely:

The term 'the arts' includes, but is not limited to, music (instrumental and vocal), dance, drama, folk art, creative writing, architecture and allied fields, painting, sculpture, photography, graphic and craft arts, industrial design, costume and fashion design, motion pictures, television, radio, tape and sound recording, the arts related to the presentation, performance, execution and exhibition of such major arts forms and the study and application of the arts to the human environment. (ACGB, 1993)

Thus the term 'arts marketing' can be considered as embracing a wide variety of human endeavours, many of which are non-profit-making in nature. Whilst the focus of this text is quite clearly not-for-profit, many of the ideas that will be presented here will be equally applicable to all arts organizations whether they be profit making or not. Indeed, whatever the goals of a particular organization, managed wisely they are all capable of making a substantial contribution to the health of the society in which they operate. Perhaps unlike any of the other nonprofit sectors reviewed in this text, the arts form an integral part of the fabric of the world in which we live. They help define the origin of societies across the globe and they legitimize and give meaning to a whole range of intellectual and individual feelings and ideas. They therefore offer opportunities for expression and personal fulfilment in a way unrivalled by any other facet of society. As the National Campaign for the Arts put it in 1990:

The arts have become indivisible from the objectives of a humane, democratic society in which personal fulfilment enhances public success.

In looking to market the arts, one therefore has to be sensitive to the nature of the 'product' in a way that is unparalleled in the realm of most consumer goods and services. In no other context does one have to be so sensitive to the need to preserve the essential essence of what is being marketed, even if from a commercial standpoint the restrictions that this imposes may be a recipe for 'failure'. Many arts organizations continue to provide access to material that is likely only to appeal to a very small segment of society. Indeed, still others may support new and emerging art forms for which an audience has yet to develop. They undertake these endeavours because they strongly believe in the merit of what they are doing and the contribution it will make to society in the medium to long term.

Despite a plethora of changes in funding frameworks and philosophical arguments about the legitimacy of many forms of art, the arts sectors in most Western societies continue to experience growth. In the USA, following the birth of the first official federal arts agency, the National Endowment for the Arts (NEA) in 1965, the number of arts organizations increased almost exponentially over just a few years. The number of symphony orchestras rose from 110–230, non profit theatres from 56–420, dance companies from 37–450, and opera companies from 27–120 (see Reiss, 1994).

A similar pattern has emerged in the UK, where there has also been a proliferation of arts organizations, the majority of which may be said to be non-profit-making in nature. Whilst this growth is undoubtedly to be commended, it is important to realize that government funding for the arts has in many countries (including the UK) declined in real terms. This has put pressure on fledgling arts organizations to become self sufficient at an early stage through the attraction of ever larger audiences. Against this backdrop, the reader could be forgiven for imagining that historically the marketing concept has been warmly embraced by arts professionals. The reader would be mistaken!

Why the Reticence?

It is probably fair to say that arts organizations have lagged some way behind most other categories of nonprofit in recognizing the utility of the marketing concept. Even as recently as ten years ago, in some arts circles one would have been severely chastised for even daring to mention the word marketing. Why should this be so? Why should arts organizations have been so reticent in accepting the need to market their services?

To answer this question it is necessary to return to a point made in Chapter 1. It should be remembered that many organizations in the nonprofit sector continue to equate marketing with selling and feel that such techniques cheapen the work that they are involved with. The same views have been held, perhaps even more acutely, by arts managers, who feel that their productions should somehow be above the need for any form of commercial approach. As Diggle (1984, 18) puts it, there was a

> religious school of thought that held art to be sacred, that audiences were made by God and any attempt to improve their sizes was profanity.

What was particularly interesting about this school of thought was that it tended to originate from artists in search of a living, or artistic directors who never bothered to consider the nature of the potential audience until the opening night, and who then wondered why their auditorium was half empty! Of course it would be too simplistic to suggest that it is possible to blindly apply marketing tools and techniques to the arts product without any form of modification whatsoever. In the arts sector there are a number of 'balances' that must be struck between the view of the arts that suggests that they have inherent worth and are worth preserving at all costs, and the view that the arts, like any other form of human activity, should be forced to 'pay their own way' and that a consideration of likely audiences should therefore be paramount. This idea of balance needs to be examined in relation to performances, portrayal, and audience.

(a) Balance in Performance

Examining first the question of the art forms or performances that should be made available to society, it seems clear that there is an inherent conflict here between the marketing concept on the one hand and the whole ethos of the arts on the other. Should arts organizations start with a thorough analysis of what their potential audiences are likely to want and then build into their programmes a mix of all the art forms desired, or should they steadfastly continue to produce art forms that they believe would be good for the society they serve, irrespective of the level of demand that will be forthcoming?

Mokwa (1980, 6) holds to the former view:

> Most might deny that the arts have lived too long in a world comprised of faith, hope and charity—the quicksand of the arts. Faith—that the arts have values, Hope—that someone will recognise the values and come to view them, Charity—that someone will pay for them (and) absorb the deficits. The faith is valid and must be kept, but the hope is of a blind nature and the charity is not forthcoming as it is needed.

Searles (1980, 69), however, supports the latter view:

> If the audience were to decide, our arts world would become narrower and narrower and increasingly sterile. All of us need to be pulled, pushed or even thrown into new artistic experiences. This part of life—the content and makeup of the US arts world—is simply too important to be entrusted to the non-artist.

Without the creative freedom to explore new art forms, creative teams will be incapable of enriching the society in which they work, yet without the income that the more popular art forms are capable of generating, individual arts organizations may simply fail to survive. There is clearly, therefore, a need to reconcile these two extremes of opinion and to strike some form of balance between the preferences of audiences on the one hand, and the needs of those producing the arts on the other. To quote Diggle (1984, 23):

> The whole art of programming for an arts organisation is based on a sensitive appreciation of who the market is, what it wants now *and what it may be persuaded to want in the future* and the relating of those perceptions to what the organisation is capable of delivering.

It would be foolish for any arts organization, no matter how pure its ideals, to completely neglect the current needs of potential audiences. Given the current funding constraints facing the sector, it is simply not realistic to design a comprehensive arts programme without recognizing the need to achieve a balance between those activities that are likely to generate a surplus and those that are likely to make a loss. Only by satisfying current audience desires can an arts organization achieve an adequate revenue stream to support the equally worthwhile fringe activities for which large audiences simply do not exist. Moreover, if audiences can be encouraged to attend a venue to view a more 'popular' art form, it may be possible to persuade a number of them to return to sample other perhaps more obscure forms of art. The adoption of such a strategy therefore guarantees that the organization will have sufficient revenue to support less popular art forms and that as wide an audience as possible can be encouraged to view them. The facilitation of this process is the real contribution that marketing can make to the sector.

Of course, marketing still has to fight for the right to make this contribution and there are often quite healthy debates in many organizations between the artistic and marketing directors, each of whom approaches the design of the next portfolio with a radically different perspective. As Keith Cooper, the first director of public affairs and marketing at the Royal Opera House, puts it:

> Art and commerce have not been happy bedfellows. If we were to be completely commercial I might have to say to the opera director: We can only do the popular productions, we can't do the modern works because they don't sell so many seats. Of course I don't say that because it doesn't get me anywhere. (quoted in Ford, 1993)

(b) Balance in Portrayal

Aside from the need to achieve a balance in terms of the art forms supported, there is often a need to decide on the extent to which an organization is prepared to 'exploit' art for commercial purposes. Just how far should our arts bodies go, for example, in popularizing artistic work to make it more accessible? Many museums, for example, have altered the way in which they present their exhibits in a bid to open up their artefacts to a wider audience. As a consequence many of the larger museums now offer displays which have much in common with theme parks. There are interactive displays, videos, special effects, and a whole new range of promotional merchandise, including children's toys and cheap replicas of historic artefacts. Whilst no one can deny that this has had the desired effect in terms of encouraging larger numbers of the public to attend, there are legitimate concerns that in presenting art in this way, one is actually degrading it. Consumers have simply been encouraged to collect momentary experiences, without any real reflection, and to move hurriedly from one 'fix' of culture to another. As Strehler (1990, 211) comments:

> reducing the presentation of an artistic work to instantaneous, consumable entertainment is consistent with the undeniable needs of the consumers, but misses the primary cultural purpose of revealing its deeper causes.

In short, something of the original experience that the artist intended is lost in the drive to popularization. It is for individual arts organizations to decide how far they are willing to permit this to happen and again, in practice, some form of balance must be struck.

(c) Balance in Audience

The third 'balance' is arguably the most difficult to achieve. As will shortly be demonstrated, the mission of many arts organizations requires them to expand the potential audience for their offerings with almost missionary zeal. Indeed many of the traditional sources of funding for arts activities require that a substantial amount of development work be undertaken to ensure that 'non-standard' audiences are encouraged to attend. Historically, this has proved to be problematic as certain groups within society appear to be openly hostile to much arts related activity (see below). In an attempt to change attitudes, organizations have had to commit valuable marketing resources to the cause and as a result have perhaps neglected their existing core audience. Mokwa *et al.* (1980, 9–10) phrases this somewhat more eloquently, narrating a story of a ship lost at sea for weeks:

> its crew dying of thirst because of no fresh water. Finally, sighting another vessel, the thirsty captain signalled: 'Water, water . . . dying of thirst!' The other ship signalled back: 'Cast down your bucket where you are.' Thinking he was misunderstood, the first captain repeated: 'Water, water . . . send us water!' 'Cast down your bucket where you are,' came the response again. The same messages were repeated again before the first captain thought to cast down his bucket. It came up full of fresh drinkable water. Although adrift on the ocean, the ship was in a sea of fresh water forming the nearly shoreless mouth of the Amazon river.

The moral of the tale, according to the authors, is that arts administrators tend to continue to look elsewhere for their help, rather than exploiting the potential close to home. Arts organizations need to strike a balance between prospecting for new audiences and looking after and cultivating their existing ones. If properly developed, this latter segment can generate much revenue which can in turn be redirected to the task of encouraging other, more reticent segments of society to attend as well.

The Vicious Circle

The achievement of an appropriate balance in each of the areas considered above continues, however, to evade many organizations and has therefore contributed substantially to marketing's delay in gaining acceptance within the sector. Indeed, even where a role for marketing has been recognized, the level of resources organizations are prepared to commit to the task is often pathetically inadequate. This in turn leads to patterns of performance that fail to meet expectations and a general air of 'well, I told you marketing wouldn't work, didn't I!' As long ago as 1991, Marketing the Arts Nationally and Regionally (MANAR) recognized this problem, describing it as a 'vicious circle'. It is illustrated in Fig. 6.1.

Fig. 6.1: **The Vicious Circle**

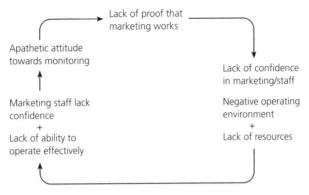

Source: The Arts Council of England. Reproduced by kind permission.

The circle can be viewed as beginning with a lack of resources being applied to the marketing task. This in turn leads to staff being unable to market the organization effectively, which in turn gives rise to a lack of confidence on the part of the relevant personnel. Since staff no longer feel they can make a difference to the enhancement of their organization, they are perhaps less than enthusiastic about monitoring their efforts. Without effective monitoring, there is no evidence to offer senior management that marketing activity is worth while and they become increasingly sceptical about both the abilities of their marketing staff to deliver and the desirability of investing valuable income in that area. As a consequence inadequate resources continue to be made available and the whole process becomes self-perpetuating.

Of course one could also become trapped in the circle by virtue of the cultural hostility that might exist towards the marketing function. Without the commitment of senior management to the marketing function, perhaps because of the misconceptions alluded to above, adequate resources will never be made available. This is to be regretted since the quality of marketing undertaken by an arts organization has recently taken on a new significance. As will be shown later, the criteria applied by the UK's major arts funding bodies require potential applicants to demonstrate their expertise in this area. Marketing can therefore no longer be avoided.

The Arts Audience

Introduction

There has been relatively little academic research conducted to date on the analysis and segmentation of arts audiences. Much of the data that is available is unpublished, of dubious quality, or highly focused on a small group of broad demographic variables. This is to be regretted since an understanding of the type of person who attends specific types of arts events and their motivations for so doing will allow an organization to develop a targeted marketing plan that will reach the prospective audience cost effectively and with a message that they will find most persuasive (Reiss, 1994). As the reader will appreciate from the previous chapter, arts organizations also need to be clear that it should be possible to segment both the market for non-attenders (who may require specific types of recruitment activity) and the market for existing attenders (who may require specific forms of development). In the case of the latter category Ashbrand (1994) reports that the McCarter Theatre in Princeton, New Jersey, has been able to both increase its cash flow and achieve a 20 per cent rise in subscription sales by installing software that enables the theatre management to target shows at individuals they know have an interest in that particular art form. Communications can hence be specifically tailored to the needs of individual groups within the overall customer database. Moreover relationships can be built and maintained with those individuals who are worth the most to the arts organization by virtue of their frequent attendance.

A review of the available research in respect of arts audiences will therefore be instructive and help suggest how an arts organization might attract and develop the potential audience for its own specific services. Moreover, the review should also highlight those audience characteristics which may be deemed to be most important and hence key to the design of an appropriate 'box office' database, a subject which will be developed more fully later.

Audience research may broadly be divided into the following three categories:

(1) studies which delineate specific segments of arts attenders;
(2) studies which examine the motivation of arts attenders;
(3) studies which attempt to profile and categorize non-attenders.

Each of these key groups will now be examined in turn.

Segmenting Arts Attenders

Given the great diversity in art forms, there is a clear potential to segment the market for different categories thereof. Most 'high' art forms, for example, tend to appeal to individuals who have a higher level of education and a higher level of income than the majority of the population (Useem and DiMaggio, 1978). It is also the case that a significantly higher proportion of professional people attend art forms such as the theatre, concerts, or the opera. These findings have been demonstrated by a number of studies in the USA (see, for example, Robbins and Robbins), and in the UK have also been verified by the BMRB (British Market Research Bureau). This latter source of information for audience profiles can be a useful starting point for marketers looking to define a market for the first time. Other commercially available sources of information such as Mintel or Keynote can also prove useful in defining, at least in general terms, what a potential audience might look like.

Useful though this preliminary investigation of arts audiences might be, the reader will recall from the preceding chapter that, within the broad spectrum of individuals who might be predisposed to attend a particular category of event, there might be further sub-segments, many of which are worth exploiting with a separate marketing mix. As an example, Seminik and Young (1979) studied the potential to segment arts audiences using data gathered from a survey of patrons of two large opera companies. The authors concluded that three distinct segments of attender existed:

(1) *Season ticket subcribers* (73.8 per cent of the sample)—individuals who rely for their information about performances on direct mailings from the opera companies themselves. Members of this segment tend to be older, from higher socio-economic groups and have a higher degree of education than the other two segments. Season ticket subscribers attend the opera because they view themselves as fans.

(2) *Infrequent attenders* (11.6 per cent of the sample)—who rely for information about performances on word-of-mouth recommendation from friends and acquaintances. They do not regard themselves as 'fans' in the same way as season ticket subscribers and will tend only to attend if a big name star is performing.

(3) *Non-subscribing frequent attenders* (14.6 per cent of the sample)—who also rely on word-of-mouth recommendation for information. This group also regards itself as being a general fan of the opera, but is younger and less well-educated than the season ticket subscriber segment.

These findings are important in so far as they suggest that an arts organization could draw a distinction between each category and apply a mix of attraction and retention activities to each. This idea is illustrated in Fig. 6.2. Subscribers are clearly committed to attendance at a particular venue. They are likely to have the most frequent pattern of attendance and be worth a significant sum of money to an arts organization over the duration of their relationship with it. The loss of even a small percentage of the members of this segment per annum will therefore result in a significant drop in revenue. It is therefore important that considerable effort is expended in keeping this segment loyal. As they are already enthusiastic about the arts 'product', they do not need to be 're-convinced' of its merits. Instead the focus with this group should be in establishing and building a meaningful relationship which builds loyalty and keeps retention rates high.

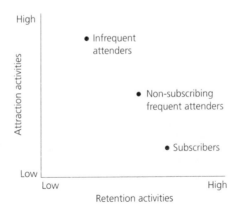

Fig. 6.2: **A Classification of Arts Customers**

Non-subscribing frequent attenders are somewhat more problematic. Evidence suggests that this segment will attend a very wide variety of different categories of event and it may be difficult to build loyalty in the face of competition from other venues which are perceived as of equal value. A mix of attraction and retention activities might hence be more appropriate.

Infrequent attenders are likely to have to be convinced of the 'need' to attend specific events and the focus with this category will hence lie in attraction. They will therefore need to be informed of the merits of a particular performance, why it represents a particular opportunity and the status of the 'star' that is performing. Efforts to develop this group further are likely to be futile since they will tend only to attend performances that are perceived as in some way unique. It is interesting to note though that many arts managers would disagree with this assessment, arguing that infrequent attenders could be developed over time and eventually become subscribers. There is no evidence however that this is actually the case. Ryans and Weinberg (1978) in a five-year study of theatre audiences attempted to verify their hypothesis that an entry pattern to subscriptions existed. The researchers felt that subscribers would begin as single-ticket buyers, progress to the purchase of several tickets in a season, and then ultimately become a season-ticket holder. They found quite surprisingly that there was a high incidence of sudden subscribers (those who subscribed without attending previously) and were hence forced to conclude that their perception of an entry pattern to the arts was invalid.

Additional studies which have examined attendance patterns at other forms of arts events have derived similar findings to those given above. Importantly, Kaali-Nagy and Garrison (1972) were amongst the first to recognize that the Pareto principle can be applied equally well to arts audiences and, in their study of the Los Angeles Music Center, found that 10 per cent of the patrons accounted for nearly 45 per cent of the attendance pattern of their sample. The authors thus concluded that a relatively small number of people constituted the core of the Center's audience. Importantly these findings have been replicated at other venues and indeed in other countries (see, for example, Sargeant, 1997).

Businesses will of course be familiar with the Pareto rule and will ensure that they expend considerable effort on those customers who generate the majority of their income. The same does not yet seem to apply to arts organizations though, and in particular to theatres. If there are certain segments of society who may be deemed regular attenders of arts events, these segments should surely be the focus of considerable effort. Such segments are by their very nature the easiest to encourage to attend and may hence be readily developed over time. Indeed, Dawson (1980, 7) identified what he saw as a paradox in arts management, namely that of

the missionary effort (taking place) to develop arts audiences from those marginally interested and the near exclusion of effort to develop the fullest possible response from that segment of society most likely to support the arts.

This latter point is worthy of some elaboration since many arts organizations still fail to recognize the need to focus on those customers who are potentially worth the most to their organization. After all, a customer who spends £500 a year with an organization is certainly worth more than a customer who spends only £5 over the same period. Many die-hard artistic directors may regard this as heresy, but they would be wrong to do so! It is important to realize that a careful cultivation of high-worth customers can yield valuable revenue which can then be applied meaningfully to the more missionary aspects of an organization's work. In short, marketing does not mean the abandonment of artistic values, it can actually enrich them.

Audience Motivation

The second important category of research into arts audiences concerns an examination of their motivations for attendance. An understanding of why people attend and what features they will be looking for in an arts event can greatly aid marketing planning, since the 'product' can be carefully adapted to the target market and promotional messages can reflect the themes that a particular audience is likely to find most appealing. Valuable though this data might be, however, comparatively few arts organizations are likely to have access to it, and there are only a few secondary studies which are available for consultation. If this form of data is required, therefore, there may be no alternative but to conduct primary research.

Usually such research will either take the form of focus groups or questionnaires. In the case of the former, a group of 8–10 customers will typically be assembled and a general discussion about an art form and/or a specific venue will be initiated. The discussion is usually led by a trained researcher and is audio or video taped for subsequent analysis. Much insight can be gained through the careful use of this technique into underlying motivations for attendance. The drawback of the approach, however, is that relatively few individuals will actually be involved and the results therefore may be difficult to generalize. They can also be costly since participants (and researchers!) have to be paid for their time.

The use of questionnaires, on the other hand, can allow an organization to take a greater sample of opinion amongst its target audience at a relatively low cost. They do, however, have the drawback that due to space/time constraints only a fraction of the data provided by a focus group can typically be collected. It is also not possible to probe respondents to discover the underlying rationale for their answers. In the arts context, questionnaires tend either to be administered by staff asking selected visitors a series of questions about their enjoyment of a visit, or through the mail—questionnaires being sent to a representative sample of known attenders. The latter form of approach is probably the least intrusive, but will typically only generate a response rate of between 10 and 15 per cent.

An excerpt from a postal questionnaire that was employed to profile theatre audiences in the South West of England is given in Exhibit 6.1. The use of even a simple questionnaire such as this one can pay enormous dividends for an arts organization. Demographic data from questions 1–6 can be cross-tabulated with the responses to question 10 to yield a profile of those most likely to attend a particular category of event. Moreover, data from question 12 can also be of value in allowing the researcher to profile more frequent attenders for the purposes described in the previous section.

However, for our purposes we are now interested in ascertaining whether a particular series of motivations might exist for attending the theatre. At a simplistic level we could simply examine the pattern of responses to question 13, but this would tell us little about how these motivations might vary between different categories of individual, and this latter information is really quite essential for the derivation of a meaningful communications campaign. Fortunately however, there are a variety of statistical techniques that can be used to help facilitate a more sophisticated level of analysis. One of the more useful, but often neglected, forms of analysis is the technique of cluster analysis. An example of its application is given in Case 6.1 below:

Questionnaire

1. Are You

☐ Male   ☐ Female

2. Year of Birth _____

3. Are you presently

☐ In full-time employment
☐ In part-time employment
☐ Retired
☐ Housewife
☐ Other

4. Are you

☐ Single
☐ Married
☐ Other

5. How many people are there in your household? _____

6. Do you have children living with you at home?

☐ Yes   ☐ No

If yes, how many? _____

What are their ages? _____   _____   _____   _____   _____   _____

7. What are your hobbies and interests?

_____
_____
_____
_____

8. What is/was your main occupation? _____

9. At what age did you complete your full-time education?

☐ Aged 16 or younger
☐ Aged 17/18
☐ Aged 18/20
☐ Aged 21+

10. How likely are you to attend any of the following categories of performance at the XYZ theatre? Please indicate your level of interest using the following scale.

1 = Not at all likely
2 = Not very likely
3 = No opinion/neutral
4 = Somewhat likely
5 = Very likely

	Likelihood of Attendance				
Category of Performance	**1**	**2**	**3**	**4**	**5**
Classic Plays					
New Plays					
Comedies					
Musical Comedies					
Dance					
Ballet					
Other (Please Specify) _____					

11. When you attend the theatre, how important are each of the following factors in influencing your selection of which theatre to attend? Please use the following scale to select your response.

1 = Not at all important
2 = Not very important
3 = No opinion/neutral
4 = Important
5 = Very important

	Importance				
Factor	**1**	**2**	**3**	**4**	**5**
Category/Type of Performance					
Reputation of Performers					
Presence of a 'Big Name'					
Cost of Tickets					
Ease of Booking					
Presence of a Bar					
Cleanliness of the Theatre					
Comfort of the Seating					

12. On how many occasions would you attend the theatre in a typical year? _____

13. For what reason do you normally attend the theatre? Please tick any boxes that apply.

☐ To Socialize with Friends and Relatives   ☐ To Enjoy a Night Out
☐ To Celebrate a Special Occasion   ☐ I Enjoy Attending Arts Event
☐ To Learn Something   ☐ Other (Please Specify) _____

14. To what extent would each of the following factors be likely to encourage you to attend the theatre more often?

Factor	Would Encourage More Regular Attendance	Would Not Encourage More Regular Attendance	No Opinion/ Unsure
Lower Prices			
Easier Booking Facilities			
Availability of a Season Ticket			
Early Booking Facility			
Availability of Discounts			
Better Range of Performances			
Other (Please Specify) _____			

15. How likely are you to attend any of the arts venues listed below during the next 12 months? Please use the following scale for your reply.

1 = Not at all likely
2 = Not very likely
3 = No opinion/neutral
4 = Somewhat likely
5 = Very likely

Venue	Likelihood of Attendance				
	1	2	3	4	5
Museums					
Concerts					
Art Gallery					
Cinema					
Arts Centre					

Case Study 6.1: **In Search of the Ageing Socialite**

This case study reports the results of theatre audience research conducted in south west England during 1995. A similar questionnaire to that illustrated in Exhibit 6.1 was administered to 500 known theatre-goers in an attempt to identify whether specific segments of theatre audience existed, each of which might have differing motivations for its pattern of attendance. The technique of cluster analysis was therefore selected as this allows the market researcher to identify potential market segments amongst the total group of individuals who respond (in this case) to a questionnaire. The cluster analysis algorithm begins by searching the dataset for those two individuals whose questionnaire responses were most alike, and pairs these two individuals off. It then looks for the next two most similarly answered questionnaires and pairs these two individuals off. As the programme works through the dataset it continues to look for the next closest match in terms of the pattern of responses. This may involve pairing off two more individuals, matching one individual to one of the newly created pairings, or even creating groups of 4, 8, 16, etc. as appropriate. This 'matching up' process continues until all the respondents are finally reunited in one large mass. Consider the example shown in Fig. 6.3. In this case there are only eight respondents to a questionnaire that we wish to analyse. The analysis proceeds as described above from stage 1, where only individual responses exist, to stage 8, where they are all combined as one group. Whilst in itself this might appear a rather fruitless task, the algorithm helpfully records the level of difference that is being combined at each stage. Between stages 1 and 2 it is comparatively easy to find respondents who have given almost identical responses to the questionnaire. Between stages 5 and 6, it remains comparatively easy, but within each group of individuals there is almost certainly now an element of variation in the pattern of responses (a difference of opinion!). Between stages 7 and 8 this variation will undoubtedly be more pronounced as individuals with ever differing responses are combined into the same group.

Fig. 6.3: **The Process of Cluster Analysis**

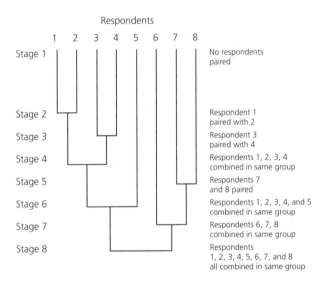

The trick in using this technique is to examine the measures of difference at each stage in the process and, when the amount of difference between the individuals within a group jumps sharply, to recognize that the pattern of responses within a new pairing is no longer coherent. In plain English one has to recognize when oranges begin to be combined with bananas! If, for example, the amount of difference measured in the responses within each group is seen to jump sharply between stages 6 and 7, the researcher would recognize that there would appear to be three distinct segments of respondents amongst the eight individuals analysed. Any attempt to further reduce the number of segments to two would be inappropriate, since the software then begins to combine into one group individuals who are not alike at all. Ideally the amount of difference in response within a segment should be as small as possible, and the amount of difference between the segments as large as possible. In our example a three-cluster solution is thus recommended—Segment 1 containing respondents 1, 2, 3, 4 and 5,

Segment 2 containing only respondent 6, and Segment 3 containing respondents 7 and 8. Of course in reality the number of respondents would have to be much greater for the analysis to be meaningful and a segment containing only a few respondents would normally be discounted, but the example does serve to illustrate how the clustering algorithm works.

In an effort to make this clearer, examine for a moment Table 6.1. The table contains the results of the cluster analysis conducted on the theatre-goers in south west England. Having performed the cluster analysis it appeared that three distinct groups of customers existed. The table presents the typical answer of each segment to each of the questions contained in the original questionnaire. Importantly the motivations for at-

Table 6.1
Cluster Profile of Theatre-goers in South West England

	Cluster 1	Cluster 2	Cluster 3
Demographics			
Education	16–18	16	21+
Age of Children at Home	Even Distribution	Parents—Younger Children 11–20	Even Distribution
Age	Predominantly Younger (35 and Under)	Predominantly Middle Aged (36–45)	Older (46+)
Marital Status	Single	Married	Even Distribution
Gender	Even Distribution	Even Distribution	Even Distribution
Preferred Performance Type			
Dance	Very Likely	Neutral	Somewhat Likely
New Play	Somewhat Likely	Somewhat Likely	Very Likely
Drama	Somewhat Likely	Neutral	Very Likely
Ballet	Somewhat Likely	Not At All Likely	Not Very Likely
Classic Plays	Somewhat Likely	Neutral	Very Likely
Musical Comedy	Even Distribution	Very Likely	Not At All Likely
Comedies	Neutral	Neutral	Neutral
Other Arts Venues Attended			
Art Gallery	Very Likely	Not Very Likely	Likely
Cinema	Very Likely	Unlikely	Neutral
Concerts	Somewhat Likely	Neutral	Very Likely
Museums	Neutral	Neutral	Neutral
Facilities Required			
Bar	Neutral	Neutral	Very Important
Ease of Booking	Neutral	Neutral	Important
Cleanliness of Theatre	Important	Important	Neutral
Comfort of Seating	Important	Important	Fairly Important
Factors Capable of Encouraging Attendance			
Lower Price	No	Neutral	Yes
Ease of Ordering	Yes	No	Yes
Purchase of a Season Ticket	Yes	No	No
Ticket Availability Guaranteed	Neutral	No	No
Early Booking	Neutral	No	Neutral
Availability of Discounts	Neutral	Neutral	Yes
Better Range of Performances	Neutral	Neutral	Neutral
Attendance Pattern			
Frequency of Attendance	Medium	Low	High
Segment Size			
Percentage of Total	27%	24%	49%

Table 6.2
**Reasons for
Audience
Attendance at
Theatre Events**

Reason	Segment 1	Segment 2	Segment 3
To Socialize with Friends and Relatives	28%	63%	56%
Celebrating a Special Occasion	38%	75%	48%
To Learn Something	45%	27%	43%
A Night Out	43%	50%	26%
Enjoy Arts Events	52%	20%	25%

Please note that the column totals do not add up to 100% since respondents were asked to tick any reasons that they felt applied

tending the theatre were also found to vary quite considerably between the segments identified. These are shown in Table 6.2. Armed with this information it is then possible to proceed to naming each segment. In this case the categories of Nouveaux Sophisticats, Blue Mooners and Ageing Socialites suggested themselves. A brief profile of each segment follows.

(a) Nouveaux Sophisticats (27 per cent of the total population)

This is the youngest of the three segments and is comprised ostensibly of young adults, many of whom may still be in full-time education. Of the three segments they are the most likely to be single and committed to attendance at a wide range of different arts events. They have an interest in most forms of art and would potentially consider viewing any type of performance at their local theatre.

They require few additional facilities from the theatre but expect that the accommodation will be clean and comfortable. Given that this segment appear committed to the arts in general they are less susceptible to price than other groups and are more likely to consider the purchase of a season ticket as a positive means of encouraging them to attend on a regular basis. It may also be the case that this segment are less susceptible to price than other segments because they already attract substantial discounts. Many theatres are, for example, willing to offer a discount on performances for those still in full-time education.

Implications for Marketing

This group is possibly the easiest to target since they are regular attenders at arts events, and leaflets distributed at other arts venues may well attract this audience. As members of this group are committed to the arts, promotional messages must surely concentrate on raising awareness of the scope and range of events available locally. Advertising themes such as product quality, variety, pleasant surroundings, aesthetics, and the theatre's facilities may be particularly appropriate.

(b) Blue Mooners (24 per cent of the total population)

The least well educated segment, Blue Mooners are so named because they are only infrequent attenders (that is, they attend only 'once in a blue moon'). They are likely to be married couples, possibly with teenage children who view a trip to the theatre as a special occasion. They do not appear to be committed to a wide range of art forms and prefer to see only a limited number of types of performance at their local theatre. In particular they are likely to attend musical comedies and modern plays. They share with Nouveaux Sophisticats a need for few additional features in the theatre itself but do require clean and comfortable surroundings. This is to be expected given the motivation of this segment for attendance at a theatrical performance. Blue Mooners are also less susceptible than other groups to any promotional method that might be aimed at encouraging them to attend on a more regular basis. Clearly there is little demand in this segment for the theatrical product except for a special occasion and this is reflected in the fact that this segment exhibits the lowest attendance rate (that is, once a year or less).

Implications for Marketing

This is potentially the most difficult segment to motivate to attend on a more regular basis, and indeed the research suggests that promotional methods aimed at persuading this group to attend more frequently will be largely ineffective. Clearly theatre management will want to make every effort to develop this segment into more frequent attenders by providing an experience of memorable quality that the individual will consider worthy of repeating. However, given that many individuals in this segment will make their purchase decision quite late and do not see early booking as an advantage, it seems probable that advertisements in local press and local radio may be most appropriate (research suggests that radio advertisements are particularly well suited to enhancing theatre audiences as the date of performance draws near).

(c) Ageing Socialites (49 per cent of the population)

The oldest segment (predominantly over 45), Ageing Socialites have a particular interest in all types of play and would also consider viewing other related art forms such as concerts, ballet, and dance. However, they appear not to be so interested in the various forms of comedy.

   The primary motivation of this group is to share in a social occasion and hence the presence of a bar is particularly important to share a drink during the performance. Theatre attendance clearly forms an integral part of their social life and this is reflected in the fact that they exhibit a higher rate of attendance than members of the other two segments. The exact nature of the performance seems less important to this group, who instead cite price, discounts, and ease of ordering as being amongst the most important factors that might influence their decision to attend.

Implications for Marketing

Members of this group are clearly motivated by the social aspects of an evening's performance and successful promotional messages will reflect this. The theatre could also emphasize the facilities that it has to offer and suggest how these can enhance the social value of the evening. Potential themes include service, comfort, ease, enjoyment, attention, entertainment, friendship, status, leisure, etc. In terms of marketing strategy an evening at the theatre could be repositioned as a venue through which individuals could meet and socialize. Promotional brochures and leaflets could be changed to reflect the social exchange that many individuals seem to require, and stark illustrations of artwork related to each performance or photographs of the performers themselves might be supplemented (or replaced) by pictures of patrons relaxing in the bar and being seen to enjoy themselves. If it is the interaction that is important to the largest percentage of the audience then such a theme should at the very least feature in a season's brochure.

It is worth emphasizing this latter point. If this segment is worth the most to an arts organization, it follows logically that the organization would wish to periodically demonstrate that it is capable of meeting its needs. An emphasis on the social aspects of an evening's entertainment could hence pay dividends in encouraging more frequent attendance. It is also worth noting that the Ageing Socialite segment has a high propensity to attend a variety of events on an extremely frequent basis. This suggests that many arts organizations would gain considerable utility from co-operation in the form of list sharing. It would appear that the highest value customers are likely to be the highest value customers of other related arts organizations.

The idea developed in the case study that the social aspects of attendance at an arts event are important is not without support in the literature. In an interesting study of attendance at live musical events Levy *et al.* (1980) conducted a series of in-depth interviews with middle class music lovers. The authors found that audiences tended to prefer this type of event because of the perceived immediacy and involvement in the creative process. The social aspect of attendance was also found to be important, although in the case of what the authors call 'high culture' events (such as opera) this manifested itself quite formally—perhaps through the inclusion of a dinner, or a meeting with friends in the interval—in the plan for the evening as a whole. In the case of rock concerts, the social aspects were equally important but rather less formal—including travelling with friends to the event, and smoking, drinking, and eating together at the event itself.

Clearly the exact relevance of the social aspect of the entertainment will vary between one category of the arts and another. The key point for marketers to recognize, however, is that this social component exists and can be extremely important to an audience. Thus if carefully cultivated it can pay enormous dividends. One organization which does recognize the importance of social interaction, and actively promotes and encourages it, is Performing Arts Management.

Case Study 6.2: **Performing Arts Management**

Performing Arts Management (PAM) was founded in 1990 and has quickly expanded to be the leader in its field. The organization provides a series of concerts held at stately homes all over the UK each summer. Over 150,000 tickets are sold per season for a variety of classical performances, including music by Vivaldi, Tchaikovsky, Rossini, and Strauss. The aim of PAM is essentially to provide a full evening's entertainment in the beautiful surroundings of some of the nation's finest stately homes. The concerts are all held in the open air and many are accompanied by fireworks, laser displays, and Dancing Waters. The latter represents quite a feat of engineering, as a complicated series of pumps and levers force jets of water up through 2,000 nozzles of different shapes, sizes, and apertures to create water formations which undulate in response to the sounds and rhythms of the music. The result is an experience which plays on a variety of the senses to draw the audience into an appreciation of the beauty of the music being performed.

The 'service' offered by PAM therefore consists of an effective mix of music, spectacle, the beauty of some of the nation's finest stately homes, and, somewhat unusually, a picnic. Since all the concerts are held in the open air, a tradition has developed for audiences to bring along their own picnic hampers and to enjoy the concert whilst eating their sandwiches, or sipping a glass of champagne. PAM have therefore determined that they are not marketing Strauss or Tchaikovsky, but rather a social event at which people can meet to enjoy good food, wine, conversation, and a high quality of entertainment in beautiful surroundings. In short, all the ingredients of the 'service' neatly complement each other and contribute to the evening's overall effectiveness.

The idea of positioning the concerts as an evening's entertainment has also been reflected very successfully in PAM's promotional literature. Rather than concentrating solely on the background to the musical works being performed, or on the biographies of the musicians, the brochure instead chooses to develop, with equal zeal, the informality and fun nature of the visit. The reader may therefore find pictures of the concerts themselves and, unusually (in arts marketing), pictures of the audience enjoying their picnic and having a good time (see Exhibit 6.2).

The organization currently sells more tickets than any other organization engaged in the same activity and has developed to be a leader in its field, increasing its audiences by approximately 3,000 per annum. Why, then, has PAM been so successful?

The key to answering this question must undoubtedly be PAM's detailed understanding of its target market. The organization targets young and settled couples, aged 25 plus, predominantly from socio-economic groups A and B. From experience PAM knows that this target group are buying 'atmosphere' and this is reflected not only in the manner in which the classical music is supported (through lasers, etc.) but also through the informal nature of the picnics. To ensure that regular feedback is obtained on the quality of the evenings, most PAM staff travel with the orchestra and socialize with the audience at each venue. As the marketing manager explains, 'we walk through the audience and chat with them'.

PAM jealously guards its database. It makes a point of not selling its contacts to other organizations who might relish the opportunity of contacting over 58,000 people with the profile given above. PAM feels that any such move would anger its clients and damage what has developed into an extremely close relationship. For similar reasons mailings are contained to a maximum of two to three per annum.

The database has been painstakingly built over the past seven years by a combination of selective advertising and leaflet drops. Details of each enquiry the organization has received as a result have been carefully recorded. No lists have ever been purchased and the organization does not envisage the need to do so. In terms of its advertising PAM has traditionally relied on a mixture of both regional and local press, carefully timed to raise awareness two to three months before a given concert date. The organization also makes use of public relations activities and so, for example, journalists are regularly given free passes to sample the atmosphere at a particular performance. By far the most potent promotional tool, however, has been word of mouth. Couples who sampled a concert for the first time one year will often return subsequently with their friends or families.

So successful has the organization been that approximately half of the concerts they provide each year sell out well in advance of the date of the performance. When one considers that a venue might typically accommodate over 7,000 people, this pays testimony to the phenomenally high loyalty rates exhibited by PAM's customers.

Exhibit 6.2 PAM
**Promotional
Literature**

Despite the affluent nature of PAM's target market, ticket prices compare very favourably with those of other arts venues and would typically be set at between £15 and £17 per person. Indeed, given that clients may typically spend up to six hours at a venue, the organization is clearly able to supply value far superior to that offered by most direct or indirect competitors. Pricing is decided largely on the basis of 'cost plus' and the organization does not currently see the need to engage in any forms of promotional pricing.

The organization selects venues each year on the basis of whether PAM believes there are sufficient members of its target audience nearby to break even. If there is a good chance that a venue will not break even the organization will elect not to perform there. However, PAM does elect to perform some music which it knows will prove less popular with potential clients but which, nevertheless, the artistic management feel they would like to do. In recent times, PAM has therefore included an evening of the music of Sibelius on its programme, even though they recognized that the concert would be unlikely to break even. Their justification for this venture was simply that they felt 'this was something we wanted to do'.

It is interesting to note that PAM consciously decided against sharing their database with other organizations (perhaps at a profit). Given the nature of their target group this could quite clearly have been a very lucrative activity. Nevertheless the organization has resisted the temptation, feeling that to share such information would betray something of the personal relationship it has built up with its customers.

It is important to note, however, that in different circumstances the sharing of information, perhaps with a commercial organization, can actually serve to enhance customer value whilst at the same time serving the interests of all the parties involved. Stanley (1995) cites the example of the Continuum Group which enters all attenders into a database by asking them to fill out a registration card in return for promotional discounts and related merchandise. The data is then made available to suitable participating advertisers to the benefit of all involved.

Organizations could also actively solicit a corporate partner which has a similar customer profile to that which the organization itself is seeking and, as Brightman (1994, 25) points out, approaches to new customers can then be made at no cost to the arts organization. She cites the example of San Diego's Globe Theatre which has sold discounted seats to members of a credit union. The union viewed the service as 'a benefit that could be offered to their members to help retain loyalty'. (For a further example of such collaborative marketing, see Selwitz, 1992).

Non-Attenders

Mention has already been made of the need for many arts organizations to broaden their appeal through societal groups that would not normally consider attending an arts event. Indeed the ability to be able to attract non-traditional audiences may be a requirement for the attraction of funding. Identifying and categorizing non-users can therefore be of equal utility to an arts organization, since different forms of non-user may prove susceptible to different forms of approach in attempts to persuade them to sample the arts for the first time. Diggle (1984) makes a particularly strong argument for this approach in recognition of the fact that many arts organizations have a mission to develop audiences across as wide a spectrum of society as possible. He concludes that there are three segments of non-attenders:

(1) *The Intenders.* These are individuals who have a positive perception of the arts and plan to go to a venue or performance at some stage in the future, but who for various reasons never quite seem to get around to it. Clearly, an organization wishing to develop this group may need to find some way to 'incentivize' them, perhaps through the creative use of sales promotion type techniques.

(2) *The Indifferent.* This group have no strong opinions about the arts and have no great motivation to set about attending. They are an interesting group, however, because they tend not to have negative perceptions of the arts and may be suitable candidates for development if positive attitudes can be encouraged.

(3) *The Hostile.* From an arts marketer's perspective this segment will hardly be worth pursuing at all. They have clear and firmly established negative attitudes towards the arts and will tend to dislike most arts forms altogether. Clearly, if an arts organization is to make an effective use of its marketing resources there will be little point in focusing specifically on this segment.

Of course, there may be some merit in attempting to address all of the segments that Diggle identifies, but the approach will be radically different in each case. In the case of the intenders, the barrier to achieving attendance is relatively small. Members of this segment need either to be given some incentive to attend, or it needs to be made easier for them to do so. Interestingly the Royal National Theatre identified a need some years ago to encourage a sub-group of intenders to attend its performances. In particular they identified that students in the London area constituted an important audience for the theatre's work, not only because they represented the potential audience of tomorrow, but also because they could potentially become an important part of the audience today. To get them to attend, however, was no easy matter as a number of barriers needed to be overcome. Price was clearly a key barrier, but the theatre also determined that inertia and the fact that this target group was unlikely to consider booking an evening's entertainment in advance were key problems that had to be overcome. Case study 6.3 describes the marketing approach that was adopted in an effort to circumvent these difficulties.

Case Study 6.3: **Royal National Theatre—Student Rep Scheme**

The National Theatre has recently implemented a new strategy designed to develop fully the potential of its student audience. In 1991 the theatre set up a student representative scheme, the aim of which was to encourage a larger proportion of the capital's student population to attend its performances. The scheme was originally developed in partnership with *Time Out* magazine as there was felt to be considerable synergy between what the two organizations could offer students in the London area.

The basic premise was that there should be as many representatives in London as possible in universities and colleges. Each representative would act on behalf of *Time Out* and the National to raise awareness amongst their peers about the services that both organizations could offer. At the most basic level of involvement, representatives would be expected to circulate publicity material and to ensure that posters were regularly displayed on their campus detailing forthcoming productions, events, etc.

To recruit its reps the National has produced a student leaflet, which provides full details of all student services including the rep scheme. These leaflets are distributed at Freshers fairs each year, which members of National staff also attend to raise awareness of the theatre amongst as many students as possible. Potential reps are asked to write in with details about themselves and why they want to join the scheme. Applicants are subsequently invited to attend for a brief informal interview. Successful students then join the scheme and attend regular meetings held alternately at the National and *Time Out* to be appraised of the new productions, student events, and promotions. The National now has fifty reps and they meet once a month during term time.

Each rep is expected to promote the services that the National can offer to students, including its very popular Student Standby scheme. By using this scheme students can gain access to performances at substantially reduced rates. Although, with the exception of the first preview of all new productions, it is not possible to purchase these tickets in advance (they can only be bought on the day, 45 minutes before curtain up), students can access a performance which might typically cost £27 for only £7.50. It is also interesting to note that the scheme operates on the basis of the best available ticket, so students can often access some of the best seats in the house for the cost of their £7.50 admission fee.

The availability of student standby is promoted by the student reps through 'Standby' posters which warn students in advance of what is likely to be available. These posters are updated each week and posted to reps for display. Availability is also flagged up in the student section of the *Time Out* magazine. Take-up of student standby has improved significantly as a result of the scheme and importantly for the theatre, take-up does not seem to be related to the general popularity of a particular production. This is important, since whilst students are afforded the opportunity to view a performance at a heavily subsidised rate, their presence may enhance the experience for all, as they increase the overall size of the audience thereby contributing to the quality of the ambience in the auditorium.

Aside from the dissemination of information, reps can often help in other ways, perhaps by organizing trips to National performances. One student rep recently organized a group of sixty-seven students who might otherwise not have thought to come. It is very clear that reps can provide an additional impetus to encourage others to attend. At Colleges where there are strong drama groups, however, it may not be necessary for reps to organize trips, as their peers will attend anyway to complement their studies. At such institutions the reps elect to promote awareness of other National services such as the Platform performances. These consist of 45 minute talks by writers or directors immediately in advance of a show, something that would quite clearly be of interest to a typical drama student.

To encourage rep loyalty the National and *Time Out* provide a number of incentives. Student reps get access to the building, to marketing staff, and to special offers or deals that they would not normally have access to. They also qualify for a free ticket to a performance when they book a group of twelve people or more. There are therefore small 'perks' and rewards, but the scheme remains essentially voluntary.

Since its conception the scheme has continued to build each year and loyalty rates are high. If people join the scheme in the first year of their degree they tend to continue in their second and third years. By doing so, they become increasingly valuable to the National as they begin to extend their contacts throughout the Student Union and the student publication office. This assists them to enhance the profile of the National, and a small number of reps even contribute reviews to student publications (see Exhibit 6.3). To assist the students who wish to do this, the National provides free press tickets to its preview performances.

The student rep scheme has become an integral part of the theatre's overall marketing mix and marketing staff regard it is an important tool for ensuring that students are encouraged to attend the National on as frequent a basis as possible. Thereafter, by providing them with a memorable experience the theatre hopes that their loyalty will be retained when they complete their degree and that they will continue to patronize the National for many years to come.

In the case of the 'indifferent' category the marketing task is clearly one of changing attitudes. An interesting piece of research by Cooper and Tower (1994, 306) suggested that many who are indifferent to the arts may not attend because:

- they lack confidence in their ability to enjoy the arts, possibly due to a lack of education or any form of background in the subject;
- of social pressure from peer groups acting to dissuade individuals from sampling the arts;
- there is a feeling that the arts are only for the upper classes;
- of the positive alternative of television which has achieved the status of myth and 'meta medium' and which comprises many consumers' social and intellectual universe.

If a more positive attitude towards the arts could be cultivated, there is a high probability that in future the members of this group could be persuaded to attend. Members of this segment will need considerable encouragement, however, and the process of persuasion may require a substantial investment in both human and financial resources. There are a number of development strategies that could be adopted with this group.

(1) *Investment in Education*. Links could be forged with schools and colleges to encourage young people to sample (and even participate in) the arts. School parties could be encouraged to visit arts organizations and encouraged to interact with staff in workshops/seminars, etc. Staff could provide guest 'lectures' in schools which support the national curriculum and in the case of some larger organizations educational material could even be produced to help young people appreciate the art form in question. One art gallery in the USA produced a series of Impressionist kits consisting of slides of twelve paintings, biographies of the artists, texts on the movement, and suggested questions for discussion. There was even a copy of Renoir's wife's famous chicken recipe.

Exposure to the arts in this way can therefore be non-threatening and may serve to demystify the arts for a new generation of young people. Indeed if an interest can be cultivated, a proportion of them may even persuade friends and relatives to sample an art form for the first time.

Exhibit 6.3

Modern times

Christina Patrick on sexliesandInternet

I'm no renowned theatre critic. Yet. But on average I see around three plays a week. That's a hell of a lot of plays per year. Some are great, some are mediocre and a few I walk out of.

Closer is without a doubt the best thing I've seen on stage this year. It's very rarely that something blows me away like this. If I made this many notes in lectures I might actually survive my degree, but somehow I need to condense ten pages of frantic scribblings on the brilliance in front of my eyes into a readable review. Tough one.

Closer is a brutally realistic and painfully clear presentation on human communication, interaction and relationships. It's incisively funny, packed with wry observational humour and unnerving insight into the human mind and its irrational workings.

There are four people: Dan and Larry and Anna and Alice, and for two hours we follow their interwoven lives through love, hate, abuse, loss, sex, revenge and a thousand emotions in between that for once aren't some epic tragedy but shown in their true habitat: real life. Communication is searingly direct and personal or detached and incomprehending.

Men want a girl who looks like a boy. She must come like a train, but with elegance... Liza Walker's tense combination of fragile child and toughened punk breathes complex life into Alice, the lost soul who meets obituarist Dan in a road accident and falls deeply, unaccountably and savagely in love with him. He uses her life story for a novel and they move up the ladder of partial success, meeting Anna (Sally Dexter), a photographer, who took Dan's dustcover picture, and Larry, a doctor at the hospital where Alice and Dan met, while their lives start to become increasingly entangled in a pleasingly balanced sort of way. Dan brings Anna and Larry together through a deliciously foul mouthed Internet sequence where Dan pretends to be a whore-ish Anna and we can see the whole "conversation" on a giant screen behind the men:

Mid 30s. Dark hair. Big mouth. Epic tits.
Perfectly timed pause.
Define epic.

It's fascinating to see the people behind the anonymous Internet connections, the harsh green words on the screen describing the most intimate acts... We are complicit in their mutual fantasies, caught in the humour of people exposing their most private thoughts, and then Marber hits you with Dan's instantly quotable sledgehammer sentences:

Life without risk is death. The best sex is anonymous. We live as we dream, alone.

Marber set out to write a Jonsonian city comedy of manners, and what he has produced is an acerbic and icily accurate reflection of modern life and thought. Phrases like "I fucking love you" for us have to be the currency of this strange thing called love, the old words are too tired, we can only inject new life into them with obscenities that are so widely used that perhaps they aren't even obscene anymore. Language is direct—more "fucks" per minute than the BBC would tolerate.

Private moments are shown to us in cringing detail: Larry's confession of sex with a New York prostitute is quickly followed by Anna's confession of her affair with Dan and the ensuing vicious interrogation: Was it good? Better than me? Where? When? The connections weave in and out of the play, covering modern sexual mores and the assumptions behind the roles men and women play and create for themselves.

The actors are all perfectly adequate, with superb comic timing, particularly Sally Dexter: "You're a man. You'd come if the tooth fairy winked at you." She has real stage presence and brings complex human depth the Anna, who would otherwise be in danger of becoming a creaky stereotype.

This play covers so many ideas—it manages to be intellectually incendiary yet still hold a taut and compelling narrative. It reminds us how "every human life has a million stories" and of the demands we make on ourselves and those we love or think we love: love, that crazy, warped, nebulous, mythical quality that still fuels our lives. It has been deconstructed and challenged by modern time, but somehow, despite all the evidence, we want to believe.

Source: The London Student, December 1997.

(2) *Facility Enhancement*. A second option concerns altering the nature of the art facility itself. Whilst this is not a move to be taken lightly, some arts organizations, particularly those with display material, can optimize the use thereof to attract new audiences. Ricklefs (1975, 169) cites the example of Washington's National Gallery which started a separate exhibition department with a full-time architect with this very thought in mind. The aim was to enhance for the public the enjoyment of the art works on display and by so doing to make them accessible to a wider proportion of society. As an example, to provide the rustic background for a show of Alaskan native art, the gallery acquired weathered boards from a man who made his living tearing down old barns. Stone statues were placed on deer hides and the lights were arranged to simulate the Arctic sunlight. 'In the old days (they) just hung things on the wall.'

Of course there is a real need not to alienate traditional audiences by being seen to cheapen the arts through the use of gimmicks, but in the example quoted above, the reader will note that the gallery had gone to great lengths to ensure that the ambience supporting their works was as authentic as possible. In short the changes introduced served to enhance the experience for both new and existing customers alike.

(3) *Portfolio Enhancement*. It may also be possible to encourage new audiences to attend a given venue by extending the range of art forms that are supported. Most categories of art contain forms that are perceived as more accessible by the general public. If these are from time to time included in the portfolio, new customers might be attracted who might otherwise not have attended. Moreover, if they enjoy their experience they may be persuaded to sample other art forms that would hitherto have lacked an appeal. In the case of museums, travelling exhibitions could for example be booked. Often these are of great public interest and, whilst they might represent something of a financial gamble because of the expense of the hire, can yield great benefits in terms of both the revenue generated and the wider spectrum of the public attracted to view. Once again, if only a small percentage of these individuals are persuaded to return to sample another (perhaps local) exhibition in the future, the recruitment strategy will have been effective.

There are therefore a variety of strategies which could be adopted to attract the indifferents to attend the arts, although none of those suggested is without some form of financial risk. Individual organizations will therefore need to determine the extent to which they are prepared to focus on recruitment activity and decide on the allocation of budgets accordingly.

The remaining category of non-attender, the 'hostile' is almost certainly the only category that will not be worth some form of recruitment expenditure. This group have absolutely no interest in the arts and are openly hostile towards any attempts to encourage them to attend. Many in this category may view the arts as inappropriate for their social grouping, a waste of public funds, or worse! Targeting this segment is hence likely to be wasteful of valuable marketing resources and, as has been shown above, this could be gainfully employed elsewhere.

The Box Office Database

Getting Started

A marketing database is an organised collection of comprehensive data about individual customers, prospects or suspects that is current, accessible and actionable for such marketing purposes as lead generation, lead qualification, sale of a product or service, or maintenance of customer relationships. (Kotler, 1994)

Given Kotler's definition above, the creation of a computerized database is the single most important investment that an arts organization can make. As we have seen in the previous chapter, the benefits offered in terms of a more detailed understanding of consumer behaviour can lead to an infinitely more effective use of marketing resources. In the context of the arts, however, the use of the database is somewhat different, as will be illustrated below.

Before taking the decision to invest in a database, it is important that an arts organization identifies clearly:

- what the primary purpose of the database will be
- what secondary functions the database will be expected to fulfil
- the other systems with which the database must interact—e.g. accounting
- the categories of data it is intended to store
- the volume of data it is intended to store
- the forms of analysis and/or segmentation the database will be expected to accomplish
- the forms of marketing it is intended to support
- the range of outputs that will be expected.

An understanding of these issues should enable an organization to select between the various options open to it in the acquisition of appropriate database software. For a typical arts organization, these are likely to include:

(1) *The purchase or lease of a commercially available software package.* There are a great many packages currently on the market and their number continues to grow almost daily. Packages will support many forms of direct marketing activity, including direct mail and telemarketing. Other more sophisticated systems will aid in market research and even allow the development of geodemographic profiles of the customers on the system.

(2) *The use of proprietary software.* This differs from packaged software in that it is usually developed by highly specialized third parties such as Marketing Computer Bureaux. These organizations usually lease the software and work with the user to help them carry out their marketing activity and analysis.

(3) *Designing a custom database.* This is clearly the most expensive of the three options and therefore beyond the reach of most arts organizations. Moreover one would need a very strong argument in favour of this alternative since the range of proprietary or packaged software is likely to meet all but the most specialized of needs perfectly adequately. Circumstances which are likely to warrant this considerable investment include the necessity to link with a wide range of other

systems, the desire for a particularly specialized function, and/or the sheer size of the database to be created.

For the majority of arts organizations, however, the purchase of a commercially available package is likely to be the most appropriate option because of both the quality of the options currently available and their relatively low cost.

What Information should be Stored?

Data relating to customers is typically held in 'files' which usually require the user to follow a set format. Each variable that is stored, for example age, gender, etc. will have a specific 'field' into which such information must be entered. More sophisticated packages also contain a number of user-definable fields so that the database can to a certain extent be customized to the needs of the individual organization. In the case of most box office systems, the data fields illustrated in Exhibit 6.4 are likely to be of most relevance.

Exhibit 6.4:

Customer Record

Name:

Title: Initials: First Name: Surname:
Qualifications (any suffix)

Addresses: Home, Business and Temporary Addresses
Number: Building Name: Street/Road: District: Post Town: County: Postcode.

Phone Numbers: STD Code and Number

Age/Year of Birth:

Social Grade: A, B, C1, C2, D, E

Profiling Classification: e.g. ACORN or Mosaic Code

Buyer Types:

the type of customer and their interests, including:
■ the performances/events attended—what they booked, how they heard of it, etc.
■ the relationship of the customer to the venue—i.e. subscriber, member, board member, respondent to particular campaign, etc.

the type of ticket bought:
child, student, pensioner, unemployed, any other concession

the number of tickets bought and price paid:
including the part of the auditorium normally occupied, prices paid, frequency of purchase

the payment method:

the time of booking:

Additional Records: for any other information, e.g. fundraising, sponsorship, and information about contacts

---

Adapted from Tomlinson (1994). Reproduced by kind permission of Roger Tomlinson and the Market Research Society.

It is interesting to note that the collection of a customer's telephone number has recently taken on a new significance as many new telephone systems are equipped with a facility known as caller recognition. This allows the system to recognize the person calling by their telephone number and to display the relevant customer file in front of an operator so that he/she can welcome the caller by name. Not only is this a more personal service, since the operator has immediate access to the customer record, but the time taken to process an enquiry is also considerably shortened—something of benefit to both parties to the transaction. Over the next ten years this facility is likely to become ever more powerful since a move is currently being made to allocate telephone users their own unique telephone number which they can then use for a lifetime, taking it with them when they move from house to house.

Database Applications

Once installed and operational a database can be used for a variety of purposes. These include:

(1) Building customer loyalty;
(2) Cross selling;
(3) Up-selling;
(4) Effective targeting.

(a) Building Customer Loyalty

Box office data can be used to add value to a client's experience with an arts organization. Frequent attenders can be rewarded for their loyalty by offering them concessions, invitations to special events, and even loyalty points which can be exchanged for either merchandise or seats at subsequent performances. It may come as a surprise to learn that even the Royal Opera House under the leadership of its new Director of Public Affairs and Marketing now operates such a scheme. Of course the creation of consumer rewards must be handled with care—it would hardly be appropriate, for example, to offer a scheme entitled Aria Miles, or in the case of a ballet company, Pirouette Points. Loyal customers to these art forms are entitled to be rewarded for their loyalty, but in a manner which is wholly appropriate for the art form in question. Often the safest way of achieving this is through the provision of points which can be redeemed for additional tickets or free seat upgrades. Indeed, given that few performances will completely sell out, a loyalty scheme can often operate at minimal cost.

(b) Cross Selling

Cross selling can take two different forms in arts marketing. The first might involve the marketer in encouraging customers for one category of event to attend and view another. Thus ballet customers could be informed of upcoming classical music concerts in an attempt to broaden their attendance pattern. More usually though, cross selling may involve developing a link with a second organization and the sharing of names/addresses so that customers are informed of appropriate events taking place at other venues in the local area. Whilst this might on the face of it sound like commercial suicide a review by DiMaggio *et al.* (1978) of 270 audience studies confirmed that high value patrons of one art form are also likely to be high value patrons of another. The sensitive sharing of names and addresses can therefore work to the benefit of both organizations.

(c) Up-Selling

Up-selling involves the marketer in trying to develop the arts customer to a higher level of value. In other words an attempt could be made to persuade customers to take higher value seats, or to attend on a more frequent basis. Ashbrand (1993) cites the example of the McCarter theater in Princeton, New Jersey, which recently installed a new client/server system which has facilitated an increase in subscription sales by about 20 per cent. As the curtain rises on each performance the system allows sales and marketing staff to begin work generating a list of all ticket holders. Current subscription holders are separated from those who do not currently have a subscription and the latter category are targeted for a telemarketing campaign the following day. Clearly, if the audience have enjoyed the evening's performance, they will be more likely to accept a subscription package whilst the enjoyment is still fresh in their minds.

(b) Effective Targeting

When an organization recognizes the buying behaviour of its clients it can use this knowledge in targeting specific campaigns at those it knows will be most likely to respond. Offers and information pertaining to performances of ballet can therefore be targeted only at those customers who enjoy this art form. Similarly, advanced information in respect of the annual pantomime can be targeted at those individuals known either to have small children, or to have attended such categories of performance in the past.

In addition, the discussion of profiling in the previous chapter is equally relevant here. Attenders at specific categories of events can be profiled and the data used to inform the purchase of lists of other individuals who might also be predisposed to attending such categories of event.

Attracting Funding

The Arts Funding Framework

The funding framework for the arts in the United Kingdom is complex. Until 1994 the organization responsible for allocating government funding to arts organizations was the Arts Council of Great Britain. The aims of this organization were simply:

(1) to develop and improve the knowledge, understanding, and practice of the arts;
(2) to increase the accessibility of the arts to the public throughout Britain;
(3) to advise and co-operate with departments of government, local authorities, and other bodies.

In general terms these objectives are still valid and the duties of the Arts Council have now been allocated to the four successor bodies: the Arts Council for England, the Arts

Council for Scotland, the Arts Council for Wales, and the Arts Council for Northern Ireland. In England, the responsibility for the allocation of funding to particular arts organizations is devolved to one of ten Regional Arts Boards (RABs) which each receive funding from the Arts Council of England, the Crafts Council, and the British Film Institute. The RABs combine this funding with that received from local authorities wishing to cultivate arts provision in their area and distribute it to a variety of arts organizations and individual artists across the full spectrum of arts activity.

The RABs have a brief to develop a rich diversity of arts provision and will thus tend not to focus funding on specific categories of organization or individual. It should thus be possible to attract funding to any category of art form provided that certain criteria are met. The RAB's selection criteria include:

(1) *General Criteria*. In the case of organizations they must show that the activity for which funding is sought is:
   (a) based in the RAB region;
   (b) organized by a registered charity or non-profit distributing group;
   (c) supportive of equal opportunities;
   (d) able to be self evaluated by the organisation.
(2) *Artistic Criteria*:
   (a) the quality of the artistic work;
   (b) the opportunities for involvement and participation;
   (c) the educational value of the work, i.e. whether it increases an understanding of creative forms of expression and of the societies in which they operate;
   (d) the contribution which the work will make to the artistic life and multi-cultural traditions of the region.
(3) *Financial and Management Criteria*:
   (a) the extent to which the budget is realistic;
   (b) the nature and extent of the financial request in relation to the RAB's own resources;
   (c) the extent to which effort has been made to secure other forms of funding;
   (d) the effectiveness of the organization's management in areas such as marketing;
   (e) clearly defined targeting of audiences and participants with appropriate marketing strategies.

The criteria for funding thus encourage applicants to give consideration to many of the 'balances' discussed earlier. Arts organizations are expected to recognize the need to make a contribution to the cultural traditions of the region in which they operate. To do so will involve a careful identification of the nature of the existing local provision and an analysis of any gaps that would contribute to the range of experiences available. These gaps can then be compared with the resources available in house to identify any opportunities that might exist for development.

Aside from the need to demonstrate a very real contribution to the cultural health of a region, potential applicants must also demonstrate the quality of their management, and in particular the quality of their marketing management. They must be able to show that they have the capability to communicate effectively with target audiences and attract (and involve) reasonable numbers of customers, given the nature of the performances/attractions provided. Marketing can therefore no longer be viewed as a peripheral activity. It must permeate the core of an organization's thinking and, moreover, be shown to have done so.

Commercial Sponsorship

A chapter on arts marketing would not be complete without a brief discussion of arts sponsorship, which remains for many organizations an important source of income. Sponsorship involves a company in exchanging (usually cash) support for a series of benefits which the arts organization, by virtue of the nature of its portfolio, or the profile of the audience it expects to attract, is able to provide.

From the corporate perspective sponsorship can offer a number of benefits, many of which are so attractive that a sizeable proportion of a marketing budget may be parted with to acquire them. The following benefits are the most common and form the basis of most solicitations initiated by arts organizations. Sponsorship can be used very effectively to:

(1) build up awareness of a corporate name or brand;
(2) add value to that name or brand by demonstrating good citizenship;
(3) generate favourable publicity for the sponsor;
(4) court important customers/distributors/staff through the provision of executive entertainment.

This latter point is worthy of elaboration, since some organizations look to their sponsorship as a means of being able to offer hospitality to important clients. As a condition of its support, the corporate sponsor insists on access to reserved seating, a special performance, or other such benefit. It can then offer free seats to selected individuals. Not only can this be an effective and non-threatening way of securing new business, it can also help reward staff, distributors, or intermediaries for their efforts over the preceding months. Corporate sponsorship was recently instrumental, for example, in allowing the management of an exhibition centre to meet the costs of hiring a touring exhibition of Chinese dinosaurs. The key condition of the support was that the sponsor would be able to host a dinner for its key personnel and clients in the building and that the evening would include an opportunity to privately view the dinosaur exhibition. Indeed the dinner was scheduled so that these individuals were actually the first to view what proved to be an enormously popular exhibition.

More commonly, however, the business places greater emphasis on the generation of favourable publicity, since if this is timed correctly, a direct impact on sales can often be measured.

> Thorntons, an independent confectionery company with a national network of its own retail outlets, has its headquarters in Belper, near Derby. When the Derby Playhouse approached it in 1986 for sponsorship of its Xmas show 'Charlie and the Chocolate Factory', a very successful deal was struck. For Thorntons a highly appropriate connection at a time of year when sales are at their most intense. And for Derby Playhouse, not only a sizeable injection of funds, but some excellent photo-opportunities when the cast of 'Oompah Loompahs' visited the factory and tried their hands at chocolate making in the real world. (Hill *et al.*, 1995)

Any arts organization looking to secure sponsorship for the first time would therefore be well advised to seek organizations that have some synergy either with the nature of their productions, or the target audience they are attempting to serve. This should not be the end of the search, however. In the author's experience it is also well worth consulting information sources such as market reports, trade and quality press, and increasingly, the Internet, since useful intelligence can often result. Companies often support arts organizations that, on the face of it, would seem difficult to justify. AT&T for example have a history of supporting arts organizations which seemingly would be able to offer little in return. The company recently supported the Almeida (a small 300-seat venue in North London) in putting on an obscure Russian satire by Sergeyevich Griboyedov. However, when one considers that AT&T take credit for producing the first transistor, the first laser, and the first commercial satellite, one begins to understand that the company is not afraid to take risks and this is reflected in the pattern of sponsorship it chooses to provide. The company likes to take risks with its sponsorship monies and to support performances that might otherwise not be seen. Nor is AT&T alone in its somewhat unorthodox pattern of sponsorship, making it essential for arts organizations serious about seeking sponsorship to look beyond the most 'obvious' lists of prospects to approach.

Before leaving the question of sponsorship, however, it is important to sound a word of caution. Whilst arts organizations will doubtless be grateful of any offer of support they receive, there are wider considerations than the mere receipt of money. The culture and/or history of an organization may make it inappropriate for gifts to be accepted from certain categories of corporate organization. Those involved in dubious environmental practices, or organizations with less than reputable connections to the Third World, are particular candidates for avoidance, although altogether more subtle reasons will often be found to exist. As with other forms of corporate fundraising there is therefore no substitute for a careful research of potential sponsors prior to the initial contact. This can conserve valuable marketing resources and avoid considerable embarrassment when the decision has to be taken to withdraw at a later stage.

Summary

In this chapter we have examined the relevance of marketing to the arts sector. It was argued that, although many of the tools and techniques of marketing are of direct relevance, there is a need to adapt the fundamental marketing concept to accommodate the need for arts organizations to take a longer-term view of the needs of the society in which they are located. It was further suggested that this modification to the marketing concept could best be articulated as a need to achieve a series of balances: the balance of performances in a portfolio, the balance in portrayal of the arts, and the balance in terms of audiences attracted.

With respect to this latter point, the results of a number of audience studies were introduced and their implications for marketing strategy discussed. The reader was also introduced to the technique of cluster analysis as a tool to delineate sub-segments of behaviour and motivation within an overall arts audience.

The development and use of a box-office database was also discussed and suggestions were offered in respect of both the most appropriate information to hold and how this might best be used for the purposes of building customer loyalty, cross selling, up-selling, and the targeting of individuals who might be most likely to respond to particular campaigns.

The final part of the chapter examined marketing's application to the attraction of funding. The criteria for Arts Council funding were evaluated and the significance of marketing in allowing an organization to satisfy these was noted. The chapter concluded with a discussion of the role of corporate sponsorship and the benefits that could accrue both to the sponsor and to the sponsored.

Discussion Questions

1. Why has the arts sector been slow to recognize the significance of marketing both as a guiding philosophy and as a functional area of management?

2. How might an understanding of the audience motivations for attending an arts event inform the development of an appropriate marketing mix? Illustrate your answer with examples.

3. You have been asked to give a talk to the Arts Marketing Association about the importance of segmenting a box-office database. What would be the key dimensions that such a talk would need to address?

4. What factors would normally be considered in the selection of appropriate database software?

5. With reference to your own arts organization, or one with which you are familiar, suggest appropriate fields of data that marketing management should look to create in the design of its customer records.

6. What are the key target groups for an organization to address in the attraction of arts funding? (Hint—look beyond the two target segments specifically addressed in this text). With reference to your own arts organization, or one with which you are familiar, design an appropriate marketing mix to secure funding from each.

References

Andreasen, A. R., and Belk, R. W. (1980) 'Predictors of Attendance at the Performing Arts', *Journal of Consumer Research*, Vol. 7, Sept, 112–20.

Arts Council of Great Britain (1993) *A Creative Future: The Way Forward for the Arts*: Crafts and Media in England, London, HMSO.

Ashbrand, D. (1993) 'Client Server System Boosts Theatre Ticket Sales', *Infoworld*, Vol. 5, No. 52/1, 50, 55.

Brightman, J. (1994) 'Selling Sibelius isn't Easy', *American Demographics*, 1994 Directory, 24–5.

Churchill, G. A. (1991) *Marketing Research: Methodological Foundations*, Hinsdale Ill., The Dryden Press.

Cooper, P. and Tower, R. (1994) 'Inside the Consumer Mind: Consumer Attitudes to the Arts', *Journal of the Market Research Society*, Vol. 34, No. 4, 299–311.

Cutts, C. S. and Drozd, F. A. (1995) 'Managing the Performing Arts', *Business Quarterly*, Spring, 62–6.

Dawson, W. M. (1980) 'The Arts and Marketing' in Mokwa, M. P., Prieve, E. A. and Dawson, W. M., *Marketing The Arts*, New York, Praeger Publishing.

Diggle, K. (1984) *Arts Marketing*, London, Rhinegold Publishing.

DiMaggio P., Useem, M. and Brown, P. (1978) *Audience Studies of the Performing Arts and Museums: A Critical Review*, Washington DC, National Endowment For The Arts.

Ford, C. (1993) 'Tuning up for Promotion', *Incentive Today*, Sept, 14–16.

Hill, E., O'Sullivan, C. and O'Sullivan, T. (1995) *Creative Arts Marketing*, Oxford, Butterworth Heinemann.

Kaali-Nagy, C. and Garrison, L. C. (1972) 'Profiles of Users and Non-Users of the Los Angeles Music Center', *California Management Review*, Vol. 15, Winter, 133–43.

Kotler, P. (1994) *Marketing Management: Analysis Planning Implementation and Control*, 8th edn, Englewood Cliffs, Prentice Hall.

Levy, S. J., Czepiel, J. A., and Rook, D. W. (1980) 'Social Division and Aesthetic Specialisation: The Middle Class and Musical Events', in *Symbolic Consumer Behaviour*, Proceedings of the Association for Consumer Research Conference on Consumer Aesthetics and Symbolic Consumption, May, 103–7.

MANAR (1991) *National Arts and Media Strategy: Discussion Document on Marketing the Arts*, London, Arts Council.

Mokwa, M. P., Prieve, E. A. and Dawson, W. M. (1980) *Marketing the Arts*, New York, Praeger Press.

Nielsen, R. and McQueen, C. (1975) 'Performing Arts Consumer Behaviour: An Exploratory Study', in *New Marketing for Social and Economic Progress*, American Marketing Association Proceedings, 392–5.

Reiss, A. H. (1994) 'The Arts Look Ahead', *Fundraising Management*, Vol. 25, No. 1, 27–31.

Ricklefs, R. (1975) 'Museums Merchandise more Shows and Wares to Broaden Patronage', *Wall Street Journal*, Vol. XCIII, No 32, 14 Aug.

Ryans, A. and Weinberg, C. (1978) 'Consumer Dynamics in Non Profit Organisations', *Journal of Consumer Research*, Vol. 5, 89–95.

Sargeant, A. (1997) 'Marketing the Arts—A Classification of UK Theatre Audiences', *Journal of Non Profit & Public Sector Marketing*, Vol. 5, No. 1, 45–62.

Searles, P. D. (1980) 'Marketing Principles in the Arts', in Mokwa, M. P., Prieve, E. A. and Dawson, W. M. (1980) *Marketing the Arts*, New York, Praeger Press.

Seminik, R. J. and Young, C. E. (1979) 'Market Segmentation in Arts Organisations', *Proceedings of the 1979 American Marketing Association Conference*, 474–8.

Seminik, R. J. and Young, C. E. (1980) 'Correlates of Season Ticket Subscription Behaviour,' *Advances in Consumer Research*, Vol. 7, 114–18.

Stanley, T. L. (1995) 'Entertainers Barter for Databases', *Brandweek*, 13 March, 6.

Strehler, G. (1990) 'The Marketing Oriented Diffusion of Art and Culture: Potential Risks and Benefits', *Marketing and Research Today*, November, 209–12.

Tomlinson, R. (1994) 'Finding out More from Box Office Data', *Journal of the Market Research Society*, Vol. 34, No. 4, 389–404.

Useem, M. and DiMaggio, P. (1978) 'A Critical Review of the Content Quality and Use of Audience Studies,' in *Research in the Arts*, Proceedings of the Conference on Policy Related Studies of the National Endowment For The Arts, Baltimore: Walters Arts Gallery, 30–2.

7

Education

Objectives

By the end of this chapter you should be able to:

(1) describe the impact of key environmental changes on the marketing of education institutions;

(2) describe how an educational institution might proceed to attain a market orientation;

(3) define key educational publics and their impact on schools, colleges, and universities;

(4) understand the process by which parents/students decide on an appropriate educational provision;

(5) design a marketing mix for use by a school, college, or university;

6) develop appropriate control procedures to ensure that the objectives of a marketing plan are met.

Introduction

It is proposed to begin this chapter by introducing some of the major changes to take place in British education over the past 30 years. Whilst such an introduction could be criticized on the grounds of provincialism, an understanding of the environment in which educational establishments are now operating provides an essential background against which to assess the immediate benefits that might accrue from addressing issues such as the attainment of a marketing orientation and, particularly, a focus on students as customers. Indeed, whilst the specific nature of the pattern of education provision will vary considerably from country to country, many of the same forces for change are in evidence. It is thus hoped that the discussion in this chapter will be equally relevant for all educational institutions, irrespective of the country in which they are based. This chapter will therefore examine what might be viewed as the generic difficulties experienced by educational establishments in achieving a market orientation and define the needs of the key publics on which a focus must be developed.

The chapter will also examine the decision-making process as it applies to two key publics, namely those of prospective students and their parents. It will then conclude with an overview of the unique nature of the educational product and some of the difficulties that are likely to be encountered in the design of an appropriate educational marketing mix.

Recent Changes in the UK Education Framework

Primary/Secondary Education

In the United Kingdom, the Education Act of 1988 unleashed the power of market forces on the management of schools for the first time. Prior to the introduction of the Act the pattern of primary and secondary education could perhaps best have been described as a series of small markets, each of which was dominated by a monopoly player. Since implementation, however, this position has altered and, in the case of some regions of the country, quite dramatically. In essence the Act has shifted power away from the schools and the staff working in those schools towards pupils and parents. Parents now have the ability to select the school that they feel is right for their son or daughter and, provided that the necessary place exists and that the child in question meets any entrance requirements, such as a particular religious affiliation, their wishes must usually be respected.

Of course, in practice there are very real constraints which act to reduce the level of parental choice. In many cases the number of local schools might be very small, making it difficult to exercise genuine choice. Alternatively parents may not have the resources necessary to transport their child to a school more distant from their home. However, the Act has had a dramatic effect in many parts of the country and school roles have genuinely begun to reflect the local pattern of parental choice, favouring 'good' schools over those which are felt to perform less well. Since the system of government funding is now based on a simple formula which reflects the numbers of children enrolled, a failure to recruit can starve a school of very necessary resources for IT, library, and sports facilities. Under these circumstances a greater percentage of the school's income will be absorbed by fixed costs, such as the maintenance of school buildings or staff salaries, which must be paid irrespective of the number of pupils enrolled. Competition is thus a very real issue for many organizations and marketing now has a crucial role to play in encouraging parents and pupils to view a particular school in a favourable light.

In an age where there is considerable public interest in levels of school discipline, and when a school reputation can often hang on this issue alone, effective communication with local communities also takes on a new significance. Relationships need to be built with all stakeholder groups in the local community to ensure that strong positive images of the role of a particular school and its pupils are built and developed over time. Moreover, a good public image, whilst doubtless aiding in the attraction of students, will also help to attract and retain new staff. It is no secret that many UK schools now find it difficult to attract suitably qualified professionals because of their poor reputation. This may have been generated by the attainment of low academic standards, by a lack of resources, by poor management, or by a perceived threat of violence from a particularly rowdy school roll. In many cases the perception may be an accurate one, and therefore difficult to counter; in others the reputation might be entirely un-justified and marketing may thus have a role to play in correcting any erroneous ele-ments thereof.

Further Education

The pattern of post-16 education has also experienced considerable change in recent years. In the UK, Further Education (FE) Colleges have traditionally bridged the gap be-tween school and university. Whilst most have always offered a traditional 'A' level route to Higher Education (HE), the strength of the FE colleges has always been their vocational provision. Students could study a range of courses that would give them a practical grounding in business, engineering, sports/leisure, nursing, beauty therapy, and a wide range of other disciplines. These vocational courses were practically based and, whilst they led to valuable qualifications in their own right, were often used by young adults to gain a place at a university in competition with students who selected the more traditional 'A' level route provided by schools. The FE college provided an en-tirely different learning environment not unlike that which would ultimately be en-countered at university, and which importantly could offer students a degree of flexibility not available in schools. Methods of assessment tended to be more varied and courses could usually be studied in full-time, part-time, or day-release modes, making it possible to work towards a university place whilst at the same time experiencing em-ployment for the first time.

FE colleges also played a vital role in their communities, providing a full range of aca-demic and practical courses for adult learners who were interested in acquiring an ad-ditional qualification, or developing new skills. Often this study may have been undertaken purely for the pleasure of learning something new, with no real goal of fu-ture progression in mind. In recent times, however, much of this provision has been adapted and extended and new routes towards part-time qualifications have been es-tablished. With many more adult learners wishing to gain a place in higher education, FE colleges have responded by creating a range of ACCESS courses, the successful com-pletion of which now usually guarantees a place at a university.

Whilst much of the preceding description of FE still holds, considerable change has recently impacted on the sector. The recent introduction by the government of the 'vo-cational A level'—the GNVQ (General National Vocational Qualification)—has blurred the academic/vocational divide and, since the GNVQ is designed to develop in students the skills demanded by the modern employer, many schools have taken the decision to add one or more of these to their sixth-form portfolio. Schools that could once have been regarded as feeder institutions to FE have now hence to be regarded as competi-tors. Indeed, given that many schools have a vested interested in promoting their own post-16 provision, FE colleges may find it increasingly difficult to gain access to poten-tial students to communicate the benefits of what they have to offer.

Moreover, at the other end of the scale, the division in portfolios between further and higher education institutions has also eroded. Government demands for a rapid expansion of access to Higher Education have fuelled the development of partnerships between FE colleges and universities. It is now not uncommon to find the first year of a degree programme being delivered in an FE college and many post-graduate professional qualifications are now also franchised to FE providers. Whilst the development of some FE/HE partnerships have clearly facilitated this blurring in distinction between the two portfolios, they have also led to the creation of considerable additional competition. FE colleges now directly compete with HE providers in their geographic regions for students. Indeed, one in ten HE students are currently enrolled in FE colleges.

These changes have led to a great deal of marketing complexity, reflected in the almost exponential increase over the past ten years in the number of institutions now making marketing appointments at a most senior level. There are, after all, considerable dilemmas facing an institution which must now compete directly with both schools and universities. Marketing resources are now split between an ever increasing number of target markets and even where sufficient resources are likely to be available it is often difficult to decide on a suitable strategy to adopt. The development of a coherent positioning strategy is particularly problematic

There have also been changes to the way in which FE is funded, deliberately aimed at encouraging competition between colleges who traditionally have always operated within their own geographical boundaries. Funding now depends not only on absolute measures of success, but also on patterns of relative success between competing institutions. Moreover, the funding mechanism itself has altered, placing a greater emphasis on student outcomes. No longer is funding awarded simply for the number of students on a course, the emphasis is now on the achievements of those students at the end of their studies. High drop-out or failure rates can now have a dramatic effect on the level of funding received. There has therefore never been a greater need to instil a market orientation amongst college administrators and staff. Simply recruiting greater numbers of students is no longer an appropriate goal.

Higher Education

Over the past thirty years the pattern of higher education in the UK has changed almost beyond recognition. A plethora of different providers now exists, catering for an equally diverse population of students. Higher Education Institutions (HEIs) have been forced by successive government policy to forge closer links with industry, research funders, and markets for education overseas. In an attempt to categorize this change Bargh *et al.* (1996) draw a distinction between what they perceive as a trend towards massification and a trend towards marketization.

(a) Massification

The growth of the HE student population has been spectacular. Total student numbers have risen from a mere 50,000 in 1939 (about 25 per cent of whom were involved in studying medicine or dentistry) to 324,000 at the time of the Robbins report in 1963, to over 1.4 million today. The ability to be able to gain a Higher Education is no longer the privilege of a select few. What was certainly until the early 1960s very much an élite system has now been transformed into a mass system with levels of access which rival those attained in most European countries and even North America.

Given the great rise in student numbers, change has been forced on the pattern of institutions providing the education. In the late 1950s there were no more than 24 universities providing a very narrow range of highly specialized courses. After the expansion of the system recommended by Robbins the number increased to 45, and after the ending of the so-called binary divide between universities and polytechnics in 1992, 93 such institutions then existed. When one considers that there are also a further 60 HEIs not classified as universities and well over 400 FE colleges—as mentioned previously, with a stake in higher education—the move to a mass system of provision is all but complete. Nor has change merely been confined to a growth in the number of providers. When the sector comprised only a handful of institutions, all governed by similar academic and professional values, there was little variation in the 'character' of each institution. The arrival of a situation where there are now 93 different universities has encouraged a greater degree of heterogeneity. One university is no longer much like another and considerable scope for the development of a unique institutional personality now exists.

In 1963 the average British university had a mere 2,750 students. Today the average university has well over 8,000 full-time equivalents and approaching 20,000 students in total enrolled. The small and historically intimate nature of most institutions has therefore been lost and the expansion in student numbers has led to the creation of ever larger sites and even split-site campuses. The task of managing this change has fallen to ever increasing numbers of professional administrators. New management frameworks have of necessity been implemented and this in turn has led to the erosion of what was once almost purely an academic culture, with its own unique set of attitudes, beliefs, and behaviours.

One of the key reasons for the growth in student numbers after Robbins was the creation of a mandatory award system that would subsidize the course fees of HE students and greatly assist the student in meeting the costs of living over the duration of their studies. This had the impact not only of encouraging participation, but also of persuading students that distance was no longer a problem and that study could therefore be undertaken at whichever UK institution they desired. The home-based student therefore became the exception rather than the rule, and moving away from home began to be seen as part of the natural process of growing up and gaining one's independence.

The difficulty for HEIs, and indeed successive governments after Robbins, has been that a greater freedom of student choice, both to enter higher education *and* to study those subjects that were individually most attractive, has meant that demand for subjects deemed to be of crucial importance to the future health of the economy—such as the sciences or engineering—was often sadly lacking. Faced with additional spaces on these programmes, universities switched their attention in these areas to the attraction of overseas students for the first time. Since the fees were subsidized (at least until the Thatcher government took office), the attainment of a British education was a very attractive option. The experience gained by universities of recruiting overseas students at this time was later to pay dividends, since the recruitment of overseas students has recently taken on a whole new significance. Not only are such individuals no longer subsidized by the UK government, but the fees charged to overseas students are also now set at rates that often greatly surpass those charged to UK or EC nationals. Moreover, at the undergraduate level, the government now controls the overall number of home students that a given university is expected to attract. Under or over-recruitment is now penalized by the funding framework. Once the quota of home students has been recruited, the only way that the revenue stream from a particular course can then be increased is through the recruitment of overseas students, who, since they are full-fee paying, are not included in the institutional quota. Such students therefore constitute an important and extremely profitable target market.

The nature of the academic product has also changed. More than a quarter of all students are now mature students and the number of part-time students has increased sharply, particularly on postgraduate programmes. The nature of provision has therefore changed to reflect the needs of these key new customer groups. There has also been a general blurring of the distinction between academic, vocational, and continuing education as HEIs have attempted to respond (in most cases) to the needs of their various constituencies.

(b) Marketization

In recent years, successive government policy has encouraged the development of a market culture. Institutions are now in a position where they must compete for scarce resources and even consider alternative sources of funding, such as that provided by private enterprise. Moreover, the new market comprising 93 competing institutions has afforded HE customers an unprecedented level of choice. This in turn has already led to the creation of an unofficial 'Ivy League' of institutions, a process recently encouraged by the decision of a number of foreign governments to limit the number of campuses to which they are prepared to send students (O'Leary, 1996).

At the undergraduate level the recent decision by the UK government to charge fees to all but the most underprivileged of students will put great pressure on institutions to communicate to potential students the benefits of continuing their education and of studying at their particular campus. Since students must now bear the cost of their studies, at least in the longer term, it is quite fair to assume that greater consideration will be given to exactly where these studies will take place. Indeed there are also internal marketing implications for this policy change. If students must now pay for their education, they are likely to have ever greater expectations of the quality of service they will receive. Institutional managers and teaching staff will in the future need to be especially sensitive to the needs of their now fee-paying clients.

In addition, universities and other institutions which provide higher education are now subject to an unprecedented level of external scrutiny; the demands made of them have expanded and expectations have changed. League tables are now published in respect of the quality of both teaching and research; and prospective students, or their sponsors, can now use such information to allow them to make a more informed choice. Indeed the level of research funding provided to each university is now highly dependent on the research rating achieved and set to become more so, as the recently published Dearing report recommends the concentration of funding amongst a select few institutions who have consistently outperformed the others. There is a very real threat that the traditions of both teaching and research being conducted alongside one another at every UK institution will shortly come to an end, creating new categories of university some of which will be perceived as being more desirable than others. Senior management will therefore have to ensure that appropriate strategies are put in place now to ensure that their desired positioning is maintained and developed over time. This will only be achievable if both the internal and external marketing activity is focused on this goal and co-ordinated to ensure that the *whole* institution moves forward in the direction required

The remainder of this chapter will therefore examine how providers might respond to these challenges, commencing with what for most institutions will be the key marketing issue, namely how a market orientation might be achieved. As will shortly be demonstrated, introducing such a radical change of emphasis is perhaps more difficult in this sector than in any other, given both its history and the traditional freedoms afforded to its academic staff.

Higher Education in the USA

Whilst the preceding discussion has focused quite deliberately on the UK, the issues identified above are matters of great concern to most government education departments, irrespective of the country in which they are based. In the USA, for example, competition is very much a key issue since, whilst student demand for places at the top 50 US degree awarding institutions still outstrips supply, the picture elsewhere in the sector is radically different. The vast majority of institutions continue to have to actively solicit student interest. There are currently over 3,000 degree awarding institutions in the USA each contributing to the production of over 2.5 million new bachelor degrees every year. The sheer number of institutions and the wide range of courses on offer make it essential that HEIs communicate effectively with their target markets and carve out a clear positioning which serves to differentiate their provision from that offered by others, in particular those within the same geographic region.

In addition to competition, the USA continues to experience a healthy growth in what has now become a large market for part-time and adult education. Moreover, fees are as much an issue in the USA as in the UK and, faced with strong domestic competition, many HEIs are now every bit as concerned with the expansion of overseas recruitment as their UK counterparts.

We may thus conclude that the issues identified above will be of equal concern to educational management in many other countries. Whilst the structure of the educational systems will certainly differ, the forces shaping the development of change will be likely to exhibit strong degrees of similarity. Indeed as we move increasingly towards a global market for education, this level of similarity can only grow in significance.

Changing Perspectives of Marketing in Higher Education

It is against this backdrop that the need for marketing can be assessed. Perhaps marketing's greatest contribution lies in its ability to facilitate the exchange process that takes place between the HEI and each of the customer groups it addresses. It can provide a detailed understanding of the needs of such customers and ensure that the institution addresses these needs in as efficient and comprehensive a manner as possible. In the competitive environment in which most HEIs now operate, enhanced customer satisfaction may be one of the few ways remaining in which institutions can create and sustain a credible source of competitive advantage. Marketing can help deliver this satisfaction and deliver much more besides. Indeed in the education context Kotler and Fox (1985) identify that marketing can offer an HEI four major benefits:

(1) greater success in fulfilling the institution's mission;
(2) improved satisfaction of the institution's publics;
(3) improved attraction of marketing resources;
(4) improved efficiency in marketing activities.

Despite the benefits, however, the HE sector has been slow to embrace the concept and, although many institutions have now appointed marketing officers, the real influence that such professionals can have is often severely limited. In a major study of marketing in further and higher education, HEIST trace the evolution of the marketing function over forty years. The authors recognize that although certain behaviours are symptomatic of a particular historical phase, examples of each stage of development are still very much in evidence.

(a) Beginnings

The impact of the Robbins report, as highlighted above, was to completely change the pattern of educational provision. Universities were faced with a need for expansion and the need to explain this to the local communities in which they were based. To plan the expansion it became necessary to negotiate with a variety of groups, such as resident groups, traders, local authorities, etc. In response, many universities appointed administrators whose primary function was to manage the institution's relationship with these publics.

(b) Placating the Press

This phase began in the late 1960s in response to developments such as the student revolts and subsequent critique by the press of university management. Press reports accused them of being too soft on the troublemakers who had instigated the problems. For the first time, media professionals were appointed, often ex-journalists themselves, to manage the difficult relationships with the press that ensued. Their primary role was to ensure that potentially damaging publicity was, as far as possible, deflected.

(c) Winning Hearts and Minds

By the mid-1970s, the press relations function had risen in importance. Senior management began to recognize the importance of a proactive rather than a purely reactive approach. In recognition of this the press office function in many institutions was renamed 'external relations'. These new departments were empowered to generate favourable publicity for the institution and to co-ordinate any lobbying activity that might prove necessary. The public image of many universities had been badly damaged by the years of student revolt and a key external relations function was to rebuild the image of higher education. However, there was also a need to communicate to government and other funders the desirability of maintaining the level of funding attracting to the sector. The mid-1970s were characterized by a period of serious public expenditure constraint.

(d) Selling the System

It was not until the early 1980s, however, that institutions recognized that their relationships with the press and government funders were not the only relationships that should be fostered at a senior level within a university. Changes in government policy had raised the significance of overseas recruitment, soliciting donations from alumni, and selling short courses and conferences, etc. At around this time, the first attempts were therefore witnessed to co-ordinate this diverse activity into a unified external relations function. Media or marketing professionals began to be recruited to manage all these important aspects of activity and, depending on the nature of the institution, some homogeneity in reporting structures was achieved. This is a matter that will be returned to below.

(e) Marketing Institutions

By the late 1980s a new trend in the marketing of education had begun to emerge. Universities had now started to integrate marketing, both as a philosophy and a management function, into the way in which their institution was managed. Formalized planning and an adherence to an institutional mission are now the norm across the sector and newly created marketing departments now help co-ordinate both departmental and institutional contact with key customer groups. Moreover, in the more enlightened organizations, these marketing departments have established a two-way dialogue with academic departments, ensuring that genuine customer input is fed back to those who have the responsibility for the design and creation of new course programmes. Without overriding academic freedom, these mechanisms serve to ensure that the programmes offered to the market reflect in part the needs of those who will ultimately consume them.

Achieving a Market Orientation—The Case of Higher Education

At the time of writing, however, comparatively few universities appear to have reached the fifth of these stages of development (section (e) above). There are usually a number of reasons as to why this might be so.

(a) Academic Values

Marketing is still perceived by many as being incompatible with the educational mission, and some academics continue to equate marketing with selling and feel that their institution should be 'above' such practices. Others feel that marketing should not be necessary because they have a strong belief in the desirability of their subject and their right to deliver it as they see fit. Academics, by virtue of their professional status, tend to be more concerned with the future of their discipline and will often focus on the narrow interests thereof. As Jarratt (1985, 33) notes, in many universities there exist

> large and powerful academic departments together with individual academics who sometimes see their academic discipline as more important than the long term well being of the university which houses them.

Boxall (1991, 12) concurs:

> The activities and priorities of universities have traditionally been determined primarily by the preferences and aspirations of their academic staff, given voice through various faculties and internal committees. Indeed, the very essence of a university has been the self-determining community of academic professionals, whose rights to set their own agenda were enshrined in the unwritten charter of academic freedom.

(b) Conflict between Management and Academic Interests

Difficulties are also encountered because of the split in responsibility for dealings with customers between departments and the institution's central administrative function. In most institutions, responsibility for marketing is split between these two areas and this can give rise to a degree of tension. Many departments have the desire to be masters of their own destiny and hence want to take responsibility for all marketing activity, whilst others express reluctance and would be delighted if the whole process could be dealt with by those working for the university's central administration. For their part university marketers usually want to maintain some control over the activities of individual departments, but are reluctant to have too much 'local' involvement as their role within the university has usually to be more strategic in nature. There is therefore a need to achieve some form of balance in this relationship, although in practice this can be difficult given the antipathy that can exist between academic and administrative staff.

> [I]n almost all HE institutions there is a them and us aspect to the manager–academic relationship, which will vary from nothing more sinister than staff club banter . . . to real conflict and tension especially at a time of cuts. (Palfreyman and Warner, 1996, 12)

(c) The Lack of a Strategic Perspective

Given the usually high number of subject specialisms that make up a particular university it is often the case that it is only the senior administration of the institution who have the capacity to take a strategic perspective and are uniquely placed to do so (Lockwood and Davies, 1985). The problem, however, lies in convincing academic staff of the need for this perspective and the need to implement any strategy that might be suggested as a result of it. Many academics fail to recognize that the desirability of offering new courses in their individual discipline must be viewed against the capacity of other developments in other subject areas to offer even greater utility for one or more of the institution's customer groups. Clearly only those developments which are optimal from the perspective of the whole institution should be supported. Very often, however, the power to make such decisions is vested in a university committee structure heavily dominated by academics, each fighting for the welfare their own specific discipline.

[U]niversities are commonly not outwardly market oriented—courses are sometimes established and maintained for the status of a department or an institution, rather than where there is clear evidence of an economic level of long term demand. (Moore, 1989, 120)

(d) The Diversity of Marketing Activity

The point has already been made above that responsibility for marketing activity can be shared between individual departments and marketers working for the central administration. Regrettably, however, marketing activity is also conducted by a variety of other players making co-ordination difficult. In a typical university these might include:

(1) *The Development Office.* Staff in this department of a university will typically be involved in raising funds from both individual and corporate donors. They also have responsibility for the fostering of links with alumni.

(2) *The International Office.* The responsibility for overseas recruitment is often devolved to an international officer, who will travel extensively visiting institutions in other countries and attending educational fairs, etc.

(3) *Schools Liaison Office.* Liaison with feeder institutions remains an important activity in aiding student recruitment. Dedicated staff will tour local schools, giving presentations and offering advice in respect of university course options.

(4) *Admissions Office.* Usually split between undergraduate and postgraduate admissions, the latter is of particular significance. Postgraduate admissions staff are often the first point of contact for students wishing to obtain information about the taught or research degrees currently being offered. The office will also be likely to deal with correspondence and, ultimately, applications from individual students. In this sense they can act as a liaison between the academic department and the individual applicant and will probably also issue the final notice of acceptance or rejection.

(5) *Press Office.* Most universities have dedicated staff whose sole function is to foster good relations with the press. Since their role is almost certainly now a proactive one, such individuals are constantly monitoring the work of academic departments to ascertain whether opportunities exist to promote the teaching, development, or research work being undertaken.

(6) *Business Relations.* Many university missions now address the need for the institution to make a contribution to the economic health of the country and/or region in which the institution is based. This often involves working closely with commercial enterprise to conduct joint research, train staff, or sell the expertise of university academics who might undertake paid/unpaid consultancy. Since successive governments have been keen to provide increasing numbers of undergraduates with business experience, this function may also have the responsibility for arranging and supervising student projects and placements.

(7) *Research Office.* Given the importance of research income, particularly for the established universities, it would now be highly unusual to find a university that did not have a fairly senior member of staff responsible for the administration of research grants and the co-ordination of bids to the respective funding agencies.

(8) *The Conference Office.* The potential to generate a very lucrative revenue stream from offering university facilities, both teaching and residential, to clients

seeking a conference facility has long been recognized. The marketing of the site and its facilities will usually be the responsibility of a dedicated team.

Whilst this list is not exhaustive it does serve to illustrate the great diversity in marketing activity that would normally be undertaken in a typical university. Co-ordination thereof can therefore be a very significant issue for senior management to address.

(e) The Influence of Research

The remuneration systems within the majority of universities, and indeed the academic 'system' in general, continues to reward individuals for excellence in research to the near exclusion of all else. Whilst many universities include in their reward structures the criteria of excellence in teaching and/or administration, in reality the quality of an individual's research output is still of overriding concern. Given this, the concept of rewarding an individual for the quality of any marketing activity they might have responsibility for is almost laughable. As one colleague put it recently, 'you can't even gain promotion for being an excellent teacher—what chance marketing?'

The incentive for many academics to devote time to marketing is therefore sadly lacking and many staff prefer, understandably, to concentrate on those aspects of their role for which they will gain some reward. Active researchers therefore jealously guard their time and can be reluctant to engage in 'peripheral' activities such as visiting schools, attending education fairs, or interviewing business clients. Indeed, it is quite ironic that, since admin work-loads in HE often reflect the level of research an individual is able to generate, it can often be the least able members of staff who find their time being allocated to marketing and administration activity.

Case Study 7.1: **Starting the Process—Achieving Change in an 'Established' University**

There are very real difficulties that will be encountered in achieving a marketing orientation in an HE setting. Whatever the route undertaken, it is likely to be fraught with difficulty and often subject to outright condemnation by senior members of academic staff. What follows is a description of the process that was initiated by a major and long established UK university in its bid to become market oriented. In essence the senior management of the university recognized the need to focus on the needs of individual customer groups, so that the university could respond more intimately to their needs. They also saw the need to design new programmes that would be attractive to the market, and to be more aggressive in promoting certain aspects of the institution's work and provision. The following steps were therefore initiated.

(a) Managing the Process

A Marketing Committee was established to consider how the process of change might be initiated, involving senior academics and administrators and a marketing facilitator. It was felt important to demonstrate the importance with which this change was viewed, and hence both the Vice-Chancellor and Registrar were in attendance.

(b) Marketing Audit

The Marketing Committee initiated a university wide audit of marketing activity. This audit had both strategic and tactical perspectives and was designed to gather data in respect of the external changes that would impact on the university over the next 5–10 year period. Data was also gathered in respect of the competition, the needs of each key customer grouping, and the relative success/failure of past marketing activity. The methodology employed consisted of a series of personal interviews with staff, students, alumni, members of the local residential/business communities, and research funders. A questionnaire was also completed by each Head of Department (see Exhibit 7.1).

(c) SWOT Analysis

Once the data had been gathered, a comprehensive SWOT analysis was conducted revealing three major weaknesses that urgently needed to be addressed.

(1) *The lack of a co-ordinated marketing intelligence system.* Most departments and administrative functions having contact with university clients maintained their own databases or records of such contact. However, there existed no way in which the data could be shared between all those who might have an interest therein. Moreover, there existed no mechanism within the university to conduct any form of primary marketing research. As a result the institution had almost no understanding of the needs of any of its key customer groups.

(2) *Habitual under-recruitment in key subject areas.* Much of the university's provision was either unattractive to potential students or poorly marketed. The university was also found to be struggling to recruit overseas students in key subject areas, and hence to maintain and build its market share in many foreign markets.

(3) *The lack of a coherent identity.* The university lacked a corporate identity and communications with customer groups were often visually poor and lacking in a common theme. A university logo was in existence, but its use was unco-ordinated and not informed through research. Moreover, university managers (and academics) were all found to have their own views on how the university should position itself in the market and this diversity tended to be reflected in the communications they had with their market.

(d) Agreement of an Action Plan

In the light of the findings of the audit, an action plan was agreed to implement change. Specifically the following steps were taken.

(1) *Creation of a marketing forum.* Heads of Department, admissions tutors, and all those involved in some way with the marketing of the university were invited to attend an occasional meeting of a new marketing forum. The format of the forum was initially flexible, being agreed upon by the participants themselves. Its role developed into a facility for individuals to share their own experiences with marketing, discuss best practice and analyse individual problems that had been encountered. Membership of the forum was open and meetings were held in lunchtimes to minimize the inconvenience to individual schedules.

(2) *Appointment of a University Marketing Officer.* It was intended that this person would form an integral part of the external relations team and have input into

Departmental Guide to the Process of Auditing Marketing Activities

Introduction

The purpose of this document is to guide you through the process of carrying out a marketing audit for your department. It should be remembered that the central purpose of the audit is to assist you in determining 'where you are now' in marketing terms and what the opportunities may be for future development. Not every question asked will be of relevance for your department but you should distinguish between those that you perceive as having no relevance and those which you are unable to answer due to a lack of information.

The Macro Environment

1. The wider environment

Factor	Details
What political (government) decisions are likely to impact on your department within the next three years?	
What macro-economic factors might impact on your department within the next three years ?	
Are there any technological developments, planned, or likely, which will occur over the next three years that could affect your department's activities?	

Customer Segments

2. Please indicate for each programme your department offers, both the total number of enquiries received and the number of students to finally enrol.

Course	1992/3		1993/4		1994/5		1995/6		1996/7	
	Enqs	Enrl	Enqs	Enrl	Enqs	Enrl	Enqs	Enrl	Enqs	Enrl

3. Examining the table above, do any trends emerge? If so please give details.

4. For each programme your department offers please indicate the profile of the student body over the past five years.

Programme Title					
	1992/3	1993/4	1994/5	1995/6	1996/7
Number of Male Students					
Number of Female Students					
Number of Full-Time Students					
Number of Part-Time Students					
Number of Mature Students					
Number of Overseas Students					

5. Examining the table(s) above, are any trends in enrolment evident? Please give details.

6. In the case of each programme please indicate where your current students first heard of Exeter's provision.

Course	Primary Methods of Communication

7. From which regions of the country do you presently recruit for your undergraduate programmes? Do you tend to recruit from certain types of school?

8. For each programme please indicate where you are currently advertising/promoting the programme.

Course	Location of Advertising/Promotional Activity (if any)

9. Comparing your answers to questions 6 and 7, can you identify any promotional activity which would appear to be ineffective? Could this be improved?

10. Comparing your answers to questions 6 and 7, can you identify communication channels that could be enhanced with an additional spend? If so, please specify.

11. Can you identify any changes which might be likely to take place in the markets for your programmes over the next three years? How are these changes being monitored? What actions do you propose to take as a result?

12. For each programme, please indicate the two institutions which you would describe as your closest competitors.

Course	Competitors

13. Do you have copies of the most recent literature produced by these institutions?

☐ Yes   ☐ No

14. Is this information circulated to course co-ordinators and admissions tutors?

☐ Yes ☐ No

15. What unique features can your department offer that the two competitors identified above cannot?

16. What unique features can competitor 1 offer that [your university] cannot? (If necessary please specify this by programme.)

17. What unique features can competitor 2 offer that [your university] cannot? (If necessary please specify this by programme.)

18. How has a knowledge of these features been integrated in the design of marketing communications?

19. If your department has an undergraduate programme (or programmes), how have the numbers of applications compared with those made to other institutions over the past five years?

Programme Title					
Instituition	1992/3	1993/4	1994/5	1995/6	1996/7

20. What forms of promotion do each of the key competitors currently undertake?

Competitor 1 (Insert name)	Competitor 2 (Insert name)

Research

21. Over each of the past five years, what is the average amount of research funding that has been attracted per staff member? (i.e. the total research income generated, divided by the number of full-time staff or equivalents.)

	1992/3	1993/4	1994/5	1995/6	1996/7
Research Income Per Staff Member					

22. How do the current year's figures compare with the national average?

☐ Well Above

☐ Above

☐ Equivalent

☐ Below

☐ Well Below

23. If the figures are below, or well below the national average, what steps will be taken to increase the level of research funding being attracted?

24. Do mechanisms exist within your department to monitor the success of individual applications for funding and to learn from the design/content etc. of those that proved successful? If yes, please give details.

25. Have members of staff from funding bodies been invited to the department to meet members of staff and discuss application procedures over the past three years? If so, please give details.

26. Do opportunities exist to involve the business community in research? Are these opportunities currently being exploited?

Other Customer Groups

27. Are there any aspects of your department activities which you feel could be of value to the local/national business community? If so, please give details.

28. What mechanisms currently exist to promote these features/facilities to the business community?

29. Could the University offer additional assistance in this regard? If so, please give details.

30. Which professional bodies do your staff belong to? Do you know the CPD requirements set out by these professional bodies for their members? Are you an accredited provider for these institutions?

Own Marketing Activity

31. Has your department considered any of the following activities:

Activity	Yes (and currently use)	Yes (and rejected)	No
Attending Educational Fairs (UK)			
Attending Educational Fairs (Overseas)			
Providing Guest Lectures in Schools			
Providing Guest Lectures for Professional Bodies			
Providing Events For School/College Tutors			
Providing Events/Competitions for Schools (not open days)			
Advertising Undergraduate Courses			
Advertising Postgraduate Courses and/ or Research			
Releasing Occasional Press Releases through External Relations			
Links with Overseas Institutions			
Providing Speakers for High Profile Events— e.g. International Conferences			

32. If activities have been considered and rejected, please indicate why this decision was taken.

33. On what basis are admissions tutors selected within your department? Are these qualities relevant to the target market?

34. What additional expertise would assist you in making your marketing more effective?

35. What market research would typically be undertaken by your department prior to the introduction of a proposed new programme?

36. What market research in respect of any key customer group would normally be undertaken by your department on an annual basis?

SWOT Analysis

This completes the marketing audit process. You should now have access to a variety of marketing intelligence data. This information should now be interpreted in terms of whether it represents a:

Strength
Weakness
Opportunity
Threat

Strengths and weaknesses are factors which relate to the internal aspects of your department's activities. The opportunities and threats relate to the information gathered about the environment external to the University (e.g. competitor activity).

Looking back over the data gathered, please interpret it in terms of whether you consider it to be a strength, weakness, opportunity or threat. You should also list any other relevant factors which occur to you as you complete this section.

Strengths	Weaknesses
a)	a)
b)	b)
c)	c)
d)	d)
e)	e)

Opportunities	Threats
a)	a)
b)	b)
c)	c)
d)	d)
e)	e)

university marketing at both a strategic and a tactical level. Specifically they were to be given responsibility for the co-ordination of the effort to achieve a market orientation and to help shape the future positioning strategy of the university. At a tactical level they would also be available to advise departments who required individual guidance and assistance.

(3) *The creation of a new permanent external affairs committee.* It was decided to add an additional committee to the university's existing governance structure. The new committee would have ultimate responsibility for all university marketing activity (i.e. all those aspects listed above). As such the new body was designed to

provide a mechanism to ensure that all marketing activity was co-ordinated and appropriate, given the institution's long-term strategic plan. Reporting directly to senate with all senior staff in attendance, the committee was also to include representatives of the key customer groups. The president of the Students' Union and representatives from local industry and commerce were thus invited to sit as members of the committee. It was further determined that given the diversity of marketing activity undertaken, it was unlikely that time would permit the committee to have anything other than a decision-making role. Three working groups, or sub-committees, were thus also established, the purpose of each of which was to address one of the three key weaknesses highlighted above (i.e creation of a marketing intelligence system, student recruitment, and the development and co-ordination of a corporate image).

(4) *Provision of marketing training.* The university's staff development unit was instructed to provide an ongoing programme of marketing training throughout the academic year. Enrolment was open to all academic and administrative staff and the training was structured to allow individuals to study towards a recognized qualification, or merely to deepen their knowledge of a particular aspect of marketing depending on their individual requirements.

(5) *Control mechanisms implemented.* The university recognized that many departments required marketing communications support in respect of how to plan and implement the promotion of their individual courses. Since each department had traditionally planned in a vacuum, the university had on one occasion placed four different advertisements in one magazine, each of which painted a slightly different picture of life on the campus. It was thus decided that all promotional activity would have to be cleared centrally by the new marketing officer, who would also offer advice regarding the appropriateness of the activities planned. He/she could also ensure that the university gained as much synergy as possible from all its activities and obtained the best possible financial deals from the media. The effectiveness of all the forms of promotion used was also to be monitored centrally, so that the advice given to departments could ultimately be informed by experience gained in the market.

The university also developed a set of guidelines which were designed to govern the use of the university logo and other materials that might be used in communications with customer groups. The aim was to standardize the production of literature so that it was immediately apparent that each brochure was part of a wider institutional 'family' of publications. As the work of the 'Image' sub-committee described above progresses, it is likely that further guidelines will be issued to departments to ensure common dimensions not only of livery, but also of style and/or content.

The reader will note that the changes implemented in the case represent quite a 'softly, softly' approach to achieving change and quite a different route to that which might typically be taken in industry. Senior management recognized the need not to overtly 'push' academic staff towards the attainment of a market orientation. They felt that the provision of training, in house marketing consultancy (by the new marketing officer), and marketing intelligence should begin to demonstrate the very practical benefits that marketing could provide. This in turn, it was felt, would help generate a much more positive perspective on what marketing could offer the institution and gradually begin to alter its culture.

Key Educational Publics

Previously in this chapter the term 'customer' has been used to refer to those groups of individuals or organizations that the organization in some way addresses. In the educational context, however, institutions often have contact with groups or individuals who, whilst they may not be involved in an exchange process with an educational institution (in a strict sense of the word), still have a vested interest in the work carried out by these bodies and the management thereof. It may therefore be helpful in attempting to achieve a market orientation to develop a focus not only on customers, but also more generally on key educational publics. Kotler and Fox (1985, 24) define the term 'public' as:

> a distinct group of people and/or organisations that has an actual or potential interest in and/or effect on an institution.

Educational institutions probably have the most diverse range of publics of any category of nonprofit. When one considers that each of these is likely to have a very unique set of expectations of an institution, something of the complexity of educational marketing can begin to be appreciated.

School Publics

Looking first at school publics, Davies and Ellison (1991) suggest that the following target groups are worthy of particular consideration by marketers.

(a) Internal Publics

Governors

Governors have the capacity to shape the future direction of the school and as such have a need to be informed about ongoing developments. They also need to be informed about changes taking place in the external environment and from time to time lobbied about the desirability of a particular response thereto. Governors may also need marketing support to communicate policy decisions and their underlying rationale to other school publics, such as pupils, staff, parents, and, increasingly, the wider community.

Staff

As the providers of the educational service, staff are arguably the most important of all the educational publics. It is staff who interact on a daily basis with the key customers of the school: parents and pupils. The attitudes and behaviour of staff can therefore have a profound impact on the performance of a school and its role in a community. Of late the role of the staff has taken on a particular significance since school performance is now measured in league table terms. Since these league tables consist almost entirely of lists of quantitative criteria such as performance in exam results, there is a danger that schools could concentrate too heavily on these aspects of their role. Teaching staff have traditionally been able to take a more holistic view of the development of individual children and have taken steps to ensure that social, artistic, physical, and academic concerns are all equally addressed. Since these aspects are all key components of the academic product, institutions need to ensure that staff are encouraged to continue to give consideration to these 'softer' aspects of their role.

Regular Visitors and Helpers

School visitors and helpers play a vital role in shaping the image that the school has within a community. If these individuals leave the school with a favourable impression they are likely to impart it to others and hence enhance the overall image and reputation of the institution.

Current Pupils

It is current pupils, however, who have the greatest capacity to shape the nature of the relationship of a school with its community. Their attitude, appearance and behaviour all have the capacity to communicate something of the quality of the educational role the school is providing. Current pupils often need to be reminded of this fact and persuaded that it is ultimately in their best interests to ensure that the school is seen in as positive a light as possible.

Current Parents

Parents represent a key public for both primary and secondary schools. In both cases they now have the right to select the institution at which their child will be educated. Schools therefore need to reassure parents that the right decision has been taken, and to enable them to do this an ongoing dialogue must be maintained. It has to be recognized that parental expectations of a school have now changed and they expect to be able to have a greater influence over the child's education. Communications with the school must thus be both frequent and informative. The days of the preparation of report cards which read simply 'could do better' have long since passed.

(b) External Publics

Prospective Parents

A key focus of external marketing activity are the parents of prospective students. For a detailed discussion of the nature of the relationship that should be developed with this target public, see the following section, 'Influencing Student Buying Behaviour'.

Prospective Staff

For many schools, the recruitment of appropriately qualified staff may be a significant issue. In a competitive market the school will have to ensure that it effectively markets its location, the quality/behaviour of its pupils, and the management culture of the school, alongside the more traditional package of direct benefits that every employer now offers.

Other Educational Institutions

Effective liaison with feeder institutions can play a major role in recruitment activity. Often, designated secondary school teachers will be given responsibility for developing relationships with key feeder schools in the immediate geographical area. The cultivation of this relationship may involve regular visits to such institutions and meetings with staff, parents, and pupils, in a bid to make the transition from one school to another as seamless as possible.

The Local Community

The local community is a public which is increasing in importance. Whilst schools have always been concerned to be seen to be living in harmony with local residents, the role of community liaison has in the past has been quite reactive in nature. Since parents often build their perception of particular schools (see the following section) from listening to the local grapevine, influencing this grapevine proactively has now become a major priority. The advent of community education has also compelled schools to specifically develop this target group. Many schools now market evening courses designed to meet the needs of local people and draw valuable income therefrom.

Commerce and Industry

With educational funding becoming increasingly restricted, many schools have now registered as charities and are attempting to solicit support from corporate donors in the same way as other charitable organizations. The educational standards set and the overall reputation of a given school will doubtless exert considerable influence over a decision of whether or not support will be granted. Good links with industry and commerce are also important to find work placements for those students who require them. If a school has a bad reputation, employers are likely to be less willing to offer its pupils placements, particularly when the administration of these can often be burdensome.

The Local Education Authority

Whilst the role of the LEA has declined in significance in recent years, they remain a key school public by virtue of the access that they can provide to discretionary funding. They are also important targets since schools may have the desire to influence funding policies at a local level and will therefore want to develop close links that can be exploited for lobbying purposes, as and when the need arises.

University/College Publics

The list of important publics for those institutions involved in the delivery of FE or HE is even longer. To those identified above we may add research funders, alumni, accredited organizations, and local/national media, although not even this list should be regarded as exhaustive.

Research Funders

Research funders constitute an important public, particularly for universities to address. These fall generally into one of two categories. The first are quasi-governmental organizations which exist to act as a conduit to channel government support into those projects or departments which are deemed most worthy of support. The destination of this form of funding is now highly dependent on the performance of a department (or more accurately a unit of assessment), in the Research Assessment Exercise (RAE) currently conducted every four years. Other government funding is available through the research councils and this may be bid for on an ad hoc basis as projects present themselves. The second category of research funders are essentially grant-making trusts which exist to support particular forms of research. The process of applying for funds from such organizations is usually, although not always, a competitive process.

Whilst one would hope that decisions taken in respect of research funding would always be objective and based on the quality of past research and/or the application submitted, the impact of a favourable image and an institution's record of gaining publicity for its research should not be underestimated.

Alumni

The careful cultivation of alumni can serve a number of purposes. Good alumni relations can greatly aid student recruitment, particularly in some overseas markets where personal recommendations can be of great importance. Alumni can also be a valuable source of publicity for the university as the achievements of past students are often newsworthy. Moreover an alumni network can unlock doors that lead to research funding, consultancy, student placements, and even quite sizeable donations of cash support.

Accredited Organisations

With the expansion of higher education a great many institutions now accredit colleges to teach one or more aspects of their provision. Franchise or accreditation arrangements are now common. In the former, a college would deliver a course programme on the university's behalf whilst, under the latter arrangement, the university would agree to recognize a college course as meeting a particular standard and award an appropriate qualification to participants on completion. In recent years the development of such arrangements has been popular not only at home, but also with educational establishments abroad. Indeed there has been a phenomenal growth in overseas links, primarily because they can prove extremely lucrative, not only in terms of the revenue generated, but also in terms of the number of future university applicants they can generate. As a consequence responsibility for the development of such links tends now to be administered at a most senior level within the majority of HE institutions.

Local/National Media

Given the significance of the output of qualified individuals from colleges and universities to the national economy, it is no surprise that there is considerable media interest in the activities of universities. The activities and successes of individual students are often of great interest as are the nature of the relationships that a university has with all its other publics. Carefully managed, the publicity that this generates can have a very positive impact on the overall image the institution is able to project.

In a short text such as this it is impossible to examine in great detail the manner in which relationships with all the 'publics' identified above could be developed. The decision was therefore taken to concentrate in the remainder of this chapter on the impact that marketing can have on arguably the most important of these—namely, that of potential students.

Influencing Student Buying Behaviour

Chapman (1986) was amongst the first to apply the buying behaviour literature to the education sector. He suggested that, in selecting a suitable institution at which to study, students (and/or their parents) will pass through a number of uniquely definable stages.

Stage 1—Pre-Search Behaviour

Students will give an early consideration to their choice of the next educational establishment to attend, although at this stage little or no effort is expended to actually gather information about the various options available. Students will quite passively 'register' the existence of information to which they are exposed. This may be general institutional advertising, or it may be casual discussions with family or friends. It is at this stage, however, that attitudes towards different providers will begin to be formed. This is a crucial stage of the process, since these attitudes, be they positive or negative, will help the student in the future to develop his/her own shortlist of potential institutions at which to study.

The marketing task at this point is to ensure that the institution maintains a relatively high profile within its target markets. Favourable publicity about the activities of students and/or staff, links with feeder institutions, open days, special events, etc. can all help create and reinforce positive attitudes towards an organization. Similarly the local grapevine can often be persuaded to act in an institution's favour through the careful cultivation of links with the broader community.

Stage 2—Search Behaviour

By the time students actively seek out course information the evidence suggests that a short list of potential providers has already been formed. For the student it is then only a matter of comparing between this limited number of alternatives. They will use a variety of sources of information to help them in this task and look for data relating to a wide range of decision criteria. Since these criteria will vary substantially between the various levels of education, this is a matter that will be returned to in some detail below.

Stage 3—Application Decision

Having researched the alternatives available, the student will then utilize the decision-making criteria referred to above to identify a small number of institutions to which an application will be made. At this stage the selected institutions will respond by either rejecting the application or making an offer of a place. It is often the case that this offer will be dependent on a specified level of performance in forthcoming examinations.

The marketing task at this point is to ensure that applications are dealt with as promptly and 'personally' as possible. In the case of higher education, whilst almost all undergraduate applications are now dealt with by UCAS (Universities and Colleges Admissions Service), the time taken to respond by a particular institution can still make a substantial difference. This is particularly true of postgraduate education where many students are keen to guarantee themselves a place as soon as the decision to study has been taken. In a market where a great similarity in portfolios now exists between institutions, those that are seen to provide a high standard of 'customer care' and respond quickly to communications will undoubtedly gain an advantage.

Stage 4—Choice Decision

The next stage of the process involves the student in accepting one or more of the offers that has been made. In most cases, this acceptance does not form the basis of a binding contract with the education provider and hence multiple acceptances are common.

It is absolutely essential that providers realize at this point that they will be competing with only a small number of other institutions. Since many still fail to maintain a dialogue with prospective students from the time at which an offer is issued, until (hopefully) the student arrives on campus, there remains a substantial marketing opportunity. Institutions which maintain a dialogue, perhaps by sending copies of information sheets, newsletters, course information, and/or reading lists have all recognized the importance of such communications in psychologically bonding a student to their institution. The reader will recall the issue of 'tangibility' in service marketing from Chapter 4. High-quality, informative communications which help prepare students for their forthcoming programmes of study can greatly raise the level of tangibility and serve to reduce the inevitable stress that will result from having to choose between the final few institutions.

Stage 5—Matriculation Decision

At the final stage of the process, the student has ultimately to decide at which institution he/she will study and register as a student on the campus. At this stage the marketing task is to welcome the new students and ensure that the transition to their new way of life is as smooth as possible. At an undergraduate level, universities have many years of experience of running informative and often highly entertaining 'Freshers Week' programmes to help ensure that students make new friends and settle in before the commencement of their studies.

In the case of mature, overseas and postgraduate students, however, their needs are likely to be somewhat different. Many may need help to arrange accommodation (often for their whole family), medical care, English Language support, religious services, and more specific help to identify all the key university services that they are likely to need during their stay. An increasing number of institutions have come to recognize the needs of these individuals and now operate separate induction programmes which ensure, as far as possible, that these are catered for.

Whilst all the stages of the decision-making process are important and marketing has a clear role to play in each, the key communication issue for most institutions (and certainly the allocation of the largest proportion of the marketing budget) revolves around stages 1 and 2. Institutions need to ensure that they communicate effectively with students early in their decision-making process. The difficulty for most providers, however, lies in deciding exactly what to say and to whom. The remainder of this section will attempt to shed some light on this issue, by analysing in some detail how decisions in respect of education provision are taken in the cases of primary, secondary, and higher education.

Primary Education

The key decision makers in respect of the appropriate provider of a primary education are now (by virtue of the recent Education Act) the parents of the individual child. Interestingly parents have been shown to give consideration to this issue at a very early stage in their child's development. Indeed many will have decided on an appropriate primary school well before their child reaches the age of two years (Bussell, 1994). Given this, one may legitimately ask what sources of information parents might use in reaching their decision. After all, most appear to have been taken before any direct contact with a school has been initiated. Bussell found that the key source of information used by parents was the local grapevine, emphasizing once again the importance for schools of maintaining close relationships with their local community.

Petch (1986), in a series of 400 interviews with parents, determined that the following evaluative criteria were used by parents to compare between the various alternatives available.

- *Happiness*—parents' perceptions of the atmosphere in a particular school. Most parents will at some stage visit prospective providers, even if the visit only serves to confirm an earlier decision. Since most visits can be timed to allow classroom activity to be viewed, the happiness of the pupils can be (albeit subjectively) assessed.
- *Location*—parents have been shown (for obvious reasons) to favour schools that are geographically closer to the family home.
- *Discipline*—level of discipline imposed on students is a significant factor for parents. Most like to feel that good standards of discipline are rigorously enforced.
- *Facilities*—the computing, library and recreational resources provided.
- *Friends*—the placement of children belonging to friends of the family.
- *Siblings*—the school selected for an older brother/sister.
- *Teachers*—the perceived quality of the teaching staff.
- *Reputation*—the overall reputation of the school.
- *Safety*—the perceived safety of the environment created by the school.

Secondary Education

By the stage at which decisions have to be taken in respect of a secondary education, the child his/herself now has considerably more say. Studies by Thomas (1991) and Alston (1985) both confirm the importance of the child in the decision-making process. Children appear to be influenced by visits from secondary school teachers and visits to their potential new schools. The most important factors in influencing a child's decision are, however—where friends will study, the facilities offered, and surprisingly the existence of a uniform. Children appear not to want to attend a school where the pupils appear scruffy, or where bullying is felt to occur (West *et al.* 1995).

The impact of written communications should also not be underestimated in communicating with potential pupils. West and Varlaam (1991) found that 70 per cent of children had read the school brochures of potential new schools. This fact has important implications for the style in which such publications are produced since they should clearly be written in a manner easily accessible by 11/12-year-olds.

The decision in respect of which school to attend appears to be taken before the last year of primary education (Stillman and Maychall, 1986), with a surprising amount of agreement between children and their parents over which school should be selected. Indeed West *et al.* (1995) found that parents and children agree in 83 per cent of cases. Despite the increasing involvement of the child in the decision, however, the levels of parental input and concern remain high. Over 87 per cent will visit the school their child will ultimately attend and 94 per cent will take the time to read the school brochure. Of the factors that have the most influence on parental choice, discipline, exam results, and happiness are all primary considerations (see for example West *et al.*, 1995, West and Varlaam, 1991 or Hammond and Dennison, 1995).

Higher Education

(a) Undergraduate Students

Grabowski (1981), in a comprehensive review of the literature, found that the following factors all appeared to have an impact on student choice:

- athletic facilities
- academic reputation of the institution
- quality of college faculty
- economic status of family
- availability of financial aid
- conversations with former students
- geographic location
- opinions of high school teachers and counsellors
- effectiveness of the institution in getting jobs for its graduates
- institution's competition
- interviews
- older brothers and sisters who attended the institution
- parents and family preferences
- physical plant and facilities
- activities of recruiters
- size of establishment
- social activities
- specific academic programmes
- visits to campus.

Whilst a knowledge that all these factors have the capacity to influence a decision is helpful, it does not leave an HE marketer with much of a sense of how to prioritize their effort. The available research suggests that prospectuses are probably the most crucial form of marketing communication, but it is important to recognize that they often serve only to confirm decisions that have already been made (Chapman and Johnson, 1979).

In respect of some of the other factors listed, Chapman and Franklin (1981) and Kealy and Rockel (1987) agree that parents, peers, high school personnel, and campus visits are all of primary importance in influencing the decision-making process. Pali-hawadana and Westwell (1996), meanwhile, conclude that perceived job prospects upon graduation are a powerful determinant of student choice.

Given the somewhat diverse nature of the conclusions drawn by these studies it would seem sensible for institutions to conduct their own research. It may be that the criteria that have the capacity to exert the greatest influence on the decision-making process will vary depending on the subject matter being studied and the academic abilities and background of a particular individual. Quite clearly, once the factors that *are* of importance in a particular case are identified, the knowledge can be employed to good effect in designing promotional campaigns and deciding on an appropriate allocation of scarce marketing resources. The following case study of the Camborne School of Mines illustrates this point well.

Case Study 7.2: **Digging for Gold—The Camborne School of Mines**

Camborne School of Mines (CSM) has a long and proud tradition of educating young people for careers in various roles within the mining and geological sector. Long established as one of the finest providers of such education the School enjoys a high profile throughout the world and its graduates are keenly sought by all the major employers. Indeed, in university circles it can now boast that it is something of a rarity, since employers actively compete to be the first to meet a particular student group on the annual 'milk round'. Competition for CSM graduates has been so keen in fact that this process has now to be carefully managed to avoid upsetting individual employers by being seen to give an advantage to one at the expense of another. Given this level of demand the reader will not be surprised to learn that historically CSM has had no difficulty in recruiting students to its world renowned facility, and the attitude of staff during the early 1990s probably reflected this. Staff were quite comfortable both with the ability of the students they were able to attract and with the overall numbers thereof. In short, there was felt to be no real need for marketing as they understood it.

By the mid 1990s, however, CSM began to notice a dramatic decline in its student numbers. A variety of environmental factors and organizational complacency in respect of recruitment had led to an across-the-board decrease in applications to all categories of course throughout the School. The details of this decline for the three major programmes offered by the School, are given in Figs. 7.1–7.3.

As can be seen from the Figures, CSM offers a variety of engineering and science based courses at both HND and Degree level. By 1995, however, it can also be seen that the recruitment levels on these courses had fallen to an all-time low. At that time the management of the School were seriously doubting their ability to be able to maintain the range of courses available to students and there were even concerns that the total number of staff employed would in future be difficult to justify. Indeed having extrapolated the trends suggested by the graphs, there were very real concerns that the school would not prove to be economically viable in 1996.

It was at this point that the management of the School began a thorough review of the changes in the market for their courses and the implications thereof for their own marketing strategy. Through research, they determined that the key problem was the image that both mining and the School itself projected. With respect to the latter, the School was felt to have a problem with its name. Whilst there was no question of it being able to change this, because of high levels of awareness throughout the mining industry, the three ingredients of Camborne, School, and Mines, were all not likely to

Fig. 7.1:
**First Year
Engineering
Degree
Enrolments**

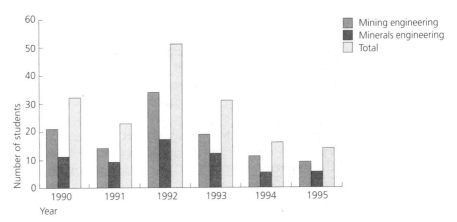

Fig. 7.2: **HND
Engineering
Enrolment**

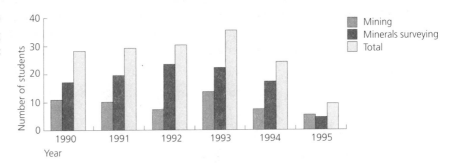

Fig. 7.3: **HND
Science
Enrolment**

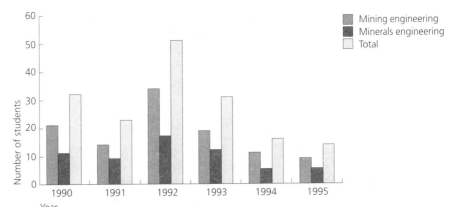

be particularly attractive to the average 18-year-old. Many would have difficulty in identifying where Camborne was, and even those that could would probably be put off by its distance from major centres of population. The word 'School' also has associations with a lower level of education and, to make matters worse, mining as a career was also found to have a long series of negatives associated with it.

The key reason for this was that the early 1990s saw the collapse of much of the remaining mining industry in the UK, leaving school leavers with the impression that mining was a dead or dying industry. Mining as a career was simply not highly regarded by school leavers and tended to be regarded as 'dirty' or in some way inferior to other forms of engineering. Indeed, as a subject, mining engineering was found to be less popular than the study of Serbo-Croat or Celtic Studies! CSM further determined that even where these negative perceptions were absent many students simply failed to understand what exactly was on offer in terms of course content. Potential students had no real idea of what studying minerals engineering and mining engineering was likely to entail. The School was therefore facing a serious communications problem. It was failing to attract students because of a whole series of negative images (which acted to persuade those who might otherwise have studied at Camborne to choose a different subject of study) and an almost complete lack of understanding of what was on offer.

It was therefore clear to CSM management that they had to take immediate action both to correct the erroneous views of the mining career and to ensure that potential students understood exactly what they could be studying at Camborne. In itself, however, this was felt to be insufficient to reverse the negative trend. CSM needed to understand more about why students did elect to study with them and to use this knowledge to their advantage. What were the positive aspects that the School could offer? To assist them in determining what these might be, the School conducted some marketing research amongst its existing students. This yielded valuable intelligence in respect of the factors which influenced the decision to study at Camborne and the key results are illustrated in Fig. 7.4.

Fig. 7.4: **Reasons for Applying to CSM**

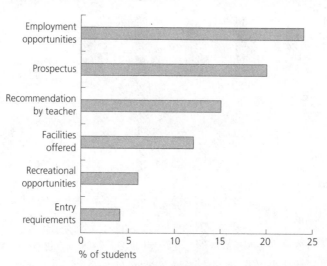

The results made clear to CSM management the key role that science teachers in schools have to play in informing students about the courses on offer and their relative merits. They are an important customer segment as they have the power to appraise students of an option they might hitherto not have considered, or to help provide criteria against which to assess the various course options available. Similarly the CSM and Exeter University (of which CSM is now part) prospectuses were found to be key forms of communication. Historically the CSM had always produced its own full-colour prospectus and the results of the survey indicated to management that this was an activity that should quite clearly be continued and that, moreover, any move to make cutbacks in either the quality of the prospectus or the quantity distributed should be strongly resisted.

Interestingly, however, almost a quarter of the students surveyed indicated that they studied at Camborne because of the job prospects that it could offer on completion of their Degree/HND. Through talking to its students about these issues CSM management further determined that many in their second or final years could command large sums of money for short periods of vacation employment. In one case a student had been able to travel to Australia during his vacation and earned £600 per week during his stay. CSM further determined that the salaries their graduates could attract far exceeded the normal salary expectations of an average graduate, irrespective of the chosen subject of study. Salaries for graduate mining engineers were typically of the order of £30,000 and posts in a variety of different countries were available. Moreover, because of a world-wide skill shortage in this area, and the excellent reputation of the CSM with employers, almost all the students in a typical intake would be able to find employment within six months of completing their course. Indeed the popularity of the School with employers has already been alluded to above.

The one key benefit that the school could offer its students was, therefore, almost a guarantee of well-paid employment both during and after the completion of their studies. It was decided to take full advantage of this major benefit in a bid to enhance recruitment to the CSM's engineering courses at both HND and Degree levels and it was this message that was to form the core of all the communications that the School had with its market during the 1995/6 academic year. In tactical terms, these communications included:

(1) *An aggressive PR campaign.* This addressed all the major local and national media. The initial PR focused on the success achieved by students in gaining vacation employment overseas and the sums of money involved. This proved to be a very popular story and it was covered by a wide variety of media.

(2) *Advertising.* Whilst advertising had traditionally been taboo for Universities, since it was felt that to be seen to advertise might somehow degrade the perceived quality of the institution, CSM flouted 'the rules' and began advertising its undergraduate courses for the first time. Advertisements not only outlined the CSM courses available, but once again communicated the successes achieved by its students.

(3) *Personal selling.* Given the results of the student survey, it was felt appropriate to be more proactive in CSM's dealings with schools. Staff were encouraged to forge closer links with key feeder institutions and where possible to actually make regular visits and talk to prospective students. Packs of information were also produced which directly related to the content of GCSE and 'A' level syllabuses and which were all designed to cultivate an interest in minerals and mining as a career.

The results of the push during 1995/6 were astounding. Figs 7.5 and 7.6 illustrate the impact that the new proactive marketing stance had on levels of student recruitment. A significant upturn was experienced on all engineering courses. CSM management are convinced that this upturn is directly attributable to the enhanced marketing activity undertaken and not to random fluctuations in the market. Their proof for this belief is the recruitment pattern experienced on the Science courses, which did not form part of the 1995/6 marketing push. The recruitment trends for this family of courses are shown in Fig. 7.7, with a clear and continuing decline indicated. Clearly, management attention will be shifting to address this problem area in the months and years ahead.

Fig. 7.5:
**First Year
Engineering
Degree
Enrolment**

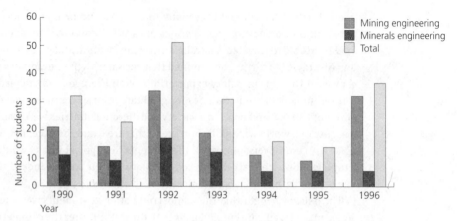

Fig. 7.6: **HND
Engineering
Enrolment**

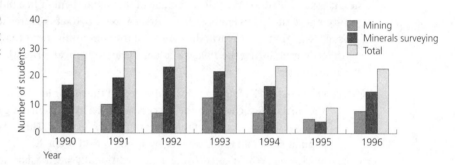

Fig. 7.7: **HND
Science
Enrolment**

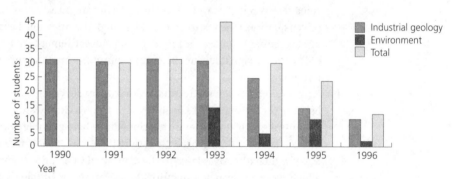

(b) Postgraduate Students

Fortunately the criteria used by postgraduate students to select between various institutions appear a little more uniform. In the largest study of its kind, HEIST (1995) identified that the factors cited in Table 7.1 were cited as having the most influence.

At a postgraduate level the nature of the course content would seem to be altogether more important than at an undergraduate level. Intense promotional activity is therefore likely to be much less effective than an early consideration of customer needs/wants and a course design that reflects these. Interestingly postgraduate students appear to seriously consider only a very small number of potential providers. In the USA , for example, it has been shown that the number of graduate schools considered by a student averages around three, with only two key sources of information

	Factor	% Of Students Citing as Primary Consideration
	Course Content	32
	Location	19
	Availability of Funding	12
	Reputation of Institution	10
	Only Institution Offering Course	7
	Recommendation	4
	Other	16

Table 7.1
Factors
Influencing
Postgraduate
Student Choice

Source: O'Neill (1995). Reproduced by kind permission of HEIST, Leeds, UK.

regarding these being utilized. Key sources of information were found to include prospectuses and peer-related contacts, a finding replicated in the UK by Palihawadana (1992).

(c) Overseas Students

The preceding discussion has focused primarily on the recruitment of home students to university courses. Since most institutions now actively recruit overseas students it is worth examining briefly what is known about the purchase behaviour of this specific group. HEIST (1994) reports that the following variables all have the capacity to influence a decision. They are listed below in descending order of importance:

- academic reputation
- content of the course
- international reputation of the institution
- guaranteed accommodation
- entry requirements
- cost of living
- level of fees.

There are a number of interesting points which emerge from this analysis. Firstly it would appear that the primary reason for studying overseas is to gain a qualification from a prestigious institution which will be recognized within the home country. This has implications for HE marketers in so far as most are quite geocentric in their approach. There is a clear need to do more than simply 'sell' in an overseas market. Institutions also need to build up a 'presence' within each market with a communications mix, the target of which is sufficiently broad to include students, parents, governments, sponsors, and employers. It is no accident, for example, that the more enlightened universities now offer graduation ceremonies in other countries for overseas students and their families to attend. Such events can raise the profile of an institution and attract generous amounts of favourable publicity. Of course, one needs sufficient numbers of students to make this latter idea work, but, since many foreign institutions now offer degrees awarded in partnership with UK universities, the opportunities to provide this kind of event look set to increase. It is no longer enough for providers to rely solely on their home reputation—a reputation in each target market must be built and studiously maintained.

The second point worthy of note from Table 7.1 is the importance of cost to the overseas student. Since most universities operate a very simple cost plus approach to their pricing, there may in the future be an opportunity to offer greater flexibility in respect of the pricing of each programme. How many institutions, for example, currently offer a lower fee rate on those courses for which it is difficult to recruit? An end to rigid accounting practices and a more flexible market-based approach could well pay dividends in overseas markets.

It is also interesting to note a further point that emerged from the HEIST study. Around 25 per cent of international students currently studying in the UK have at some time previously studied in this country. Indeed, of these, some four-fifths were studying in the country at the time of their HE application. These facts have a major significance for HE providers in that it once again emphasizes the importance of the schools liaison function in developing close links with potential feeder institutions.

As one would expect given the often great geographical distance between the country of origin and the institution at which it has been decided to study, the range of information sources that a student will utilize are considerably more diverse. The other contributory factor to the use of this range of information sources is undoubtedly the element of risk associated with study at an overseas institution. In most cases the student will never have visited the institution and can hence not 'sample' the lifestyle that will be encountered. Moreover, living and working in a foreign culture can be a daunting prospect and students need a much greater assurance that they are making the right decision. It is not surprising therefore that personal contacts are amongst the most significant influences on the decision-making process. Indeed HEIST (1994) determined that personal sources were often the trigger to considering a particular institution in the first place. The results of the study are reported in Table 7.2.

Table 7.2
First Source of Information about Overseas Institution

Source of Information	% of Students Indicating
Friend	18.5
Education Directories	13.8
Prospectus	8.0
Member of Family	7.8
British Council	7.4
Subject Lecturer	5.7
Careers Adviser	5.3
Exhibition in Own Country	5.3
University Links with Feeder Institution	4.7
Through the Media	4.7

Source: Allen and Higgins (1994). Reproduced with the kind permission of HEIST, Leeds, UK.

The key recruiting tactic employed by educational institutions addressing overseas markets has long been attendance at overseas exhibitions. Academics and administrators travel to a selection of fairs and meet face to face with individual students. For a great many institutions this will be the only contact that they will have with their market in a given year. Only a minority will take the trouble to establish a regular programme of visits to feeder institutions; only a few will have regular contacts with British

Council employees, careers advisers, and employers; and still less will actually make their presence known by advertising in the local press. What is perhaps most deplorable, however, is the fact that many universities continue not to exploit their local alumni. The achievements of many overseas students would be newsworthy in their home countries and most students return enthusing about their experiences. This enthusiasm could be employed to much greater effect in raising the local awareness of the institution and making it a topic of conversation with many of those listed in Table 7.2. Universities must learn to adopt a broader focus within each of their target markets, and to give adequate consideration to communicating with all those who can influence the decision-making process if they are to continue to meet their recruitment targets.

Education Marketing—Planning and Control

Marketing Strategy

It will be apparent from the foregoing that the task of marketing an educational institution is perhaps more complex than would be the case for almost any other category of nonprofit. A diversity of publics with an equally diverse set of needs and wants makes it almost impossible to derive one plan that will adequately serve the needs of the whole institution. It is therefore normal practice to address the marketing strategy that will be followed at an institutional level and to delegate authority for the production of individual tactical plans to specific departments or centres. Each of these can then develop a tactical mix that will be appropriate for the one or more educational publics that they deal with on a daily basis.

Clearly, at a strategic level, decisions in respect of the overall direction of the institution will be taken, perhaps utilizing Ansoff as a framework. Market segmentation and positioning are also likely to be decided centrally as they are both issues likely to have profound implications for the development of subsequent tactical plans. In particular the positioning selected by an education institution will pervade every aspect of the work that it subsequently engages in. Unlike many consumer markets where individual offerings can be separately positioned, in education markets it is rare to be able to escape from the overall 'image' that a particular supplier has in the market. Whilst most students recognize that departments in a university will vary in quality and will try to take a subject rather than an institutional perspective, it would be a brave marketer who would claim that the overall positioning of the university, in terms of perceived quality and status, would not have a considerable impact on student choice. There are a small number of institutions, for example, who tend to be selected as a fallback position by students if they fail to be accepted at one of the Oxbridge universities. Interestingly this group of institutions are continually selected as the second choice, irrespective of the subject being studied. At a postgraduate level this phenomenon is perhaps less in evidence, since students are often motivated to apply by the research ranking achieved by an individual department. Even in these cases, however, students will doubtless be mindful of how the institution will be perceived in the minds of potential employers on completion of their studies.

The positioning can also have a profound impact on the success or failure of fundraising initiatives and attempts to work closely with commerce/industry. Those institutions that are perceived as being either of high quality or as in some way unique are likely to have the greatest success in these areas.

The difficulty for senior managers, however, is that the positioning strategy selected needs to be consistent and hence capable of implementation in each of the very diverse markets that the institution serves. Accomplishing this is no easy matter, the temptation being to select a positioning strategy which is based on vague academic values such as excellence in teaching or research. There cannot be many institutions who do not perceive themselves as striving for excellence in both these key areas! A good positioning strategy should be genuinely unique and summarize neatly the key facets of the organization, thus allowing some scope for modification in response to the requirements of each individual market.

Marketing Tactics

The responsibility for the development of tactical plans will vary considerably from institution to institution. In the case of schools, it is likely that one plan will be developed centrally with the help of senior teaching staff and administrators. In the case of an FE college a central institutional plan is also likely to exist, although responsibility for marketing individual courses is likely to be devolved to the members of academic staff who have the responsibility for co-ordinating each programme. In a university, the picture is likely to be somewhat more complex with separate tactical plans being developed by a multitude of different administrative and academic departments. In this environment it is absolutely essential that some mechanism exists to co-ordinate the actions of each. Greater co-ordination can lead to a considerable number of benefits, including the placement of joint advertising (leading to overall cost reductions), greater buying power, a sharing of ideas and experience, and the careful planning of support activities. A department within one well-known institution recently advertised its presence in clearing for the first time and was swamped with high numbers of phone calls. No additional administrative staff had been devoted to the task of dealing with enquiries and none of the operators who took the calls were even aware that the advert had been placed. What could have been a very effective promotion was thus sabotaged by a failure to communicate with other key 'marketing' staff.

Control

The issue of control is of particular significance for educational institutions. Given the great diversity in marketing activities taking place right across a typical organization it is essential that effective control mechanisms are put in place to ensure that all these activities are co-ordinated. Where control is lacking, conflicting decisions can often be taken resulting in organizations sending two or more very different messages to their target market. Indeed these decisions may well bear no resemblance to those envisaged by senior management in the overall institutional plan. A lack of control can also result in lost opportunities to minimize cost and the inefficient use of promotional media. One institution in the author's experience once placed four separate advertisements in the same educational journal, each with a very different and conflicting message about the nature and size of the organization's campus.

Control activity can best be categorized under the following headings.

(a) Strategic Control

At a strategic level, the emphasis is largely on ensuring that the organization 'gets to where it wants to be'. Senior management will have taken a range of decisions relating to the strategic direction of the institution, segmentation issues, and positioning. They will also doubtless have had considerable input to portfolio matters, pricing, and promotion. Strategic control therefore needs to ensure that the decisions taken were implemented in the manner envisaged and that the desired effect in terms of the strategic health of the organization has been realized (i.e. that the marketing activity has been effective). The key strategic control is thus the marketing audit referred to earlier which should be undertaken on an ongoing and regular basis.

(b) Efficiency Control

Institutions will also want to ensure that they are making an efficient use of their resources. Marketing activity could well be effective in the sense that it is aiding the achievement of the institutional objectives, but it may be costing the organization rather more than is strictly necessary. The efficiency of the marketing activity undertaken is thus an important issue on which to focus control. Typically this might be undertaken at a functional level, measuring, for example, the efficiency of various forms of promotional activity (for example, attendance at overseas fairs, advertising, direct mailshots, etc.). Desired levels of efficiency can be compared against actual and remedial action instigated where necessary.

(c) Profitability Control

The profitability of each activity also needs to be controlled. Setting targets for each course, department, faculty, etc. may be one way of achieving this. Alternatively, an institution-wide perspective could be adopted and profitability measured by key customer segment.

(d) Annual Plan Control

A key focus of control activity is the annual institutional plan. Marketers would need to measure:

(1) *Sales/Market Shares*—Comparing actuals with the budgeted figures.

(2) *Sales/Expense Analysis*—In many institutions this is referred to as the allowable cost per sale. Organizations need to decide in advance just how much they are prepared to spend to secure each sale and monitor performance against this target.

(3) *Conversion Rates*—Institutions will wish to ensure that a sufficient number of enquiries are actually converted into sales. If the conversion rate appears to be dropping in the case of one department, this may indicate that its portfolio is becoming less attractive, or that the marketing thereof is of poor quality.

(4) *Drop-out Rates*—A key test of the quality of marketing activity in education is the extent to which it allows individuals to self select the courses that are right for

them. Monitoring drop-out rates can therefore be a helpful control mechanism in ensuring that a high quality of contact is maintained with each target group. Individuals should have no difficulty in determining in advance which courses are right for them and taking action accordingly.

Despite the length of the foregoing list, however, it is important that a balance be struck between ensuring that adequate control mechanisms do exist and allowing individual marketing functions sufficient scope to develop their own creativity. Departments should be encouraged to explore the utility of new marketing techniques and not be afraid on occasion to experiment with new ideas, even if this means an occasional 'failure'. The control procedures employed within a particular organization should therefore allow sufficient scope for this to take place without compromising the integrity of the overall institutional position.

Summary

In this chapter we have examined a number of the key environmental influences for change on education at all levels within the UK. Issues of competition and enhanced student choice are now matters of concern to all education marketers irrespective of where they might happen to work within the sector. Importantly these changes should not be viewed as taking place only in the UK—in many other countries the same environmental forces are shaping the manner in which educational frameworks are developed and maintained.

Against this backdrop it has been argued here that the singularly most important marketing issue for educational institutions to address is the early attainment of a genuine market orientation. By definition this would involve organizations in fostering greater degrees of collaboration between internal departments, monitoring the performance and activities of key competitors and developing a focus on a wide range of institutional publics.

To date, research undertaken into the needs/wants of these publics has been comparatively sparse, although the findings of a number of the more important studies have been reported here. If institutions are to successfully develop course provisions that are attractive to the market, they need to have a detailed understanding of the needs thereof. Indeed an understanding of how and when decisions are taken in respect of educational provision is absolutely essential if providers are to effectively market their provision to what are undoubtedly the key organizational publics of potential students and their parents. Only when such a knowledge has been gained can organizations hope to develop meaningful strategic and tactical plans which will genuinely capture the imagination of their market and lead ultimately to superior performance therein.

Discussion Questions

1. What are likely to be the key institutional barriers to the attainment of a marketing orientation in the education sector? How might these be overcome?

2. How might a competitive focus be accomplished? What categories of data should an educational institution look to capture in respect of its key competitors?

3. To what extent might marketing at a philosophical level be likely to conflict with the traditional concept of academic freedom? Are the two necessarily incompatible?

4. In the case of your own institution, or one with which you are familiar, list its key publics. How might relationships with each of these key publics be developed and maintained over time?

5. Why is the concept of marketing 'control' of particular relevance to Higher Education Institutions? What difficulties are likely to be encountered in attempting to control the marketing activities undertaken? How could these difficulties be overcome?

References

Allen, A. and Higgins, T. (1994) *Higher Education—The International Student Experience*, HEIST, Leeds.

Alston, C. (1985) *The Views of Parents before Transfer*, Secondary Transfer Project, Bulletin 3 (RS991/85) Inner London Education Authority.

Bargh C., Scott P. and Smith, D. (1996) *Governing Universities: Changing the Culture?*, SRHE and Open University Press, Buckingham.

Boxall, M. (1991) 'Positioning the Institution in the Marketplace', in *Universities in the Marketplace*, CUA Corporate Planning Forum, Conference of University Administrators in Association with Touche Ross.

Bussell, H. (1994) 'Parents and Primary Schools: A Study of Customer Choice', *Proceedings of 1994 Marketing Education Group Conference*, Coleraine.

Chapman, R. (1986) 'Toward a Theory of College Selection: A Model of College Search and Choice Behaviour', in *Advances in Consumer Research*, Vol. 13, (eds), Lutz, R. J. and Association for Consumer Research, Provo, Utah.

Chapman, R. G. and Franklin, M. S. (1981) 'Measuring the Impact of High School Visits: A Preliminary Investigation', *AMA Educators Conference Proceedings*, Chicago.

Chapman, D. W. and Johnson, R. H. (1979) 'Influences on Students' College Choice: A Case Study', Ann Arbor, Mich: Project CHOICE, School of Education, University of Michigan.

Davies, B. and Ellison, L. (1991) *Marketing the Secondary School*, Longman Industry and Public Services Management, Harlow.

Grabowski, S. M. (1981) *Marketing in Higher Education*, AAHE ERIC Higher Education Research Report, No. 5, Washington.

Hammond, T. and Dennison, W. (1995) 'School Choice in Less Populated Areas', *Educational Management and Administration*, Vol. 23, No. 2, 104–13.

HEIST (1995) *The Role of Marketing in the University and College Sector*, HEIST, Leeds.

Jarratt (1985) *Report of the Steering Committee for Efficiency Studies in Universities*, CVCP, London.

Kealy, M. J. and Rockel, M. L. (1987) 'Student Perceptions of College Quality: The Influence of College Recruitment Policies', *Journal of Higher Education*, Vol. 58, No. 6, 683–703.

Kotler, P. and Fox, K. (1985) *Strategic Marketing for Educational Institutions*, Englewood Cliffs, Prentice Hall.

Lockwood, G. and Davies, J. (1985) *Universities, The Management Challenge*, NFER Nelson, Windsor.

Moore, P. G. (1989) 'Marketing Higher Education', *Higher Education Quarterly*, Vol. 43, No. 2, 108–24.

O'Leary, J. (1996) 'The Future of Higher Education' *The Times*, 21 Jan, 5.

O'Neill, I. (1995) *Taught Postgraduate Education—The Student Experience*, HEIST, Leeds.

Palfreyman and Warner (1996) *Higher Education Management: The Key Elements*, The Open University Press, Buckingham.

Palihawadana, D. (1992) *Marketing Higher Education: A Case Study Related to the Strathclyde Business School*, unpublished PhD Thesis, Dept of Marketing, University of Strathclyde, Glasgow.

Palihawadana, D. and Westwell, R. (1996) 'Information Search and Choice Behaviour in Higher Education', *MEG Conference Proceedings*, 1165–77.

Petch, A. (1986) 'Parental Choice at Entry to Primary School', *Research Papers in Education*, Vol. 1 No. 1, 26–47.

Porter, M. E. (1985) *Competitive Advantage*, The Free Press, New York.

Stillman, A. and Maychell, K. (1986) *Choosing Schools: Parents, LEA's and the 1980 Education Act*, NFER-Nelson Publishing Company.

Thomas, A. and Dennison, W. (1991) 'Parental or Pupil Choice—Who Really Decides in Urban Schools?', *Education Managemnet and Administration*, Vol. 19, No. 4, 243–51.

West, A., David, M., Hailes, J. and Ribbens, J. (1995) 'Parents and the Process of Choosing Secondary Schools: Implications for Schools', *Educational Management and Administration*, Vol. 23, No. 1, 28–38.

West, A. and Varlaam, A. (1991) 'Choosing a Secondary School: Parents of Junior School Children', *Educational Research*, Vol. 33, No. 1, 22–30.

8

Healthcare Marketing

Objectives

By the end of this chapter you should be able to:

(1) understand and describe the healthcare environment;

(2) understand and describe the importance of service quality in obtaining a competitive advantage in healthcare;

(3) understand and describe the changing relationship between healthcare providers and their patients;

(4) design, develop, and implement a marketing plan for a primary healthcare organisation;

(5) design, develop, and implement a marketing plan for a nonprofit hospital.

Introduction

The relevance of the marketing concept to the delivery of healthcare services has long been recognized and it was as early as 1971 when the first journal article on the subject by Zaltman and Vertinsky appeared in the *Journal of Marketing*. Since then a variety of other writers have entered the fray and two particularly key healthcare marketing textbooks by MacStravic (1975) and Kotler and Clarke (1987) have now been added to our bookshelves. In their turn these have been followed by a veritable deluge of new journal articles covering almost every conceivable aspect of the subject.

Despite the academic interest in the subject, however, marketing has still not been fully embraced by the healthcare community. Many of the common misconceptions of marketing alluded to in Chapter 1 are still widely held and much of the sector still suffers from an acutely malignant form of product orientation!

Many healthcare organizations still have no conception of the term 'customer', and remain steadfastly focused on management issues related to the product/service being provided. The reader will recall from Chapter 1 that the primary goal of any product-driven organization is to 'deliver goods that it thinks would be good for the market' (Kotler and Clarke, 1987, 29). In the case of the delivery of health care this approach essentially regards the patient as being in passive receipt of their treatment and affords little scope for a genuine interaction to take place between the healthcare provider and its patients. There is regrettably a considerable amount of evidence to support the proposition that much of the UK's healthcare provision, in particular, is delivered in such a manner. Teasdale (1992, 62), for example, notes that:

> a major criticism of the NHS (National Health Service) has always been that it is a very large organisation which decides for itself what is best for patients, and then develops its services accordingly. Patients are expected to be grateful for what they are offered, and to put up with delays or other inadequacies because we tell them we are short of resources.

Indeed whilst calls for a patient-centred approach to the delivery of physician services have been made for some time (see, for example, Pendleton and Hasler, 1983), in the UK at least, the evidence of many years of complaints suggests that the idea of a customer focus is still anathema (BMA, 1995).

In this chapter we will therefore examine a number of the structural reasons why this might be so, beginning with an overview of both the UK and US models of healthcare provision. We will then consider a number of ways in which providers could 'get closer' to their patients and in particular consider the role of service quality in enhancing overall customer satisfaction. This latter issue is now of great significance since attending to the important dimensions of service quality may be one of the few ways in which healthcare providers can in the future establish a truly sustainable form of competitive advantage.

The chapter will then conclude by considering the relevance of marketing to two key categories of healthcare provider, namely hospitals and those responsible for the delivery of primary health care, such as General Practitioners (GPs). A number of the key marketing issues faced by each category of organization will be discussed.

Healthcare Systems

It is important to begin this section of the text, however, by defining exactly what we mean by the expression 'healthcare system'. The World Health Organization (WHO) defines health as 'a state of complete physical, mental and social well being and not merely the absence of disease or infirmity'. (WHO, 1986, 1). The system established by every member of the WHO should hence be capable of responding to a wide range of physical, chemical, infectious, psychological, and social problems. In short the concept of health care is much wider than many people believe. Health care, as Edgren (1991) argues, should be viewed as much broader in scope than mere medical care. Healthcare systems thus need not only to give consideration to medical treatment but also to a range of social, cognitive, and emotional factors—societies must not only be clinically healthy, they should feel healthy too. Marketing thus has a key role to play in managing the expectations of customers and matching these as far as possible to the range of services provided. Marketing can also help in developing the quality of communications with various healthcare communities and in encouraging individuals to adopt healthier lifestyles, thus minimizing the use of unnecessary resources. Importantly, however, marketing can also help improve the nature of healthcare relationships and gently prise some physicians away from a view of the world in which they offer daily consultations to a range of clinical complaints rather than the human beings that are suffering from them. As West (1994, 29) notes, the medical profession has always been effective in attempting to cure disease; regrettably, however, many physicians and indeed healthcare organizations have left patients with the impression 'that what matters least of all is the average human life . . . its comfort and its happiness.'

The root of the problem in some countries has been the manner in which the healthcare framework has developed. In the UK, for example, the National Health Service has prided itself on its ability to provide high quality health care, free of charge, to anyone who might require it. Whilst, broadly speaking, it has proved successful in achieving this goal, its success has come at a price. Until recently patients had very few rights in respect of the treatment they received and from whom—it was necessary to take whatever was on offer. Individuals attended the family doctor that they had always attended and accepted any referrals that were recommended to whichever hospital happened to serve their locality. Since patient choice was not an issue, the medical institutions had a virtually captive audience for the services they provided. It was not surprising therefore that under such circumstances an inward-looking product-oriented focus began to develop.

Interestingly this manifested itself not only in declining levels of customer service, but also in wide variations in clinical care from one region of the country to another. The idea that one should both serve customer requirements and monitor the performance of 'competitors' to ensure that only the highest industry standards were maintained was anathema.

In an attempt to heighten standards of service and to raise the performance of all healthcare organizations to that of the best, the UK government introduced a number of changes into the way that UK health care was delivered and managed in the NHS and Community Care Act 1990. The key changes introduced in the Act were as follows:

(1) Money now 'follows the patient'. Essentially NHS funds are now allocated to reflect the size of the population local to particular healthcare providers. Adjustments are made to account for different demographic patterns and patterns of need. A facility also exists for GPs to refer patients to a hospital of their choice, which may not necessarily be the local one. Under such circumstances funding will follow the patient to the hospital selected for treatment.

(2) An internal market has been created. A distinction may now be drawn between purchasers and providers. Under the old system all health services were purchased on behalf of GPs by the District Health Authorities. In the new internal market there are now two key purchasers, the District Health Authorities and those GPs that have elected to hold their own budget for healthcare services—GP Fundholders. Both categories of purchasers are responsible for obtaining the best value-for-money care that they can for their patients.

(3) Regulation of the market has been achieved through written contracts. Contracts are now drawn up between purchasers and providers which specify in detail the nature of the services to be provided, how many patients will benefit, and at what cost. Incidentally the term 'contract' is now very little used by marketing practitioners in the sector—the latest buzzword is 'agreement'.

(4) Healthcare providers now have greater management autonomy. Providers are free to compete for service contracts and have the freedom to structure themselves in an appropriate manner in order to facilitate this process. Business units may, for example, be constructed around key competencies.

(5) Greater accountability—healthcare providers are now subject to medical audits to monitor the quality of health care provided. The audit commission has also been given responsibility for conducting what might be termed 'value for money' audits as part of the new financial framework.

The reader will appreciate the central role that GPs have to play as both purchasers and providers within the new style NHS. GP fundholders are essentially larger practices which have elected to hold some public monies which they may then use to buy the healthcare provision for patients on their list. Such monies would previously have been held by the relevant District Health Authority. These fundholding practices are then able to select those providers whom they see as offering the best value for money to their patients. Whilst the number of referrals to a particular hospital may be small, it should be noted that these fundholders have considerable power, since the money for those referrals would hitherto have been guaranteed income for a local hospital. Even a small drop in the same may force a particular hospital to consider rationalizing its services and/or to consider redundancies.

GP practices have been able to opt for fundholding status since 1991 and approximately 60 per cent of Britain's 33,000 GPs have now selected such a status. The patients under their care have availed themselves of a greater range of options in respect of their treatment as their GPs have been able to 'shop around'.

Hospitals have responded by actively marketing their services for the first time. Many now have dedicated marketing or 'development' roles, whose primary function is to solicit business from health authorities and GP fundholders. Hospitals have also been forced to think very carefully about the nature of their provision, giving careful consideration to the relative skills of other providers in their area. Under the old regime consultants could afford to develop specific areas of medicine governed by their own interests. Under the new regime, hospital portfolios must carefully match the needs of their specific market, thus ensuring that adequate levels of demand can be maintained.

The changes in the UK have also switched the emphasis from cure to prevention, creating the need for the first time for GPs to actively encourage their patients to attend the surgery for a range of preventative treatments and healthcare advice. Moreover GPs are now obliged to see their patients on a regular basis irrespective of whether they are sick or not. This monitoring system has compelled GPs to play a greater role in enhancing the overall health of the nation and for the first time many have had to consider researching the ongoing needs of those individuals comprising their local community. Marketing skills are therefore beginning to be sought for the first time and a number of larger practices now have a dedicated individual responsible for fulfilling such a role. Typically this might involve researching demand, promoting a range of health/wellness clinics, the attraction of new patients, and the general facilitation of healthier lifestyles in the local community.

In the USA both the need for, and the application of, marketing has historically been rather different. Under the US healthcare system income-earning Americans are obliged to have their own healthcare insurance, in many cases provided as a benefit by their employer. Healthcare insurers then pay on their clients' behalf for any healthcare treatment that might prove necessary in the hospitals that are associated with their scheme. As the system is in essence a fee-paying one, Americans have traditionally had a much greater choice in respect of where they will receive their medical treatment. In addition, individual doctors are remunerated not by the State but by fees reflecting the quality of their individual reputation. Marketing has therefore long played a role in communicating with the healthcare market and the promotion of all forms of medical care is quite commonplace.

Only the very poorest members of American society are looked after by the State through the Medicaid and Medicare systems. The federal government, for example, pays over 60 per cent of the cost of Medicaid, with the balance being met from the finances of each individual US state. Tough decisions thus have to be made at a local level both about the cut-off point at which Medicaid cover will be triggered and the range of services that will be provided. Often there is a trade off between the two (Ranade, 1994).

Thus the 'old style' NHS, before its recent reforms, and the US system could be viewed as opposite ends of a healthcare continuum reflecting substantial variations in the level of financial support volunteered by the State. The NHS reforms introduced in 1990 served to introduce quasi-markets into the UK system and thus established a 'halfway' house between these two extremes. Many other countries are now experimenting with similar systems, for example Sweden, Finland, New Zealand, and a number of the newly independent Eastern European states.

Whilst the need for the application of the marketing concept at a philosophical level is universal, since all societies have the right to expect that their healthcare systems will reflect the needs and wants of their people, the need for its application at a functional level will differ substantially from country to country. Whilst in the USA, for example, it is usual to encounter communication campaigns promoting practitioners in all branches of health care, only the private institutions in the UK currently find it necessary to maintain such a heightened public profile. In the USA general practitioners openly advertise to attract patients, since they rely almost entirely on fees to survive. In the UK, however, where levels of income have, at least until recently, been guaranteed, advertising is all but non-existent. It is interesting to note though that British GPs are having to learn some new marketing communications skills as individual practices begin to face up to the need to encourage patients to attend a range of health and wellness clinics.

The Healthcare Marketing Challenge

Healthcare marketing is undoubtedly one of the most challenging of all the forms of nonprofit marketing. To begin with, the healthcare product is probably the most intangible of all the services previously described. For example, the consumer has no real way of being able to assess the competence of a surgeon either before, or after, an operation has been completed. They have simply to put their faith in the skills of the medical profession and take everything on trust. Of course, patients can and do form opinions about the quality of the healthcare product, based on a whole series of observations, including their physical surroundings and the 'bedside manner' of their physician. Ironically it is thus possible for a patient to leave a hospital dissatisfied with the service they have received, even if their operation was performed to the very highest of technical standards. Unfortunately the reverse is probably also true and physicians that are amongst the least competent of the whole profession can still attain very high levels of customer satisfaction by a careful attention to other aspects of the service encounter. Putting aside the ethics of the latter approach to health care, it does seem clear that marketing has much to offer professionals in allowing them to do justice to their image, by supporting the excellence achieved in clinical care with good quality customer service.

Intangibility is, however, only one of the particular difficulties that healthcare marketers need to overcome. France and Grover (1992), for example, list a number of other factors which serve to complicate the marketing task:

1. *Mismatch between customer expectations and actual delivery.* Whilst all service encounters offer a multitude of opportunities for the provider to fall short of the customer's expectations, this is, perhaps, particularly a risk for healthcare providers. Whilst a given individual may have set expectations about the outcome of a particular treatment, his/her physiology and psychology will in practice mitigate this substantially. In the case of the former, no two individuals are alike, and they will enter a programme of treatment suffering from various degrees of the ailment and having different demographic characteristics and different levels of physical strength and recuperative powers. All these individual characteristics are quite beyond the control of the physician and yet will impact substantially on the outcome achieved. Similarly, whatever the quality of the medical outcome, the psychology of the patient will determine how this is actually perceived. Moreover, psychology will also determine the emphasis that patients will place on the various components of the overall service. Thus some patients require a greater degree of hand-holding and/or information than others. Practitioners therefore have the difficult task of formulating a judgement about the degree of support required, and acting accordingly.

2. *The number of service providers.* In a healthcare setting, the individual patient will encounter a variety of different categories of personnel. During the course of attending a hospital for a routine operation, for example, patients will have to deal with administrative staff, nurses, anaesthetists, catering staff, hospital porters, a variety of physicians, and their own surgeon. Thus a variety of opportunities exist for the encounter to go awry.

3. *Unpredictable demand.* It is almost impossible to predict with any degree of accuracy what the demand for a healthcare service will be. Newly emerged strains of virus, serious accidents, natural disasters, and even armed conflicts make planning something of a minefield. Provision clearly has to be set at a level that will meet all foreseeable demands, but perishability can then become a problem. Under-utilization of a service can cause serious financial problems during a 'lean' period. Marketing can hence have an important role to play in attempting to even out demand as far as is practical.

4. *Derived demand.* One of the major difficulties for healthcare marketers is that it can be difficult to know when to market and to whom. The key decision maker will often not be the patient, but rather their GP, a specialist, or a member of their immediate family. This is particularly an issue for healthcare providers in the United States where considerable choice in respect of an appropriate provider can be exercised.

Of all these difficulties, the inherent intangibility is perhaps the most difficult for healthcare marketers to come to terms with. The increasingly competitive environment is making it essential for those working in this arena to clearly differentiate their provision from that available elsewhere in the market. The most obvious route to the achievement of this goal is to position an organization as providing excellence in clinical care. Since, however, the patient has no way of evaluating this aspect of the provision, the search for some form of competitive advantage is problematic. Moreover, many categories of healthcare provider (for example, hospitals) provide such a wide range of clinical services that to position an institution as being 'a provider of excellent standards of clinical care' would be meaningless. Excellence in which field?

According to San Augustine *et al.* (1992) organizations which learn to deal with this complexity will in the future lead the field. Positioning, the authors argue, is set to become *the* key marketing strategy in achieving a sustainable competitive advantage in health care. Given the observations above, perhaps there are two primary dimensions of the healthcare service that could be used as the basis for a strong market positioning.

1. Providers could aim to position themselves as 'the best in the world at . . .' Quinn (1992). Hence, the key clinical benefit of sending a patient to a particular institution would be clear to all healthcare purchasers. Indeed the portfolio of services could support the identified area of expertise, providing clinical service in related areas and building up appropriate resources accordingly.

2. Where a wide portfolio of existing provision is already in evidence however, the healthcare marketer may be more advised to seek elements of positioning which can have a direct benefit for the attraction of patients to every clinical service the organization can offer. There are comparatively few ways in which such a 'global' positioning might be accomplished and a reliance on some aspect of the overall service quality provided has hence become commonplace. If a particular organization can build a reputation in the market-place for being a provider of a high quality service, greater numbers of customers will be attracted. From the perspective of the provider this means a concentration not only on clinical care, but also on the wider range of surrogate observations which patients use to build up their own perceptions of the quality of their experience.

Given the importance of service quality in health care, the next section will identify those 'ingredients' that have in the past been found to have the greatest impact on patient perceptions thereof.

The Dimensions of Healthcare Service Quality

There is now a consensus emerging from the available research to suggest that patients actually define the quality of their healthcare provision as a function of three separate intangible factors. Bopp (1990) suggests, for example, that these can be viewed as:

(1) expressive caring;
(2) expressive professionalism;
(3) expressive competence.

Since the competence of staff is particularly intangible, the author argues that this will be assessed using a number of other cues as surrogates. To determine what these might be, it is worth returning briefly to the service quality literature introduced in Chapter 2. Lytle and Mokwa (1992) effectively adapt the SERVQUAL model for use in conceptualizing the overall healthcare experience. Their view of the healthcare 'product' is depicted in Fig. 8.1.

Fig. 8.1:
Healthcare Product Bundle of Benefits

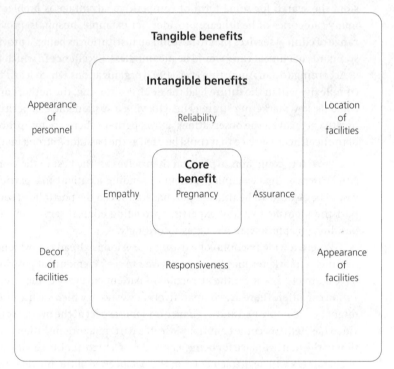

Core benefit   The nucleus of the product offering
Intangible benefits   Physician/patient/staff interactions
Tangible benefits   Physical environmental surroundings

Source: Reprinted with permission from Journal of Health Care Marketing, Lytle and Mokwa (1992), 12(1).

(a) Core Benefit

The core benefit is the outcome that the patient is seeking from the treatment he/she receives. This expectation will be shaped by conversations with family or friends, literature that they might have read in connection with their illness, and the advice and opinions of their physicians. Patients will clearly evaluate their experience according to the extent to which their expectations of its outcome have been met. They can obviously not assess the clinical skills of their physician, but they can assess the difference in how they feel, after the healthcare intervention has taken place.

(b) Intangible Benefits

The intangible benefits are received from the quality of the interaction which takes place between the patient and the physicians and their staff. The four SERVQUAL dimensions of reliability, empathy, assurance, and responsiveness are each key areas for the healthcare provider to address as it is relatively easy for the patient to form an opinion on these. In the case of comparatively minor interventions, where clinical benefits may be difficult to assess, it is these intangible elements that will in themselves form the basis of the majority of the overall assessment of service quality.

(c) Tangible Benefits

The expressive competence referred to earlier in the work of Bopp is difficult for a patient to assess. They have no way of being able to compare their surgeon's level of competence with that of another. They can however appraise the appearance of the facilities, the extent to which the latest technology appears to be being utilized, the comfort afforded by the physical surroundings, and the overall appearance of the personnel. It is these aspects when combined that will allow the patient to form a perception of the overall competence of their healthcare provider.

Whilst an attention to all these aspects of the healthcare encounter may be warranted, it is important for healthcare marketers to establish some sense of priority. Should priority be given to improving the quality of the physical environment, improving the interpersonal skills of staff, or reducing the length of time it is necessary to wait for treatment? From which of these areas would the patient be likely to draw the most value from potential improvements? These questions will be addressed below.

Enhancing Service Quality

The reader will recall from Chapter 2 that customer satisfaction can be modelled by looking at the five gaps proposed by Parasuraman *et al.* (1988):

Gap 1—between consumer expectations and management perception;
Gap 2—between management perception and service quality specification;
Gap 3—between service quality specifications and service delivery;
Gap 4—between service quality and external communications;
Gap 5—between perceived service and expected service.

Of all the gaps Gap 1 is undoubtedly the most important. Gap 5 cannot be managed directly, as it is merely the sum of all the others, and the size of Gaps 2 to 4 will largely be governed by the extent to which providers actually understand the expectations of their customers. Thus, for example, an attempt to address faulty service specifications without first acquiring a detailed understanding of what matters to the customer is likely to be both futile and costly. Any attempt to improve customer satisfaction with health care should hence commence with a thorough analysis of the nature of Gap 1.

In an interesting study of this gap in the healthcare context O'Connor *et al.* (1994) concluded that clinical contact employees (such as nurses), physicians, and administrators consistently underestimate patient expectations for each of the five SERVQUAL dimensions. In particular, physicians were found to have the poorest understanding, and the dimensions of empathy and responsiveness were the least well understood.

To achieve meaningful improvements in perceived service quality, therefore, healthcare providers would be advised not to focus solely on the enhancement of tangible factors. The greatest impact will be obtained if physicians, and to a lesser extent clinical contact employees, are educated about the importance of good communication with customers, promptness, helpfulness, and the facilitation of easy access.

Indeed there is much support for this view throughout the healthcare marketing literature and there has been considerable research conducted over the past thirty years to determine the components of medical care most likely to affect patients' perceptions of service quality. Ware *et al.* (1978), in a detailed review of the literature, identified eight satisfaction dimensions which they were subsequently able to reduce (through factor analysis) to four in the healthcare setting (i.e. physician conduct, availability of services, continuity/confidence, and efficiency/outcomes of care). Brown and Swartz (1989) meanwhile identify physician interactions as being the most important in determining satisfaction. The authors also conclude that a fifth dimension of convenience/access should be added to those proposed earlier by Ware *et al.*

Allied to the factor 'ease of access' is the concept of waiting time which may also warrant consideration, particularly by primary physicians. A number of studies have confirmed that the time spent waiting for a doctor is inversely related to patient satisfaction (see, for example, Lu Ann and Andersen, 1980). When one considers that Maister (1985) identified that anxiety can increase the perception of waiting time this additional factor's relevance to the healthcare setting becomes readily apparent.

More recently Sage (1991) identified five key factors which may be used to measure the quality of healthcare outcomes, namely: access, choice, information, redress, and representation. In the context of the primary healthcare practice, meanwhile, Gabbott and Hogg (1994) established that factors relating to the nature of the individual practice, such as the range of services offered and the ease of access to them, are important factors, as are the responsiveness and empathy of the physician.

The physical environment can also affect customers' perceptions of quality and Lych and Schuler (1990) suggest that hospital patients in particular will evaluate the service quality received, in part by assessing their physical environment. Andrus and Buchheister (1985) identify that pleasant and comfortable surroundings are important factors in determining patient satisfaction, in their case, with dental care.

In the USA a number of other studies are also of interest—each of which has examined patient satisfaction with medical services. These include Larsen and Rootman (1976), Hall and Dornan (1988) and Singh (1990). They broadly agree that the following factors all have the capacity to influence patient satisfaction:

(1) physician's manner;
(2) quality of information;
(3) professional and technical competence of physician;
(4) interpersonal and relational skills of physician;
(5) nature of the patient's medical problems;
(6) demographic background of patient.

The reader will appreciate from the foregoing that there has been considerable academic interest in this field. A variety of healthcare studies have shown that many different factors have the capacity to influence levels of patient satisfaction and there is not always much agreement between authors on the specifics thereof. Health-marketing professionals would hence be well advised to treat patient satisfaction as situation specific and to conduct their own primary research before embarking on any form of service improvement programme.

Healthcare Information

Whilst space does not permit a detailed analysis of all the factors capable of influencing patient satisfaction it is worth enlarging for a moment on the question of the provision of healthcare information. Healthcare information has the capacity to influence satisfaction both directly and indirectly and, in an age when consumers are increasingly expected to make their own decisions in respect of treatments and providers, the role of marketing in communicating effectively with customers will become increasingly crucial.

Healthcare communications can be either internal or external. With regard to the latter we have already established above that the nature of expectations in respect of the core healthcare product can be shaped by the exposure of a particular individual to a variety of communications messages. These messages which can now come from a plethora of different sources help to inform patient perceptions of both their complaint and the likelihood of a successful outcome deriving from a medical intervention. A key task for healthcare marketers is thus to manage these flows of information to ensure that the patient's perceptions of the outcome of their treatment is as realistic as possible.

Moreover, most healthcare systems now actively encourage the development of consumer choice—the ability to select one's own physician and to be able to discuss with him/her the relative merits of each course of action available. This dimension of the healthcare framework can only function adequately if physicians understand the range of information sources that are now available and understand the nature of their own role in relation to these.

The increased availability of good quality healthcare information has led to many individuals becoming what Berkowitz and Flexner (1980) refer to as 'activist health care consumers', a lifestyle category evidenced by rapidly increasing sales of home diagnostic equipment, greater involvement in decisions, and a general move (at least in the USA) towards increased doctor shopping. This is a relatively new phenomenon, since medical information only a few years ago used to be the preserve of the medical profession and was disseminated solely through scholarly journals and specialized conferences (Bunn, 1993). Patients were ill-informed and could hence exercise little judgement over the suitability of the treatment their physician was recommending. In the modern era, the doctor is no longer even the primary source of medical information (Jenson, 1987), with a wide range of communication channels now available for 'consultation'. These include:

- health magazines
- medical textbooks
- libraries
- pre-recorded health messages—such as those supplied by a number of food manufacturers

- television/radio/general interest magazines
- Trusts/Foundations specializing in a particular medical complaint
- other medical professionals.

One result of this explosion in healthcare information has been a move towards medical terminology finding its way into everyday language (Johnsson, 1990) and the facilitation of a healthcare system in which consumers are encouraged to take a greater responsibility for their own health by adopting healthier lifestyles, etc.

Healthcare information can also be viewed as flowing internally between the provider and the patient whilst they are under the care of that institution. Patients have a need to be kept informed about the progress of their treatment and now have a right to expect that healthcare providers will share the details of the advantages and disadvantages of particular forms of treatment. This in turn has created a need for many staff to be re-trained to transform what used to be only a one-way exchange of information into a genuine dialogue. There is hence a clear role for internal marketing within healthcare institutions to instil a mindset that makes staff aware of the importance of this process for both the well-being and the satisfaction of their patients.

Marketing Primary Health Care

There are a range of marketing issues that primary healthcare practitioners (such as GPs) now need to address, including the following.

(a) Identification of Market Needs

A careful identification of the needs of those within their geographical catchment area is essential for every GP practice. An analysis of current and future healthcare needs will allow a practice to plan its particular portfolio of services. For example, GP practices sited in an area with an increasingly elderly population may need to plan for the inclusion of chiropody or physiotherapy services at some stage in the foreseeable future. If demand is likely to be high it may be more cost-effective for these to be provided within the confines of the practice rather than contracting other institutions to provide it. An analysis of need may also yield valuable information in respect of the range of preventative clinics that would best serve the community. Practice nursing staff may run a range of highly specialized clinics dealing with issues such as drug abuse, smoking, alcoholism, obesity, arthritis, asthma, and, perhaps more commonly, motherhood.

(b) Promotion of Healthcare Clinics

Once a decision has been taken about the appropriateness of running a particular clinic, its existence will need to be carefully promoted amongst the patients of the surgery most likely to benefit. At a superficial level this might require the staff to produce posters which could be sited in the waiting room, or in local libraries and community centres. More imaginative practices will use database records to promote the clinic specifically to those individuals they perceive would derive the greatest of benefit.

(c) Information/Education

GPs are increasingly recognizing the importance of good healthcare information to the well-being of their society. Recent meningitis scares and the emergence of a number of vicious strains of flu virus have placed an onus on GPs to supply up to date and timely information to those most at risk. It is no longer sufficient for practice staff to 'fire-fight' problems as they arise. A marketing perspective can help plan communications mechanisms that can easily be activated should the unthinkable occur. Moreover, as the society in which we live continues to age, it is likely that ever greater demands will be placed on the healthcare service. It will therefore be increasingly in the GP's interest to educate patients in the self-diagnosis of a range of minor ailments so that they can select their own treatments and avoid unnecessary consultations. Similarly there can be few GPs that have not spent at least one sleepless night attending to a range of relatively minor call-outs which could easily have waited until the following day for a routine appointment at the surgery. Marketing can help educate patients to recognize how best to use the services that the GP can provide.

(d) Enhancement of Customer Satisfaction

Perhaps the greatest contribution that marketing can make to health care lies in its ability to be able to direct resources to those areas most likely to increase overall customer satisfaction. The preceding discussion has already highlighted the dimensions of the service encounter that could offer the greatest utility in this regard and it is a matter for individual practices to determine the factors of most relevance to their own circumstances. An understanding of how patients evaluate the quality of the health care that they receive can allow those responsible for managing a GP practice to 'value engineer' the service they provide, concentrating resources in those areas most likely to enhance the overall experience of their clients. Similarly, cost savings could be made in those areas where little or no value is currently being perceived.

(e) Motivation Of Practice Staff

If the marketing concept is adopted at a philosophical as well as at a functional level, GPs will be encouraged to view their own practice staff as customers and treat them accordingly. There have been a number of instances reported of late where GPs have instructed their practice nurses to run a particular category of clinic and then failed to offer any additional support that might prove necessary. Internal marketing could hence have much to offer GPs and act to compel them to consider the requirements of their staff for adequate training and support.

(f) Attraction of Patients

The new healthcare framework rewards GPs, amongst other things, for the number of patients they are able to attract. Whilst in most regions of the country a general shortage of doctors means there is no shortage of demand, those practices that do face direct competition will need to carefully assess its impact and plan their marketing strategy accordingly. Marketing skills can also be immensely valuable for new practices which are only just beginning to attract patients for the first time. In such cases, patients need to be given sufficient reason to switch from their existing practice and to register with a new GP. Marketing's role in such circumstances is to assist practice managers in overcoming consumer apathy and giving patients enough encouragement to ensure that sufficient numbers make the transition.

Marketing Hospital Services

The quality of hospital marketing varies considerably from country to country. In the USA it has long been recognized that marketing has a significant role to play in the attraction of patients, although there still remain some small pockets of resistance amongst hospital administrators (McDevitt and Shields, 1985). Given that Wrenn (1994) determined that as little as a 10 per cent improvement in a hospital's marketing orientation could be associated with a $25 million increase in total net patient revenues and an 8 per cent increase in occupancy rates, it is no surprise that a change in perception is presently ongoing.

In the USA over 79 per cent of individuals have a preferred hospital, although the strength of this bond would not appear to be particularly strong. Inguanzo and Harju (1985) determined that fewer than 50 per cent of these individuals would characterize this preference as strong. The strongest degrees of loyalty would appear to be exhibited by people living towards the East of the country, in cities housing between 50,000 and 5,000,000 people, aged 55 or older and with household incomes less than $15,000. We may thus conclude that most segments of US society would be willing to change healthcare provider if given a sufficient reason to do so. Factors such as the level of new technology employed, the courtesy of staff, cost, and the recommendation of a primary physician have all been shown to influence switching behaviour. Healthcare marketers within a hospital thus have a key role to play in the development of future hospital business.

In the UK, however, the framework within which most hospitals work is rather different. Until recently hospital income was guaranteed and as a consequence the requirement to view healthcare purchasers as customers was anathema. As hospitals now begin to face competitive pressures a few are starting to recognize the need to market their services and to employ full-time marketers to assist them in this task. In particular NHS hospital trusts require marketing skills to:

(1) *Redefine their catchment areas*. Since hospitals are no longer restricted to treating patients within their immediate geographical area there is a need to redefine the target market, concentrating particularly perhaps on those areas which have the densest populations and hence the greatest demand for healthcare resources.

(2) *Define the competition*. In many regions of the country it may be possible to avoid damaging, direct competition with neighbouring hospitals by emphasizing those aspects of the service that complement the other provision available locally. Even in cases where this proves not to be possible it will be necessary to monitor competitor activity and to benchmark hospital performance accordingly.

(3) *Network*. Despite the prevailing aura of competition it may well be in the interests of some hospitals to co-operate. Where service gaps do exist, collaborative agree-

ments could be developed to ensure that adequate coverage of all medical specialisms is provided within one geographical region.

(4) *Get close to customers.* Given that fundholding GPs now have the power to purchase hospital services from wherever they choose, it may well be appropriate for a hospital to consider appointing a GP practice co-ordinator who will tour the local practices explaining the range of services available and the unique advantages of sending patients to their particular institution. Indeed, since many NHS trusts now have such an appointment, a hospital which fails to get close to its customers in this way may well find itself at a significant disadvantage.

(5) *Identify the customers.* Hospitals need to identify those individuals who have the greatest capacity to influence the healthcare decision. In the USA where patients arguably have a greater choice this is a key issue, as the decision-making unit can often be complex. Moreover, the cultivation of customer loyalty becomes extremely important in retaining family business. Phillips (1980) identified that the key to sustaining loyalty might lie in the careful targeting of female patients. Women account for 70 per cent of all hospital admissions and have been shown to be responsible for over 70 per cent of their family's healthcare decisions—they therefore represent an important target market.

(6) *Involve customers in new service developments.* Whilst it may be difficult to involve the end users of healthcare services in this way, there is no reason why intermediaries such as GPs should not be actively involved in the design of new hospital services. Having contributed actively to the birth of a new service, GPs are thereafter more likely to use it for the benefit of their patients. The process of service development is also likely to strengthen relationships between GPs and key management/clinical staff within the hospital.

(7) *Develop employees.* Given the key role of all hospital staff in delivering an appropriate level of service quality, hospital staff should be treated as internal customers of the organization and treated as the administration would have them treat external customers. Good internal communications and customer-care training programmes should be initiated and the results monitored to ensure the achievement of the desired outcomes.

(8) *Conduct internal promotion.* There is still much resistance to marketing, particularly in UK hospitals. In order to win the hearts and minds of clinical staff, marketing staff need to promote their successes. Only when clinical staff understand the benefits that accrue to the hospital in increased patient throughput, job security, and enhancements to service quality, will marketing build a better reputation for itself. Marketing successes should hence be unashamedly promoted throughout the whole organization.

(9) *Incorporate three areas into institutional development: cost, quality, customer satisfaction.* Careful costing of all activities, together with a detailed analysis of service quality, should allow hospital marketers to engineer the value that they deliver to their customers. This in turn should greatly enhance levels of customers satisfaction.

(10) *Not underestimate the impact of change.* The health services of most developed countries are currently in a state of flux. Ageing populations and a time of economic constraint are forcing governments to take a long hard look at the way in which health care is managed and delivered. Healthcare marketers therefore

need to monitor their external environment particularly closely to ensure that they stay in touch with both proposed and actual change. Only by responding to environmental challenges ahead of the competition will the long term stability of any healthcare organisation be truly assured.

The above analysis is adapted From Crowther (1995) and Petrochuk and Javalgi (1996). The following case study illustrates the role that marketing can play in respect of many of these issues.

Case Study 8.1: **Richmond Community Healthcare Hamlet**

Background

Richmond has enjoyed the services of a local hospital for over 130 years. The Royal Hospital in Kew Foot Road, Richmond on Thames, has stood on its current site since 1868 when it was first opened by Earl Russell. Interestingly the purchase of the original building was no more than a happy accident of fate. Following the marriage of HRH the Prince of Wales in 1863 the local community decided to celebrate the occasion by providing a very special dinner for the benefit of the local poor and children under the age of 7 years. Having successfully fundraised for the event and purchased the necessary foodstuffs the organizing committee found themselves with the princely sum of £40 6s 2d remaining. Anxious to invest this sum in 'some charitable purpose of a more permanent character' the decision was taken to put the money aside as the nucleus of a fund for the creation of a local hospital—The Royal Hospital was born.

By 1869 115 patients had been treated with the average duration of each stay being 35 days. Interestingly, the average cost of each in-patient at the time was a mere £6 0s 10d—somewhat less than it would be today! In the years that followed, the hospital saw a gradual expansion of both its in-patient and out-patient provisions and a number of new ground breaking clinics were added, including an Ophthalmic wing in 1908. The hospital also looked after servicemen and local air-raid victims during the two World Wars and from 1939–45 a minimum of 45 beds were put aside for this specific purpose.

The National Health Service Act 1946 brought the hospital into the new national healthcare system and by 1956 it had grown into a general hospital with 121 beds. Unfortunately, however, by the 1970s the buildings were becoming increasingly costly to maintain and much of the equipment was beginning to look dated. This, combined with improvements at other hospitals, compelled the district health authority to shut down the hospital in 1984. Aside from a brief spell as a homeless hostel the buildings were hardly used from that time until 1988 when the earlier decision was revoked and provision started at the hospital once more. However, this reprieve was to be short-lived due to a serious fire which destroyed most of the building in 1992.

A New Healthcare Concept

With such a proud tradition of healthcare provision behind it, however, it was perhaps inevitable that this would not be the end of the Royal's story. The necessary monies were ultimately found to completely refurbish the buildings and only a few months after the fire the Richmond, Twickenham and Roehampton Healthcare NHS Trust (based at Queen Mary's University Hospital, Roehampton) was formed, following the National Healthcare reforms of 1991. One of the primary aims of this new organization was to consider the situation of the Royal Hospital and to give it a new lease of life. The Trust thus decided that the site should form part of its 'Right Place' strategy—a radical new concept in healthcare provision. In essence the Royal was set to become a centre of a health resource for the whole Richmond community. The new Richmond Community Healthcare Hamlet, as it was to become known, was formed to house a variety of medical services including district nursing, health visiting, mental health services, a rehabilitation unit, and ultimately a general medical out-patients department.

In April 1996 the first wing was completed and the first medical services began to be installed in their new facility. The mental health service and community services (for example, district nursing) were the first to take up residence although, in view of the size of the buildings, a decision was later taken to provide an out-patients department in an attempt to maximize the usage thereof. This move was also consistent with the desire of the local Trust to outreach into their local community. Indeed the primary motivation for all the provision at the site had always been the desire to take the services that were likely to be in most demand by the community and place them actually *in* that community. The creation of an ENT (Ear, Nose, and Throat) out-patients clinic, for example, would have been consistent with this goal, as some 20 per cent of patients attending at GP surgeries fall within the remit of this discipline, and for this reason one of the local acute providers is currently in discussions to provide this clinic at the Hamlet.

In the new era of NHS competition it was further realized that it was no longer appropriate for the Trust to expect patients to travel distances to consult their hospital specialist. Whilst it may have been managerially optimal to see all out-patients at the Trust's primary facility (Queen Mary's), the Trust had now to actively go out and seek patients, or face the possibility of losing them to Trusts based in other areas. Indeed a number of NHS Trusts had already expressed an interest in 'poaching' business from the catchment areas of neighbouring organizations.

Interestingly, this latter point has become less of an issue with the passage of time as Queen Mary's itself is now facing a de-merger. Historically Queen Mary's services were purchased by two health authorities—Kingston and Richmond and Merton, Sutton and Wandsworth—because the hospital was located virtually on the boundary between the two. However, since each district health authority has its own general hospital the decision has been taken to move Queen Mary's services slowly out into these and to leave only out-patients clinics provided at a local level. With such a radical change in organization ongoing, concerns about the impact of competition on the Hamlet are therefore much less of an issue than improving the utilization of the assets on the site to ensure survival. With the out-patients facility only operating one day per week, and the X-ray facility for only half a day, the unit costs of treatment are currently very high.

The Marketing Challenge

With this latter point in mind, the management of the Hamlet have decided to encourage other healthcare providers to use the facilities of the site. Consultants from other NHS Trusts form a key target market for this initiative. There was seen to be no *a priori* reason why consultants from neighbouring healthcare Trusts could not use the facilities of the Hamlet as long as the majority of the provision was seen to be complementary and to the overall benefit of the people of Richmond. Clinics will therefore be operated at the Hamlet provided by a variety of different healthcare Trusts each of whom will pay an agreed amount for the use of the facility. The initiative thus improves the amount of income accruing to the Hamlet and facilitates a greater degree of competition in the local area by allowing for neighbouring Trusts to offer services to the local GPs. This will mean that patients will have access to specialist clinics and therefore a greater level of 'choice', thus ensuring that the existence of the healthcare Hamlet will very much improve the quality of the medical service provided to the people of Richmond.

Aside from encouraging other Trusts to utilize the facilities, Hamlet marketers are also considering the opportunities offered by the provision of private medical care. Richmond has traditionally been a very wealthy suburb of London where, as a consequence, the demand for private health care has always been strong. The establishment of a local clinic that specialists could use as their base for treating patients close to their own home is therefore likely to be attractive. Moreover, since the Hamlet buildings have been completely refurbished to the highest of standards (due to the existence of listing orders on some parts of the building) private patients attending the site for treatment would be unlikely to notice any significant difference in standards between those of the Hamlet and those of some private hospitals. Encouraging the provision of private health care at the site therefore also represents a possible growth opportunity.

Allied to this latter point, the Hamlet has recently been approached by providers of various forms of complementary medicine who also wish to make use of its facilities. Local demand for homeopathy, osteopathy, etc. is likely to be strong and the reputations of the various practitioners would doubtless be enhanced by an association with their local community hospital. From the Hamlet's perspective encouraging as wide a form of medical provision as possible would greatly enhance the degree of asset utilization and lead in the future to a gradual expansion of the hours during which the site would be open for business. This latter point is a particular issue, since until access is expanded, the Hamlet is unlikely to be perceived by local people as a genuine community resource.

To assist in this, the decision was also taken to encourage associated voluntary organizations to use the building, and space was hence set aside for the local branch of the mental health charity RABMIND and the Kingston and Richmond Alcohol Counselling Services. Aside from deepening the already strong relationship between the healthcare and voluntary sectors, in the case of the Hamlet, the presence of these organizations would also ensure that rooms were used out of hours for additional patient support, counselling, self help groups, etc.

The Launch

Whilst the Hamlet has been open since April 1996, it has been a phased opening as each block of the building was completed. The Hamlet's portfolio is only now approaching that which was originally envisaged at the commencement of the project. For this reason the Hamlet's official opening did not take place until December 1997. The event was seen as being of considerable importance since it afforded Hamlet marketers their first real opportunity to genuinely promote the site to each of their three target markets.

The first of these is undoubtedly the general public. A key message on the day of the launch was that the 'Hamlet is here and open for business'. Whilst there has been a hospital on the site for over a century, there were many individuals who simply did not know that the site had now re-opened and/or that it had been completely refurbished. For this reason local press and radio were sought to help publicize the existence of the new community resource. Moreover, on the day of the launch the site was open to all visitors and the various healthcare providers erected displays detailing the nature of the services provided and, where appropriate, the benefits thereof.

Whilst this approach undoubtedly served to raise public awareness, it was less effective at encouraging awareness specifically amongst members of the medical profession. Indeed, in the case of GPs in particular, a much greater degree of information must be imparted than simply 'we are open for business'. GPs need to understand the benefits that could accrue to their patients from the full range of provision and to experience something of the process that their 'customers' will encounter when they attend for a particular clinic or service. The problem, however, lies in persuading this target group to attend the site. They are particularly busy individuals with little time to simply walk around or be given some form of tour. Hamlet marketers have therefore encouraged the various providers who will be using the site to run CPD (Continuous Professional Development) workshops which GPs can attend to obtain credit towards their annual target of training hours. These workshops would hence have an educational function in that they would serve to deepen GP understanding of some form of mainstream or even complementary medicine, but they would also bring individuals into the site where they can be appraised of the full range of services provided.

The third target market for the launch is clearly the healthcare providers themselves. Individuals who might potentially use the facilities to operate their own clinics can be encouraged to attend to view for themselves the quality of the refurbishment and the accommodation available.

The Future

Clearly the official launch of the new facility will be only the first key role for marketing as a function to perform within the Hamlet. As the portfolio of services is extended there may be many opportunities for the Hamlet as a whole to benefit from collective marketing activities such as contacts with GPs and other healthcare purchasers, or even local events hosted for the benefit of the Richmond community. The advantages of a united approach to marketing are likely to be considerable and hence marketing has been highlighted as one of the key issues that will be discussed at monthly meetings of the Hamlet's management committee. It is intended that these meetings will be attended by representatives from all the healthcare providers currently utilising the Hamlet, so that all may have a say in its future.

Summary

In this chapter we have reviewed the healthcare frameworks of both the USA and the UK. In the case of the latter, substantial changes have recently been introduced in the manner in which the NHS is managed through the creation of quasi-markets in which healthcare purchasers now have a greater right to choose their provider. This structural change has created a real need for marketing skills within the sector as institutions begin to respond for the first time to the threat of competition.

As in the case of the education sector discussed earlier, positioning is likely to become *the* key marketing issue for healthcare marketers to address in the years ahead. Indeed this drive towards the attainment of some unique position in the market will undoubtedly compel healthcare institutions to give greater consideration to the genuine needs of their patients and the quality of service they are afforded. This chapter has included a brief review of the available literature in this respect and concluded that service quality matters are best regarded as situation-specific, requiring the provider to conduct their own research to establish real priorities for the improvement thereof.

Discussion Questions

1. In your role as the Marketing Director of an NHS Trust, prepare a briefing document for a newly recruited marketing colleague, explaining the changes that have recently taken place in the healthcare environment and the additional need for marketing that this has created.
2. In what ways might the marketing of a healthcare service differ from the marketing of other nonprofit services described in this text? Why should this be so?
3. What are the key service quality dimensions that should be addressed by hospital marketers in a bid to enhance overall customer satisfaction?
4. As the newly appointed marketing manager of a GP Fundholding Practice what steps would you take to enhance patient satisfaction with the service provided?
5. Why is the provision of good quality information becoming an increasingly important issue for healthcare marketers to address.
6. With reference to your own healthcare organization, or one with which you are familiar, describe the issues that would need to be addressed under each of the headings of the 'typical' marketing plan introduced in Chapter 4.

References

Andrus, D. and Buchheister, J. (1985) 'Major Factors Affecting Dental Consumer Satisfaction', *Health Marketing and Consumer Behaviour*, Vol. 3, No. 1, 57–68.

Berkowitz, E. N. and Flexner, W. (1980) 'The Market for Health Services: Is there a Non Traditional Consumer?', *Journal of Health Care Marketing*, Vol. 1, No. 1, 25–34.

BMA (1995), 'Declining Standards in Community Care', as reported in *British Journal of Nursing* (Editorial), Vol. 4, No. 8, 425–6.

Bopp, K. D. (1990) 'How Patients Evaluate the Quality of Ambulatory Medical Encounters: A Marketing Perspective,' *Journal of Healthcare Marketing*, Vol. 10, No. 2, 6–15.

Brown, S. W. and Swartz, T. A. (1989) 'A Gap Analysis of Professional Service Quality', *Journal of Marketing*, Vol. 53, April, 92–8.

Bunn, M. D. (1993) 'Consumer Perceptions of Medical Information Sources: An Application of Multidimensional Scaling', *Health Marketing Quarterly*, Vol. 10 No.3, 83–104.

Crowther, C. (1995) 'NHS Trust Marketing: A Survival Guide', *Journal of Marketing Practice: Applied Marketing Science*, Vol. 1, No. 2, 57–68.

Edgren, L. (1991) *Service Management Inm Svensk Halso-Och Sjukvard*, Lund, Sweden, Lund University Press.

France, K. R. and Grover, R. (1992) 'What is the Health Care Product?', *Journal of Health Care Marketing*, Vol. 12, No. 2, 31–8.

Gabbott, M. and Hogg, G. (1994) 'Care or Cure: Making Choices in Healthcare', Unity in Diversity, *Proceedings of the MEG Conference*, University of Ulster.

Hall, J. H. and Dornan, M. C. (1988) 'Meta Analysis of satisfaction with Medical Care Description of Research Domain and Analysis of Overall Satisfaction Levels', *Social Science and Medicine*, Vol. 27, No. 6, 637–44.

Inguanzo, J. M. and Harju, M. (1985) 'What Makes Consumers Select a Hospital', *Hospitals*, 16 March, 90–4.

Jenson, J. (1987) 'Most Physicians Believe Patients Obtain Health Care Information from Mass Media', *Modern Health Care*, Vol. 17, No. 19, 113–14.

Johnsson, B. C. (1990) 'Focus Group Positioning and Analysis: A Commentary on Adjuncts for Enhancing the Design of Health Care Research', *Health Education Quarterly*, Vol. 7, No. 1/2, 152–68.

Kotler, P. and Clarke, R. N. (1987) *Marketing for Health Care Organisations*, New Jersey, Prentice Hall.

Larsen, D. E. and Rootman, I. (1976) 'Physician Role Performance and Patient Satisfaction', *Social Science and Medicine*, Vol. 10, No. 1, 29–32.

LuAnn, A. and Andersen, R. (1980) *Health Care in the USA*, Beverly Hills, Sage Publications.

Lych, J. and Schuler, D. (1990) 'Consumer Evaluation of the Quality of Hospital Services from an Economics of Information Perspective', *Journal of Health Care Marketing*, Vol. 10, June, 16–22.

Lytle, R. S. and Mokwa, M. P. (1992) 'Evaluating Health Care Quality: The Moderating Role of Outcomes', *Journal of Health Care Marketing*, Vol. 12, No. 1, 4–14.

MacStravic, R. Scott. (1975) *Marketing Health Care*, Gaithersburg, Aspen Publishers.

Maister, D. H. (1985) 'The Psychology of Waiting Lines' in Czepiel, J., Solomon M. R. and Suprenant, C. F. (eds) *The Service Encounter*, Lexington, Mass., Lexington Books.

McDevitt, P. K. and Shields, L. A. (1985) 'Tactical Hospital Marketing: A Survey of the State of the Art', *Journal of Health Care Marketing*, Vol. 5, No. 1, 9–16.

O'Connor, S. J., Shewchuk, R. M and Carney, L. W. (1994) 'The Great Gap', *Journal of Health Care Marketing*, Vol. 14, No. 2, 32–9.

Parasuraman, A., Zeithaml, V. and Berry, L. (1988) 'SERVQUAL: A Multiple Item Scale for Measuring Consumer Perceptions of Service Quality', *Journal of Retailing*, Vol. 64, No.1, 12–40.

Pendelton, D. and Halser, J. (1983) *Doctor Patient Communication*, London, Academic Press.

Petrochuk, M. A. and Javalgi, R. G. (1996) 'Reforming The Health Care System: Implications for Health Care Marketers', *Health Marketing Quarterly*, Vol. 13, No. 3, 71–86.

Phillips, C. R. (1980) 'Single Room Maternity Care for Maximum Cost-Efficency' *Perinatology-Neonataology*, March/April, 21–31.

Quinn, J. B. (1992) *Intelligent Enterprise*, New York, The Free Press.

Ranade, W. (1994) *A Future for the NHS*, Harlow, Longman Group Ltd.

Sage, G. C. (1991) 'Customers and the NHS', *International Journal of Health Quality Assurance*, Vol. 4, No. 3, 23–34.

San Augustine, A., Long, W. J. and Pantzallis, J. (1992) 'Hospital Positioning: A Strategic Tool for the 1990s', *Journal of Health Care Marketing*, Vol. 12, No. 1, 16–23.

Singh, J. (1990) 'A Multifacet Typology of Patient Satisfaction with a Hospital', *Journal of Health Care Marketing*, Vol. 10, Dec, 8–21.

Teasdale, K. (1992) *Managing the Changes in Health Care*, London, Wolfe.

Ware, J. E., Davies-Avery, A. and Stewart, A. L. (1978) 'The Measurement and Meaning of Patient Satisfaction', *Health and Medical Care Services Review*, Vol. 1, Jan/Feb, 14–20.

West, P. (1994) 'In the Temple of Pain', *Harper's Magazine*, Dec, 29–30.

World Health Organization (1986) *Basic Documents: 36th edition*, Geneva, Switzerland, World Health Organization.

Wrenn, B. (1994) 'Differences in Perceptions of Hospital Marketing Orientation between Administrators and Marketing Officers', *Hospital and Health Services Administration*, Vol. 39, No. 3, 341–58.

Zaltman, G. and Vertinsky, I. (1971) 'Health Services Marketing: A Proposed Model', *Journal of Marketing*, Vol. 35, July, 19–27.

9

Social Marketing

Objectives

By the end of this chapter you should be able to:

(1) **define social marketing;**
(2) **distinguish between social marketing and social communication;**
(3) **understand the contribution of market research techniques to the field of social behaviour;**
(4) **design a social marketing communications campaign.**

What is Social Marketing?

Social marketing first emerged as a distinct concept in the early 1970s when Kotler and Zaltman (1971, 5) recognized that marketing tools and techniques typically applied to products and services could be applied equally well to the marketing of ideas. The authors define social marketing as:

> the design, implementation and control of programmes calculated to influence the acceptability of social ideas and involving considerations of product planning, pricing, communication, distribution and marketing research.

The wording of this definition is quite precise. The authors have deliberately avoided any reference to education or the facilitation of a change of attitudes or values. This is because social marketing is concerned with neither of these processes. The ultimate goal of any form of marketing is to influence behaviour. This may be to influence a particular individual to purchase an organization's product/service, or it may be to influence an individual to start recycling a proportion of his/her household waste. In either case a concrete change in behaviour has resulted. Marketing and the variant social marketing are therefore conceptually different from the process of education, where the ultimate goal is knowledge, not necessarily a change in behaviour. Similarly marketing should be viewed as distinct from a process designed merely to elicit a change of attitudes or values. Individuals or organizations concerned with this process may essentially be regarded as lobbyists, since once again behavioural changes are not involved.

To understand the key difference between marketing as we have discussed it thus far and social marketing it is necessary to examine the question of objectives. In the generic marketing discussed thus far, some form of benefit has usually accrued to the marketing organization as the result of its marketing activity, for example, increased patronage, enhanced levels of voluntary donation, etc. Thus, even if the objective of the organization is not to make a profit and the work of the organization is quite philanthropic, some form of 'benefit' will nevertheless accrue to the marketing organization. In social marketing this is not the case. The marketing activity is aimed at a society with the aim of inducing a change in the behaviour in that society for the good of all.

Of course the word 'good' in the last paragraph is a relative term, and it does rather depend on your viewpoint just how 'good' you would perceive the effects of social marketing to be. Indeed a number of researchers have recently questioned the ethics and desirability of social marketing (see, for example, Laczniak *et al.*, 1979). The reader will doubtless be relieved to learn, however, that it is not my intention to 'muddy the water' by entering into a complex philosophical debate at this stage. Rather it is important merely to realize that there is a distinction between the objectives of generic marketing and the objectives of social marketing. It is this distinction which makes the latter concept unique.

Fox and Kotler (1980) draw a further distinction between what they term 'social communication' and social marketing. The authors view the former as a paradigm of thought which majors on the use of mass media advertising, public relations, and personal selling. The aim of social communication is simply to take advantage of all possible opportunities to communicate a message to a target group. The social marketing paradigm, however, adds at least four more dimensions which are typically missing from a purely social communication approach, and these are discussed in the following sections.

(a) Marketing Research

The social marketer begins work on a campaign only after the target market has been thoroughly researched. The size of the overall market, its needs/wants, attitudes, behavioural patterns, and the likely costs and benefits of addressing individual market segments will all be carefully evaluated. Appropriate campaigns can thereafter be designed for those segments it is felt most appropriate to address.

The power of effective marketing research cannot be understated. It can greatly improve the relevance and ultimate impact on behaviour of a social marketing campaign. It was recently identified for example that prostitutes in Tijuana, Mexico, had little fear that they might die of AIDS. Traditional social communications messages extolling the virtues of safe sex were therefore largely ineffectual with the members of this important target group. Research, however, identified that the prostitutes were very much afraid of leaving their child without a mother. The emphasis of the resulting social marketing campaign was hence switched from 'I want to live' to 'I want to protect my child'.

(b) Product Development

Assume, for example, that the purpose of a campaign is to influence consumers to adopt a recycling behaviour. The social communicator will tend to see the problem as one of a need to 'exhort' people to change their behaviours. The social marketer, on the other hand, will in addition seek to promote the necessary means to facilitate this change more easily. The campaign would highlight the technology that is available to assist in recycling and offer practical opportunities for the behavioural change to be adopted at minimal cost. In short, the 'product' being promoted is not just a need to change behaviour, but also the means by which it is possible to do so.

Two decades ago, for example, international health experts recognized that simply telling people about birth control was unlikely to have any significant impact on behaviour. Their early attempts were hindered by misconceptions about contraceptives for example, that they would make women ill or children sick, that they were expensive, or that unfavourable religious beliefs prohibited their use. A social marketing approach was then adopted by many organizations which took account of these difficulties and segmented the market according to the sets of perceptions that were held. The emphasis was changed from mere mass communication to the creation of support frameworks which were tailored to the needs of each market segment.

A further example from social marketing folklore is the story of a project developed at Johns Hopkins University in partnership with USAID and a number of Mexican Agencies. The aim was to encourage Latin teenagers to become more sexually responsible, something which had hitherto proved difficult to achieve by mere mass communication alone. The team therefore sought a means of appealing to the teenagers that would not be perceived as a 'lecture' on the subject of birth control. Moreover, the team wished to ensure that as high a percentage as possible of teenagers had access to appropriate advice. The solution was to create two pop songs 'Stop' and 'When We Are Together' performed by Tatianna and Johnny, which contained lyrics that made it clear that sex need not be part of a loving relationship. The two songs were a great success and, when teenagers purchased the record, the sleeve opened out into a poster which contained information about where to obtain birth control information.

(c) The Use of Incentives

Social marketing can involve the use of incentives to encourage the desired behaviour change. Thus some campaigns in South America or the Third World have offered small gifts to those who agree to use a particular service. Similarly, price incentives have been offered to encourage take-up rates amongst the poorest groups in a given society. The use of such 'sales promotion' type activities can pay rich dividends in a good social marketing campaign (see, for example, Sihombing, 1994 or Schellstede, 1986).

(d) Facilitation

The social marketer is concerned not only with the communication of a message, he/she must also attempt to make the adoption of a behavioural change relatively easy to achieve. Thus community recycling initiatives which galvanize the whole community into action (and where, hence, individuals can draw support from each other) may be more effective than a simple advertising campaign alone. Similarly, if individuals are to be encouraged to adopt safer sexual practices, access to appropriate advice and contraception must be convenient and freely available. In Uganda, for example, contraceptives were almost impossible to sell in conventional retail stores. Social marketers therefore created booths in traditional markets and sold contraceptives at prices acceptable to the target market.

Social Marketing Domains

Social marketing has been used to good effect to tackle many social issues world-wide. Perhaps the greatest success has been achieved with family planning campaigns to control the size of the population in a variety of countries. In Sri Lanka, for example, where market research indicated that although there was widespread support for birth control there was little knowledge of the techniques available, the government introduced a brand of condom called 'Preeth' (meaning happiness) and sold it to consumers at extremely low prices. The product was supported by promotion in local films, radio, and print, and the overall campaign proved to be very successful in lowering the birth rate in that country. However, the domain of social marketing is not related merely to birth control issues. Social marketing campaigns have also tackled issues such as:

- HIV infection and sexual responsibility (e.g. Black, 1979, Luthra, 1991, or Ramah and Cassidy, 1992)
- the dangers of smoking (e.g. Elder, 1994)
- drunk driving (e.g Braus, 1995)
- pollution/business ethics (e.g Abratt and Sacks, 1988)
- recycling/energy conservation (McKenzie-Mohr, 1994)
- drug/alcohol abuse (e.g. Smith, 1992).

The reader will appreciate that many of these are difficult issues and the behaviours concerned may be firmly entrenched. Marketing may therefore offer no magic solution. Even with the most finely tuned social marketing campaign the targeted behaviours may prove difficult, if not impossible, to change. According to Kotler and Andreasen, there are three major dimensions which determine just how difficult it may be to achieve such a change:

(a) whether the behaviour is high or low involvement;
(b) whether the behaviour is a one-time or continuing;
(c) whether the behaviour is exhibited by individuals or groups.

Examples of each of the eight categories of social marketing produced by these dimensions are given in Table 9.1.

(a) High Involvement/Low Involvement

The more 'involved' with a purchase decision a consumer is, the more thought they are likely to give to alternative solutions and the costs and benefits associated with each. It is thus important for marketers to recognize whether a decision is high or low involvement as this will impact on the amount of factual information provided. There is, however, regrettably no consensus on what constitutes 'involvement' (see, for example,

Table 9.1
A Categorization of Social Behaviours

	Low Involvement	High Involvement
One-Time Behaviour		
Individual	Donating money to a charity	Donating blood
Group	Election of a local council	Creation of a neighbourhood watch scheme
Continuing Behaviour		
Individual	Not smoking in elevators	Stopping smoking or drug intake
	Recycling newspapers	Recycling all household waste
Group	Driving within the speed limit	Supporting a woman's right to abortion

Source: Kotler/Andreasen, *Strategic Marketing For Nonprofit Organisations*, 5th edn, © 1996. Adapted by permission of Prentice-Hall, Inc., Upper Saddle River, NJ.

Kapferer and Laurent, 1986, or Ratchford, 1987). Most researchers would agree, though, that consumers will be more 'involved' in a situation if they perceive it as having immediate and personal relevance to themselves. Moreover, if the situation is perceived as having a high degree of risk associated with it, the level of involvement will also be enhanced. The choice of a method of birth control, for example, would for most constitute a high involvement decision, since it is of immediate personal relevance and the social and financial risks of an unwanted pregnancy are very real.

Low involvement decisions on the other hand are typically of little importance to the consumer as the outcome of the decision will not have a major impact on their lifestyle. Such decisions involve little thought, do not involve a detailed search for information in respect of the alternatives, and carry few penalties if the wrong decision is taken. Thus, in the social context, low involvement behaviours may be somewhat easier to change than those requiring high involvement. If a particular behaviour pattern is not deemed significant, and changing it would expose the individual to little social risk, it will be somewhat easier for the marketer to encourage a change to take place. Persuading car drivers to switch to non-alcoholic lager might thus be somewhat easier than persuading them to switch to soft drinks, since they can still be seen to enjoy a pint with their friends at a party. They can hence offset any social pressure that they might feel to join in and have a drink.

Interestingly, there are a variety of products and services which are capable of evoking high levels of involvement purely on the basis of the emotional appeals that are associated with them. Tobacco is one such product, and understanding the reasons why this is so might significantly aid social marketers in a bid to reduce deaths from heart disease and lung cancer. Hirschman and Holbrook (1982) found, for example, that many smokers imagined themselves as 'Marlboro Men' and felt that their habit (and brand) was a statement of both their masculinity and their desire to imagine themselves as idealized cowboys. The weakening of this association might thus be one issue for social marketers to address.

(b) One-Time versus Continuing Behaviour

One-time behaviour changes are usually somewhat easier to instigate than longer-term adjustments. They require the target merely to understand the communication message and to take action on the basis thereof. Of course, the easier it can be for the target audience to take the desired action, the more likely it is that they will actually take it.

Communicating the benefits of a change in behaviour is therefore not enough in itself, thought must be given to how easy an individual will find it to act on the information presented. Thus immunization programmes in the Third World will visit individual rural communities rather than expect people to travel to major towns and cities for treatment. In this way as large a percentage of the population as possible can be affected. Similarly political parties of all persuasions will usually offer free rides to the polling station for the elderly or infirm to ensure that they turn out to vote—hopefully in the manner desired!

Persuading individuals to change their behaviour patterns permanently is a little more problematic. Over time, behaviour can become habitualized, in the sense that it happens without any thought on the part of the individual. Moreover the justification for the behaviour can become firmly entrenched in an individual's value systems. People have to be convinced of the need for them to change and of the benefits that might accrue as a result. They also have to be convinced that these benefits will be substantive enough to warrant the effort necessary to instigate the change in behaviour. In the case of low-involvement decisions this may only involve an occasional reminder of the need to behave in a particular way. High-involvement, continuing behaviours are the most difficult to change. In many cases these may prove impossible to alter without resorting to legislative change to provide a final backdrop of enforcement.

(c) Individual versus Group

Group behaviour is inherently more difficult to change than the behaviour of particular individuals. The complex dynamic of relationships that exists within a societal group act to reinforce and legitimize the attitudes and values of the members of that group. Acceptance of any form of change can be interpreted as disloyalty to the collective identity of the group, and for individuals brave enough to deviate from the norm there may be a number of social penalties imposed on them as a result.

To address changes in group behaviours it is important to recognize the distinction between (i) opinion leaders, (ii) opinion formers, and (iii) opinion followers. Communication strategies that acknowledge the significance of the opinion leaders and formers are far more likely to effect the desired change in behaviour.

(i) Opinion Leaders

Opinion leaders are those individuals that have the ability to influence behaviour because of their perceived status within their social group. Reynolds and Darden (1971) identified that these individuals tend to be more gregarious and self-confident than non-leaders and, importantly from a marketing perspective, also tend to have a greater exposure to the mass media. Clearly if group behaviours are to be modified, it is the opinion leaders within those groups who must be targeted in particular with the communications message. Given that they tend to read more publications than others in society, are amongst the first to return promotional coupons, and have a propensity to take and enjoy risks, they are not impossible to identify.

(ii) Opinion Formers

Unlike opinion leaders, opinion formers exert influence over group behaviour because of their actual authority, education, or status. In essence, opinion formers may be looked to for advice because of the *formal* expertise that they have in a particular area.

Thus government ministers, community group leaders, newspaper editors, etc. can all be viewed as opinion formers. Once again, since this group have a great capacity to be able to influence others, they will form an important target group in any social marketing campaign. Fortunately they are somewhat easier to identify than the former category since, by virtue of their position, they normally seek to be seen as having an important impact on the attitudes and behaviours of others. Targeting them is therefore not problematic.

(iii) Opinion Followers

The majority of members of society can be categorized as opinion followers. They are unlikely to set a new trend in behaviour themselves unless such a behaviour change has previously been legitimized and endorsed by their societal group. They look for advice in respect of appropriate behaviours both from opinion formers and opinion leaders.

Researching Social Behaviours

The research of social issues is undoubtedly one of the most difficult facets of marketing that nonprofit practitioners ever have to deal with. Many traditional primary research techniques are difficult, or even downright inappropriate, to apply to this field. People are quite understandably reluctant to talk about sensitive personal matters and when one considers that a high proportion of postal questionnaires asking respondents about the relatively innocuous topic of personal income will often be returned with the relevant section incomplete, something of the difficulty researchers face in this sensitive area becomes readily apparent. Indeed the various forms of questionnaire—i.e. telephone/postal—will be particularly difficult to apply in this context, making the collection of quantitative data problematic.

For this reason much of social research is qualitative in nature and as a consequence conducted with smaller numbers of subjects, although often in considerably more depth. Of the techniques that are most helpful in accumulating this category of data, personal interviews and focus groups are probably the most commonly used.

Interviews

Personal interviews with subjects from a particular societal group can play a pivotal role in a social marketing research project. Although they are relatively costly to administer the researcher is able to take his/her time with the research and to establish a rapport with each subject before more intimate and personal details are probed later in their discussion. The researcher can also benefit from being able to observe the body language of the subject and hence be sensitive to those aspects which he/she finds it particularly difficult to talk about.

Interviews can be either fully structured, semi-structured or conducted in a free format more closely resembling that of an everyday conversation. In the case of the former, the researcher has a prescriptive list of the questions that will be posed and has decided in advance the order in which they will be delivered. The interviewer has little or no authority to adjust the wording of the questions in each case, making it easier to compare the findings of the interviews undertaken, but potentially stifling a debate of any interesting issues that might emerge. For this reason a semi-structured approach is more common since, although the researcher must follow a prescribed pattern for the interview, there is more scope for him/her to tailor the conversation to follow up on matters of particular interest in the case of a given individual.

At the other end of the scale, a free-format interview is one in which the researcher has only an idea of the subjects that will be covered, and the interview is conducted as far as possible as a natural conversation. These naturalistic 'conversations' are normally tape-recorded so that the researcher is free to concentrate on the development of the interaction between him/her and the subject. This technique is commonly used in social marketing research since the subject can more easily be put at their ease and approached with questions that reflect the natural order of the conversation taking place.

Focus Groups

By contrast, focus groups involve the researcher assembling a 'panel' of six to eight members of the subject group. A trained facilitator then explores with this group the issues under research. The discussion is usually quite unstructured in the sense that the researcher has a clear idea of the ground that must be covered, but is happy for the group to emphasize those aspects of the discussion that they find particularly exciting or of relevance to them. Once again it would be normal practice to either audio or video tape the proceedings so that the facilitator is free to concentrate on the development of the discussion and ensure that each individual has the opportunity to contribute.

As with personal interviews, focus groups can be used to investigate difficult social issues and the key findings can be developed from a careful analysis of the tape of the discussion after it has taken place. Focus groups often yield valuable insight into the underlying motivations for particular categories of behaviour, and as participants begin to recognize that they are not alone in holding a particular view, quite open and honest discussions often emerge.

A good recent example of the use of focus groups to inform social marketing practice is reported in Case Study 9.1. In this case the agency employed to design a campaign aimed at encouraging younger females to adopt safer sexual practices decided to use focus groups as the vehicle for discovering why it was that a great many such individuals were still failing to take adequate birth control precautions. Many of the focus group participants indicated that they would sometimes take a gamble by not using birth control and especially when younger they did not use any form of contraception at all! The following statements represent a selection of direct quotes from focus-group participants, giving some clue as to why this might be the case.

> Luckily, I haven't gotten pregnant, but yeah, it's certainly been a gamble, you know, and if I'm in a situation where nothing's available, you know, just those situations you can get into. . . . I know it's stupid but, you know, at the time that's not as real as the moment is.

> I was so immature that it was like almost a game to me, to say, 'Oh, no, it won't matter this time,' you know. Or 'Don't worry about it' or 'I can't get pregnant.' I know so many girls that say 'Oh, I can't get pregnant. I think I must be one of those women that can never get pregnant.' I thought that until I got pregnant.

> When I first started having sex and stuff, I honestly believed that I could not get pregnant.

The quotes given above were used by the creative agency to directly inform the development of the poster in Fig. 9.1. As the reader will appreciate it was designed specifically to get across the vital statistic that 90 per cent of young women who do not use birth control become pregnant within a year. In short, it was designed to counter the belief that 'it can't happen to me'. The preliminary artwork for the poster was itself subsequently the subject of a focus-group discussion to ensure that it was likely to be successful in imparting the required message to the target group. In this latter case, members of the group were asked to interpret the message contained in the poster. Their responses were:

> Your odds of getting pregnant are pretty good.
>
> Start using birth control. You're not always lucky.
>
> This one's really easy to understand. It's concrete and believable.
>
> It's eye-catching. If I saw this somewhere I'd stop and look at it.

Full details of the campaign and its development are given in the following case study.

Case Study 9.1: **The 'Don't Kid Yourself' Campaign**

The 'Don't Kid Yourself' campaign is the result of a collaboration among the Title X Family Planning grantees in Public Health Service Region VIII—Colorado, Montana, North Dakota, South Dakota, Utah, and Wyoming. The grantees pooled their funds in order to create a social marketing campaign to reduce unintended pregnancies in the region. They selected Weinreich Communications, a social marketing firm in Washington, DC, to plan, develop, and implement the programme. Every element of the 'Don't Kid Yourself' campaign was developed based upon social marketing research conducted by Weinreich Communications. An initial set of five focus groups were conducted in Butte and Salt Lake City with members of the target audience—low-income women aged 18 to 24. These focus groups provided insight into how they think about birth control and pregnancy, as well as how best to reach them with campaign messages. Based on the results of the initial research, draft materials and campaign ideas were developed and tested in six additional focus groups before being finalized. In addition, eight individual interviews were conducted with target audience members to be used as a source of sound-bites for the radio spots. The campaign was then pilot-tested in Butte and Salt Lake City.

In Salt Lake City, the number of phone calls to Planned Parenthood's clinics increased by 72 per cent during the two months the pilot campaign was implemented. In Butte, the number of people listing the Butte Family Planning clinic as a place they would go for answers about sexual health or birth control issues nearly doubled after the campaign.

The campaign included the following elements.

Radio Advertisements (ten 30-second spots)

Most of the radio ads used the actual voices of members of the target audience to model attitudes, change misconceptions, and spark thoughts and conversations about the topic. Radio was selected as a key element of the campaign for several reasons. First, in the focus groups, nearly all participants said that they listened to the radio regularly. Secondly, radio allows the campaign to reach a very specific audience; it is possible to precisely target women aged 18 to 24 and reach a large percentage of that population. Thirdly, because radio is ever-present in many people's lives, the target audience may hear messages when they are in a situation in which they should use birth control—the radio spot may thus serve as a reminder and make it more likely that they use it. Fourthly, the spots may play when friends or partners are together and promote conversations about birth control issues. Finally, the older people who are more likely to be offended by the ads are less likely to be listening to the same stations as the 18 to 24-year-olds.

Posters (4 designs)

A set of four posters was developed to get the campaign message out through community organizations, including clinics, schools, businesses, government agencies, recreational facilities, and local 'hangouts'. The tag-line on all the posters and visual materials, 'Don't Kid Yourself,' came from a focus group participant who was summing up the point of the poster visuals. Although she didn't realize it at the time, these words provide a clever *double entendre* for this campaign. This idea of 'kidding oneself' came up often in the focus groups, with many young women saying that they often had unprotected intercourse because they thought that pregnancy couldn't happen to them or that they would be safe 'just this once'. The bright neon colours, rough drawings, and text typeface of the posters were designed to draw attention from the 18 to 24-year-old age group and younger.

Newspaper Ads (4 designs)

Four newspaper ads were designed in several different sizes. The focus group research showed that many of the women read particular types of newspapers or sections of the paper. Newspaper ads were felt to be helpful in reaching those who respond better to visual information, or who do not hear the radio ads. They also provided the phone number and campaign messages in a form that could be cut out and kept until someone is ready to call.

Drink Coasters

Bright pink drink coasters with campaign messages were designed for distribution to bars and clubs. The focus group participants said that bars, clubs, and coffee-houses were good places to reach women aged 18 to 24. These venues were particularly appropriate, since potential sexual partners or groups of friends might be drinking together and can use the coaster as a method of initiating conversations about birth control.

Brochures (2 topics)

Two 3-colour brochures were developed, based on the needs identified by focus group participants. One brochure presented birth control options, while the other assisted in talking to a sexual partner about birth control. They provided in-depth information and skills-building content at an appropriate reading level, using the target audience's language. The brochures also served as a proxy for those who would not come into the clinic to speak with a counsellor. They were easily placed in locations frequented by the target audience, including schools, grocery stores, bars and clubs, public libraries, and doctors' offices.

The Social Marketing Mix

The reader will appreciate that, since in a social marketing context we are no longer concerned with physical products or even services, the traditional marketing mix introduced in Chapter 4 is somewhat more difficult to apply. Whilst this is so, it is possible to extend and adapt the marketing mix to generate a greater relevance to the marketing of ideas. Since marketers seem to prefer to talk about Ps, a 6 P framework for use by those of us working in the social arena is proposed below.

1 Product

The product in this context is the 'idea' that the marketer wishes to get across to stimulate a change in behaviour. Unlike traditional marketing which advocates the development of the product carefully designed to mirror customer preferences, the social marketer strives to engineer a change that (in their opinion) would be good for society as a whole. The element of persuasion is therefore important since the behaviour change must be marketed on the basis of the benefits that could accrue either directly or indirectly as a result. The product might hence be a change in sexual behaviour, a change in recycling behaviour, or the stimulation of demand for health programmes to counter social problems such as drug or solvent abuse.

2 Price

The price may be regarded as the monetary costs associated with adopting a change in behaviour. Attendance on a health programme may require the individual to fund some of the treatments that might be suggested. More usually, however, the important costs of a change in behaviour will be social. Individuals may suffer embarrassment and even ridicule within their social group for responding to a social marketing campaign. One can even place a cost on the fear that individuals might have of attending a health programme such as an annual mammogram. Some women may simply feel that they could not deal with the stress of having a lump discovered and may take the conscious decision that it is better not to know.

Cost is also an issue in the realm of recycling and Shrum *et al.* (1994) conclude, after a review of the literature, that cost viewed in terms of inconvenience acts as a very powerful motivator to avoid recycling. Identifying all the potential costs is therefore important as the social marketing campaign can take account of these and make every attempt to minimize them as far as possible.

A final point on price that experience has taught social marketers is that it is often better to make some form of charge for any products that they might be involved in distributing. Simply giving away free items runs the very real risk that little value will be placed on them. It is often better to sell at a cheap price to encourage a perception of value amongst members of the target segment. Indeed, doing so may also help engage the support of the local infrastructure which will be necessary if the programme is to have any form of long-term impact. It is therefore not unusual, for example, for a small charge to be made for contraception, even in some of the world's poorest societies.

3 Place

Place refers to the location at which any service component of the social marketing campaign will be delivered. In the case of many birth-control programmes, for example, access to the programme must be straightforward and provided at a location geographically close to the target market. Place can also refer to the channels of information that are used to reach the target market. Information on the dangers of HIV, for example, might be conveyed to the target market by distributing leaflets via schools, colleges, universities, general practitioners, family planning clinics, etc.

4 Promotion

Social marketers will make use of most of the promotional tools described in Chapter 4. Many campaigns utilize advertising, public relations, sales promotion, and direct marketing to communicate with their target audience. The mechanics of exactly how this might be achieved and the stages involved in developing a typical communications plan are outlined in detail later in this chapter.

5 Partnerships

It has already been suggested that certain categories of behaviour are not easy to influence. Many nonprofits may simply be too small to make much of an impact on their own. They may lack the necessary resources in terms of both staff time and monetary backing. As a consequence many nonprofits involved in social marketing look for potential partnerships with other organizations with similar goals. This may involve working closely with a wide variety of different organizations in both the private and public sectors. Clearly social marketers will need to identify and liaise with potential allies for a particular campaign to ensure that the overall approach to society is as co-ordinated as possible.

6 Policy

The difficulties of influencing continuing behaviours have already been discussed above. In many cases the only method of achieving the desired outcome may be to compel individuals/groups to institute the change in behaviour required. Ultimately, for example, it may become necessary for governments to ban all forms of tobacco advertising to reduce sales. Simply trying to persuade individuals to give up smoking of their

own volition may work up to a point, but ultimately there will be a few 'die hard' smokers who simply will never have either the necessary will-power or desire to give up their
habit. For these reasons marketers also have to be aware of the social policies that
influence behaviour, and attempt to influence those who have the power to instigate
legislative change.

Thus, it is possible to utilize an adapted marketing mix in a social marketing context.
The familiar concepts of product, price, place, and promotion all have their role to play
in the creation of an effective social marketing campaign, even where the provision of
no physical products, or even services, may be involved.

Since Part B of this text has already examined the use of the marketing mix in different nonprofit contexts, it is intended to focus specifically in the remainder of this chapter on the development of a social marketing communications campaign, and to
examine in detail the stages that are involved in its creation.

Designing a Communications Campaign

There are seven steps that are normally followed in designing a communications campaign, namely:

(1) specification of the target audience;
(2) communications objectives;
(3) specification of promotional message;
(4) media selection;
(5) schedule;
(6) budget;
(7) monitoring/control.

Each of these will now be examined in turn.

Specification of the Target Audience

Chapter 3 has already highlighted a variety of criteria that could be used to define the
target audience. They may be specified in terms of their geographic, demographic, geodemographic, behavioural, or lifestyle characteristics. However, in a social marketing
context, it would also be usual to specify in detail the behaviours within each segment
and the current pattern thereof. With only finite resources available social marketers
will usually have to select only those segments that they perceive as being of particular
importance. Bennett (1996), for example, in a survey of twenty Health Education
Officers identified that homosexual men were almost unanimously perceived as being
the most important target for AIDS awareness campaigns and that resources were
being allocated accordingly.

If a variety of segments are to be addressed the behaviours of each should be clearly
identified so that planners can be clear about the point from which the behaviour
change will be started. Such a specification will aid in setting campaign objectives and
will be essential if the overall effectiveness of the campaign is to be assessed.

2 Communications Objectives

Communications objectives, like any other form of objective, should be specific, measurable, achievable, relevant, and time-scaled. They are written to address various aspects of the campaign, so that the resulting communications strategy is focused clearly on achieving the goals of the initiating organization. Colley (1961) developed a model for setting communications objectives entitled DAGMAR (Defining Advertising Goals for Measured Advertising Results). Although Colley's ideas were originally developed to assist in the assessment of advertising effectiveness, the model he developed can be applied to all forms of social marketing promotion. Colley believed that the process of communications was essentially hierarchical in nature and hence, for our purposes, if an idea is to be effectively communicated consumers should be moved through the following five stages:

- Unawareness
- Awareness
- Comprehension
- Conviction
- Action

Clearly before a social idea can gain acceptance, the target audience must be appraised of the concept and made to realize that alternative behaviours exist. Third World communities thus need to be made aware that birth control methods exist and that pregnancy can be avoided. Similarly in the marketing of oral rehydration therapy, mothers in parts of Asia need to be made aware that diarrhoeal disease need not necessarily be fatal, given the proper (and rudimentary) treatment.

Simply making an audience aware of alternative behaviours is unlikely to be enough in itself to encourage a change, however. The social marketer must strive to ensure that the target audience actually understands the benefits that a change in behaviour could bring. Taboos or fallacies about the use of birth control methods must hence be overcome. Similarly, information about the success and simplicity of oral rehydration tablets in treating diarrhoeal disease must also be conveyed.

Having achieved a certain level of understanding in the target market it is then necessary to generate a sense of conviction. Smokers, for example, may be aware of the dangers of their habit and understand the relationship between it and fatal diseases such as heart disease and cancer, but they may lack the necessary conviction to quit. Establishing conviction in such a high-involvement decision is not an easy task, however, and a variety of carefully targeted messages may be necessary to secure it.

The final stage of Colley's model can be viewed as the ultimate goal: securing a change in behaviour. Communications messages could be used to guide their recipients through the steps necessary to effect a change in behaviour. A Freephone number could, for example, be provided to give individually tailored advice to callers about health or welfare issues.

Colley held the view that communications objectives could be written to reflect any of the four important stages of the model. Hence, one could write objectives in terms of the number of people who are aware that alternative behaviours are available/acceptable (awareness), the number of people who understand why a behavioural change might be necessary (comprehension), the numbers of people who express an intention to change in the future (conviction), and, finally, the numbers of people who actually implement a change in behaviour (action). Social communication objectives typically address all four of these areas.

3 Specifying the Promotional Message

There are a number of considerations which must be addressed in the design of appropriate promotional messages. These include the level of involvement a particular behaviour invokes, the content of the message, and the manner in which it will be conveyed. Each of these issues will now be explored in turn.

(a) Level of Involvement

Fill (1995) argues that the effectiveness of a message, from a receiver's perspective, depends on two factors. The first is the amount and quality of information communicated, whilst the second is the overall judgement made about the manner in which it is presented. There is therefore a need to strike a balance between an individual's need for information and their need to enjoy the consumption thereof. However, different styles of message may be appropriate depending on the nature of the behaviour that it is intended to influence. As Fig. 9.2 makes clear, decisions that are high involvement in nature require that the individual is presented with detailed information about the alternatives available and the benefits thereof. This is because such decisions will require the individual to use his/her cognitive functions and the decision-making processes are hence relatively (although not exclusively) rational in nature. What is termed a central route to persuasion is therefore adopted, consisting of strong, well-documented and supported arguments in favour of the idea being raised. After the recent BSE crisis in the UK, for example, numerous agencies were involved in a large social marketing campaign to convince the public that British Beef was safe. Given that the question of which meats to eat had become a high-involvement decision for most UK households, it was decided to convey a series of very rational reasons why British Beef was safe to eat and considerable background detail was thus communicated to the public in an attempt to allay any fears.

Low-involvement decisions on the other hand require rather less thought from the individual and messages will hence be more effective if they concentrate on imagery. The aim here is to engender an emotional response which reflects an individual's ego, or self image, and marketers hence follow the peripheral route to persuasion through an emphasis on non-content message ingredients such as music, lighting, scenery, or the use of celebrity endorsements. The advertising that preceded the compulsory use of seatbelts in the UK for example focused on the use of powerful imagery which illus-

Fig. 9.2: **High Involvement versus Low Involvement Decisions**

High involvement	Rational product attribute appeal
Central route	Information provision Benefit claims
Peripheral route	Emotional, image-based appeal
Low involvement	Social, ego, hedonic orientation

Source: Fill, C. (1995) *Marketing Communications*. Reproduced with the kind permission of Prentice Hall.

trated the suffering and pain that could be caused to family members by a failure to comply with the new regulations. Celebrity endorsement was also offered by Jimmy Saville who coined the catchy advertising strap line 'Clunk Click, Every Trip'.

(b) Content of the Message

There are a number of issues relating to message content that social marketers must consider, including the following.

(i) One and Two-sided Messages

Some promotional messages contain only 'one side' of the argument. They convey only the positive impacts of the change in behaviour required whilst ignoring any drawbacks completely. Other messages may be termed two-sided in that they present a more balanced view to the audience and present both the advantages and disadvantages of a given behaviour change. In general, research would seem to indicate that one-sided messages are more effective where the recipient group already has a favourable view of the behaviour change, or where their level of education is low. Conversely the use of two-sided messages would be preferred where the recipients are either highly educated or hold a very negative view of the behaviour change presented.

(ii) Drawing Conclusions

Marketers must also decide whether the message they intend to convey will draw a firm conclusion about the need for a change in behaviour, or whether the message will be left open and the individual encouraged to draw his/her own conclusions. There is of course no easy way in which to choose between these two options but a variety of factors have been found to impact on the most appropriate form of message to use (Hovland and Mandell, 1952). Specifically the desirability of drawing a conclusion for the audience has been found to depend on the following factors:

The level of education of the message recipients. The higher the level of education possessed by the audience, the more likely it is that they will prefer to draw their own conclusions. There is a danger that members of a highly educated group will feel patronized by an approach which claims to know categorically what is right for them. Those with lower levels of education, however, may be incapable of drawing the correct conclusion from the data presented for themselves and may require it to be drawn for them.

Level of complexity. If the idea being marketed is technically complex, or multifaceted, it may be less easy for the recipient to see the end to which they are being led. Guidance may hence have to be more specific where complexity is encountered. Similarly, completely new ideas may need a greater degree of explanation and conclusion-drawing than those that have been around for some time.

When action is required. In the case of the marketing of the oral rehydration tablets mentioned earlier, the action required of the recipient is often immediate. Any delay in decision making may substantially reduce the chances of saving a child's life. Promotional messages in such circumstances must therefore be quite forceful and the results of inaction spelt out very clearly. If, on the other hand, the timescale for action is somewhat longer, the necessity for immediate action is diminished and the need for firm conclusion-drawing is less pronounced.

Level of involvement. As one would expect, given our earlier discussion, high-involvement decisions are best approached by furnishing individuals with the appropriate facts to make their decision alone. Any attempt to 'force' a change in behaviour on individuals in these circumstances is likely to be counter-productive. Indeed recipients may actively resent such messages (see, for example, Sawyer and Howard, 1991).

(iii) Framing the Presentation

In presenting any new social ideas to a potential audience, there will always be a variety of arguments that could be used to attempt to persuade. Of course, not all of these messages will have an equal impact on the target group; some will be seen as weak arguments, whilst others will not be as easy to counter. The issue for marketers then becomes the order in which these messages should be presented. Should a promotional message begin with the stronger points or the weaker ones?

Once again we must return to the question of the level of involvement that the audience has with the idea. If the audience has a low level of involvement it may be necessary to begin with a strong message which serves to generate attention. It is also true that if the audience holds a strongly opposing view, a weak argument at the beginning of the message will only serve to raise counter-arguments in the minds of recipients and the remainder of the message may be filtered out as a result. Of course, the converse of these points is also true. Messages which begin with weaker points and 'build up' to the strongest arguments at the end, tend to be more appropriate where the position adopted is not controversial, or where the issue evokes a strong but positive sense of involvement.

Social marketers must also decide whether to use positively framed messages (that is, messages which refer primarily to the benefits of the desired change in behaviour) or negatively framed messages (which draw attention to the drawbacks of *not* implementing the change in behaviour). So, for example, a campaign directed at persuading people to stop smoking, will need to decide whether the campaign will be positively framed and feature the details of how much better they will feel if they stop, or whether it should focus on the health implications of not giving up (negatively framed messages). Maheswaran and Meyers-Levy (1990) conclude that positively framed messages are more appropriate in situations where the individual does not have to process information (low involvement), and negatively framed messages more appropriate where a detailed level of information processing is required (high-involvement decisions).

(iv) The Nature of the Appeal

There are a variety of ways in which a social idea can be communicated in a promotional message. If individuals are highly educated, or where the decision is a high-involvement decision, we have already seen that a factual appeal may be the most appropriate to use. However, where the target audience is less well-educated, or where the appeal is addressing low-involvement behaviours, the social marketer may find that an emotional appeal is more effective. Indeed even where an appeal is largely factual there may still be scope for the social marketer to design campaigns which make an indirect use of fear, humour, or sexual imagery. The advantages and disadvantages of each of these approaches will now be considered in turn.

Fear Appeals

Fear is an emotion often evoked to good effect by social marketers. This may be an immediate fear, such as the fear of contracting a particular disease, or it may be more longer term in nature and reflect a concern for issues that will have a greater impact on future generations (for example, some recycling behaviours). Fear may also be catego-rized according to whether it is a health-related fear or a fear of social disapproval, re-sulting from taking (or not taking) a particular form of action. Clearly social marketers may utilize a variety of messages from each category.

Many researchers working in the field of 'fear' in advertising have found that there is a negative relationship between the strength of a fear appeal and its ability to be able to persuade a target market. In other words, appeals which evoke a strong sense of fear are likely to be less effective than those which use fear to only a very mild extent. Schiff-man and Kanuk (1994) explain this phenomenon as a reaction to what is termed '*cogni-tive dissonance*' in the minds of recipients. In the case of a strong fear appeal used to target cigarette smokers, the recipients cannot reconcile their need to continue using the product with the strong sense of fear the advertising has generated. In psychologi-cal terms they experience dissonance. The only way they can reconcile this dissonance is either by giving up the habit or rejecting the content of the fear message. As Schiff-man and Kanuk (1994, 308) put it:

> Since giving up a comfortable habit is difficult, consumers more readily reject the threat. This they do by a variety of techniques including denial of its validity ('There still is no real proof that smoking causes cancer'), the belief that they are immune to personal disaster ('It can't happen to me') and a diffusing process that robs the claim of its true significance ('I play it safe by only using filter cigarettes').

It is therefore important to test any campaign relying on a fear appeal to ensure that an appropriate level of fear is induced. Used properly it can be an important weapon in a social marketer's armoury, since Strenhal and Craig (1982) conclude that fear appeals are a particularly powerful way of persuading audiences to change their attitudes. Re-grettably the relationship between the use of fear appeals and actual behaviour change is rather less clear cut. For those that are interested Janis (1967) provides a concise re-view of the literature in this area.

Appeals Based On Humour

Numerous studies over the years have addressed whether humour can enhance the ef-fectiveness of a promotional campaign. Helpfully, Weinberger and Gulas (1992) pre-sent a review of the relevant literature which concludes that:

- humour attracts attention;
- humour does not harm comprehension (indeed, in some cases it can aid it);
- humour is not more effective at increasing persuasion than other promotional messages;
- humour enhances 'liking'. Individuals are more likely to develop a favourable im-pression of advertising that utilizes humour;
- humour that is relevant to the product is superior to humour unrelated to the product;
- audience characteristics (gender, ethnicity, age) affect the response to humorous appeals;
- the nature of the product affects the appropriateness of a humorous treatment.;
- humour is more effective with existing products than with new products;
- humour is more effective with low involvement decisions than those with a high involvement.

Sexual Appeals

The very nature of many social marketing campaigns ensures that a percentage of marketers working in this area will have to address the level of sexual messages/imagery that will be contained in the messages they have to convey. The use of sex in advertising can take many forms, such as nudity, *double entendre*, or perhaps more subtle devices such as that depicted in Fig. 9.3. The extent to which blatantly sexual imagery will be appropriate will vary from society to society and from year to year. In the mid 1980s, for example, visual sexual imagery was commonplace in many forms of advertising. By the end of the decade, advertisers had reverted to the use of more romantic imagery in response to an increased awareness of the threat of AIDS.

Fig. 9.3: **Health Education Council Advertising**

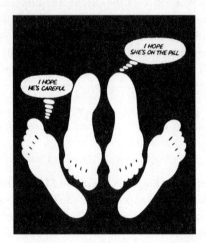

Source: Health Education Council.

The key advantage of an appeal based on sex is simply that it is unrivalled in terms of its power to attract attention. Studies have shown that advertising with a sexual appeal is capable of arousing the immediate attention of both men and women. Regrettably, however, attention does not necessarily equate with interest in the product or idea being marketed. Social marketers may therefore find that they attract immediate interest amongst the target group, but ultimately they fail to learn anything about the ideas the marketer is attempting to communicate. Nudity in particular has been found to impact negatively on the ability to communicate a message.

If used, sexual imagery must therefore be used with care. Research suggests that the key seems to lie in:

- using the sexual content largely as a device to attract attention;
- using the sexual component only where it is necessary to display a product function—or the expression of an idea;
- using sex symbolically rather than overtly—sexual imagery tends to be more effective than overt portrayals of sex *per se*. Nudity is also less effective in advertising than the use of sexual symbolism

Cartoons/Animation

Animation techniques have begun to rise in popularity in recent years. Although campaigns featuring animated characters have tended to address a younger audience, several big names have recently used animated campaigns aimed at adults to good effect in the for-profit sector. Tetley Tea, Direct Line, and National Savings are three campaigns for potentially very dull products that have been greatly enlivened by the use of creative animation. Thus, when considering the marketing of some social ideas, a greater degree of attention may be attracted if animated characters are used to convey the idea. Houston and Markland (1976), for example, quote the example of Marcus Rabbit MD being used to convey immunization messages to parents of small children in Missouri, USA.

Media Selection

There are a variety of different media which can be utilized in a social marketing campaign, each with their own advantages and disadvantages. These include the following.

Television

If the campaign is to be directed at broad target groups within society, the cost of reaching each individual within that market will be comparatively low if television is selected as an appropriate medium. Television also lends a certain status to a campaign, in that organizations that advertise on television are generally perceived as being more reliable and trustworthy than those that don't. Thus the credibility of a social idea may be greatly enhanced by even an occasional airing on television. Of course, given that a typical television commercial is only a few seconds long, it may be necessary to repeat the message on several occasions to ensure that the idea has been effectively communicated. This in turn increases the absolute level of cost associated with the campaign and, when one adds in the costs of producing the commercial in the first place, the overall cost can often be prohibitive.

Print

Print media represent a very flexible communications opportunity for the marketer. Advertisements of all shapes and sizes can be presented using a wide range of colours and effects. Adverts can be targeted specifically at those newspapers or magazines known to have a high readership amongst the target audience and, because of the enhanced segmentation this provides, messages can be tailored to suit the environment of the publication in which they are housed. Print also offers opportunities for inserts (which, incidentally, are six times more likely to be read than advertising carried on the pages of a magazine) and cut-out coupons, which can be completed to obtain further information, etc.

The weaknesses of press advertising relate to the fact that increases in circulations have tended to lag somewhat behind increases in advertising rates, gradually making print financially a less attractive option. The other major difficulty with press advertising is that readers of the publication will not necessarily read the ad. Readers can, and do, select those advertisements which they feel they want to read. Magazines have the further weakness that it is often necessary to book space months in advance of the intended publication date. Given that at this stage the details of the promotional campaign are unlikely to have been finalized this can create significant problems.

Radio

Expenditure on radio advertising has been cyclical over the past fifteen years. It recovered from a dip in the mid 1980s to level off at approximately £160m per annum in the UK in 1990. More recently the sector has experienced another rise in its fortunes and expenditures are currently closer to £200m. Radio advertising is thus clearly becoming an increasingly attractive option for many organizations. Largely this is because it is possible to identify quite specific audiences tuning in to various stations at various times of the day. Radio campaigns are relatively cheap to produce and comparatively easy to modify should this become necessary. Radio also has the advantage that it can often utilize the imagination of the recipient, and effects can be achieved which would be unthinkable on television.

On the down side, radio advertising clearly lacks any form of visual stimulus which can be helpful in gaining attention. The other difficulty with radio is that listening can often be a background activity and the level of attention advertising receives can, as a consequence, be low. Radio is a useful medium, however, for reinforcing other forms of promotional activity, because sound triggers can be used to aid recall of, for example, a television commercial.

Outdoor

All forms of posters and signs are usually referred to as outdoor media. Outdoor media traditionally receive less attention than others and overall expenditure is a very small percentage of promotional spend in general. The amount of information that can be conveyed on a poster is relatively limited and for this reason many poster campaigns elect to focus on the creative use of imagery. As with radio, poster campaigns can be very effective at reinforcing messages conveyed by other media and very large numbers of people have the opportunity to see (OTS) promotional messages conveyed in this way. Poster sites are sold on the basis of the number of 'sheets' that make up the display panel and these vary in size from 1 to 96 sheets (see Fig. 9.4). Similarly the purchase would typically be made of a package of sites, rather than a series of one-offs. Posters can be much more effectively targeted than many people believe. The introduction of the OSCAR system in the UK (Outdoor Site Classification and Audience Research) now enables advertisers to select those sites likely to be most effective in reaching their target audience. Locations can be selected on the basis of key demographic variables and targeting greatly enhanced as a result.

Fig. 9.4: **Poster Advertising Sheet Specification**

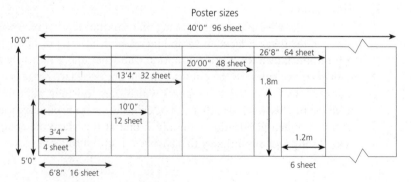

Source: Media Pocket Book, NTC Publications Ltd.

The key disadvantages of outdoor advertising are the long lead times. Many sites are booked up months/years in advance particularly if the site is one of the ever increasing number of three dimensional displays, which tend by their very nature to command a greater degree of attention. There are of course many other, often very creative, forms of outdoor advertising. One can book advertising space on the sides of most forms of transport, hire balloons, airships, or even, as the Devon Wildlife Trust did recently, create a six-foot replica of a dodo and 'release' it into the wild!

Electronic

There has been a proliferation in the availability of other electronic media over the past twenty years. Aside from the fragmentation of the television industry and the proliferation of new channels, advertising space can also now be bought on the accompanying teletext pages. With over 50 per cent of homes in the UK estimated to have the necessary technology to receive teletext, this represents a significant new media opportunity.

Video displays are now being provided in major retail outlets where promotional material can be viewed while you wait to be served. Viewdata systems are now commonplace in most major post offices for example. The use of the Internet has already been addressed in Chapter 3.

Schedule

To ensure that all the communications activities undertaken are fully integrated it would be usual to specify the exact timings of each on a Gantt chart (see Chapter 4), which can then be used by those responsible for the campaign to ensure that not only does each activity commence on the prescribed date, but also that opportunities for synergy are fully exploited. Thus, for example, if it is intended to run a brief television campaign, outdoor and radio advertising can be implemented as a follow-up in subsequent months to ensure that enhanced levels of awareness of the social idea are maintained cost effectively and for as long as possible in the minds of the target market.

It is also important to note that the original objectives for the campaign can impact on the schedule that it is intended to follow. Campaigns which are ground-breaking and designed to raise awareness of a totally new concept may thus require that promotional effort is concentrated in a major initial burst, in order to expose as many members of the target audience to the social ideas as early as possible. This can then be supported with periodic reminders at various points throughout the year. If, on the other hand, the campaign is designed merely to extend and develop an idea already established in the minds of the targets, the need for an expensive initial burst is likely to be greatly reduced. Indeed, in such circumstances it is rather more likely that the promotional budget will be evenly allocated across the whole duration of the campaign, allowing a gradual infusion of learning to take place.

Budget

As in the case of the marketing plan referred to in Chapter 4, it would be usual in a communications plan to specify the overall budget and the manner in which it will be allocated across the various activities to be undertaken. Variances between proposed and actual expenditure can then be easily monitored and, where necessary, corrective action initiated.

Evaluation and Control

There are essentially four types of evaluation which would typically be undertaken in a social marketing context. These are:

(1) *Formative Evaluation*. This form of evaluation is undertaken to pre-test the materials that will be used during the campaign. This would typically include the copy, design, and layout of any advertising, together with an assessment of the effectiveness of any sales promotion techniques that it is intended to use.

(2) *Process Evaluation*. The process of implementation will also be subject to review. Each stage of the communications plan will be evaluated to ensure that the campaign objectives will ultimately be achieved and that appropriate messages have been received and understood by members of the target market.

(3) *Outcome Evaluation*. This would typically consist of a detailed analysis of whether or not the desired change in behaviour has been facilitated. Of course there are many variables that could be examined for the purpose of outcome evaluation. These include:

   (i)   the number and form of requests for information;

   (ii) the source of requests for information—the profile of respondents;

   (iii) the awareness, recall, and acceptance of the campaign messages. Changes in attitude may also be measured;

   (iv) the extent to which the target market has been exposed to the message—the coverage achieved by the campaign;

   (v)   the nature and extent of behavioural change achieved within the target segment.

(4) *Impact Evaluation*. It may be impossible to measure the impact of a social marketing campaign in the short term. The campaign could be concerned with changing societal behaviours which would only impact on society in the longer term. Thus, whilst one would obviously be concerned with the immediate impact on behaviour achieved by a campaign, it may also be necessary to track those behaviours over time to ensure that they are sustained. Some social marketers may even attempt to evaluate the benefits that have accrued to society as a result of the behavioural changes achieved. It is worth noting, however, that such forms of evaluation are seldom used for communication programmes alone because the costs of conducting this form of research are formidable.

Control procedures would normally be set up to monitor each stage of the campaign. The overall objectives would usually be broken down to derive a set of targets for each month (or aspect) of the campaign to achieve. Any deviance from these interim targets would be recorded and if significant variations have occurred corrective action may be implemented to ensure that ultimately the campaign objectives are met in full. Typically around 5–10 per cent of the communications budget would be set aside to allow for such contingencies.

Summary

In this chapter we have defined social marketing as the marketing of ideas with the specific intent of influencing social behaviours. It is this latter dimension which distinguishes the concept from mere education or lobbying activities. The relevance of social marketing to various social domains was established, including efforts to alter forms of sexual, smoking, drug/alcohol abuse, pollution, and recycling behaviours. In each case social marketers have no concrete product or service which they can 'sell' to a target market—they only have an idea which, if accepted by the selected segments, could impact favourably on the whole of society. Of course, one's perception of what would be a favourable outcome will differ from individual to individual and there are thus strong ethical dimensions to any social marketing campaign.

A number of factors were introduced that have been found to affect the extent to which it is possible to influence behaviour, namely whether the behaviour is high or low involvement, whether the behaviour is one-off or continuing, and whether the behaviour is exhibited by groups or individuals. Those continuing behaviours exhibited by groups were introduced as being the most difficult to alter, largely because group dynamics serve to legitimize and support anti-social behaviours which may otherwise be discarded.

This chapter introduced the concept of a social marketing mix which could assist in changing these behaviours, adding two additional 'Ps' to the traditional four 'P' mix, namely partnerships and policy. These additional elements together allow the social marketer to recognize the desirability for many organizations of forging links with others in order to exert greater influence over their target market. They also acknowledge what is often a final necessity—namely, that of convincing governments to instigate legislative change, when less forceful attempts at persuasion have failed.

The chapter concluded with a review of the contents of a typical communications plan and the key considerations which must be borne in mind by a social marketer as each stage is developed. A surprising amount of research has been conducted, for example, into issues such as the suitability of various forms of emotional appeals, message order effects, and the manner in which information is presented. Only by taking account of such research can social marketers ensure that they benefit from knowledge gained through past failures and ensure that their particular campaign is as effective and efficient as possible.

Discussion Questions

1. To what extent does the element of persuasion inherent in a social marketing campaign conflict with the marketing philosophy of satisfying customer requirements?
2. Distinguish social marketing from the processes of social communication, education, and lobbying.
3. What primary data would you advise a social marketing organization to gather in an attempt to inform the design of a campaign designed to reduce levels of teenage smoking? How might this data be gathered?

4. You are a consultant employed by the communications manager of Waste Concern, an organization whose primary aim is to encourage households to recycle as much of their domestic waste as possible. How could this organization proceed to segment the 'market' for its communications? For each segment you identify, design appropriate communications messages and specify the media that you would recommend the organization to utilize to deliver them.

5. Design a marketing communications plan for your own social marketing organization, or one with which you are familiar.

References

Abratt, R. and Sacks, D. (1988) 'The Marketing Challenge: Towards Being Profitable and Socially Responsible', *Journal of Business Ethics*, Vol. 7, 497–507.

Bennett, R. (1996) 'Implementation of HIV/AIDS Awareness and Prevention Campaigns: The Case of the London Boroughs', *Proceedings, MEG Conference*, University of Strathclyde.

Black, T. R. L. (1979) 'The Application of Market Research in Contraceptive Social Marketing in a Rural Area of Kenya', *Journal of the Market Research Society*, Jan, 30–43.

Braus, P. (1995) 'Selling Good Behaviour', *American Demographics*, Nov, 60–4.

Colley, R. (1961) *Defining Advertising Goals for Measured Advertising Results*, New York , Association of National Advertisers.

Elder, J. P. (1994) *Motivating Health Behaviour*, Albany NY, Delmar Publishers.

Fill, C. (1995) *Marketing Communications*, Hemel Hempstead, Prentice Hall.

Fox, K. A. and Kotler, P. (1980) 'The Marketing of Social Causes: The First 10 Years', *Journal of Marketing*, Vol. 44, No. 3, 24–33.

Hirschman, E. C. and Holbrook, M. B. (1982) 'Hedonic Consumption: Emerging Concepts Methods and Propositions', *Journal of Marketing*, Vol. 46, 92–101.

Houston, F. S. and Markland, R. (1976) 'Public Agency Marketing—Improving the Adequacy of Infant Immunisation', in *Proceedings: American Institute for Decision Sciences*, 461–63.

Hovland, C. I. and Mandell, W. (1952) 'An Experimental Comparison of Conclusion Drawing by the Communicator and the Audience', *Journal of Abnormal and Social Psychology*, Vol. 47, July, 581–8.

Janis, I. L. (1967) 'Effects of Fear Arousal on Attitude Change: Recent Developments in Theory and Experimental Research', in Berkowitz, L. (ed) *Advances in Experimental Social Psychology*, New York, Academic Press.

Kapferer, J. N. and Laurent, G. (1985) 'Consumer Involvement Profiles: A New Practical Approach to Consumer Involvement', *Journal of Advertising Research*, Vol. 25, No. 6, 48–56.

Kotler, P. and Andreasen, A. (1991) *Strategic Marketing for Nonprofit Organisations*, Englewood Cliffs, Prentice Hall.

Kotler, P. and Zaltman, G. (1971) 'Social Marketing: An Approach to Planned Social Change', *Journal of Marketing*, Vol. 35, No. 2, 3–12.

Laczniak, G. R., Lusch, R. F. and Murphy, P. E. (1979) 'Social Marketing: Its Ethical Dimensions', *Journal of Marketing*, Vol. 43, No. 1, 29–36.

Luthra, R. (1991) 'Contraceptive Social Marketing in the Third World: A Case of Multiple Transfer', *Gazette*, Vol. 3, 159–76.

Maheswaran, D. and Meyers-Levy, J. (1990) 'The Influence of Message Framing and Issue Involvement', *Journal of Marketing Research*, Vol. 27, Aug, 361–7.

McKenzie-Mohr, D. (1994) 'Social Marketing for Sustainability: The Case for Residential Energy Conservation', *Futures*, March, 224–33.

Ramah, M. and Cassidy, C. (1992) 'Social Marketing and Prevention of AIDS', in *AIDS Prevention through Education*, New York, Oxford University Press.

Ratchford, B. (1987) 'New Insights about the FCB Grid', *Journal of Advertising Research*, Aug/Sept, 24–38.

Reynolds, F. D. and Darden, W. R. (1971) 'Mutually Adaptable Effects of Interpersonal Communication', *Journal of Marketing Research*, Vol. 8, Nov, 449–54.

Sawyer, A. G. and Howard, D. J. (1991) 'Effects of Omitting Conclusions in Advertisements to Involved and Uninvolved Audiences', *Journal of Marketing Research*, Vol. 28, Nov, 464–74.

Schellstede, W. (1986) 'Social Marketing of Contraceptives', *Draper Fund Report*, December, 21–6.

Schiffman, L. G. and Kanuk, L. L. (1994) *Consumer Behaviour*, Englewood Cliffs, Prentice Hall.

Shrum, L. J., Lowrey, T. M. and McCarty, J. A. (1994) 'Recycling as a Marketing Problem: A Framework for Strategy Development', *Psychology and Marketing*, Vol. 11, No. 4, 393–416.

Sihombing, B. (1994) *Overview of the Indonesian Family Planning Movement: The Blue Circle and Gold Circle Social Marketing Policies*, Jakarta, National Family Planning Co-ordinating Board.

Smith, M. A. (1992) *Reducing Alcohol Consumption among University Students: Recruitment and Programme Design Strategies Based on Social Marketing Theory*, unpublished dissertation, University of Oregon.

Sternthal, B. and Craig, C. S. (1982) *Consumer Behaviour: An Information Processing Perspective*, Englewood Cliffs, Prentice Hall.

Weinberger, M. G. and Gulas, C. S. (1992) 'The Impact of Humor in Advertising', *Journal of Advertising*, Vol. 21, No. 4, 35–59.

Bibliography

Aaker, D. (1989) 'Managing Assets and Skills: The Key to Sustainable Competitive Advantage', *California Management Review*, Vol. 31, No. 2, 91–106.

Abell, D. F. (1980) *Defining the Business: The Starting Point of Strategic Planning*, Englewood Cliffs, Prentice Hall.

Abratt, R. and Sacks, D. (1988) 'The Marketing Challenge: Towards Being Profitable and Socially Responsible', *Journal of Business Ethics*, Vol. 7, 497–507.

Addison, J. (1993) 'The Selling of Giving', *Sales Promotion*, Oct, 30–3.

Ajzen, I. and Fishbein, M. (1973) 'Attitudinal and Normative Variables as Predictors of Specific Behaviour', *Journal of Personality and Social Psychology*, Vol. 27, No. 1, 41–57.

Allen, A. and Higgins, T. (1994) *Higher Education—The International Student Experience*, HEIST, Leeds.

Allen, J. and Maddox, N. (1990) 'Segmenting Blood Donors by their Perceptions and Awareness about Blood Donations', *Health Marketing Quarterly*, Vol. 7, No. 1, 177–93.

Allt, B. (1975) 'Money or Class: New Light on Household Spending', *Advertising Quarterly*, Vol. 44, Summer, 6–9.

Alston, C. (1985) *The Views of Parents Before Transfer*, Secondary Transfer Project, Bulletin 3 (RS991/85) Inner London Education Authority.

Andreasen, A. R. and Belk, R. W. (1980) 'Predictors of Attendance at the Performing Arts', *Journal of Consumer Research*, Vol. 7, Sept, 112–20.

Andrus, D. and Buchheister, J. (1985) 'Major Factors Affecting Dental Consumer Satisfaction', *Health Marketing and Consumer Behaviour*, Vol. 3, No. 1, 57–68.

Ansoff, I. (1968) *Corporate Strategy*, London, Penguin Books.

Arts Council of Great Britain (1993) *A Creative Future: The way Forward for the Arts*, Crafts and Media in England, London, HMSO.

Ashbrand, D. (1993) 'Client Server System Boosts Theatre Ticket Sales', *Infoworld*, Vol. 5, No. 52/1, pp. 50, 55.

Babakus, E. and Boller, G. W. (1992) 'An Empirical Assessment of the SERVQUAL Scale', *Journal of Business Research*, Vol. 24, 253–68.

Baker, K. (1982) quoted in Clark, E. (1982) 'Acorn Finds New Friends', *Marketing*, 16 Dec, 13.

Bargh, C., Scott, P. and Smith, D. (1996) *Governing Universities: Changing the Culture?*, SRHE and Open University Press, Buckingham.

Beik, L. L. and Smith, S. M. (1979) 'Geographic Segmentation: A Fundraising Example', *Proceedings*, American Marketing Association, 485–8.

Bennett, R. (1996) 'Implementation of HIV/AIDS Awareness and Prevention Campaigns: The Case of the London Boroughs', *Proceedings, MEG Conference*, University of Strathclyde.

Berkowitz, E. N. and Flexner, W. (1980) 'The Market for Health Services: Is there a Non-Traditional Consumer?', *Journal of Health Care Marketing*, Vol. 1, No. 1, 25–34.

Berry, L. L. (1981) 'The Employee as Customer', *Journal of Retail Banking*, Vol. 3, March, 33–40.

—— (1987) 'Service Marketing is Different', *Business*, Vol. 30, No. 2, 24–9.

Black, T. R. L. (1979) 'The Application of Market Research in Contraceptive Social Marketing in a Rural Area of Kenya', *Journal of the Market Research Society*, Jan, 30–43.

Bliss, M. (1980) *Market Segmentation and Environmental Analysis*, unpublished MSc thesis, University of Strathclyde.

BMA (1995) 'Declining Standards in Community Care', as reported in *British Journal of Nursing* (Editorial), Vol. 4, No. 8, 425–6.

Bonoma, T. V. and Shapiro, B. P. (1983) *Segmenting the Industrial Market*, Lexington, USA, Lexington Books.

Booms, B. H. and Bitner, M. J. (1981) 'Marketing Strategies and Organisation Structures for Service Firms, Marketing of Services', in Donnelly, J. and George, W. R. (eds) *Marketing of Services*, Chicago, American Marketing Association.

Bopp, K. D. (1990) 'How Patients Evaluate the Quality of Ambulatory Medical Encounters: A Marketing Perspective', *Journal of Healthcare Marketing*, Vol. 10, No. 2, 6–15.

Borden, N. H. (1964) 'The Concept of the Marketing Mix', *Journal of Advertising Research*, June, 2–7.

Bowen, D. E. and Schneider, B. (1985) 'Boundary Spanning-Role Employees and the Service Encounter: Some Guidelines for Management and Research' in Czepiel, J., Solomon, M. and Suprenant, C. (eds) *The Service Encounter*, Lexington, Lexington Books, 127–45.

Boxall, M. (1991) 'Positioning the Institution in the Marketplace', in *Universities in the Marketplace*, CUA Corporate Planning Forum, Conference of University Administrators in Association with Touche Ross.

Boyd, H. W. and Levy, S. H. (1967) *Promotion: A Behavioural View*, Englewood Cliffs, New Jersey, Prentice Hall.

Braid, M. (1994) 'Children's Charity in Drive for Recognition', *Independent*, 1 Feb, 1.

Braus, P. (1995) 'Selling Good Behaviour', *American Demographics*, Nov, 60–4.

Brightman, J. (1994) 'Selling Sibelius Isn't Easy', *American Demographics*, 1994 Directory, 24–5.

Brown, J. D. (1992) 'Benefit Segmentation of the Fitness Market', *Health Marketing Quarterly*, Vol. 9, No. 3, 19–28.

Brown, S. W. and Swartz, T. A. (1989) 'A Gap Analysis of Professional Service Quality', *Journal of Marketing*, Vol. 53, April, 92–8.

Bruce, I. (1995) 'Do Not For Profits Value their Customers and their Needs?', *International Marketing Review*, Vol. 12, No. 4, 77–84.

—— and Raymer, A. (1992) *Managing and Staffing Britain's Largest Charities*, VOLPROF, Centre for Voluntary Sector and Not-for-Profit Management, City University Business School, London.

Bryce, H. (1992) *Financial and Strategic Management for Non-Profit Organisations*, Englewood Cliffs, Prentice Hall.

Bunn, M. D. (1993) 'Consumer Perceptions of Medical Information Sources: An Application of Multidimensional Scaling', *Health Marketing Quarterly*, Vol. 10, No. 3, 83–104.

Bussell, H. (1994) 'Parents and Primary Schools: A Study of Customer Choice', Proceedings of 1994 Marketing Education Group Conference, Coleraine.

CAF (Charities Aid Foundation) (1994) *Individual Giving and Volunteering in Britain*, West Malling, CAF.

—— (1996) *Dimensions of the Voluntary Sector*, West Malling, CAF.

Cermak, D. S. P., File, K. M. and Prince, R. A. (1994) 'A Benefit Segmentation of the Major Donor Market', *Journal of Business Research*, vol. 29, No. 2, 121–30.

Chapman, D. W. and Johnson, R. H. (1979) 'Influences on Students' College Choice: A Case Study', Ann Arbor, Mich: Project CHOICE, School of Education, University of Michigan.

Chapman, R. (1986) 'Toward a Theory of College Selection: A Model of College Search and Choice Behaviour', in *Advances in Consumer Research*, Vol. 13 (eds) Lutz, R. J., Association for Consumer Research, Provo, Utah.

—— and Franklin, M. S. (1981) 'Measuring the Impact of High School Visits: A Preliminary Investigation', AMA Educators Conference Proceedings, Chicago.

Chisnall, P. (1992) *Marketing Research*, Maidenhead, McGraw Hill.

Churchill, G. A. (1991) *Marketing Research: Methodological Foundations*, Hinsdale Ill., The Dryden Press.

—— and Suprenant, C. (1982) 'An Investigation into the Determinants of Customer Satisfaction', *Journal of Marketing Research*, Vol. 19, 491–504.

Colley, R. (1961) *Defining Advertising Goals for Measured Advertising Results*, New York, Association of National Advertisers.

Commonwealth Federation (1996) *NGOs What They Are and What They Do*, The Commonwealth Foundation, Webpage (http://carryon.oneworld.org/com).

Cooper, P. and Tower, R. (1994) 'Inside the Consumer Mind: Consumer Attitudes to the Arts', *Journal of the Market Research Society*, Vol. 34, No. 4, 299–311.

Crespi, I. (1977) 'Attitude Measurement, Theory and Prediction', *Public Opinion Quarterly*, Vol. 41, No. 3, 285–94.

Crimp, M. (1985) *The Marketing Research Process*, 2nd edn, London, Prentice Hall.

Crosby, J. (1979) *Quality is Free*, New York, McGraw Hill.

Crowther, C. (1995) 'NHS Trust Marketing: A Survival Guide', *Journal of Marketing Practice: Applied Marketing Science*, Vol. 1, No. 2, 57–68.

Cutts, C. S. and Drozd, F. A. (1995) 'Managing the Performing Arts', *Business Quarterly*, Spring, 62–6.

Darby, M. R. and Karni, E. (1973) 'Free Competition and the Optimal Amount of Fraud', *Journal of Law and Economics*, Vol. 16, April, 67–86.

Davies, B. and Ellison, L. (1991) *Marketing the Secondary School*, Longman Industry and Public Services Management, Harlow.

Dawson, W. M. (1980) 'The Arts and Marketing' in Mokwa, M. P., Prieve, E. A. and Dawson, W. M., *Marketing the Arts*, New York, Praeger Publishing.

Delozier, M. (1976) *The Marketing Communication Process*, McGraw Hill.

Deng, S. and Dart, J. (1994) 'A Multi-factor, Multi-items Approach', *Journal of Marketing Management*, Vol. 10, 725–42.

Deshpande, R. and Webster, F. (1993) 'Corporate Culture, Customer Orientation and Innovativeness in Japanese Firms: A Quadrad Analysis', *Journal of Marketing*, Vol. 57, 23–37.

Dichter, E. (1964) *Handbook of Consumer Motivations*, New York, McGraw Hill.

Diggle, K. (1984) *Arts Marketing*, London, Rhinegold Publishing.

DiMaggio, P., Useem, M. and Brown, P. (1978) *Audience Studies of the Performing Arts and Museums: A Critical Review*, Washington DC, National Endowment for the Arts.

Dominguez, L. V. and Page, A. (1984) 'Formulating A Strategic Portfolio of Profitable Retail Segments for Commercial Banks', *Journal of Economics and Business*, Vol. 36, No. 3, 43–57.

Donaldson, L. (1994) 'Charities: A Man with a Mission', *Independent*, 29 Sept, 31.

Doyle, P. (1987) 'Marketing and the British Chief Executive', *Journal of Marketing Management*, Vol. 3, No. 2, 121–32.

Drucker, P. (1990) *Managing the Non-Profit Organisation*, Oxford, Butterworth Heinemann.

Drucker, P. F. (1955) *The Practice of Management*, London, Heinemann.

Edgren, L. (1991) *Service Management Inm Svensk Halso-Och Sjukvard*, Lund, Sweden, Lund University Press.

Elder, J. P. (1994) *Motivating Health Behaviour*, Albany NY, Delmar Publishers.

Fendley, A. and Hewitt, M. (1994) 'When Charity Begins with a Pitch', *Marketing*, 23 June, 14–15.

Fenton, N., Golding, P. and Radley, A. (1993) 'Thinking About Charity: Report of a Pilot Study into Public Attitudes to Charities and Volunteering', in *Researching the Voluntary Sector*, West Malling, Charities Aid Foundation.

Fill, C. (1995) *Marketing Communications*, Hemel Hempstead, Prentice Hall.

Fishbein, M. (1967) *Attitude Theory and Measurement*, New York, John Wiley and Sons.

Ford, C. (1993) 'Tuning up for Promotion', *Incentive Today*, Sept, 14–16.

Fox, K. A. and Kotler, P. (1980) 'The Marketing of Social Causes: The First 10 Years', *Journal of Marketing*, Vol. 44, No. 3, 24–33.

France, K. R. and Grover, R. (1992) 'What is the Health Care Product?', *Journal of Health Care Marketing*, Vol. 12, No. 2, 31–8.

Frank, R. E. (1967) 'Correlates of Buying Behaviour for Grocery Products', *Journal of Marketing*, Vol. 31, No. 4, 48–53.

Gabbott, M. and Hogg, G. (1994) 'Care or Cure: Making Choices in Healthcare', *Unity in Diversity*, *Proceedings of the MEG Conference*, University of Ulster.

George, W. (1990) 'Internal Marketing and Organisational Behaviour. A Partnership in Developing Customer Conscious Employees at Every Level', *Journal of Business Research*, Vol. 20, No. 1, 63–70.

George, W. R. and Berry, L. L. (1981) 'Guidelines for the Advertising of Services', *Business Horizons*, Vol. 24, July–August.

George, W. R. and Gronroos, C. (1989) 'Developing Customer Conscious Employees at Every Level—Internal Marketing', in Congram, C. A. and Friedman, M. L. (eds), *Handbook of Services Marketing*, AMACOM.

Gilmore, J. and Carson, C. (1995) 'Managing and Marketing to Internal Customers', in Glynn, W. J. and Barnes, J. G. (eds), *Understanding Service Management*, Chichester, Wiley.

Go, F. M. and Pine, R. (1995) *Globalization Strategy in the Hotel Industry*, London, Routledge.

Grabowski, S. M. (1981) *Marketing in Higher Education*, AAHE ERIC Higher Education Research Report, No. 5, Washington.

Green, P. E. (1977) 'A New Approach to Market Segmentation', *Business Horizons*, Vol. 20, No. 1, 61–73.

Gronroos, C. (1981a) 'Internal Marketing—An Integral Part of Marketing Theory', *Proceedings, AMA Services Marketing Conference*, 236–8.

—— (1981b) 'Internal Marketing—Theory and Practice', *Proceedings, AMA Services Marketing Conference*, 41–7.

Hair, J. F., Anderson, R. E., Tatham, T. and Black, W. C. (1995) *Multivariate Data Analysis with Readings*, New Jersey, Prentice Hall.

Haley, A. T. (1968) 'Benefit Segmentation: A Decision Oriented Research Tool', *Journal of Marketing*, Vol. 32, No. 3, 30–5.

Halfpenny, P. and Lowe, D. (1993) *Individual Giving and Volunteering in Britain 1993*, West Malling, Charities Aid Foundation.

Hall, J. H. and Dornan, M. C. (1988) 'Meta Analysis of satisfaction with Medical Care Description of Research Domain and Analysis of Overall Satisfaction Levels', *Social Science and Medicine*, Vol. 27, No. 6, 637–44.

Hammond, T. and Dennison, W. (1995) 'School Choice in Less Populated Areas', Educational Management and Administration, Vol. 23, No. 2, 104–13.

Hansler, D. F. and Riggin, D. L. (1989) 'Geodemographics: Targeting the Market', *Fund Raising Management*, Vol. 20, No. 10, 35–43.

Harvey, T. (1995) 'Service Quality: The Culprit and the Cure', *Bank Marketing*, June, 24–8.

HEIST (1995) *The Role of Marketing in the University and College Sector*, HEIST, Leeds.

Hems, L. and Passey, A. (1996) *UK Statistical Almanac*, London, NCVO.

Hill, E., O'Sullivan, C. and O'Sullivan, T. (1995) *Creative Arts Marketing*, Oxford, Butterworth Heinemann.

Hind, A. (1995) *The Governance and Management of Charities*, Barnet, Voluntary Sector Press.

Hirschman, E. C. and Holbrook, M. B. (1982) 'Hedonic Consumption: Emerging Concepts, Methods and Propositions', *Journal of Marketing*, Vol. 46, 92–101.

Horne, S. and Moss, M. (1995) 'The Management of Collecting Boxes: Analysis of Performance and Site Location', *Journal of Nonprofit and Public Sector Marketing*, Vol. 3, No. 2, 47–62.

Houston, F. S. and Markland, R. (1976) 'Public Agency Marketing—Improving the Adequacy of Infant Immunisation', in *Proceedings: American Institute for Decision Sciences*, 461–3.

Hovland, C. I. and Mandell, W. (1952) 'An Experimental Comparison of Conclusion Drawing by the Communicator and the Audience', *Journal of Abnormal and Social Psychology*, Vol. 47, July, 581–8.

Howitt, D. and McCabe, J. (1978) 'Attitudes do Predict Behaviour—In Mails at Least', *British Journal of Social and Clinical Psychology*, Vol. 17, No. 3, 285–6.

Inguanzo, J. M. and Harju, M. (1985) 'What Makes Consumers Select a Hospital', *Hospitals*, 16 March, 90–4.

Janis, I. L. (1967) 'Effects of Fear Arousal on Attitude Change: Recent Developments in Theory and Experimental Research', in Berkowitz, L. (ed), *Advances in Experimental Social Psychology*, New York, Academic Press.

Jarratt (1985) *Report of the Steering Committee for Efficiency Studies in Universities*, CVCP, London.

Jenson, J. (1987) 'Most Physicians Believe Patients Obtain Health Care Information from Mass Media', *Modern Health Care*, Vol. 17, No. 19, 113–14.

Johnsson, B. C. (1990) 'Focus Group Positioning and Analysis: A Commentary on Adjuncts for Enhancing the Design of Health Care Research', *Health Education Quarterly*, Vol. 7, No. 1/2, 152–68.

Jones, J. (1996) 'Doing Good while Doing Well', *Black Enterprise*, Vol. 26, No. 7, 178–84.

Jones, T. O. and Sasser, W. E. (1995) 'Why Satisfied Customers Defect', *Harvard Business Review*, Nov/Dec, 88–99.

Kaali-Nagy, C. and Garrison, L. C. (1972) 'Profiles of Users and Non-Users of the Los Angeles Music Center', *California Management Review*, Vol. 15, Winter, 133–43.

Kapferer, J. N. and Laurent, G. (1985) 'Consumer Involvement Profiles: A New Practical Approach to Consumer Involvement', *Journal of Advertising Research*, Vol. 25, No. 6, 48–56.

Kealy, M. J. and Rockel, M. L. (1987) 'Student Perceptions of College Quality: The Influence of College Recruitment Policies', *Journal of Higher Education*, Vol. 58, No. 6, 683–703.

Kelley, B. (1991) 'Cause Related Marketing', *Sales and Sales Management*, March, 60.

Kohli and Jaworski (1990) 'Market Orientation: The Construct, Research Propositions and Managerial Implications', *Journal of Marketing*, Vol. 54, April, 1–18.

Koponen, A. (1960) 'Personality Characteristics of Purchasers', *Journal of Advertising Research*, Vol. 1, No. 1, 6–12.

Kotler, P. (1982) *Marketing for Nonprofit Organisations*, 2nd edn, Englewood Cliffs, Prentice Hall.

—— (1994) *Marketing Management: Analysis, Planning, Implementation and Control*, 8th edn, Englewood Cliffs, Prentice Hall.

—— (1997) *Marketing Management: Analysis, Planning and Control*, 9th edn, Englewood Cliffs, Prentice Hall.

—— and Andreasen, A. (1991) *Strategic Marketing for Nonprofit Organisations*, Englewood Cliffs, Prentice Hall.

—— and Clarke, R. N. (1987) *Marketing for Healthcare Organisations*, Englewood Cliffs, Prentice Hall.

—— and Fox, K. F. A. (1985) *Strategic Marketing for Educational Institutions*, Englewood Cliffs, Prentice Hall.

—— and Levy, S. (1969) 'Broadening the Concept of Marketing', *Journal of Marketing*, Vol. 33, January, 10–15.

—— and Zaltman, G. (1971) 'Social Marketing: An Approach to Planned Social Change', *Journal of Marketing*, Vol. 35, No. 2, 3–12.

Laczniak, G. R., Lusch, R. F. and Murphy, P. E. (1979) 'Social Marketing: Its Ethical Dimensions', *Journal of Marketing*, Vol. 43, No. 1, 29–36.

Lamb, C. W. (1983) 'Non Profits Need Development Orientation to Survive', *Fund Raising Management*, August, 26–30.

Lansing, J. B. and Kish, L. (1957) 'Family Life Cycle as an Independent Variable', *American Sociological Review*, Vol. 22, No. 5, 512–19.

Larsen, D. E. and Rootman, I. (1976) 'Physician Role Performance and Patient Satisfaction', *Social Science and Medicine*, Vol. 10, No. 1, 29–32.

Levitt, T. (1981) 'Marketing Intangible Products and Product Intangibles', *Harvard Business Review*, Vol. 59, May/June, 94–102.

Levy, D. R. (1992) 'Segment Your Markets', *Association Management*, Vol. 44, No. 8, 111–15.

Levy, S. J., Czepiel, J. A. and Rook, D. W. (1980) 'Social Division and Aesthetic Specialisation: The Middle Class and Musical Events', in *Symbolic Consumer Behaviour*, Proceedings of the Association for Consumer Research Conference on Consumer Aesthetics and Symbolic Consumption, May, 103–7.

Lewis, B. (1989) 'Quality in the Service Sector. A Review', *International Journal of Bank Marketing*, Vol. 7, No. 5, 4–12.

Lockwood, G. and Davies, J. (1985) *Universities, the Management Challenge*, NFER Nelson, Windsor.

Lovelock, C. H. and Weinberg, C. B. (1990) Public and Nonprofit Marketing, 2nd edn, San Francisco, The Scientific Press.

LuAnn, A. and Andersen, R. (1980) *Health Care in the USA*, Beverly Hills, Sage Publications.

Luthra, R. (1991) 'Contraceptive Social Marketing in the Third World: A Case of Multiple Transfer', *Gazette*, Vol. 3, 159–76.

Lych, J. and Schuler, D. (1990) 'Consumer Evaluation of the Quality of Hospital Services from an Economics of Information Perspective', *Journal of Health Care Marketing*, Vol. 10, June, 16–22.

Lynn, P. and Smith, D. (1992) *The 1991 National Survey of Voluntary Activity in the UK*, Berkhamsted, Volunteer Centre UK.

Lytle, R. S. and Mokwa, M. P. (1992) 'Evaluating Health Care Quality: The Moderating Role of Outcomes', *Journal of Health Care Marketing*, Vol. 12, No. 1, 4–14.

MacDivitt, H. and Asch, D. (1989) *Block 1: Formulating Policy*, B881 Strategic Management, Milton Keynes, Open University Press.

MacStravic, R. Scott (1975), *Marketing Health Care*, Gaithersburg, Aspen Publishers.

Maheswaran, D. and Meyers-Levy, J. (1990) 'The Influence of Message Framing and Issue Involvement', *Journal of Marketing Research*, Vol. 27, Aug, 361–7.

Maister, D. H. (1985) 'The Psychology of Waiting Lines' in Czepiel, J., Solomon, M. R. and Suprenant, C. F. (eds) *The Service Encounter*, Lexington, Mass, Lexington Books.

MANAR (1991) *National Arts and Media Strategy: Discussion Document on Marketing the Arts*, Marketing the Arts Nationally and Regionally (MANAR), London, Arts Council.

Market Research Society (1984) *Market Research Society Yearbook*.

May, L. (1988) 'How to Build a Simple Segmentation System', *Fundraising Management*, May, 67–71, 111.

McGuiness, J., Jones, A. P. and Cole, S. G. (1977) 'Attitudinal Correlates of Recycling Behaviour', *Journal of Applied Psychology*, Vol. 62, No. 4, 376–84.

McCarthy, E. J. (1960) *Basic Marketing: A Managerial Approach*, Illinois, Richard Irwin.

McDevitt, P. K. and Shields, L. A. (1985) 'Tactical Hospital Marketing: A Survey of the State of the Art', *Journal of Health Care Marketing*, Vol. 5, No. 1, 9–16.

McDonald, M. H. B. (1984) *Marketing Plans: How to Prepare Them, How to Use Them*, London, Heinemann.

McKenzie-Mohr, D. (1994) 'Social Marketing for Sustainability: The Case for Residential Energy Conservation', *Futures*, March, 224–33.

Mescon, T. S. and Tilson, D. J. (1987) 'Corporate Philanthropy: A Strategic Approach to the Bottom Line', *California Management Review*, Winter, Vol. 29, 49–61.

Miller, S. J. (1974) 'Market Segmentation and Forecasting for a Charitable Health Organisation', *Proceedings of the Annual Conference*, Southern Marketing Association, Atlanta, Georgia.

Mindak, W. A. and Bybee, H. M. (1971) 'Marketing's Application to Fundraising', *Journal of Marketing*, Vol. 35, No. 2, July, 13–18.

Mokwa, M. P., Prieve, E. A. and Dawson, W. M. (1980) *Marketing the Arts*, New York, Praeger Press.

Monk, D. (1970) *Social Grading on the National Readership Survey*, London, Research Services Ltd (JICNARS).

Moore, P. G. (1989) 'Marketing Higher Education', *Higher Education Quarterly*, Vol. 43, No. 2, 108–24.

Narver, J. C. and Slater, S. F. (1990) 'The Effect of a Market Orientation on Business Profitability', *Journal of Marketing*, October, 20–35.

Nelson, P. (1974) 'Advertising as Information', *Journal of Political Economy*, Vol. 81, July/August, 729–54.

Nichols, J. E. (1991) *Targeted Fundraising*, Illinois, Precept Press.

—— (1995) 'Developing Relationships with Donors', *Fundraising Management*, August, 18, 19, 47.

Nicosia, F. and Wind, Y. (1977) 'Behavioural Models of Organisational Buying Processes', in Nicosia, F. and Wind, Y. (eds) *Behavioural Models of Market Analysis: Foundations for Marketing Action*, Hinsdale, Ill, Dryden Press, 96–120.

Nielsen, R. and McQueen, C. (1975) 'Performing Arts Consumer Behaviour: An Exploratory Study', in *New Marketing for Social and Economic Progress*, American Marketing Association Proceedings, 392–5.

O'Connor, S. J., Shewchuk, R. M. and Carney, L. W. (1994) 'The Great Gap', *Journal of Health Care Marketing*, Vol. 14, No. 2, 32–9.

O'Leary, J. (1996) 'The Future of Higher Education', *The Times*, 21 Jan, 5.

O'Neill, I. (1995) *Taught Postgraduate Education—The Student Experience*, HEIST, Leeds.

Ogwo, O. E. (1980) *An Analysis of the Psychographic and Demographic Correlates of Consumer Credit Behaviour*, unpublished doctoral dissertation, University of Strathclyde.

Ostergard, P. M. (1994) 'Fasten Your Seat Belts', *Fundraising Management*, March, 36–8.

Ovretveit, J. A. (1992) 'Towards Market Focused Measures of Customer/Purchaser Perceptions of Service', *Quality Forum*, Vol. 18, No. 1, 21–4.

Pagan, L. (1994) 'Testing Out Support', *Marketing*, 12 May, 43.

Palfreyman and Warner (1996) *Higher Education Management: The Key Elements*, The Open University Press, Buckingham.

Palihawadana, D. (1992) *Marketing Higher Education: A Case Study Related to the Strathclyde Business School*, unpublished PhD thesis, Dept. of Marketing, University of Strathclyde, Glasgow.

—— and Westwell, R. (1996) 'Information Search and Choice Behaviour in Higher Education', MEG Conference Proceedings, 1165–77.

Palmer, A. (1994) *Principles of Services Marketing*, Maidenhead, McGraw Hill.

Parasuraman, A., Zeithaml, V. and Berry, L. (1988) 'SERVQUAL: A Multiple Item Scale for Measuring Consumer Perceptions of Service Quality', *Journal of Retailing*, Vol. 64, No. 1, 12–40.

Passey, A. (1995) 'Corporate Support of the UK Voluntary Sector' in CAF, (1995), *Dimensions of the Voluntary Sector*, West Malling, Charities Aid Foundation, 57–61.

Pendelton, D. and Halser, J. (1983) *Doctor–Patient Communication*, London, Academic Press.

Petch, A. (1986) 'Parental Choice at Entry to Primary School', Research Papers in Education, Vol. 1, No. 1, 26–47.

Petrochuk, M. A. and Javalgi, R. G. (1996) 'Reforming the Health Care System: Implications for Health Care Marketers', *Health Marketing Quarterly*, Vol. 13, No. 3, 71–86.

Pharoah, C. (ed) (1997) *Dimensions of the Voluntary Sector*, West Malling, Charities Aid Foundation.

Philips, L. W. and Sternthal, B. (1977) 'Age Differences in Information Processing: A Perspective on the Aged Consumer', *Journal of Marketing Research*, Vol. 14, No. 4, 444–57.

Phillips, C. R. (1980) 'Single Room Maternity Care for Maximum Cost-Efficiency', *Perinatology-Neonataology*, March/April, 21–31.

Piercy, N. and Morgan, N. A. (1994) 'The Marketing Planning Process: Behavioural Problems Compared to Analytical Techniques in Explaining Marketing Plan Credibility', *Journal of Business Research*, Vol. 29, No. 3, 167–78.

Pifer, A. (1987) 'Philanthropy, Voluntarism and Changing Times', *Journal of the American Academy of Arts and Science*', Winter, 119–31.

Pinson, C. and Roberto, E. L. (1973) 'Do Attitude Changes Precede Behaviour Changes?', *Journal of Advertising Research*, Vol. 13, No. 4, 33–8.

Porter, M. E. (1985) *Competitive Advantage: Creating and Sustaining Superior Performance*, New York, Free Press.

Quinn, J. B. (1992) *Intelligent Enterprise*, New York, The Free Press.

Rados, D. L. (1981) *Marketing for Non-Profit Organisations*, Dover, Massachusetts Auburn House.

Ramah, M. and Cassidy, C. (1992) 'Social Marketing and Prevention of AIDS', in *AIDS Prevention Through Education*, New York, Oxford University Press.

Ranade, W. (1994) *A Future for the NHS*, Harlow, Longman Group Ltd.

Ratchford, B. (1987) 'New Insights about the FCB Grid', *Journal of Advertising Research*, Aug/Sept, 24–38.

Reiss, A. H. (1994) 'The Arts Look Ahead', *Fundraising Management*, Vol. 25, No. 1, 27–31.

Resnik, A. J., Turney, P. B. B. and Mason, J. B. (1979) 'Marketers Turn Towards Countersegmentation', *Harvard Business Review*, Vol. 57, No. 5, 100–6.

Reynolds, F. D. and Darden, W. R. (1971) 'Mutually Adaptable Effects of Interpersonal Communication', *Journal of Marketing Research*, Vol. 8, Nov, 449–54.

Richards, A. (1995) 'Does Charity Pay?', *Marketing*, 21 Sept, 24–5.

Ricklefs, R. (1975) 'Museums Merchandise More Shows and Wares to Broaden Patronage', *Wall Street Journal*, Vol. XCIII, No. 32, 14 Aug.

Rivlin, A. (1990) 'New Way to Manage a Database', *Fundraising Management*, July 1990, 33–8.

Rubinger, M. (1987) 'Psychographics Help Health Care Marketers Find and Serve New Market Segments', *Marketing News*, Vol. 21, No. 9, 24 April, 4–5.

Ryans, A. and Weinberg, C. (1978) 'Consumer Dynamics in Non Profit Organisations', *Journal of Consumer Research*, Vol. 5, 89–95.

Sage, G. C. (1991) 'Customers and the NHS', *International Journal of Health Quality Assurance*, Vol. 4, No. 3, 23–34.

Salamon, L. M. and Anheier, H. K. (1992) *In Search of the Non-Profit Sector II: The Problem of Classification*, Johns Hopkins Comparative Non-Profit Sector Project, Baltimore, Johns Hopkins Institute for Policy Studies.

San Augustine, A., Long, W. J. and Pantzallis, J. (1992) 'Hospital Positioning: A Strategic Tool for the 1990s', *Journal of Health Care Marketing*, Vol. 12, No. 1, 16–23.

Sargeant, A. (1995) 'Market Segmentation in the Charity Sector—An Examination of Common Practice', *Proceedings of the MEG Annual Conference*, Bradford, July, 693–702.

—— (1996) 'Market Segmentation—Are UK Charities Making the Most of the Potential?', *Journal of Non Profit and Voluntary Sector Marketing*, Vol. 1, No. 2, 132–43.

—— (1997) 'Banishing the Battleship Ladies!—The Emergence of a New Paradigm of Corporate Giving', *Proceedings Academy of Marketing Conference*, Manchester, July, 903–16.

—— (1997) 'Marketing The Arts—A Classification of UK Theatre Audiences', *Journal of Non Profit & Public Sector Marketing*, Vol. 5, No. 1, 45–62.

—— and Bater, K. (1996) 'Market Segmentation in the Charity Sector—Just What is the Potential?' *Working Paper 96/05*, University of Exeter.

—— and Bater, K. (1997) 'Trust Fundraising—Learning to say Thank You', *Journal of Nonprofit and Voluntary Sector Marketing*, forthcoming.

—— and Kaehler, J. (1998) *Benchmarking Charity Costs*, West Malling, Charities Aid Foundation.

—— and Stephenson, H. (1997) 'Corporate Giving—Targeting the Likely Donor', *Journal of Nonprofit and Voluntary Sector Marketing*, Vol. 2, No. 1, 64–79.

Sawyer, A. G. and Howard, D. J. (1991) 'Effects of Omitting Conclusions in Advertisements to Involved and Uninvolved Audiences', *Journal of Marketing Research*, Vol. 28, Nov, 464–74.

Schellstede, W. (1986) 'Social Marketing of Contraceptives', *Draper Fund Report*, December, 21–6.

Schiffman, L. G. and Kanuk, L. L. (1994) *Consumer Behaviour*, 5th edn, Englewood Cliffs, Prentice Hall.

Schlegelmilch, B. B. (1979) 'Targeting of Fund Raising Appeals', *European Journal of Marketing*, Vol. 22, 31–40.

—— and Tynan, A. C. (1989) 'The Scope for Market Segmentation within the Charity Sector—An Empirical Analysis', *Managerial and Decision Economics*, Vol. 10, 127–34.

Searles, P. D. (1980) 'Marketing Principles in the Arts', in Mokwa, M. P., Prieve, E. A. and Dawson, W. M. (1980) *Marketing the Arts*, New York, Praeger Press.

Seminik, R. J. and Young, C. E. (1979) 'Market Segmentation in Arts Organisations', *Proceedings of the 1979 American Marketing Association Conference*, 474–8.

—— and —— (1980) 'Correlates of Season Ticket Subscription Behaviour', *Advances in Consumer Research*, Vol. 7, 114–18.

Shapiro, B. P. (1988) 'What the Hell is "Market Oriented" ', *Harvard Business Review*, November–December, 119–25.

Shrum, L. J., Lowrey, T. M. and McCarty, J. A. (1994) 'Recycling as a Marketing Problem: A Framework for Strategy Development', *Psychology and Marketing*, Vol. 11, No. 4, 393–416.

Sihombing, B. (1994) *Overview of the Indonesian Family Planning Movement: The Blue Circle and Gold Circle Social Marketing Policies*, Jakarta, National Family Planning Co-ordinating Board.

Simpson, J. A. (1994) 'Market Segmentation for Appraisal Firms', *Appraisal Journal*, Vol. 60, No. 4, 564–7.

Singh, J. (1990) 'A Multifacet Typology of Patient Satisfaction with a Hospital', *Journal of Health Care Marketing*, Vol. 10, Dec, 8–21.

Slocum, J. W. and Matthews, H. L. (1970) 'Social Class and Income as Indicators of Consumer Credit Behaviour', *Journal of Marketing*, Vol. 34, No. 2, 69–74.

Smith, A. (1776) *The Wealth of Nations*, Letchworth, Dent and Sons Ltd.

Smith, M. A. (1992) *Reducing Alcohol Consumption among University Students: Recruitment and Programme Design Strategies Based on Social Marketing Theory*, unpublished dissertation, University of Oregon.

Smith, S. M. and Beik, L. L. (1982) 'Market Segmentation for Fundraisers', *Journal of the Academy of Marketing Science*, Vol. 10, No. 3, 208–16.

Smith, W. R. (1956) 'Product Differentiation and Market Segmentation as Alternative Marketing Strategies', *Journal of Marketing*, Vol. 21, No. 3, 3–8.

Stanley, T. L. (1995) 'Entertainers Barter for Databases', *Brandweek*, 13 March, 6.

Stanton, W. J. (1978) *Fundamentals of Marketing*, 5th edn, New York, McGraw Hill.

Staudt, T. A., Taylor, D. A. and Bowersox, D. J. (1976) *A Managerial Introduction to Marketing*, Englewood Cliffs, Prentice Hall.

Sterne, L. (1994) 'Giving as they Grow', *Foundation News and Commentary*, 35(5), 42–3.

Sternthal, B. and Craig, C. S. (1982) *Consumer Behaviour: An Information Processing Perspective*, Englewood Cliffs, Prentice Hall.

Stewart, K. L. (1991) 'Applying a Marketing Orientation to a Higher Education Setting', *Journal of Professional Services Marketing*, Vol. 7, No. 2, 117–24.

Stillman, A. and Maychell, K. (1986) *Choosing Schools: Parents, LEA's and the 1980 Education Act*, NFER-Nelson Publishing Company.

Strehler, G. (1990) 'The Marketing Oriented Diffusion of Art and Culture: Potential Risks and Benefits', *Marketing and Research Today*, November, 209–12.

Stroup, M. A. and Neubert, R. L. (1987) 'The Evolution of Social Responsibility', *Business Horizons*, Vol. 30, March, 22–4.

Tansuhaj, P., Randall, D. and McCullough, J. (1988) 'A Service Marketing Management Model: Integrating Internal and External Marketing Functions', *Journal of Services Marketing*, Vol. 2, Winter, 31–8.

Teasdale, K. (1992) *Managing the Changes in Health Care*, London, Wolfe.

Thomas, A. and Dennison, W. (1991) 'Parental or Pupil Choice—Who Really Decides in Urban Schools?', *Education Management and Administration*, Vol. 19, No. 4, 243–51.

Tomlinson, R. (1994) 'Finding out more from Box Office Data', *Journal of the Market Research Society*, Vol. 34, No. 4, 389–404.

Twedt, D. W. (1964) 'How Important to Marketing Strategy is the Heavy User?', *Journal of Marketing*, Vol. 28, No. 1, 301–35.

Tynan, A. C. and Drayton, J. (1987) 'Market Segmentation', *Journal of Marketing Management*, Vol. 2, No. 3, 301–35.

Useem, M. and DiMaggio, P. (1978) 'A Critical Review of the Content Quality and Use of Audience Studies', in *Research in the Arts*, Proceedings of the Conference on Policy Related Studies of the National Endowment for the Arts, Baltimore: Walters Arts Gallery, 30–2.

Varadarajan, P. R. and Menon, A. (1988) 'Cause Related Marketing: A Co-alignment of

Marketing Strategy and Corporate Philanthropy', *Journal of Marketing*, Vol. 52, No. 3, 58–74.

Vincent, R. (1988) 'Charity Administration: Is it Time for an Institute of Charity Trustees?', *New Law Journal*, 29 April, 2–4.

Ware, J. E., Davies-Avery, A. and Stewart, A. L. (1978) 'The Measurement and Meaning of Patient Satisfaction', *Health and Medical Care Services Review*, Vol. 1, Jan/Feb, 14–20.

Webster, F. E. (1988) 'The Rediscovery of the Marketing Concept', *Business Horizons*, May–June, 29–39.

Weinberger, M. G. and Gulas, C. S. (1992) 'The Impact of Humor in Advertising', *Journal of Advertising*, Vol. 21, No. 4, 35–59.

Wells, W. D. (1975) 'Psychographics: A Critical Review', *Journal of Marketing Research*, Vol. 12, No. 2, 196–213.

— and Gubar, G. (1966) 'Lifecycle Concept in Marketing Research', *Journal of Marketing Research*, Vol. 3, No. 4, 355–63.

— and Tigert, D. J. (1971) 'Activities, Interests and Opinions', in Engel, J. F. (ed), (1972) *Market Segmentation, Concept and Applications*, Holt and Rinelot Winston.

West, A. and Varlaam, A. (1991) 'Choosing a Secondary School: Parents of Junior School Children', *Educational Research*, Vol. 33, No. 1, 22–30.

— David, M., Hailes, J. and Ribbens, J. (1995) 'Parents and the Process of Choosing Secondary Schools: Implications for Schools', *Educational Management and Administration*, Vol. 23, No. 1, 28–38.

West, P. (1994) 'In the Temple of Pain', *Harper's Magazine*, Dec, 29–30.

Wilson, R. M. S., Gilligan, C. and Pearson, D. J. (1994) *Strategic Marketing Management*, Oxford, Butterworth Heinemann.

Wind, Y. and Cordozo, R. (1974) 'Industrial Market Segmentation', *Industrial Marketing Management*, Vol. 3, No. 1, 153–65.

Wokutch, R. E. and Spencer, B. A. (1987) 'Corporate Saints and Sinners', *California Management Review*, Vol. 29, Winter, 72.

World Health Organization (1986) *Basic Documents: 36th edition*, Geneva, Switzerland, World Health Organization.

Wrenn, B. (1994) 'Differences in Perceptions of Hospital Marketing Orientation between Adminstrators and Marketing Officers', *Hospital and Health Services Administration*, Vol. 39, No. 3, 341–58.

Yankelovich, Skelly and White Inc (1985) *The Charitable Behaviour of Americans, Management Survey*, Washington DC, Independent Sector.

Yavas, U., Riecken, G. and Paremeswaren, R. (1980) 'Using Psychographics to Profile Potential Donors', *Business Atlanta*, Vol. 30, No. 5, 41–5.

Young, S. (1971) 'Psychographics Research and Marketing Relevancy', in King, C. W. and Tigert, D. J. (eds) *Attitude Research Reaches New Heights*, Chicago, American Marketing Association, 220–2.

Zaltman, G. and Vertinsky, I. (1971) 'Health Services Marketing: A Proposed Model', *Journal of Marketing*, Vol. 35 July, 19–27.

Zeithaml, V. A. (1985) 'How Consumer Evaluation Processes Differ between Goods and Services', *Journal of Marketing*, Fall, 186–90.

— and Bitner, M. J. (1996) *Services Marketing*, New York, McGraw Hill.

Index